CANADIAN ANNUAL REVIEW OF POLITICS AND PUBLIC AFFAIRS 2006

Canadian Annual Review of politics and public affairs 2006

EDITED BY DAVID MUTIMER

Published with the support of York University by
University of Toronto Press
Toronto Buffalo London

Toronto Buffalo London
www.utppublishing.com
Printed and bound by CPI Group (UK) Ltd, Croydon, CR0 4YY

ISBN 978-1-4426-4569-1

Printed on acid-free, 100% post-consumer recycled paper with vegetable-based inks.

A cataloguing record for this publication is available from Library and Archives Canada.

University of Toronto Press acknowledges the financial assistance to its publishing program of the Canada Council for the Arts and the Ontario Arts Council.

Canada Council for the Arts Conseil des Arts du Canada

ONTARIO ARTS COUNCIL
CONSEIL DES ARTS DE L'ONTARIO
50 YEARS OF ONTARIO GOVERNMENT SUPPORT OF THE ARTS
50 ANS DE SOUTIEN DU GOUVERNEMENT DE L'ONTARIO AUX ARTS

University of Toronto Press acknowledges the financial support of the Government of Canada through the Canada Book Fund for its publishing activities.

This book was published with the support of York University.

Copies of the *Canadian Annual Review* published annually for 1989 and 1991–2005 are available.

Contents

Contributors xiii

Canadian calendar 2006 xv

Editor's introduction – the year in review 3

Parliament and politics *by Robert Everett* 11

THIRTY-NINTH GENERAL ELECTION 13
Contestants 13; Major party platforms and issues 14; Swing to the Conservatives 16; Results 17; Liberal leadership transfer 19; The NDP and Bloc hold steady 22; Green Party leadership 23

NATIONAL INSTITUTIONS 23
Cabinet 23; Speech from the Throne 24;
Branding Canada's 'new government' and the Conservatives' style 26;
House by-elections and caucus changes 27;
Fixed election dates 28; Government accountability 29;
Patronage commissioner 29; Senate reform 30; Supreme Court 31;
Auditor general 32; Ethics commissioner 33

NATIONAL ECONOMY 33
Economic indicators 33; The Conservatives' first budget 34; Trimming the fat, stirring the pot 35;
Autumn economic update 37 Income trusts 39; Trade 39

MAJOR POLICY AREAS 40
Aboriginal affairs 40; Recognition of the Quebecois 41;
Crime and punishment 42; Kyoto and greenhouse emissions 44;
Same-sex marriage reopened … and closed 45;

Extending the Afghanistan mission 46

SPECIAL COMMISSION AND INQUIRIES 47
Gomery Commission and the sponsorship scandal 47;
Maher Arar inquiry 49; Air India bombing inquiry 50

PERSONALITIES AND CONTROVERSIES 51
David Emerson and the ethics commissioner 51;
Wheat Board 52; Office of the Correctional Investigator 53

Foreign affairs and defence *by Christopher Spearin* 54

FOREIGN AFFAIRS 57

Terrorism and Canada 57
Prophet Mohammed cartoons 57; Toronto 18 58; Air India 59;
Canadians kidnapped in Iraq 60; The Khadrs 61; Arar inquiry 63;
Crisis in Lebanon 67

Major trade issues 70
World Trade Organization 70; Softwood lumber 71; North
American borders 72; Canada-China relations 73; International
AIDS Conference 74

DEFENCE POLICY 75

Afghanistan 75
Mission and debate 75; Canadian casualties in Afghanistan 77;
Prime Minister Harper's visit to Kandahar 79

Arctic 80

Defence procurement 81

Ballistic Missile Defence (BMD) 82

North American Aerospace Defence Command (NORAD) 84

General Rick Hillier 84

Municipal affairs *by Emmanuel Brunet-Jailly, Serena Kataoka, and Warren Magnusson* 87

CITIES IN THE MARKETPLACE 87

THE CULTURE OF CITIES 91

REGIONAL GOVERNANCE 93

LOCAL DEMOCRACY 95

CITIES IN THE CONFEDERATION 98

First Nations *by Kristin Burnett* 99

FEDERAL DEVELOPMENTS 99
Uncertain times – the federal election 99; The Congress of Aboriginal Peoples (CAP) 100; Realignment of federal spending 101; The budget 101; Aboriginal Affairs Committee 102; The First Nations Governance Act 102; Human Rights Act 103; Indian residential school settlement 103; United Nations Declaration on the Rights of Indigenous Peoples 105; AFN election 105

PROVINCIAL AND TERRITORIAL DEVELOPMENTS 106

British Columbia 106
Government spending 106; The Aboriginal Pilot Sales Program 106; Treaty firsts 107

The West 108
The Gateway Pipeline 108; The United Nations 108; Governance 109

Ontario 109
Caledonia and the Haudensaunee 109; Ongoing water crises 111; Kitchenuhmaykoosib Inninuwug (KI) 112

Quebec 113
Lawsuit 113; Rupert River Diversion Project (RRDP) 113; Quebec Native Alliance (QNA) 114

Maritimes: Treaty rights 114

The North 115
Mackenzie Valley Pipeline Project 115; The Nunavut Project 116

British Columbia *by Carey Hill* 118

FEDERAL ELECTION 119

EMERSON FALLOUT AFTER THE ELECTION 119

FEDERAL CABINET INCLUDES FOUR B.C. MINISTERS 121

THRONE SPEECH 121

BUDGET 123

LABOUR ISSUES: MARATHON PUBLIC-SECTOR BARGAINING 123

LABOUR ISSUES: TEACHERS BARGAINING 124

FERRY SINKING 126

HIGHWAY OF TEARS 126

INTERPROVINCIAL COOPERATION 126

KELOWNA ACCORD 127

SOCIAL SERVICES: THE HUGHES REPORT 129

HEALTH SYSTEMS ISSUES 131

MINING ACCIDENT 131

SOFTWOOD LUMBER 131

FOREST FIRES 133

MARC EMERY 133

LOOKING FORWARD TO THE OLYMPICS 133

SPIRIT BEAR: ENVIRONMENTAL PROTECTION 134

SALMON FARMING 134

AIR INDIA 135

PICKTON TRIAL 135

NEW PRESIDENT AT UBC 136

CMA CHOOSES BRITISH COLUMBIAN 136

BOIL WATER ADVISORY 136

ECONOMY 137

Alberta *by Harold Jansen* 139

THE BOOM 139

MANAGING THE CONSEQUENCES OF GROWTH 140

A NEW PREMIER 144

2006 FEDERAL ELECTION 148

ANOTHER HEALTH CARE REFORM FOUNDERS 149

THE LEGISLATURE 151

OTHER NEWS 152

Saskatchewan *by Joseph Garcea* 153

ELECTIONS 153

POLITICAL PARTIES 154

LEGISLATURE 155

EXECUTIVE 157

BUDGET 157

ECONOMY 158

JUDICIARY 159

INTERGOVERNMENTAL RELATIONS 160

ABORIGINAL AFFAIRS 162

Manitoba *by Geoffrey Lambert* 164

ECONOMIC DEVELOPMENTS 164

THE BUDGET 166

THE LEGISLATIVE SESSION 167

POLITICS AND POLITICAL PARTIES 169

THE FEDERAL ELECTION OF 2006 170

OTHER EVENTS 171

The Territories *by Ken Coates and Greg Poelzer* 172

THE NORTH IN NATIONAL POLITICS 172

TERRITORIAL POLITICS 177

ECONOMY 180

SOCIAL ISSUES 181

Ontario *by Robert Drummond* 184

HEALTH 185

EDUCATION 191

ENERGY 194

FIRST NATIONS 196

SOCIAL, LABOUR, AND LEGAL ISSUES 200

Quebec *by Daniel Salée and Richard Bisaillon* 203

CONSENSUS ON REJECTION, BUT NOT ON DIRECTION 204

QUESTIONING STATE BUREAUCRACY 206

DEALING WITH PUBLIC DISAPPROVAL OVER POLICY 209

THE LABOUR FRONT: JOBS LOST AND ADDED, OLD CONFLICTS RESOLVED 211

ETHNICITY AND DIFFERENCE: SENSITIVITIES OVER QUEBEC'S NATIONAL IDENTITY 212

QUEBEC IN CANADA: COMMITTING TO FEDERALISM 217

BRACING UP 220

New Brunswick *by Richard Wilbur* 222

PREMIER LORD'S LAST SESSION 222

THE GENERAL ELECTION 224

THE EVER-CHALLENGING PUBLIC SECTOR 227
NB Power 227 Health 229; Education 230

NATURAL RESOURCES SECTORS CONTINUE THEIR DECLINE 231

OTHER STORIES THAT CAUGHT PUBLIC ATTENTION 233

The Miramichi Hospital fraud case 233; The case of the Grand Manan Five 233; The fight over Lord Beaverbrook's art gifts 234; Agent Orange fallout at Camp Gagetown 235

LIBERAL PREMIER GRAHAM'S CAUTIOUS APPROACH TO GOVERNING 235

Prince Edward Island *by Peter E. Buker* 238

ECONOMY 238

FISCAL EVENTS 239

POLITICS AND THE LEGISLATURE 240

OTHER EVENTS 242

Nova Scotia *by Robert G. Finbow* 244

POLITICS 244

THE LEGISLATURE 246

THE ECONOMY 249

INTERGOVERNMENTAL RELATIONS 251

Newfoundland and Labrador *by Melvin Baker and Peter Neary* 255

Obituaries 267

Election tables 271

Index of names 273

Index of subjects 283

Contributors

MELVIN BAKER, Archivist / Historian, Memorial University, Newfoundland

RICHARD BISAILLON, Assistant Professor in the Department of Political Science at Concordia University, Montreal

EMMANUEL BRUNET-JAILLY, Associate Professor, School of Public Administration, University of Victoria

PETER EDWARD BUKER, PHD, Independent Scholar, Prince Edward Island

KRISTIN BURNETT, Assistant Professor in History and Adjunct in Indigenous Learning, Lakehead University

KEN COATES, Professor, Department of History, University of Waterloo

ROBERT DRUMMOND, Professor, Political Science and Public Policy and Administration, York University

ROBERT EVERETT, University Secretariat, York University

ROBERT G. FINBOW, Professor, Department of Political Science, Dalhousie University

JOSEPH GARCEA, Associate Professor, Department of Political Science, University of Saskatchewan

CHRIS HENDERSHOT, Doctoral Candidate, Department of Political Science, York University, Compiler of the calendar and obituaries

CAREY HILL, Independent Researcher, Ottawa, Ontario

HAROLD JANSEN, Associate Professor, Department of Political Science, University of Lethbridge

SERENA KATAOKA, Doctoral Candidate, Department of Political Science, University of Victoria

GEOFFREY LAMBERT, Professor, Department of Political Studies, University of Manitoba

WARREN MAGNUSSON, Professor, Department of Political Science, University of Victoria

DAVID MUTIMER, editor of the *Canadian Annual Review of Politics and Public Affairs*, Associate Professor, Political Science,

York University, and Director, York Centre for International and Security Studies

PETER NEARY, Professor Emeritus, Department of History, University of Western Ontario

GREG POELZER, Associate Professor, Department of Political Studies, University of Saskatchewan

DANIEL SALÉE, Professor of Political Science and in the School of Community and Public Affairs, Concordia University

CHRISTOPHER SPEARIN, Associate Professor, Department of Defence Studies, Canadian Forces College, Toronto

SHANNON STETTNER, Managing Editor of the *Canadian Annual Review of Politics and Public Affairs*

RICHARD WILBUR, Journalist / Historian, St Andrews, New Brunswick

Canadian calendar 2006

JANUARY

6 Canada's junior men's hockey team wins its second straight gold medal at the World Junior Hockey Championship in Vancouver.

Statistics Canada reports that rates of employment remained relatively unchanged for December 2005. Overall, 2005 saw employment increase 1.4 per cent with the addition of 233,000 full- and part-time jobs.

10 Statistics Canada reports that the value of building permits issued in November 2005 dipped under $5 billion for the first time since July. The value of permits issued totalled $4.9 billion – a 5.7 per cent drop from October 2005.

16 Canadian diplomat Glyn Berry is killed following a suicide attack on his convoy in southern Afghanistan.

18 Statistics Canada reports that according to the Consumer Price Index (CPI) goods and services cost 2.2 per cent more in December 2005 than they did in December 2004.

20 The movie *Karla*, based on the crimes of Karla Homolka and Paul Bernardo, is released in Canada.

23 The Conservative Party of Canada secures a minority government in Canada's thirty-ninth general election. The Conservatives win 124 seats, the Liberals 103, the Bloc 51, and the NDP 29. One seat goes to an independent.

Paul Martin announces his intention to resign as leader of the Liberal Party of Canada. Bill Graham will serve as interim Opposition leader in the House of Commons.

26 Hamas wins 76 of 132 seats in Palestinian general elections.

The acquisition of the Hudson's Bay Company by American business person Jerry Zucker is approved by the HBC board of governors.

27 Statistics Canada reports that employment in Canada's manufacturing sector has dropped 6.4 per cent or 149,000 jobs since 2002. Two-thirds of this decline took place in 2005. However, employment in the construction and natural resources sectors is up 19 per cent (167,000 jobs) and 15 per cent (40,000 jobs) respectively over this time period.

31 Statistics Canada reports that according to the report *Access to Health Care Services in Canada* wait times remain the most significant obstacle for Canadians who had difficulty obtaining specialized medical treatment in 2005.

FEBRUARY

1 Justice John Gomery releases the final report from his inquiry into the federal sponsorship scandal. The inquiry is reported to have cost upwards of $14 million.

6 Stephen Harper is sworn in as Canada's twenty-second prime minister.

Stephen Harper reveals his cabinet. The cabinet includes the controversial appointments of Liberal David Emerson as minister of international trade and the unelected Michael Fortier as minister of public works and government services.

Statistics Canada reports that the value of building permits issued in 2005 surpassed $60 billion for the first time as contractors took out $60.7 billion worth of permits. The value of permits issued in December totalled $6.3 billion – another record high. The 9.3 per cent increase over 2004 represents the tenth consecutive year that the value of building permits has increased in Canada.

7 Statistics Canada reports that according to a study of Canadian health care services, chronic conditions, and not education or wealth, represented the most significant determinant in how many times senior citizens consulted a physician and / or used medication.

Statistics Canada reports Canada's three primary retirement programs – registered pension plans, registered retirement savings plans, and Canada / Quebec Pension Plans – doubled in value between 1990 and 2003. Total value for the three programs exceeds $1.3 trillion.

9 Statistics Canada reports that a study of women over the age of 65 who suffered from financial and / or psychological stresses in 1994–5 were more likely to die in the following eight years than those senior women who did not experience such stresses.

10 Statistics Canada reports an increase of 26,000 jobs in January. However, the unemployment also increased 0.1 per cent to 6.6 per cent as more people entered the labour market.

11 Rodney MacDonald is elected leader of the Progressive Conservative Party in Nova Scotia.

15 Statistics Canada reports that in 2003 Canada's trade surplus in beer with the United States totaled $265 million – a $43 million increase from 1999.

21 Statistics Canada reports that only 19 per cent of Canadian firms required some form of debt financing in 2004. This represents a 24 per cent decrease from the number of firms who sought debt financing in 1999.

22 Statistics Canada reports that the CPI rose 0.5 per cent in January. Rising energy prices were primarily responsible for the increase.

Statistics Canada reports that in 2002–3 20 per cent of workers in Canada were within 10 years of retirement, a twofold increase from 1987–8 numbers.

23 The sale of the Hudson's Bay Company to American Jerry Zucker is approved by the federal Ministries of Industry and Canadian Heritage.

Stephen Harper announces the nomination of Federal Court of Appeal judge Marshall Rothstein to the Supreme Court of Canada. Rothstein will be the first nominee to sit before the Ad Hoc Committee on Supreme Court of Canada Appointments before he can be appointed.

24 Rodney MacDonald is sworn in as Nova Scotia's twenty-sixth premier.

Statistics Canada reports that Canadian corporations reported record operating profits in 2005. Owing in large part to a booming oil and gas sector, profits were up 12.1 per cent from 2004 and totalled $217 billion.

26 The 2006 Winter Olympics close in Turin, Italy. Bolstered by the five-medal performance of speed skater Cindy Klassen, Canadian athletes win a total of 24 medals.

27 The Ad Hoc Committee on Supreme Court of Canada Appointments questions Marshall Rothstein.

28 A small group of protesters from the Grand River Territory reserve occupy the Douglas Creek Estates construction site to prevent further development of the subdivision in Caledonia, Ontario.

Brigadier General David Fraser assumes command of 8,000 NATO soldiers, including 2,200 Canadian troops, in southern Afghanistan.

Statistics Canada reports that real gross domestic product (GDP) for the fourth quarter of 2005 rose 0.5 per cent.

MARCH

1 Marshall Rothstein is appointed to the Supreme Court of Canada.

Statistics Canada reports that according to a study, one-third of male immigrants age 25 to 45 who came to Canada between 1980 and 2000 emigrated within 20 years of their arrival.

6 Statistics Canada reports that the value of building permits for January totalled $5.1 billion. This is a 19.3 per cent decrease from the record high in December 2005.

7 Statistics Canada reports that women accounted for 47 per cent of Canada's workforce in 2004, with 58 per cent of women age fifteen years and older holding paid employment, which is a 16 per cent increase from 1976 numbers. However, women continue to earn only 71 per cent of what men earn. Likewise, 27 per cent of the female workforce are employed in part-time positions.

10 Statistics Canada reports that 25,000 jobs, predominantly part-time, were added in February. The unemployment rate dropped 0.2 per cent to 6.4 per cent – matching November 2005's 30-year low.

The developer of the Douglas Creek Estates obtains an injunction that orders Six Nations protesters to end their occupation. Protesters are given until 22 March to vacate the construction site.

12 Stephen Harper and minister of defence Gordon O'Connor make a surprise visit to Canadian troops in Afghanistan.

14 Ralph Klein announces his intention to resign as leader of the Alberta Progressive Conservative Party and subsequently as premier of Alberta. Klein plans to stay on until October 2007.

Canadian soldiers shoot and kill an Afghan taxi driver after the driver fails to stop at a security checkpoint. An investigation into the shooting is launched by Afghan police.

15 Statistics Canada reports that the rate of abortions in Canada decreased by 1 per cent in 2003 to 15.2 abortions per 1,000 women. Abortions for women under the age of twenty continued to decline from 15.7 to 14.5 abortions per 1,000 women. The crude birth rate for women under the age of twenty also fell to 12.1 births per 1,000.

16 Statistics Canada reports that falling fuel prices pushed the CPI down from 2.8 per cent in January to 2.2 per cent in February

17 Statistics Canada reports that national net worth topped $4.5 trillion or $137,300 per person in the fourth quarter of 2005.

19 Paul Martin officially resigns as leader of the Liberal Party of Canada. Bill Graham is appointed interim leader.

22 Six Nations protesters continue to occupy a construction site in Caledonia, Ontario, despite a court injunction that ordered them to leave.

Two passengers die after the *Queen of the North* ferry strikes a rock and sinks south of Prince Rupert, British Columbia – 99 passengers are rescued. An investigation later reveals that human error is at fault for the accident.

23 Two Canadian aid workers, James Loney and Harmeet Singh Sooden, are freed following a British-led military operation in

Iraq. Loney and Singh Sooden had been held captive for close to four months.

24 Statistics Canada reports that according to a study men and women who participated in adult education and obtained a post-secondary certificate between 1993 and 2001 earned 8 per cent and 10 per cent more, respectively, than those workers who did not obtain similar credentials.

28 Statistics Canada reports that the number of youth taken into some form of judicial custody dropped by almost half in the year following the 1 April 2003 implementation of the Youth Criminal Justice Act.

29 One Canadian soldier is killed during fighting in southern Afghanistan.

Statistics Canada reports that a study of working hour patterns of people age 24 to 54 between 1997 and 2001 found that only 32 per cent worked a standard number of hours in a year. The standard number of work hours was between 1,750 and 2,400.

30 After receiving only 55 per cent of support from delegates at the Progressive Conservative Party's convention, Alberta premier Ralph Klein announces his intention to resign in September, clearing the way for the selection of a new leader in December.

Canada cuts aid to the Palestinian Authority with the opening of a Hamas-controlled Palestinian parliament.

Statistics Canada reports that the median after-tax income of Canadian families with two or more people increased to $54,100 in 2004 – an inflation-adjusted increase of about 2 per cent from 2003.

31 Statistics Canada reports that the Canadian economy expanded by 0.2 per cent in January driven mainly by the strength of the service sector. However, this increase represents a slight decrease from the previous three months.

APRIL

4 Statistics Canada reports that a study found that 79 per cent of visible-minority immigrant youth are interested in obtain-

ing at least one post-secondary degree, whereas 57 per cent of Canadian-born non-visible minority youth signalled interest in post-secondary education.

5 A Conservative-led federal government faces a Question Period in the House of Commons for the first time in 13 years.

Statistics Canada reports that 54 per cent of children age six months to five years were in some form of child care in 2002–3. This represents a 12 per cent increase from 1994–5 levels. The three most prominent forms of child care include day-care centres, care outside the home by a non-relative, and care by a relative either inside or outside the home.

6 Statistics Canada reports that the value of building permits in February increased 3.6 per cent to $5.3 billion.

Statistics Canada reports that in 2001 about 20 per cent of workers who held a university degree were overqualified for their job. Younger people, immigrants, and people who studied commerce, arts, and / or humanities in university were the most likely to be overqualified.

Steelmaker Dofasco is acquired by ArcelorMittal of Luxembourg.

7 Paul Coffin, the first person charged in relation to the sponsorship scandal, is sentenced to 18 months in jail.

Statistics Canada reports an increase of 51,000 jobs in March and the unemployment rate decreased 0.1 per cent to 6.3 per cent – a 30-year low. For the 2004–5 fiscal year 330,000 new jobs were created, a 2.2 per cent increase.

8 Eight members of the Bandidos motorcycle gang are murdered outside the town of Shedden, Ontario.

20 During the night Ontario Provincial Police move in on Six Nations protesters and arrest 16 people. Hundreds of protesters return to the construction site in Caledonia in the morning.

Statistics Canada reports that the 12 -month CPI remained unchanged at 2.2 per cent in March.

24 Close to 500 residents of Caledonia move to confront Six Nations protesters. Ontario Provincial Police block the group before they reach the construction site.

26 Canada and the United States reach a deal on the trade of softwood lumber. The United States agrees to return about 80 per cent of the $5 billion in duties that had been collected since 2001.

Statistics Canada reports that economic growth in Canada's western provinces, particularly Alberta, outstripped the national rate of growth for the second consecutive year in 2005. Although lower than growth rates in 2004, Alberta and British Columbia posted 4.5 per cent and 3.5 per cent gains.

Statistics Canada reports that a study of how Canadian students (in 2002–3) pay for their post-secondary education found personal savings to be the most common source of funding for students followed by funds from employment, parents, and other relatives. However, the study found that only 24 per cent of students enrolled in programs that cost more than $4,000 could cover the cost with personal savings. Furthermore, only 50 per cent of students enrolled in programs costing $4,000 or less reported the ability to cover all the cost through one source of funding.

27 Statistics Canada reports that over the past eight years student rates of employment steadily increased. In 2005 summer rates of employment for students planning to return to school in the fall averaged 51.7 per cent, which is up 48 per cent from the employment rates in 1998. However, this number is well below rates of employment in 1989–90 when 61.4 per cent of students found summer employment.

28 Statistics Canada reports that the Canadian economy grew 0.2 per cent – the same rate as the previous month.

MAY

2 Statistics Canada reports that according to the *Ethnic Diversity Survey*, conducted in 2002, close to 50 per cent of people who do not regularly attend a religious service practice some form of religious activity in their homes at least once a month.

4 The value of the Canadian dollar reaches US$0.90 for the first time since 1978.

Statistics Canada reports that the value of building permits increased 5.3 per cent to $5.5 billion in March.

5 Statistics Canada reports that 22,000 new jobs were added in April, leading to a 0.8 per cent increase in jobs in the first quarter of 2006, which is more than double the rate from 2005.

9 Minister of foreign affairs Peter MacKay visits Canadian troops in Afghanistan. The visit comes amidst the release of recent polls that reveal that less than half of Canadians support the mission in Afghanistan.

Statistics Canada reports that the number of hours worked in 2005 increased by 0.8 per cent, which is a substantial decrease from the increases of 2.9 per cent in 2004 and 1.5 per cent in 2003.

11 Statistics Canada reports that in 2001 scientists and engineers represented 5.6 per cent of all paid employees in Canada's major metropolitan areas compared to 5.1 per cent in the United States.

Statistics Canada reports that according to a study jointly conducted by Human Resources and Social Development Canada and the Research Data Centre program, the level of household income almost always determines the physical, emotional, cognitive, social, and behavioural well-being of children.

13 Provincial politicians in Nova Scotia hit the campaign trail as a provincial election is called.

17 Following extensive debate, the House of Commons votes to extend Canada's mission in Afghanistan by two years. Canadian troops are now slated to begin withdrawal in 2009.

The first Canadian female combat soldier is killed after the vehicle she is travelling in sustains a direct hit from a rocket-propelled grenade.

18 Statistics Canada reports rising fuel costs pushed the 12-month CPI to 2.4 per cent.

23 After two tense days, Six Nations protesters dismantle their blockade of Highway 6; however, the occupation of the Douglas Creek Estates construction site continues.

24 Statistics Canada reports that foreign direct investment in Canada in 2005 totalled $415.6 billion – an increase of $34.6 billion from 2004.

25 Kenneth Lay, founder of Enron, is convicted on six charges including conspiracy to commit securities fraud.

Statistics Canada reports that operating profits for all Canadian corporations totalled $56.1 billion, a 2.6 per cent decrease, for the first quarter of 2006.

29 A wildcat strike by Toronto's transit workers shuts down the city's transit system for 11 hours.

31 Statistics Canada reports that the real GDP increased 0.9 per cent in the first quarter of 2006.

JUNE

1 Statistics Canada reports that employment opportunities in Canada have increased at an average of 2 per cent a year over the previous 13 years. In 2005 17.3 million or 67.2 per cent of Canadians held some form of paid employment.

Statistics Canada reports that Canadians consumed 4.1 per cent less sugar in 2005 than they did in 2004. On average each Canadian consumed 24.4 kg of sugar, which is a 24 per cent decrease from the peak consumption year of 1987.

2 Upwards of 400 police officers conduct raids in Mississauga and Toronto, arresting 15 people on suspicion of planning to carry out terrorist attacks in Toronto and Ottawa. Two other people who were already incarcerated are also linked with the plot.

Statistics Canada reports that foreign control of Canadian corporations changed little in 2004, with foreign interests accounting for 21.9 per cent of assets and 30 per cent of operating revenue in Canada.

3 Seventeen people are officially charged under Canada's Anti-Terrorism Act. The trial for the four youngest of the accused will not be held until January 2007.

5 Statistics Canada reports that the top one-quarter of Canadians who donate in excess of $325 to charitable organizations in 2004 account for 82 per cent of the total value of donations.

6 The person at the centre of the sponsorship scandal, Chuck Guité, is convicted on five fraud charges.

Statistics Canada reports that the value of building permits fell to its lowest level since November 2005 down 10.6 per cent to a total of $5 billion.

Statistics Canada reports that 21 per cent of Aboriginal people reported that they suffered abuse from either a current or a previous common-law partner or spouse. This compares with 6 per cent of non-Aboriginal persons who reported familial abuse.

7 Statistics Canada reports that increased age and educational attainment account for increased earning for lone mothers age 40 and older since 1980.

8 Statistics Canada reports that according to a study of Montreal neighbourhoods, crime in Canadian cities does not occur randomly. This study cites demographic, socio-economic, and land use factors as the three primary determinants of the level and types of crime to occur in a neighbourhood.

9 Statistics Canada reports that the unemployment rate in May fell to a 32-year low of 6.1 per cent on the back of an increase of 97,000 new jobs.

13 The Progressive Conservatives win a slim minority in Nova Scotia. The Progressive Conservatives win 22 seats with the NDP winning 20 seats – the most the party has ever won.

15 Statistics Canada reports that combined surplus of all levels of government in Canada totalled $26 billion for the 2005–6 fiscal year – the second highest consolidated surplus in 20 years.

16 The Government of Ontario announces that it bought out the developer of the Douglass Creek Estates as well as providing aid to Caledonia businesses for any losses incurred over the previous month.

Police arrest three more people in connection with the April killings of eight members of the Bandidos biker gang in Ontario. A total of eight people are charged in relation to the murders.

19 Chuck Guité is sentenced to three and half years in jail for his role in the sponsorship scandal.

The Carolina Hurricanes defeat the Edmonton Oilers 3–1 in game seven of the Stanley Cup playoffs.

20 Statistics Canada reports that the 12-month CPI increased 2.8 per cent between May 2005 and May 2006.

22 Prime Minister Stephen Harper makes an official apology for the Chinese Head Tax that charged Chinese immigrants up to $500. The tax was repealed in 1947.

23 Statistics Canada reports that national net worth topped $4.6 trillion or $141,000 per person for the first quarter of 2006.

28 Statistics Canada reports that according to a study conducted in 2001 of Canadian marital patterns, less than 1 per cent of Canadians marry more than twice. The study concluded that commitment to the institution of marriage was a key factor in determining the success of a marriage.

29 The softwood lumber deal between Canada and the United States is signed by representatives of both countries in Geneva.

30 Statistics Canada reports that 330 book publishers in Canada brought in $2 billion in revenues in 2004. Foreign-controlled publishers, 19 corporations in total or 6 per cent of publishers, accounted for 47 per cent of total publishing revenue in Canada.

JULY

1 Canada celebrates its 139th birthday.

Stephen Harper's promise to cut the Goods and Services Tax (GST) by 1 per cent goes into effect.

5 Statistics Canada reports that the number of people age 22 to 24 who graduated from a post-secondary institution increased drastically between 1997 and 2003. In 2003 44 per cent of people age 22 to 24 were graduates of a postsecondary institution, up from 7 per cent in 1997.

6 Statistics Canada reports that the value of building permits increased 6.9 per cent to $5.4 billion in May.

Statistics Canada reports that over 25 per cent of Canadians age 30 to 50 derive more than 35 per cent of their caloric intake from fat. Moreover, Canadians of all ages derive 20 per cent of their caloric intake from foods other than fruits, vegetables, milks, grains, and meat.

7 Statistics Canada reports that the unemployment rate remained unchanged in June. Employment for the first half of 2006 is up 1.6 per cent, which is double the growth for the first half of 2005.

9 One Canadian soldier is killed in fighting west of Kandahar.

10 Statistics Canada reports that a study of dates from 1993 to 2003 found that senior women experience more economic hardship than senior men in the five years following the death of a spouse or partner. In the five years following the death of a spouse or a partner 72 per cent of senior women and 51 per cent of senior men suffered a loss of adjusted income.

11 A series of coordinated bombings on Mumbai's commuter train system kills 190 people.

12 Israel begins siege of Lebanon following Hezbollah incursions into northern Israel.

Statistics Canada reports that Canadians spend upwards of 12 full days a year commuting to work based on a national daily average of 63 minutes in transit.

13 Statistics Canada reports that the 2006 edition of the *Family Violence in Canada: A Statistical Profile* found that between 1995 and 2004, 80 per cent of spousal abusers were reported to the police only once. According to the study a large number of factors determine how and when police are called and hence this number is not likely representative of the number of actual incidences of spousal abuse. Furthermore, the 2004 General Social Survey found that only 28 per cent of people who experienced spousal abuse reported it to the police.

17 Statistics Canada reports that 63 per cent of rural residents with a university degree did some form of volunteer work in 2003 compared to 42 per cent of urban residents.

19 Canada begins a massive evacuation of citizens from Lebanon following the intensification of combat between Israeli and Hezbollah forces. The two-week mission evacuates 14,000 people.

Statistics Canada reports that the average total workday for people age 24 to 55, including both paid and non-paid work, amounted to 8.8 hours in 2005. Although the gap is closing, women still do the majority of unpaid household work.

20 Statistics Canada reports that the national crime rate decreased 5 per cent in 2005, despite a spike in serious crimes such as murder, robbery, and sexual assault. The homicide rate increased 4 per cent, but the overall violent crime rate remained unchanged.

21 Statistics Canada reports that the 12-month CPI increased 2.5 per cent between June 2005 and June 2006.

22 Two Canadian soldiers are killed after a suicide attack on their convoy in southern Afghanistan.

23 A Canadian carpenter is killed in northern Afghanistan. Mike Frastacky, of Vancouver, was in Afghanistan working on the construction of a school.

26 Statistics Canada reports that people age 55 to 64 are spending more time in the paid labour force and less time on leisure activities. In 2005, men age 55 to 64 averaged 4.4 hours a day doing paid work, 3.5 hours doing leisure activities, and 3.1 hours doing unpaid work. The paid work average represents a 1.2 hour increase from the 1998 average.

Statistics Canada reports that 35 million people visited Canadian zoos, art galleries, and museums in 2004.

31 Statistics Canada reports that Canada's crude birth rate decreased to 10.5 live births per 1,000 people in 2004 – the crude birth rate in 2003 was 10.6 births per 1,000 people.

AUGUST

1 Fidel Castro temporary cedes control of Cuba to his brother and minister of defence, Raúl.

3 Four Canadian soldiers are killed during heavy fighting in southern Afghanistan.

4 Statistics Canada reports that employment numbers remained unchanged for the second straight month in July.

8 Statistics Canada reports that the value of building permits decreased 1.4 per cent in June to $5.3 billion.

11 The first Canadian medic to be killed in action since the Korean conflict is killed during an attack on a resupply convoy heading to Kandahar.

Sleeman Breweries Ltd. is acquired by Sapporo Breweries of Japan.

13 The sixteenth International AIDS Conference opens in Toronto. Prime Minister Stephen Harper is conspicuous in his absence.

14 The UN brokers a cease-fire between Israel and Hezbollah, bringing Israel's 34-day siege of Lebanon to an end. The conflict claims the lives of 850 Lebanese, 150 Israelis, and 1 Canadian UN observer.

15 Statistics Canada reports that in 2005 an estimated 16.8 million or 68 per cent of Canadians spent time on the Internet for non-business purposes. Only 58 per cent of Canadians living in small towns or rural areas accessed the Internet.

22 One Canadian soldier and three others are injured after a suicide attack on their patrol in southern Afghanistan.

Statistics Canada reports that the 12-month CPI fell for the second consecutive month as Canadians paid 2.4 per cent more for goods and services in July 2005 than they did in July 2004.

Statistics Canada reports that 23 per cent of Canadians over the age 18 are obese. According to the 2004 *Canadian Community Health Survey* 20 per cent of adults living in a census metropolitan area (CMA) can be considered obese, whereas 29 per cent of adults living outside a CMA can be considered obese.

23 Statistics Canada reports that in 2003, 29 per cent of women in Canada were the primary source of the income for their families, up from 11 per cent in 1967. However, primary-earning women only made an average of $41,200 compared to the $57,800 averaged by primary-earning men.

24 Statistics Canada reports that operating profits for all corporations in Canada increased 0.7 per cent to $57 billion in the second quarter of 2006.

26 Elizabeth May becomes the ninth leader of the Green Party with a first ballot victory.

31 Statistics Canada reports that Canada's real GDP increased 0.5 per cent in the second quarter of 2006.

SEPTEMBER

1 Statistics Canada reports that students attending a post-secondary institution will pay an average of 3.2 per cent more for tuition in 2006 than they did in 2005.

3 Four Canadian soldiers are killed and nine others are injured during a massive assault on Taliban positions in southern Afghanistan.

4 A friendly fire incident claims the life of one Canadian soldier in southern Afghanistan. According to reports American aircraft mistakenly fired upon a platoon of Canadian troops involved in a major anti-Taliban operation.

7 Statistics Canada reports that the value of building permits fell 2.3 per cent to $5.3 billion in July.

8 Statistics Canada reports that employment numbers remained unchanged for the third consecutive month, with the unemployment rate increasing 0.1 per cent to 6.5 per cent.

13 Armed with three guns, a lone gunman kills one and wounds nineteen at Montreal's Dawson College. The gunman takes his own life after being engaged by police.

Statistics Canada reports that total alcohol sales in Canada increased 3.8 per cent to $16.8 billion in 2004–5. Per capita spending totalled $638.60, a $15 increase from 2003–4.

15 Statistics Canada reports that national net worth rose to $4.7 trillion or $142,900 per person in the second quarter of 2006.

18 Shawn Graham becomes New Brunswick thirty-first premier after his Liberal Party secures a majority government in the province's general election.

Four Canadian soldiers are killed in southern Afghanistan by a suicide attacker.

19 Statistics Canada reports that the 12-month CPI increased 2.1 per cent between August 2005 and August 2006.

20 Ralph Klein officially resigns as leader of the Alberta Progressive Conservative Party.

22 During an official state visit to Canada, Afghan president Hamid Karzai asserts that Canada's mission in Afghanistan 'is a must.'

27 Statistics Canada reports that 254,000 people immigrated to Canada between 1 July 2005 and 1 July 2006.

29 One Canadian soldier is killed after triggering a roadside improvised explosive device in southern Afghanistan.

OCTOBER

2 Statistics Canada reports that the number of reported incidents of spousal abuse has been on the decline since 2000, whereas reported incidents of partner abuse in heterosexual couplings has increased. Incidents of sexual assault continue to be one of the most under-reported forms of abuse as only about 10 per cent of incidents were reported in 2004.

3 Two Canadian soldiers are killed in southern Afghanistan. Five other soldiers sustain injuries.

4 Statistics Canada reports that according to the Survey of Intellectual Property Commercialization in the Higher Education Sector, universities and hospitals reported 1,432 inventions, created 50 spinoff companies, and requested 397 patents in 2003–4.

5 Findings from the inquiry into the Maher Arar affair conclude that there is absolutely no evidence that Arar ever posed a security threat.

Statistics Canada reports that the value of building permits increased 8.3 per cent to $5.8 billion in July.

6 After serving five months of a 30-month sentence for his involvement in the sponsorship scandal, former Groupaction head Jean Brault is granted parole.

Statistics Canada reports that the unemployment rate dipped 0.1 per cent to 6.4 per cent in September.

7 One Canadian soldier is killed in fighting in the Panjwaii district of Afghanistan.

9 The Democratic People's Republic of Korea (DPRK) claims to have detonated a nuclear device.

The DPRK becomes the eighth country to join the nuclear club.

11 Statistics Canada reports that in 2004–5, 32,100 people were being held in federal penitentiaries or in a provincial or territorial jail. Factoring in inflation, the total cost for all correctional services increased 2 per cent to $2.8 billion.

12 Statistics Canada reports that 7,300 or 7 out of 1,000 went bankrupt in 2005. This is the lowest yearly rate of bankruptcy in 25 years.

14 Two Canadians soldiers die after their unit is ambushed in southern Afghanistan.

17 Statistics Canada reports that 6 per cent of Canadian workers are not satisfied with their jobs and 2 per cent are not at all satisfied according to data taken from the 2002 Canadian Community Health Survey.

20 Statistics Canada reports that the 12-month CPI for September 2005 and September 2006 rose a miniscule 0.7 per cent as gasoline prices fell 18.7 per cent over the month.

26 Statistics Canada reports that the median age for all Canadians rose to 38.8 years in 2006 from 38.5 years in 2005.

30 Julian Fantino assumes the position of the commissioner of the Ontario Provincial Police.

Statistics Canada reports that 4 out of 10 residents of the Yukon, Nunavut, and the Northwest Territories reported experiencing a crime in 2005–6, whereas 28 per cent of provincial residents reported experiencing a crime.

31 Minister of finance Jim Flaherty reneges on a campaign promise and announces a new tax on income trusts. The value of the income trust index sheds 15 per cent in the following 12 hours.

Statistics Canada reports that Canada's real GDP grew 0.3 per cent in August.

NOVEMBER

1 After eight months in charge, Canada hands over command of NATO forces in southern Afghanistan to the Netherlands.

3 Statistics Canada reports that the unemployment rate decreased 0.2 per cent to 6.2 per cent in October.

6 Statistics Canada reports that the value of building permits fell 2.5 per cent to $5.7 billion in August.

7 Midterm elections are held in the United States. The Democrats secure control of the House of Representatives and gain a slim majority in the Senate.

Statistics Canada reports that 1.01 million people enrolled in Canadian universities in 2004–5. This is the first time that enrolment has surpassed the 1 million mark.

Statistics Canada reports that Canadian universities granted 209,100 degrees, diplomas, and certificates in 2004 – a record number. The number of master's degrees granted totalled 31,600 and the number of PhDs awarded totalled 4,200.

8 Donald Rumsfeld resigns as secretary of defense for the United States.

Statistics Canada reports that 658 homicides were committed in 2005–222 of these were committed with a firearm. This is an increase of 34 gun homicides from 2004 and is the second consecutive year that the national homicide rate increased.

9 Statistics Canada reports that transportation-related activities accounted for 25 per cent of Canada's greenhouse gas emissions in 2004.

15 Statistics Canada reports that as of 15 May 2006, 62,500 police officers were on duty in Canada – an increase of 1,400 from 2005. Spending for all police-related activities totalled $9.3 billion or $288 per person.

19 The BC Lions defeat the Montreal Alouettes 25–14 to win the 94th Grey Cup.

23 Statistics Canada reports that operating profits for all Canadian corporations increased 2.8 per cent to $58.4 billion in the third quarter of 2006.

27 The House of Commons passes a motion that says Québécois form a nation within a united Canada. As no constitutional changes are required the motion is deemed to be largely symbolic.

Two Canadian soldiers are killed following a suicide attack on their convoy in southern Afghanistan. Canadian troop fatalities in Afghanistan for 2006 include 40 combat deaths and 4 non-combat deaths.

30 Statistics Canada reports that real GDP grew 0.4 per cent in the third quarter of 2006.

DECEMBER

1 Statistics Canada reports that the unemployment rate increased 0.1 per cent to 6.3 per cent in November as more people entered the labour force.

Statistics Canada reports that the number of educators in Canada totalled 502,000 in 2005, a 45,000 increase from 1999. Elementary and secondary school teachers comprise 73 per cent of this number, with college and university teachers comprising 15 and 12 per cent respectively.

2 Stéphane Dion is elected leader of the Liberal Party of Canada. Receiving the support of Toronto MP Gerard Kennedy after the second ballot, Dion bests the heavily favoured Michael Ignatieff on the fourth round of balloting.

Ed Stelmach defeats Jim Dinning on the second round of balloting to become the new leader of the Alberta Progressive Conservative Party.

6 Statistics Canada reports that the total value of building permits increased 6.1 per cent to $6 billion in September.

7 Statistics Canada reports that the value of total assets for Canada's 13.3 million family units reached $5.3 trillion in 2005. However, Canadians also carried a $760 billion debt load. The median debt load increased from $32,300 in 1999 to $44,500 in 2005.

11 Statistics Canada reports that according to the *National Survey of the Work and Health of Nurses*, 31 per cent of female nurses reported high job strain, compared to 26 per cent for all female workers.

12 Statistics Canada reports that average household spending increased 5.1 per cent to $66,860 in 2005. Increased gasoline and utilities prices account for the majority of this increase.

13 Statistics Canada reports that the top 20 per cent of Canada's wealthiest family units controlled 75 per cent of total wealth in Canada in 2005. Total wealth for this group increased from $336,000 to $465,000 in 2005, whereas the value of total assets for the bottom 20 per cent of families never exceeds the value of their debt during this time period.

14 The Toronto Stock Exchange (TSX) closes at 13,021.77, the first time the index surpasses the 13,000 mark.

Ralph Klein officially resigns as premier of Alberta.
Ed Stelmach assumes the position, becoming Alberta's thirteenth premier.

15 A severe windstorm downs and damages an estimated 3,000 trees in Vancouver's Stanley Park.

Statistics Canada reports that national net worth reached $4.8 trillion or $146,700 per person in the third quarter of 2006.

Statistics Canada reports that 30 per cent of adults who spent time in correctional institution re-offended within 12 months of their release. This compares to an 11 per cent re-offence rate for adults who served their sentence under community observation.

18 A report from the Atlantic Provinces Economic Council reveals that 13,000 workers left the Atlantic Provinces for work in Alberta between July 2005 and July 2006.

19 Statistics Canada reports that the 12-month CPI rose to 1.4 per cent between November 2005 and November 2006.

20 Statistics Canada reports that life expectancy for all Canadians increased to 80.2 years in 2004. Life expectancy reached 77.8 years for men and 82.6 years for women.

31 Ban Ki-moon assumes position of UN secretary general.

CANADIAN ANNUAL REVIEW OF POLITICS AND PUBLIC AFFAIRS 2006

EDITOR'S INTRODUCTION – THE YEAR IN REVIEW

The year 2006 was bookended by elections. It began with a federal general election campaign in full swing, an election which produced the most significant change in government in more than a decade, and ended with the election of a new leader for the erstwhile 'Government Party.' The year in between was largely shaped by these two events, with 'Canada's New Government' working to put its Conservative mark on the country in the context of a minority parliament, while the Official Opposition Liberals spent the year embroiled in its long leadership contest.

The year began in the middle of an election campaign. The Martin government had been defeated on 28 November in the aftermath of the Gomery Inquiry, and the election was called for 23 January. Indeed, the turn of the year was also the turning point in the campaign. Until the end of December the Liberals held a consistent lead in the polls despite the general disgust at the revelations of Gomery. On 30 December, however, that all changed with the announcement by the Royal Canadian Mounted Police (RCMP) of an investigation into a leak of a key provision of November's federal budget. There seemed some evidence that the budget's position on income trusts, exempting them from tax, had been leaked. The suggestion of yet more corruption around the Liberals, this time touching directly on the present prime minister, appeared too much for the country to take. The Conservatives took the lead in the polls immediately following the new year and never relinquished it. The results on election day saw the Conservatives gain 25 seats to 124 (on 36 per cent of the vote) and the Liberals lose 32 seats to 103 (30 per cent). 'Canada's New Government,' as the Conservative government led by Prime Minister Stephen Harper would style itself, was well short of commanding a majority in Parliament, but the Liberals had clearly lost the confidence of the country as well as that of the House.

Paul Martin, who had for so long fought to gain the Liberal leadership, gave it up once the election results were in. Martin's announcement started a leadership contest in the Liberal Party that would run through the year, with the convention to elect a new leader not held until 2–3 December. A number of those who would have been expected to run declined in various ways over the course of the year, including Sheila Copps (who had finished a distant second to Martin in 2003), John Manley, Alan Rock, Brian Tobin, and, perhaps most surprisingly, Frank McKenna. By the time of the convention there were eight candidates, but only four seemed to have a realistic chance of winning: Michael Ignatieff, Bob Rae, Stéphane Dion, and Gerard Kennedy. As the voting progressed, it seemed to be a race between Rae and Ignatieff, but a deal between Kennedy and Dion saw Stéphane Dion become the new Liberal leader, much to the surprise of everyone in the room, possibly including the new leader!

While the Liberals searched for renewed leadership, the Conservatives set about governing. For a number of reasons, reform of the democratic institutions of the country was considered a priority of the new government. They had been elected in large part because of the revelations of the inquiry into the sponsorship scandal, which seemed to demand a change in the way in which Ottawa was run. In addition, the Conservatives were the product of a merger on the right, the larger part of which was the Reform Party, whose guiding mission was the reform of Canada's governing institutions. Certainly, the new government introduced some measures to change the structures of Canadian governance, but whether it was the fact of a minority Parliament or the general reluctance of a governing party to alter the tremendous levers of power the Westminster system provides, the reform was at best halting. In direct response to the sponsorship scandal, the government introduced the Federal Accountability Act in an attempt to limit untoward influence on government and to rein in the patronage system that had been built in Ottawa over decades. The act spent most of the year making its way through Parliament, and it was extensively amended in the Senate, but on 8 December it did pass Senate. A month earlier Parliament had accepted the government's Bill C-16, which set fixed election dates for Canada. Rather than being held at the pleasure of the Prime Minister, elections would be held the third Monday in October of the fourth calendar year following an election, beginning with 19 October 2009 – although with a minority Parliament, there seemed little chance of the government making it that far. Central to the Reform Party's agenda had been Senate reform, and the government made some noises about limiting senators' terms and holding voluntary, non-binding elections for vacant Senate seats. Even these modest proposals – particularly compared to the Reform Party's call for a 'Triple E Senate' ('equal, elected, effective') – were going nowhere by the year's end.

The Gomery Inquiry, which had dominated the political agenda in 2005 and produced the new government in 2006, released its recommendations shortly after the election, in February. The new government used the recommendations in crafting the Accountability Act but did not accept them all. Perhaps most ironically, Justice Gomery laid the lion's share of the blame for the scandal on the ever-increasing centralization of power in the Prime Minister's Office (PMO), a trend which had been ongoing at least since the time of Pierre Trudeau. The irony was that the government led by Stephen Harper appeared set on becoming the most centralized, controlling, and opaque government in Canada's history. The PM quickly moved to limit press access to himself and his cabinet, with ministers fleeing from the traditional scrums and Harper announcing that he would only answer questions submitted in advance at his press conferences. Memos leaked over the course of the year gave details of the centralized control of the message, with all ministerial statements having to be pre-cleared by the PMO.

Gomery's was not the only inquiry to report in 2006. On 18 September the inquiry into the Maher Arar affair released its first report. Arar was the Ottawa-area engineer who had been detained by the United States while in transit back to Canada from a family holiday and then sent to Syria for eight months of torture. Justice Dennis O'Connor's first report was wide-ranging, addressing a variety of issues related to Arar's detention and the campaign to discredit him that followed his release. The commissioner began by vindicating Arar: 'I am able to say categorically that there is no evidence to indicate that Mr. Arar has committed any offence or that his activities constitute a threat to the security of Canada.' He was rather more scathing, however, on the role of the RCMP. He found that they had contributed significantly to the ordeal but that their officers were not experienced or well supervised in handling the complexities of national security. Not surprisingly, the commissioner of the RCMP, Giuliano Zaccardelli, came under significant scrutiny. He finally appeared before a Parliamentary Committee on 28 September, and although he apologized to Arar, he indicated he would not resign. However, over the next few months he was tripped up over inconsistencies in his statements concerning what he knew and when, and he ultimately recognized his position was untenable and offered his resignation on 6 December. The next week O'Connor released a second report with a number of recommendations for resolving the problems with the RCMP he had identified.

Arar's was not the only case of Canadians being caught up in the US War on Terror, and the release of Justice O'Connor's second report coincided with Harper announcing a judicial review of the case of three others held by Syria: Abdullah Almalki, Ahmad El-Maati, and Muayyed Nureddin. Unlike the case of Arar, the review by Justice Frank Iacobucci was not to be a public inquiry but an internal review to assess the role, if any, of federal agencies in their detentions. Another Canadian, Omar Khadr, continued to be held in the US prison at Guantanamo Bay, and even a ruling by the US Supreme Court that cast the quasi-judicial 'military commissions' process into disrepute did not result in his release. Khadr was the only Western citizen still held in Guantanamo and had been only fifteen at the time of his alleged crime, but the United States refused to release him, and the Canadian government refused to press for that release. At the same time, Khadr and other members of his family lost a wrongful death suit that had been filed against them in the United States and were ordered to pay a staggering $102.6 million.

Canada's own history of terrorism was also on the agenda in 2006, as on 1 May the government fulfilled one of its election promises and launched a full judicial inquiry into the bombing of Air India Flight 182 in 1985, the worst terrorist attack in Canadian history and the worst act of aviation terror prior to those of 9/11. Two of those charged in the bombing had been acquitted in 2005, and so the government launched a wide-ranging inquiry into the events and their subsequent investigation and appointed retired Supreme Court justice John Major to conduct the inquiry. A month later, Canadians were reminded that they could still be a target for terrorism. The police arrested 15 people, including 5 youths, on 2 June in what came to be known as the 'Toronto 18' plot (two additional suspects were already in custody and the eighteenth was arrested in August). The Toronto 18 were accused of constituting a 'homegrown' terror cell, of 'training' north of Toronto, and of planning a number of violent attacks on Canadian institutions and individuals, including the prime minister.

The Toronto 18 arrests raised a number of difficult issues for the government, including engagement with the Muslim communities in Canada and our relations with the United States. Perhaps foremost among them, however, was the effects of the Canadian involvement in Afghanistan. The Conservative government inherited the decision from 2005 to take on a much greater role in the south of Afghanistan, centred on Kandahar. The increase in Canadian troops had begun in 2005 with the creation of the Provincial Reconstruction Team, and by the spring of 2006 it had reached a contingent of 2,300. Harper moved quickly to make the mission his own, seeking to extend the expanded commitment until 2009. Reluctantly, he put the question to a vote in Parliament and managed to get the extension passed by a bare majority, 149–145. The split was mirrored in the country, where support and opposition to the mission were nearly equal, prompting the government to bring Afghan president Hamid Karzai to Canada to try to bolster support in September. With the growth of the mission and the change in focus, the costs to Canada became rather more evident. From the beginning of Canada's involvement until 2005, eight members of the Canadian Forces had been killed; in 2006 36 soldiers died together with one Department of Foreign Affairs and International Trade (DFAIT) official.

Afghanistan was not the only war attracting Canadians', and the Canadian government's, attention in 2006. In July Israel launched a war against the militant group Hezbollah, which was based in Lebanon. Israel was responding to a Hezbollah attack into Israel which killed or injured 15 soldiers and resulted in the capture of two others. The response saw Israel blockade Lebanon, bomb Beirut, and conduct military operations deep into Lebanese territory. Canada was resolutely pro-Israeli through the course of the war that lasted into August. The Conservative government had shifted Canada's Middle East policy even further towards Israel than had traditionally been the case, and this war provided an opportunity for Harper to demonstrate how resolute that was meant to be. The Canadian line was that Israel's response was reasonable, where by contrast the UN called it 'disproportionate' and 'a violation of international law.' The strongly pro-Israeli position was not altered even on 25 July when an Israeli bombardment killed the lone Canadian peacekeeper stationed in the area, an attack the UN secretary general described as 'apparently deliberate.' Canadian civilians were also killed in the war as the government came under fire for moving too slowly to evacuate Canadian nationals.

The Conservatives sought to distinguish themselves from their Liberal predecessors at home as well as abroad. The defeat of the previous Liberal government had been delayed by the opposition, including the Conservatives, in order to allow then prime minister Martin to attend the Kelowna Conference with Canada's First Nations. The result of that meeting was the Kelowna Accord, which was to provide a long-term framework for reshaping the relationship between the federal government and Canada's indigenous peoples. It was an ambitious agreement and an expensive one, involving the commitment of \$5.1 billion from the federal government. The Conservatives were coy on Kelowna, with

Harper pledging to meet the five- and ten-year targets on poverty reduction, but of the spending commitments he only agreed to honour the $2 billion for the deal the Liberals had reached with former residential school students. The degree to which the government would back away from the Kelowna commitments became clear in the 2 May budget. Kelowna had included spending commitments of $800 million in 2006 alone, yet the budget provided for only $450 million over two years.

Indeed, the Conservative approach to the First Nations communities was a significant change from that of previous Canadian governments. Although the new government did continue with the implementation of the residential schools settlement agreement, they adopted a much harder line than had the Liberals on verifying the claims, despite the evident difficulty some survivors would have in adducing the required proofs. The government also announced its intention to reintroduce a version of the First Nations Governance Act, designed to increase the accountability of native governments. The act had been introduced by the Liberals in 2003 but had been withdrawn after the opposition of the First Nations became clear. However, nothing demonstrated the change in attitude towards First Nations in Ottawa more than the government's *volte face* on the Declaration on the Rights of Indigenous Peoples. Throughout the negotiation process that produced the declaration, Canada had been in the lead. It was seen as one of the primary movers of and advocates for the declaration, but on the 29 June meeting of the UN Human Rights Council, Canada was one of only two votes against the declaration – the other was Russia.

Canada effected a second reversal on a UN-negotiated treaty in 2006, and this one the country had already ratified. In 1997 the members of the UN Convention on Climate Change adopted what has come to be known as the Kyoto Protocol, which among other things set targets for significant reductions on greenhouse gas emissions. Canada signed the Protocol in 1998, and after it was ratified in 2002 it entered into force for Canada in February 2005. The new government proclaimed a commitment to fighting climate change in their first throne speech, but first with the budget and then with the introduction of the Clean Air Act (C-30) in October, it became clear that what the Conservatives called a 'made in Canada' solution did not include living up to Canada's treaty commitments under Kyoto. Of the various half measures and delays included in the Clean Air Act, the one that drew the most criticism was a shift from the absolute targets of Kyoto to so-called intensity targets. Kyoto had called for marked reductions in the actual amount of greenhouse gases its parties emitted, but the Canadian act called only for a reduction in the emission per unit of activity, which meant that even if intensity reductions were achieved, greater economic activity would produce absolute increases in emissions.

The Conservatives acted on two other politically sensitive, high-profile issues in 2006. In September Liberal leadership contender Michael Ignatieff had weighed in on the Quebec question by suggesting that Quebec is a nation. In his academic life, Ignatieff is known for his championing of a notion of 'civic' nationalism, an inclusive nationalism built around shared institutions, in contrast to the 'ethnic' nationalism of language, culture, and colour. The response from Quebec nationalists should have been, and perhaps was, predictable. The Quebec wing of the Federal Liberals passed a resolution calling for the recognition of Quebec as a people within Canada; the Bloc took this call to the Commons and gave notice it would introduce a motion on these lines when it had the chance in November. The government pre-empted the Bloc, introducing its own motion to recognise Quebec as a 'nation within a united Canada.' The Bloc, of course, objected to the qualification, but the Conservative motion passed, which allowed the Bloc's leader, Gilles Duceppe, to point out that as a consequence no one can deny the nationhood of Quebec. Of course, the membership of that 'nation' was far from clear. Ignatieff clearly had meant it as the province as a whole, a civic nation built on a different history and set of institutions than the rest of Canada. For the separatists, however, the nation is that of the French Quebecois, an ethnic nation with a singular claim to the territory of Quebec. It remains to be seen what the effects of the recognition of this nation, of whatever type, will be on the ongoing – although recently largely quiet – question of Quebec's place in Canada.

In 2005 Canada had become one of the first countries in the world to legalize same-sex marriage. The Supreme Court had upheld the federal government's right to define marriage, with several courts already having struck down the denial of marriage to same-sex couples on the basis of then current legislation. The response of the Liberal government had been a law to include same-sex unions within the legal definition of marriage, making Canada the third country after Belgium and the Netherlands to do so. Stephen Harper had promised to revisit the law if elected, with a free vote in the Commons. He fulfilled this promise in the autumn of 2006, introducing a motion which would direct the government to revisit the law if it passed. The Conservatives and Liberals were free to vote their consciences on the motion, while the NDP and Bloc members were whipped. The result was a sizeable majority in favour of same-sex marriage, with 175 voting for and only 123 opposed. Six members of the Cabinet voted with the majority, and opposition among the Liberals was also down from the previous year's vote. Harper responded to the vote by saying that the result was clear, and he saw no reopening of the question in years to come.

The federal government was not the only one to change in 2006. Two conservative premiers had departed by year's end, although in rather different circumstances. Perhaps the more surprising was the sudden end to the premiership of Ralph Klein in Alberta. Given the dominance of the Progressive Conservatives in the province's politics, the pressure on Klein to leave the job he first took in 1992 could only have come from within the party. It seemed to begin with criticism of the Oil Sands developments from Klein's most successful predecessor, Peter Lougheed. It moved from there to produce a fully fledged crisis of leadership, which resulted in Klein announcing that he would resign in 2007 and leave office after a leadership convention in early 2008. However, this did not satisfy the party, and at its convention a few days after the announcement, Klein's leadership received only 55 per cent of support, prompting him to accelerate his leaving. He was replaced in December by Ed Stelmach. In New Brunswick, Bernard Lord's government was also undone from the inside, but in this case the result was not an internal changing of the guard but a general election that was won by the Liberals led by Shawn Graham.

Change was the great theme of 2006. Canada had been governed by the Liberals since 1993, and in the meantime the opposition on the right of the political spectrum had fractured and reconstituted itself as the Conservative Party under Stephen Harper. Although the new party contained the remnants of the old Progressive Conservatives, it was clearly a distinctive political project. Canada, therefore, had a 'new government' in a number of ways in 2006. It was a government constrained by its lack of an overall majority in the House of Commons, but it still demonstrated over the course of the year differences from its predecessors in both style and substance. As 2006 came to a close, the nature and extent of this change was far from clear. The government faced a surprising new Opposition leader in Stéphane Dion, and with only a minority in the Commons another election was always on the cards as the new year dawned.

ROBERT EVERETT

Parliament and politics

As he beamed down at election-night revelers gathered in Calgary on 23 January, Conservative Party leader Stephen Harper savoured a sweet victory. Minutes earlier, Liberal prime minister Paul Martin had conceded defeat in Canada's thirty-ninth general election, and Harper stood poised to lead the country's next government. The Liberals, in power since 1992, had been reduced to inglorious second-party status after a bitter campaign, one in which support for the winners had increased nearly everywhere. Even federalists in pockets of Quebec had abandoned their stubborn devotion to the Liberals and embraced the Conservatives. Harper had insisted that moral turpitude made the Liberals unfit to govern, and he had been vindicated. A swing to the right that had begun with the previous election gained added momentum, and the change craved by conservatives of various stripes for so long was now in reach.

Yet the triumph was far from absolute. Campaign-end polls showing the Conservatives within tantalizing reach of an outright majority proved ephemeral. The Conservatives fell short of full command of Parliament, and, like their Liberal predecessors, they were obliged to manage an unpredictable House of Commons that was, theoretically, stacked against them on key issues. Moreover, Canadians refused in large numbers to sign on to the Conservative agenda despite the powerful incentives supplied by the lingering odor of Liberal-era scandals and concerted, withering critiques of Martin's star-crossed campaign. The Atlantic region was especially wary of the rejuvenated Right. Urbanites, too, were reluctant to surrender the partisan attachments that lifted up the Liberals for so long. Electoral dynamics altered by the softening centre opened up new possibilities for others, and the leftist New Democratic Party (NDP) of Jack Layton also capitalized on the Liberals' troubles, parlaying them into a gain of 10 precious seats. The sovereignty-minded and generally progressive Bloc Québécois led by

Gilles Duceppe actually shed a few ridings but continued to dominate in Quebec.

Canadian minority governments have seldom collapsed quickly. Although chatter about the timing of an early election never was incessant, the Conservatives' capacity to endure was never in real doubt despite a relatively narrow margin. The Conservatives were gifted by the swift capitulation of Martin as leader and the crawling pace at which the Liberals named his successor, Stéphane Dion. With the Liberals awash in debt and distracted by a year-long leadership contest, their disarray made it hard to imagine any serious attempt by the official Opposition to topple the Conservatives and precipitate an election. Only in December, with the new leader in place, did the Liberals dare muse about the possibility of bringing down the government. This was more in the vein of a boisterous overture from Dion than a genuine threat. Opposition reticence provided the ruling party with a luxurious cushion during which to gear up for the next round of balloting. The real question turned on whether or not the Conservatives had the strength, daring, and fortune to engineer the sort of fundamental reorientation of the state and civil society pined for by fervent adherents.

The Conservatives boldly pronounced themselves 'Canada's new government.' Deeds did bear this out, but symbols were frequently the truest markers of transformation. Fresh from a victory owing much to charges of Liberal corruption, the government rolled out legislation to enhance accountability. Other governance reforms were instituted or floated, including the possible renovation of the Senate and the actual setting of fixed dates for general elections. The Cabinet was far leaner than at any time in recent memory, and, yoked by an ever- vigilant Prime Minister's Office, it focused relentlessly on core priorities adumbrated in the campaign. Few chances were missed to distinguish the government from the outgoing Liberals. This led to the reversal of major decisions made by Parliament during the Martin era of 2004–5 or, in a phrase that was uttered repeatedly by Conservative stewards, to 'clean up messes' the government had assumed. Harper's government backed away from Canada's Kyoto Protocol environmental commitments, the national gun registry, and the milestone deal with Aboriginal peoples struck in 2005. It reopened, in vain but with conviction, the vexed issue of same-sex marriage. It promoted tax cuts, family values, and tough criminal and penal legislation. Ideological inclinations were tempered by the realities of a minority. Even so, change had indeed come to Canada in the form of small-c conservatism.

Thirty-ninth general election

On 28 November 2005 the Liberal government was defeated in a vote of confidence for which three disparate opposition parties finally converged to terminate a rocky eighteen-month mandate. The short life of Paul Martin's Liberal government was marred by acrimony and enervation. The campaign trail was muddy. Biliousness was abroad even before candidates took their first steps on the hustings, and Gloria Galloway of the *Globe and Mail* saw portents that the 'campaign will set new standards of viciousness' (25 Nov.). Harper helped set the stage for the descent when he chastised Liberals for willingly associating with an 'organization that was found to have been involved in a massive corruption ring using organized crime to defraud taxpayers' during his speech on the confidence measure. Liberal lawyers countered with warnings of a lawsuit if the Conservative leader dared reprise this calumny outside of the protected precincts of the House. These were at once the last spasms of a decaying body politic and the opening volleys of the fracas to come. The stakes were high for all parties. The Liberals and Conservatives jockeyed for supremacy, while the Bloc, NDP, and Green Party sought in their varying ways to peel away segments of the Liberals' complex base.

At dissolution the party standings were thus: Liberals 133, Conservatives 98, Bloc Québécois 53, New Democrats 18, and independent members, by choice or expulsion, 4. There were two vacancies when the writs were dropped.

Contestants

Each of the three national parties represented in the House contested all 308 seats, as did the budding Green Party. The Bloc fielded a full slate of 75 candidates in Quebec. Ninety independents offered themselves against long odds. Ten minor parties were also certified by Elections Canada:

- Animal Alliance Environment Voters (running a single candidate)
- Canadian Action (34 candidates)
- Christian Heritage (45 candidates)
- Communist (21 candidates)
- First Peoples National (5 candidates)
- Libertarian (10 candidates)

- Marijuana (23 candidates)
- Marxist-Leninist (69 candidates)
- Progressive Canadian (25 candidates)
- Western Bloc (4 candidates).

Major party platforms and issues

A number of concrete issues came to the fore during the campaign. Some reflected planks adopted by the parties in their platforms. Others emerged from the give and take. The Liberals remained on the defensive throughout the seven-week campaign over the notorious sponsorship scandal, an alleged leak of information about its plans for taxing income trusts, and cost overruns associated with a national registry of firearms (which the Conservatives wanted to terminate altogether). Perennial election favourites such as health care, the allocation of resources flowing out of budget surpluses, and the social safety net made cameo appearances. Canada's involvement in Afghanistan was among the issues that had less traction. Continentalism made a surprising return to the spotlight when the Liberals and Conservatives began jawing about Canadian-American relations and (to the Liberals) unwelcome insertion of US-style practices on domestic politics. Abortion and same-sex marriage also featured in the campaign, not least because the Liberals used them as shorthand signifiers of the Conservatives' values (masked as evolving Canadian values). The random slaying of a Toronto teen on a Boxing Day family outing in the city's downtown poignantly brought crime into the mix.

In the previous campaign, the Conservatives effectively employed a strategy of unveiling their platform in daily, headline-grabbing doses. In 2006 they offered up a series of teasers until Harper announced, at the midpoint, that his government would prioritize five objectives (2 Jan.). Having dished out this easily digestible platter, they rehashed it repeatedly. The Conservatives promised to reduce taxes (starting with the much-maligned Goods and Services Tax), cut waiting times for medical treatment, dole out money directly to parents of young children for preschool care, enhance government ethics, and remedy the so-called fiscal imbalance between Ottawa and the provinces. Reminiscent of 1990s electoral gambits such as the Republican Party's successful 'Contract with America' or the Ontario Tories' streamlined platform, this simplification was meant to make other parties look unfocused and insensitive. The five priorities were wrapped in a slogan of 'Stand Up For Canada.' Harper and his team also targeted Quebec. This tactic startled many observers given the province's customary diffidence, but it yielded enough seats to eke out the plurality.

Strategists worked overtime to overcome the Liberals' compounded disadvantages. Vulnerable on patronage and frustratingly unrequited for their stewardship of a salubrious budget, they settled on assaying yet another effort to portray the Conservatives as antithetical to contemporary Canadian values. Harper and his colleagues were tarred as spiteful traditionalists in the thrall of American overlords, polluters, and religious fundamentalists. 'Choose Your Canada' was the campaign theme from the start, but Martin's awakened passion (or growing desperation) on this score may have saved the Liberals' from a greater disaster.

The New Democrats positioned themselves as a refuge for progressive-minded but disenchanted Liberal backers. This led to an emphasis on the kinds of social programs that many Canadians cherished. The party knew that it could not form a government but insisted a strong position in a minority government scenario would result in 'Getting Results for People.' The NDP also pitched its distinctiveness on matters of foreign policy. The Bloc Québécois (BQ) pressed, as always, for greater fiscal generosity towards the provinces, whereas the Liberals in particular challenged the BQ's stance on Quebec sovereignty. Towards the end, and fearing a hostile takeover of its near monopoly in parts of the province, the BQ party cast the Conservatives as wholly beholden to oil barons in Alberta and indifferent to the causes dearest to the hearts of Quebecers, whether sovereigntist or not. Running under the banner of 'Thankfully, Here It's the Bloc,' the party downplayed specific proposals even as it spoke in general terms about the risks of globalization, the need for greater stability for food producers, and the necessity of curbing greenhouse gas emissions. Under newish campaign laws, the Green Party had enough funding to sow its message farther and wider. However, lacking parliamentary seats and the prestige of participation in the leader debates, it proved difficult to penetrate deeply into the consciousness of voters. Beyond an obvious environmentalist message, Jim Harris and his fellow candidates offered up a mixed bag of proposals that were surprisingly conservative by the standards of international green parties.

Four televised leader debates were held during the campaign. Vancouver hosted a pair early on (15 and 16 Dec.). Leaders reconvened for encounters held in Montreal on 9 and 10 January. The English-language rendezvous on 10 January in Montreal was considered crucial. The Liberals were now trailing in the polls, and Harper and Martin fenced through the evening, exchanging ripostes over economic policy, ethics, and one another's national unity credentials. Curiously, heat was generated by a somewhat arcane dispute over the *Charter of Rights and Freedoms*. Martin boasted that the Liberals were prepared, as their first act, to amend the constitution to prevent the federal government from invoking the 'notwithstanding' clause to override *Charter* protections. Court rulings, he insisted, should not be trumped by the whims of politicians when jurisprudence was overwhelming on fundamental rights. Harper expressed contentment with current arrangements (*Ottawa Citizen*, 10 Jan.). Viewers may have scratched their heads about the details; but Martin's probe was intended to delineate substantive differences between the parties over the legalization of same-sex marriage, a fact in law that the Conservatives continued to resist. The Conservative and Liberal leaders also challenged each other's patriotism and values. Martin, now an aggressive underdog, eagerly portrayed Harper as a right-winger moulded by an alien ideology and scolded that 'America is our neighbour. It is not our nation.' He also took on Duceppe over Quebec's role in confederation, insisting that shared values kept the nation together. Sparring spilled over to the French-language debate the following night. Volatility meant that Quebec was suddenly in play, and all of the leaders angled. In this regard, as the *Toronto Star* reported, this second debate 'demonstrated vividly that [Duceppe] now has two rivals in the Quebec race, doling out attacks equally on Harper and Martin' and finding them 'equally guilty for trying to buy Quebecers' loyalty with federal money' (11 Jan.). Although Jack Layton tried mightily to highlight his party's platform on both occasions, his interventions on behalf of the NDP were overshadowed by the blusterous main events.

Swing to the Conservatives

The Liberals never trailed in public opinion samples in December 2005. The Conservatives maintained their lead throughout January 2006. The consensus fulcrum was the announcement by the Royal Canadian Mounted Police (RCMP) on 30 December that they were actively investigating an alleged leak of a November 2005 decision by the Liberal government not to tax income trusts. The Securities and Exchange Commission in the United States subsequently confirmed that it, too, had taken a special interest in the matter. Prodded by the NDP and others, the Mounties set out to determine if any government insiders had tipped off investors. It may have been coincidence or prescience, but the markets tracked in suspicious ways just prior to the formal announcement. No less a person than finance minister Ralph Goodale

Voter preferences by political party and date select Ipsos polls, December 2005 to January 2006

Party	20–2 December	2–5 January	10–12 January	17–19 January	17–22 January	Result
Conservatives	32	35	39	38	38	36.3
Liberals	33	31	29	26	27	30.2
NDP	16	18	18	19	19	17.5
Bloc Québécois	13	10	9	11	12	10.5
Greens	5	5	5	5	4	4.5

was interviewed by the Mounties on 3 January. Liberals denied and denounced but were forced into cover mode. All of this played into the hands of opposition parties. They had been busily condemning other lapses on the part of the Liberals. Still a significant number of voters were in a forgiving mood. From that point on, however, Harper and his party held sway. As the polls climbed in their favour, a majority government appeared plausible. At one point Ekos Research, surveying for the Liberal-friendly newspapers *Toronto Star* and *La Presse*, made the 'difficult decision' to redo a sample that showed the Conservatives safely home (*Ottawa Citizen*, 10 Jan.). It was a wise move, for the electorate was not yet prepared to fully subscribe to the cosmetically buffed conservatism proffered by Harper.

Results

Although a majority eluded the Conservatives, and the Liberals' made a modest, last-ditch recovery, the outcome was broadly consistent with predictions. Conservatives swept Alberta and piled up seats in virtually every electoral region. As is so often the case in Canadian elections, the large central Canadian provinces of Ontario and Quebec were pivotal to the result. Liberal fortunes tumbled in both. The party captured only 54s eats in Ontario as the Conservatives (at 40 seats) and NDP (with 10) pounced. The punishment of Liberals in Quebec was less severe given the Bloc's prevailing strength, but sudden shifts resulted in a shredding of the party's representation. Conservatives took 10 seats in Quebec. The Liberals hung on to 24 ridings in the Atlantic region and took the solitary seats in Nunavut and the Yukon in the north (losing to the NDP in the Northwest Territories). It was small consolation. Newcomer Liberal stars fell aplenty, and stalwarts such as Cabinet ministers Pierre

Pettigrew, Anne McLellan, Liza Frulla, Tony Valeri, Jacques Saada, and Ethel Blondin-Andrew went down to defeat.

New Democrats added 10 seats overall, generally at the expense of the Liberals, and rose modestly in the popular vote. Unable to woo Quebec, the NDP managed to add seats in the Atlantic, Ontario, the prairies, and British Columbia. Party leader Jack Layton professed himself satisfied but ever forward-looking. Ambitious and confident at the outset, the Bloc laid plans to build on an already solid foundation in Quebec (where it had garnered nearly half of the votes and won more than 70 per cent of the seats in the previous election). Duceppe was fiery after the Conservative raid on his territory: 'We are not going in the same direction ... Quebec needs to have all of the powers of a sovereign country' (*Globe and Mail*, 24 Jan.). The Green Party was dismayed by its meagre haul. It took no ridings and saw its share of the vote grow imperceptibly despite having access to public funding for the first time. Greens were noticeably stronger in the west, taking 6.5 per cent in Alberta and 5.3 per cent in British Columbia, and requalified for funding. Minor party totals were minuscule. Even the most successful also-ran, Christian Heritage, ended up losing ground. As was true in the previous election, a single independent member was elected. In 2004 British Columbia's Chuck Cadman won. This time it was the turn of provocative Quebec radio host Andre Arthur, victorious in Portneuf-Jaques Cartier.

Voter turnout rose to 64.9 per cent. This at least reversed a troubling downward trajectory. Even so, the low participation rate was indicative of ongoing alienation and indifference. Despite efforts to promote participation by youth, only 43.8 per cent of those in the 18-to-24 age bracket voted. This rate was up by a mere 6.8 per cent from 2004. The data were worrisome from the standpoint of engagement. Moreover, as Linda McQuaig noted, the generational imbalance appeared to skew the results. Citing polling analyses, done by EKOS research, she argued that Conservative support was concentrated among 'affluent, older, predominantly male Canadians,' who are 'politically active, well- connected and dominant in public debate' (*Toronto Star*, 22 Jan.). By contrast, younger Canadians were cooler to conservatism and decidedly more sympathetic to progressive causes.

The number of women in the Commons, already low, settled at 65. This meant that females made up just 21.1 per cent of MPs in the new House. Only 24.8 per cent of the candidates nominated by major parties were women. A third of the candidates running for the NDP were women, and with 12 elected, the NDP had the highest proportion of

2006 Election results with changes from prior election

Party	Ridings won in 2006	Change in ridings from 2004 election	Popular vote in 2006 (per cent)	Change in popular vote from 2004 election
Conservatives	124	+25	36.27	+6.64
Liberals	103	−32	30.23	−6.50
New Democrats	19	+10	17.48	+1.71
Bloc Québécois	54	−3	10.48 (Quebec 42.1)	−1.90
Greens	–	–	4.48	+0.19
Independents	1	1	0.55	−0.07
Other Parties	–	–	0.02	n / c

females of any caucus in Canadian history. The Conservatives had the smallest percentage of both female candidates and MPs. Prominent feminist Doris Anderson lamented that 'it's like pushing a boulder up a cliff under our present electoral system' and called, once more, for an earnest effort by the parties to recruit female candidates, especially in winnable ridings (*Toronto Star*, 24 Jan.). The Senate had a higher share of women. Organizations such as Equal Voice vowed to keep pressing for change in the electoral system.

Liberal leadership transfer

Having quickly signalled his intention to step down, Paul Martin was replaced as interim leader of the Liberals by veteran MP Bill Graham. Martin formally resigned on 19 March. He retained his seat in the House and kept up a busy schedule. He authored a private member's bill to implement the 2005 Kelowna Accord and travelled widely to stump for the concept of an expanded multilateral forum dubbed the L-20 group which would include countries such as China, India, and Brazil as well as the powerful G8 summit countries (*Toronto Star*, 1 June).

The lightning-fast decision by Martin to step down as the Liberal Party leader was followed by a marathon leadership contest that culminated in a convention in Montreal on 2–3 December. Candidates endured a protracted run-up that involved serial debates and a preliminary sounding of party faithful to nominate riding delegates. Before the final field was established, a handful of potential candidates stepped aside. They included Sheila Copps (the distant but persistent runner-up to Martin in 2004), John Manley (Martin's nearest rival until he withdrew), and erstwhile Cabinet ministers Alan Rock and Brian Tobin, both touted as possible successors in the 1990s and early part of the new century. Frank McKenna, once New Brunswick's premier and briefly Canada's ambassador in Washington, bowed out somewhat unexpectedly given pundit enthusiasm.

Ultimately, the main contenders were:

- Nova Scotian Scott Brison, a one-time candidate for the leadership of the Conservatives who, finding the party too right-wing, crossed to the Liberals and wound up as minister of public affairs in the Martin government;
- Quebec's Stéphane Dion, an academic by profession, who had served as a (hard-line) minister of intergovernmental affairs and an increasingly avid minister of the environment;
- former professional hockey standout Ken Dryden, a Toronto MP and minister of social development under Martin;
- Martha Hall Findlay, a Toronto lawyer and the sole woman on the ballot;
- historian and novice MP Michael Ignatieff, fresh from a return to Canada and successful debut on the partisan stage;
- poverty activist, Ontario MP, and former provincial minister of education Gerard Kennedy, making his first imprint on the federal scene;
- Bob Rae, a former NDP premier of Ontario, who had grown disenchanted with social democracy and gravitated to the party where his brother John had long been a powerful strategist;
- suburban Toronto MP Joe Volpe, one-time minister of citizenship and immigration and human resources management, whose candidacy was buffeted by blunders.

Another four entrants – three of them ex-Cabinet ministers – set out on the journey only to withdraw. Toronto-area MP John Godfrey threw his hat into the ring but had to depart for health reasons (12 April). Another Ontarian, Maurizio Bevilacqua, ended his run on 14 August. MP and Toronto-based physician Carolyn Bennett stepped aside on 15 June. British Columbia's Hedy Fry gave up the chase on 25 September. The quartet all supported Bob Rae.

Ignatieff was installed as a slight early favourite on the basis of his faintly Trudeauesque glide into partisan politics from globe-trotting academia. Squaring off against him at the top was an old university roommate, Rae. Both had enviable backing inside the federal caucus. With the field largely composed of Toronto-area politicos (the Liberals having a tradition of alternating between leaders from Quebec and the rest of Canada), there could be an opportunity for someone outside of southern Ontario to drive a wedge. Dion was destined to wear that mantle. He attracted environmentalists and youth and earned plaudits from several newspapers for his spirited defence of national unity as minister of intergovernmental affairs. The *Globe and Mail* described him as 'arguably the most courageous politician of his generation [for] establishing the federal government's case against unilateral secession and limiting the potential for separatist trickery' (26 Nov.).

Liberals had much to ponder. They had gravitated en masse to Martin after his long rivalry with Jean Chrétien had been resolved. Simply put, Martin underperformed. This time around there was a buffet of choices to consider, of strengths and weaknesses to assess. If they were serious about reclaiming power, the Liberals would surely have to think along with the Conservatives. In a memorandum obtained by the *Toronto Star* (28 Sept.), senior Conservative adviser Doug Finley sized up the prospects with these snapshots:

- Ignatieff would be the most 'formidable' foe, with the capacity to lure away swing voters in key demographics if he could conduct himself in a more disciplined fashion;
- Rae was a decent soul who would nevertheless be an ideal opponent because of his blemished history as the NDP premier of Ontario;
- despite a compelling personal story, Kennedy's candidacy was premature and his stage persona was weak;
- Dion was a dull policy wonk who would have difficulty getting distance from the tarnished Liberal past.

The selection process had two stages. The party's executive authorized a preliminary round of delegate selection by riding associations, clubs, and groups. When this phase concluded with a 'super weekend' of at-large delegate balloting, Ignatieff grabbed the reins, followed by Rae, Kennedy, and Dion (1 Oct.). The frontrunner also enjoyed a lead among ex officio convention goers willing to tip their hand.

Before first ballot voting began, Volpe withdrew and announced for Rae. (Volpe made news when it was revealed that he had accepted money from executives of a pharmaceutical company through their spouses and children. He lost his campaign chair over a disagreement on Middle Eastern policy that flared into a curious tiff over campaign promises that required police intervention and was accused of taking on workers from a federally supported charity.) This move did little to alter the balance, and results on the first ballot mirrored pre-gathering preferences shown by delegates of all stripes. Ignatieff took the top spot with 29.3 per cent, followed by Rae (20.3), Dion (17.8), Kennedy (17.7), Dryden (4.4), Brison (4.0), and Volpe (3.4 despite having ended his run). Hall Findlay was eliminated after trailing with 2.7 per cent. She threw her support behind Dion. Brison, retiring promptly, endorsed Rae. Dion and Kennedy had made no secret of their mutual admiration, and they vowed to support whichever had the strongest hand. For the moment, they carried on as individuals.

The second ballot represented an opportunity for one of two favourites to pull ahead. Ignatieff continued to lead with 31.8 per cent but gained little ground. Stagnation also plagued Rae (up just 2.8 per cent), Dion (doing best with a rise of 3.0 per cent), and Kennedy (1.1 per cent to the good). Dryden was dropped off and headed into the Rae fold. In a defining moment, Kennedy moved to the swelling sea of green-clad Dion backers. The tacit alliance between the two had become reality. Talks between the Ignatieff and Rae camps about the possibility of coalescing behind one or the other did not bear fruit. Both carried on against the upstart Dion and his band of outsiders.

The Dion-Kennedy coalition, backed by Hall Findlay's loyalists, stuck together on the third ballot and catapulted Dion ahead. Ignatieff fell to second place. Rae's support had risen, but he was automatically struck off. The final ballot was a straight stand-off that seemingly pitted the old guard against a dynamic, neophyte brigade. In a dramatic showdown, Dion captured 2,521 votes on the final ballot and upset Ignatieff by a margin of 54.7 per cent to 45.3 per cent. The result immediately put Liberal solidarity to the test.

The NDP and Bloc hold steady

Energized by their gains in the election, the New Democrats stood behind leader Jack Layton and relished their role as foil to the Conservatives while the Liberals were distracted by questions of leadership. Gilles Duceppe, content in Ottawa, disavowed any interest in leading the Bloc's like-minded provincial counterparts, the Parti Québécois. Neither party was keen to force an early election (although the Bloc signalled at year's end that it was intrigued by a joint manoeuvre with the Liberals that would topple the Conservatives in 2007). Both leaders were safe.

Green Party leadership

Hopes dashed by the election results in January, the Greens looked to replace Jim Harris with a more compelling leader. On 26 August they chose Elizabeth May. May earned her environmental stripes as executive director of the Sierra Club of Canada. This gave her considerable stature. Yet May had limited experience as a legislator or party head (having run unsuccessfully for the obscure Small Party in 1980). She was not shy about entering the fray. Seizing the first opportunity to vie for a seat, she finished a heartening second to a Liberal in a 27 November by-election in Ontario.

National institutions

Cabinet

The first Harper Cabinet was sworn in on 6 February. Unlike all ministries since 1972, the group included no ministers of state (that is, junior ministers normally outside of the Cabinet per se). This was meant to symbolize a sense of equality. Egalitarianism was reinforced by the absence of a designated deputy prime minister. With a relatively lean roster of 27, many ministers took on multiple portfolios. Individuals with old Reform and Democratic Alliance credentials were in abundance but did not predominate. Room had to be cleared for Conservatives who had earned their stripes in Ontario and Quebec.

There were proportionally fewer women than in Liberal Cabinets of the twenty-first century. Just six of 27 ministers were female, and one of those was a senator. Most of the positions held by women were junior. There were no members from the three northern territories or the province of Prince Edward Island, where the Conservatives had been shut out. Nine were from Ontario and five from Quebec. The west was rewarded with a disproportionate share based on population, with five new ministers who hailed from British Columbia; Alberta was home to four, Saskatchewan two, and Manitoba one. The Atlantic was represented by one minister from each of Nova Scotia, New Brunswick, and Newfoundland and Labrador.

Eyebrows were raised by two of Harper's picks. The first controversy involved the selection of David Emerson as the minister of international trade, the Pacific gateway, and the 2010 Vancouver-Whistler Olympics. Emerson was experienced, having served in the Martin government as environment minister. It was galling that, just two weeks after campaigning and winning as a Liberal, he jumped ship. Emerson justified the abrupt turnabout on the grounds that the Conservatives had constructed a beckoning 'centrist' ideological home. Livid donors and constituents demanded Emerson's resignation. Another choice provoked anger when Harper reached outside of Parliament to name the unelected Michael Fortier, a Conservative strategist, as a senator and minister of public works. The Conservatives had to fend off accusations of hypocrisy. Fortier insisted that he accepted a 'temporary' Senate appointment in order to serve the greater good. He had declined to run in the election at the urging of his family (7 Feb.). Writing in the *Globe and Mail*, Jeffrey Simpson argued that the Conservatives had adopted cynical practices they had roundly condemned; although Harper insisted that he was motivated by the need to create strong regional representation in his inner circle, Simpson argued that the 'political history of Canada suggests, however, that the natural governing party is the one that speaks for the whole country through the federal government, not as a reflection of the composite desires of every province' (7 Feb.).

Only one change in this line-up occurred during the year. Michael Chong, whose primary job was minister of intergovernmental affairs, resigned over legislation recognizing the Quebecois as a people (27 Nov.). In a straightforward promotion, Ontario backbench MP Peter van Loan was summoned to take on all three of Chong's portfolios (sport, intergovernmental affairs, and Privy Council president).

Speech from the Throne

In a prelude to the short first session of Parliament, governor general Michaëlle Jean read a crisp Speech from the Throne as Parliament opened (4 April). The succinct forecast reiterated the Conservatives' principal campaign planks – reducing the Goods and Services Tax, transferring money to parents with young children, and taking a tougher stance on crime and government accountability. The government also trumpeted a strong military, harmony with the United States, and sundry governance innovations. It was, in the words of a *Toronto Star* editorial, 'far from being socially progressive' even though it made nods to 'more than just the hard-core Conservatives [by] making a few welcome comments about improving opportunity for all Canadians, including Aboriginal peoples and new immigrants, about improving the security of seniors, promoting a more competitive and more productive economy and solving the problem of fiscal imbalance between Ottawa and the provinces' (5 April). The NDP and Bloc had been consulted

First Conservative ministry February 2006

Minister	Portfolio
Stephen Harper	prime minister
Robert Nicholson	leader of the government in the Commons minister for democratic reform
Marjory LeBreton	leader of the government in the Senate
James Flaherty	minister of finance
Peter MacKay	minister of foreign affairs minister for the Atlantic Canada opportunities agency
Vic Toews	minister of justice / attorney general of Canada
David Emerson	minister of international trade minister for the pacific gateway minister for the 2010 Vancouver-Whistler Olympics
John Baird	president of treasury board
Tony Clement	minister of health minister for the federal economic development initiative for Northern Ontario
Gordon O'Connor	minister of defence
Stockwell Day	minister of public safety
Gregory Thompson	minister of veterans affairs
Chuck Strahl	minister of agriculture and agri-food minister for the Canadian Wheat Board
Loyola Hearn	minister of fisheries and oceans
Jim Prentice	minister of Indian affairs minister for northern development federal interlocutor for Métis and non-status Indians
Lawrence Cannon	minister of transport, infrastructure, and communities
Monte Solberg	minister of citizenship and immigration
Rona Ambrose	minister of environment
Gary Lunn	minister of natural resources
Michael Chong	president of the Queen's Privy Council minister for intergovernmental affairs minister for sport
Jean-Pierre Blackburn	minister of labour minister for the economic development agency of Canada (regions of Quebec)
Michael Fortier	minister of public works and government services
Maxime Bernier	minister of industry
Carol Skelton	minister of national revenueminister for western economic diversification
Diane Finley	minister of human resources and social development
Bev Oda	minister of Canadian heritage minister for the status of women
Josée Verner	minister of international cooperation minister for La Francophonie minister for official languages

prior to the speech and pledged to work with the government. In rhetoric, the Liberals were less phlegmatic, and interim leader Bill Graham reminded the Conservatives that it was Liberal acumen that had provided the government with the budgetary flexibility they enjoyed.

Branding Canada's 'New Government' and the Conservatives' style

The Conservatives were keen to distance themselves from their Liberal predecessors, preternaturally so, and to forge a distinctive identity coterminous with a rebranded government. Control over the agenda was centralized in the Prime Minister's Office, and the PMO adopted stringent measures to maintain a tight grip over messages consistent with the Conservative brand. Cabinet ministers were often muzzled, and the press gallery chafed under strict limitations on access.

Communications officers were given their marching orders in a circular leaked to the *Globe and Mail.* Ministers were directed to avoid situations in which their unguarded or interview-guided statements might distract from the government's five priorities. PMO officials vetted all ministerial appearances and exerted authority over all written communications (17 March). In early March media personnel were asked to abandon their habitual stake-outs while Cabinet meetings were in progress. Ministers had already begun fleeing from scrums set up following the daily Question Period in the House. All this was said to stem, in part, from anxieties over the performance of novices, coupled with an obvious desire to condition media coverage. Some thought it was driven by distrust or dictatorial inclinations. According to insiders, Harper was convinced that the media were antithetical to conservatism and Conservatives. The restrictions began to colour and cool relations with many journalists. Tightening controls over news workers ultimately led to a brief boycott of a prime ministerial news conference by two dozen accredited press gallery denizens. Citing the need to create more orderly events, the PMO had begun collecting questions in advance of Harper's news conferences. When it was announced, at a news conference on 23 May, that the prime minister would not field questions since none had been submitted ahead of time, all but a handful of journalists walked out. It was a first. The contretemps reinforced suspicions on both sides, and Harper let it be known that he doubted a Liberal leader would have been subjected to the same treatment.

The situation was ironic. The Conservatives came to power on a pretext of more open government, and they were certainly prepared to be more transparent when it came to disclosing the wrongdoings of their predecessors (*Toronto Star*, 27 Jan.). It was also consistent with an overall approach to governing that emphasized differentiation. The home pages of the highly regarded and popular government Web site were made over in Conservative blue, adorned with likenesses of the prime minister, and reconfigured as portals to government initiatives. An emeritus scientist with the Geological Survey of Canada, Dr Andrew Okulitch, made a minor splash when he questioned a directive requiring that communications from his branch bear the legend 'Canada's New Government' rather than 'Government of Canada.' His correspondence was deemed sufficiently cutting as to merit Okulitch's dismissal. When a furor erupted, the brave (or curmudgeonly) employee was reinstated (19 Sept.). The government also clarified that not everyone was obliged to use the terminology. These retractions did little to mollify those who thought the Conservatives' guilty of violating ethical standards.

House by-elections and caucus changes

Two by-elections were necessitated during the year. On 28 August Benoit Sauvageau, Bloc MP for Repentigny, succumbed to injuries suffered in an automobile accident while en route to a constituency event. BQ leader Gilles Duceppe recalled him as 'a very good member of Parliament and a very good sovereignist,' who was 'respected not only in the sovereignist camp but also by our adversaries' (*Montreal Gazette*, 29 Aug.). After eighteen years in the House, Joe Fontana, Liberal MP in Ontario and minister of labour under Paul Martin, resigned in order to run for mayor of his native London. As it turned out, Fontana was beaten handily in the race.

By-elections were held for these two ridings on 27 November. In Repentigny, Raymond Gravel successfully defended the seat for the Bloc. Gravel, an outspoken Catholic priest, needed special dispensation to stand for public office. Greater interest was sparked by the run-off in London North Centre. It was there that the Greens' new leader, Elizabeth May, sought to make a breakthrough. Although May pulled off a second-place showing, Liberal Glen Person held the riding for the Grits.

Conservative Garth Turner said on 10 February he knew it was coming. After taking David Emerson to task for crossing to the Liberal Party without submitting to a by-election and recording other criticisms of the government on his personal blog, the Ontario MP was ostracized

Party standings 31 December 2006

Party	Seats
Conservatives	124
Liberals	102
Bloc Québécois	51
New Democrats	29
Independent	2 (1 elected, 1 expelled from caucus)

by his putative mates. Eventually he was suspended on 18 October from the Conservative caucus altogether on a charge of breaking confidentiality. Having stumped on behalf of Green Party leader Elizabeth May during her run for a seat in a November by-election, the maverick MP was courted by May's party. He could have been the first Green member of the party in Parliament but demurred. At the end of the year party standings were little changed from the 23 January election.

Fixed election dates

In April the Conservatives floated the idea of adopting fixed election dates. A four-year cycle had already been adopted in British Columbia, Ontario, and Newfoundland and Labrador. The goal, said Harper, was to 'stop leaders from trying to manipulate the calendar simply for partisan political advantage' (*Globe and Mail*, 26 May). Advocates also contended that predictability would loosen party discipline by taking away the prime minister's ability to coerce MPs with the prospect of an election. Critics complained that plotting elections was at odds with age-old prerogatives and the Westminster-inspired principle of requiring ongoing affirmations of confidence in the rulers. Legislation was introduced on 30 May as Bill C-16. Under the proposal elections would be held on the third Monday in October during the fourth calendar year after the previous election, beginning with 19 October 2009. It passed, with support from the NDP and Bloc, on 6 November. Notably, there was no serious movement at the federal level on proportional representation, a system favoured by several national parties and advocacy groups who faulted the first-past-the-post electoral system for distorting popular sentiments.

Government accountability

The government's cornerstone Federal Accountability Act was introduced on 11 April. The *Globe and Mail*'s Bill Curry provided readers with this summary the following day:

- a ban on donations from unions and corporations to political parties together with the ceiling for individual donations lowered from $5,000 to $1,000;
- a stipulation that Cabinet ministers, their staffs, and senior public servants could not lobby government for five years after leaving their posts and obligations for lobbyists to document contacts with senior officials;
- a new parliamentary budget authority giving MPs and parliamentary committees financial estimates at odds with ministerial projections;
- a new director of public prosecutions who would act as a permanent independent prosecutor for bureaucrats who breach federal laws other than the *Criminal Code*;
- a system whereby government appointments would be based on merit rather than political connections;
- an auditor of procurements to ensure fairness in the awarding of contracts;
- enhanced powers for the auditor general to analyse expenditures made on individuals, companies, and Aboriginal communities that were not self-governing; and
- a reinforcement of the capacities of the ethics commissioner and statutory recognition of the integrity commissioner's responsibilities to address complaints from public servants.

The act wound up spending more days in the Senate than in the House and was amended approximately ninety ways. It was finally approved on 8 December.

Patronage commissioner

As part of its repertoire of governance reforms, the government announced that it would establish a public appointments commission to oversee the choice of political appointees to government posts. Although this was acceptable in principle to other parties, the Opposition pushed back on the individual tapped by Harper to be the inaugural incumbent.

In a moment of unbridled candor, Gwyn Morgan, a former executive in the energy sector, had linked crime and violence with immigration in a speech roughly coinciding with his entrance into public affairs. He was, moreover, a Conservative fundraiser. Members of the parliamentary vetting committee, who were in a majority position, asked him to withdraw. When he refused, members proceeded to vote down his selection along party lines (16 May). In retaliation, a peeved prime minister quickly canned the idea of a patronage commissioner.

Senate reform

The old Reform Party of 1987 to 2000 had made Senate reform central to its creed. Its mantra of an 'equal, elected, effective Senate' echoed in a Conservative initiative to change the membership of the Upper House. On 30 May a Senate bill was introduced to amend the Constitution Act to limit the term of newly appointed senators to eight years (Bill S-4). Current senators would be exempted and permitted to serve until the mandatory retirement age of seventy-five. Because it proposed to amend the constitution, the provinces would have to ratify such a change. Companion legislation emerged in the House on 13 December in the form of Bill C-43. This was intended to enable citizens to express their senatorial preferences or, in the words of the bill, to provide for the 'consultation of the electors.' The bill was somewhat tentative. Until the constitution was amended, those passing muster in elections would not be automatically guaranteed the right to serve in the Senate: the prime minister would retain the right to recommend senators. Eventually Senate ballots would be tied to federal or provincial general elections. Only Alberta and British Columbia had instituted a voter mechanism. New Liberal leader Stéphane Dion called the bill irresponsible and asked why the government had not rather thought to redress an imbalance which gave Alberta an allocation of 6 Senate seats while much smaller Nova Scotia had 10. Harper took the unusual step of appearing before the Senate Committee to stump for his Senate bill on 7 September.

No change in the distribution of seats among the provinces and territories was contemplated in the government's bills. A pair of senators, Lowell Murray (Ontario, Conservative) and Jack Austin (British Columbia, Liberal), took this matter into their own hands on 22 June. Under a formula tabled that day, the Senate would grow to 117 members. British Columbia would be severed from the west to become a fifth

Senate 'division' or region. It would also be entitled to twelve senators rather than six. Alberta (10), Manitoba (7), and Saskatchewan (7) would also see a rise in number. Ontario, Quebec, and the eastern division – lumping together Nova Scotia, New Brunswick, Newfoundland and Labrador, and Prince Edward Island – would remain steady at twenty-four senators each. Proponents wanted the government of the day to have the ability to name an additional 'five to ten' non-designated senators – up from a range of four to eight. A special committee on Senate reform endorsed the idea on 26 October. An amendment to the bill whereby British Columbia would have twenty-four senators was moved by Senator David Tkachuk on 11 December.

Supreme Court

In April 2005 the Liberal government revised the process by which justices are named to the Supreme Court. Under that formula, the minister of justice undertook public consultations leading to the development of a short list of three prospective candidates by a special advisory committee composed of members of each parliamentary party, a nominee of the provincial attorneys general, a law society representative, and two individuals outside of legal circles. The justice minister would decide on the individual and justify the choice before a House committee. The nominee was spared testifying in public. Although a recommendation on the replacement for outgoing justice John Major had been made to the Liberal government in late November 2005 under this process, a final decision was deferred pending the election of a new government.

Three weeks after taking office, Harper announced a new wrinkle (20 Feb.). An all-party House committee would have three hours to question the nominee after which it could recommend or reject but not veto an appointment. The prime minister retained the prerogative to appoint. Conservatives who favoured a greater say by parliamentarians considered this a halfway measure. Critics thought it unseemly to drag a high-ranking justice through a potentially embarrassing and unedifying grilling.

Justice Marshall Rothstein was the first candidate to be named in this fashion. One of three short-listed individuals (Peter MacKinnon and Constance Hunt were the others), Rothstein testified before an Ad Hoc Committee to Review a Nominee for the Supreme Court of Canada, chaired by York University law professor Peter Hogg, on 27 February. Parameters established by Harper perversely prevented interlocutors from probing Rothstein's judicial philosophy. Even so, it was clear enough that he eschewed the kind of activism which condoned courts substituting their judgment for the will of Parliament. Niceties over, Rothstein was appointed 1 March.

Auditor general

Auditor General Sheila Fraser provided the House with two major reports. The first covered progress made in addressing previously identified problems or implementing past recommendations (16 May). The annual report was tabled on 28 November. Revelations about the conduct of the ombudsperson for federal inmates captured the spotlight. The incumbent, Ron Stewart, was accused of negligence, extravagance, and excessive generosity when it came to granting himself expenses and vacation time. The *Ottawa Citizen*'s summary of other findings underlined this list of concerns:

- although no treaty had been signed with British Columbia First Nations since 1993, negotiations and legalities had cost close to $750 million;
- the budget of Health Canada was insufficient to monitor commonly used products, and the agency had entered into a contract for non-insured benefits even though no bidder had passed muster;
- overpayments made to seniors were not being recouped;
- there were ongoing setbacks in the development and adoption of large-scale information technology initiatives;
- criteria for outlays of money were outdated for times of budget surpluses;
- oversight on new initiatives was adequate, but procedures for reviewing ongoing program funding were lacking (although new spending initiatives were not subjected to sufficiently rigorous tests as to whether or not enough time had been allotted for project completion);
- an external investigation of problems with the RCMP's pension fund did not have the appearance of impartiality;
- there were irregularities in the awarding of a contract for moving public servants; and
- employees at the Department of Public Safety were not convinced that managers were taking seriously their complaints about fraud, abuse, and misconduct.

Ethics Commissioner

Former McGill University principal Bernard Shapiro was named as the first paid, full-time, publicly appointed, parliamentary-mandated ethics commissioner in 2004. Sterling credentials aside, Shapiro ran into difficulties from the start. He and parliamentarians clashed over his interpretation of the office's mandate and his investigative prowess. Relations with Harper soured early in the year and were never repaired. When the Federal Accountability Act was unveiled, it contained a new provision such that the commissioner would require a judicial or quasi-judicial background. Shapiro lacked this experience. Although the job description was expanded (by an NDP amendment) to include expertise in ethics, the writing was on the wall for Shapiro. Nevertheless, he had not packed by year's end.

National economy

Economic indicators

Conventional indicators of economic performance in 2006 were mixed. Inflation fell to 2.2 per cent from 2.8 per cent in the previous year. This defiant drop was all the more surprising given a sharp uptick in gasoline prices as crude prices soared. While motorists and other consumers moaned as fuel prices edged above $1 per litre, energy-rich Alberta thrived. Growth continued to be the principal litmus test. The gross domestic product fell a notch, from 2.9 per cent to 2.8 per cent, as outputs stalled in the eastern half of the country. Canada had fared well compared to other G8 countries in the first years of the millennium, but the United States and the United Kingdom were two among many nations now registering higher GDP gains. Unemployment fell to 6.3 per cent, down by one-half of a percentage point. Employment was up overall (by 1.9 per cent), as was the participation rate (at 63 per cent). Six provinces set thirty-year highs for employment. Jobs were created in bulk in the western provinces thanks to a booming natural resources sector. The construction sector was notably strong. Housing starts peaked at 227,400 as low interest rates kept the real estate market buoyant.

Indexes of the country's principal stock exchange in Toronto zoomed up for a fourth consecutive year. The rise was in double digits. Mergers and acquisitions also soared in value during 2006. Canadian companies were both the target and the pursuer. One of the largest deals involved the takeover of the copper giant Falconbridge by Xstrata of Switzerland. Asset swapping was highest in the mining and energy sectors. Economic vitality remained reliant to a large extent on trade. Both exports and imports climbed to record levels. Yet the trade surplus fell to its lowest point since 1999. Outbound shipments worth $458.17 billion were up by 1.1 per cent, but imports valued at $404.5 billion represented a 4.3 per cent rise. This translated into an 11.1 per cent dip in the surplus to $53.6 billion. Exports to the United States were down for the first time in three years, and, although they accounted for 79 per cent of exports, this figure was down from 81 per cent. At $96.5 billion, the net surplus on exchanges was at 2003 levels.

In 2006 the service sector accounted for fully two-thirds of economic activity in Canada. The makeover of the country's economy was not easy, and many individual wage-earners suffered from the cruel caprices of market economics. Manufacturing lost ground, with the result that prospects in central Canada, the nominal engine of growth, were bleaker. Poverty levels were fractionally lower, but the prosperity goals set by the House of Commons in 1989 remained elusive. Unemployment rates remained high in Aboriginal communities and the Atlantic region. Economic activity also remained dependent upon oil and gas for production and transportation. Although carbon emissions were down slightly for the year, this was anomalous. Little impact on consumption habits was made by conservation and alternative energy sources.

The Conservatives' first budget

For a former Ontario finance minister, the routine on 2 May was a familiar one when Jim Flaherty rose to read his first budget speech in the House of Commons. The federal government's still-flush coffers made it possible to redeem Conservative pledges to reduce taxes, and it was reckoned that 28 tax-easing measures were contained in the budget. Perhaps the most popular was a cut in the Goods and Services Tax by 1 per cent effective 1 July. This fulfilled a promise central to the Conservatives' election platform. Rates in the lowest income bracket were pegged a half-point higher, making the cut-off 15.5 per cent. A Canada Employment Credit was established to offset expenses such as computers, uniforms, and office supplies. Claimants could get up to $500 in 2006 and $1,000 the following year. Post-secondary scholarships were completely exempted from tax, and a credit would be available to offset the cost of books.

Unlike the Opposition parties and most provinces, the government was disinclined to fund child care spaces. Instead, the Conservatives cut monthly cheques of $100 for each preschool child. Proponents of funding for spaces decried this about-face from the ostensibly solid federal-provincial framework and wondered why affluent parents should receive the same amount as those struggling to raise their offspring.

Flaherty was rather more parsimonious on the spending side. The *Globe and Mail* of 3 May pointed to these outlays:

- an additional $1.1 billion spread over two years for the military (a figure that was less than anticipated given the Conservatives' complaints while out of office about Liberal penury when it came to the armed forces);
- $161 million over two years to hire 1,000 extra RCMP officers and federal prosecutors as part of a more aggressive approach to illegal drugs, corruption, and security;
- $1 billion over five years to better prepare for pandemics;
- $52 million per year invested in cancer control;
- a package of $450 million over two years for Aboriginal housing, education, social programs, and water quality and up to $300 million for off-reserve housing (below the figures estimated when the 2005 Kelowna Accord was signed).
- $3 billion set aside to reduce an accumulated debt of $486 billion.

The *Globe and Mail* article also pointed to areas in which there were no plans to loosen the purse strings at all:

- redressing the fiscal imbalance between Ottawa and the provinces;
- reduction of hospital waiting times;
- meeting Kyoto's climate change targets (although money was hived off Liberal environmental programs to fund a tax credit for regular public transit commuters).

Oddly and uniquely, the budget passed on 6 June without a single Opposition member speaking or asking for a recorded vote. This was attributed to miscommunication between party House leaders.

Trimming the fat, stirring the pot

Was it political savvy, blinkered ideology, or partisan payback that motivated the Conservatives to swathe billions from the budget? Following up on election promises and budget commitments, finance minister Jim Flaherty and treasury president John Baird teamed up to identify significant reductions on 25 September. Savings of $1 billion would come from the outright elimination of entire programs or funding purges. Another billion would be realized from what Baird described as 'tighter management' of the coffers over a two-year period. This news came at the same time that Flaherty crowed about a budget surplus of $13.2 billion, some $5.2 billion higher than forecast in May. The windfall was used to pay down the federal deficit.

The far-ranging cuts entailed:

- scaling back adult literacy programs, shifting the load to provinces and local governments ($17.7 million), for assistance to museums ($4.6 million) and to Technology Partnerships Canada to supported innovative research and product development by high-tech companies ($42.2 million);
- revocation of GST refunds for visitors to Canada ($78.8 million);
- halving of the Youth Employment Strategy for those who might not otherwise find jobs ($55.4 million);
- restructuring of the Status of Women Canada (untouched in 2006–7 but with $5 million in annual administrative cuts the following year);
- smaller Cabinet ($46.8 million);
- elimination of marijuana science funding ($4 million), the RCMP's drug-impaired-driving program's training ($4.6 million), programming earmarked for a new citizenship act ($20 million), the Centre for Research and Information on Canada ($6.5 million), and encouragement of volunteerism ($9.7 million);
- efficiencies in Canada Mortgage and Housing Corporation ($45 million) and the Canada Firearms Centre ($6 million);
- elimination of Court Challenges Program ($5.6 million) and cuts to the Law Commission of Canada ($4.2 million);
- cancellation of High-Frequency Surface Wave Radar Project ($13.9 million) and consolidation of foreign missions ($4.5 million);
- removal of unused funding on the books for the Northwest Territories devolution ($50 million), softwood-lumber trade litigation ($15 million), and the western mountain pine beetle infestation initiative ($11.7 million) (*Canadian Press*, *Toronto Star*, and *Globe and Mail*, 26 Sept.).

Flaherty also promised that he would be upfront about the government's fiscal situation and that there would no longer be the kind of surprise surpluses that were common with Liberal governments of the recent past (*Globe and Mail*, 26 Sept.).

The House erupted in protest on 26 September. Vociferous groups across the country also registered their fury. Opponents charged that the Conservatives had taken aim at marginalized groups in society. Opposition leader Bill Graham asked, 'Why on earth is the Prime Minister eliminating research on the health of visible minorities, on child abuse, on trafficking in women, support for voluntary groups, for soup kitchens, and training for Canadians with disabilities? Are they not Canadians, too?' (*Toronto Star*, 27 Sept.). The government dismissed this as hysteria, an overreaction to changes intended to make program delivery more effective as well as economical. The cuts would also make it possible to reduce tax burdens for all Canadians. Reaction to the Court Challenges Program was especially harsh. While the government was unwilling to pay to have its own decisions litigated, others fretted that access to the courts would be impaired for a host of groups.

Autumn economic update

The traditional autumn update on the country's finances was presented to the House Finance Committee on 23 November. Spanning ninety-two pages, the update was accompanied by a long-range outlook entitled 'Advantage Canada: Building a Stronger Canada for Canadians.' The document pivoted around such goals as establishing the lowest tax rate on new business investment in the G7; eliminating total government net debt by 2021; reducing unnecessary regulation and red tape; increasing competition in the Canadian marketplace; creating a world-leading workforce in terms of education, skill, and flexibility; and modernizing infrastructure. Productivity and competitiveness were critical to the design.

Gazing towards the near horizon, the finance minister forecast real GDP of around 2.75 per cent in both 2006 (adjusted after a healthy opening quarter) and in 2007. Tax revenues were up, and the budget for 2006–7 was trending above forecasts. Whereas domestic demand was solid, slowing in the American economy was exerting a drag on exports. As in 2005, conditions in North America – slackening in the United States combined with a high Canadian dollar and cresting commodity prices – posed the biggest dangers to sustained output. The government had renewed a covenant with the Bank of Canada to squeeze inflation into a range of 1 to 3 per cent. In general, a premium was put on tax-cutting in what most observers easily discerned as an election platform in waiting should the Conservative minority be defeated. As summarized in the 25 November edition of the *Globe and Mail*, the update contained these highlights:

- all savings realized from debt reduction would go towards personal tax breaks, beginning with $800 million resulting from lower interest payments, and the Goods and Services Tax would drop by another 1 per cent;
- a pledge that program spending rise less than economic growth;
- paperwork for businesses would be cut by 20 per cent;
- cut the GST by another 1 percentage point (unlikely until 2010);
- capital gains taxes would be dropped.

One aspect of Flaherty's statement that invited dissent was his bold prediction that Canada's total 'net debt' – an agglomeration of all outstanding public obligations – could be wiped away within fifteen years. This would be plausible only if the federal government retired debt, provinces balanced their books, and the assets held by the Canada Pension Plan and the Quebec Pension Plan grew sufficiently over that time. The federal debt alone had fallen by $81 billion during a decade of Liberal rule, and the national debt expressed as a percentage of total economic output was at its lowest level in 24 years (*Globe and Mail*, 26 Sept.). Reaching higher seemed defensible. Critics did not see it that way. If, as the Conservatives said, debt would be paid down at a pace of $3 billion annually, the numbers did not add up. They argued that the gap would have to be closed, of necessity, by hiking pension plan premiums or lowering benefits for seniors.

Liberals were skeptical of the overall plan, and the NDP criticized the emphasis on tax cuts. In a mostly approving editorial, the *Globe and Mail* found many 'sensible,' 'prudent,' and 'laudable' aspects and expressed approval of the accent on productivity. Nevertheless, the editorial board was anxious about a narrowing construction of the role of the federal government in the lives of Canadians (24 Nov.). Editorialists in *The Toronto Star* treated the statement with even less equanimity, finding that the rhetoric provided cover for an anti-egalitarian streak and a potential hollowing out of Ottawa's role in social programs and aid to the provinces (24 Nov.).

Income trusts

In November 2005 the Liberal government decided not to tax income trusts, an attractive means by which corporations could pay out dividends to investors before corporate taxes were calculated. They did this despite a drain on federal revenues. On 31 October the Conservatives reversed this decision. Henceforth, new income trusts would be denied an advantage over other corporations. Grandfathered trusts would begin paying tax in 2011. At the same time, tax loads would be reduced for all traded investments and the impact on federal revenues would be neutral. By backtracking on campaign promises, they antagonized the investor, business, and pension management communities. Why had the government changed course? Flaherty said that the accelerating conversion to income trusts, left unchecked, would rob the federal government of billions. Pressure to dole out the lion's share of profits was also bleeding companies of money for innovation. Liberals, who took an opposite tack while in power, took exception to the turnabout.

Trade

Just before moving to Washington, new ambassador to the United States Michael Wilson identified the resolution of the long-running stalemate over softwood lumber as a high priority (16 Feb.). Although North American Free Trade Agreement (NAFTA) rulings continued to favour Canada, the World Trade Organization (WTO) tended to favour the Americans. In November 2005 the Americans signalled their reluctant compliance with a NAFTA panel's ruling that duties on imports of supposedly subsidized Canadian softwood were too high. Duties were then recalibrated at 10.8 per cent. The impasse was broken on 26 April. American would return about $4 billion of the duties it had collected over four years (or 78 per cent). Total Canadian shipments would be capped at the current level of 34 per cent of the US market, and Canada could impose an export tax if the price dropped below $360 (US) per thousand board feet. The deal, covering seven years with a possible extension of twenty-four months, would also preclude any new American litigation and provide for the binding resolution of disputes by neutral arbitrators. There was a catch. Either country could opt out after three years. Renewed talks required six months' notice before unilateral abrogation and precluded new duties for twelve months. An imposed ceiling would also have the effect of fixing a share that was below historic levels and certainly fell short of historic highs. Provinces and regional producers were not entirely happy with the terms. Ontario's natural resources minister David Ramsay was said to be 'furious' at having been undermined by Canadian negotiators and left by Ottawa with a take-it-or-leave-it offer (*Toronto Star*, 27 April). Future instability could not be ruled out. Clearly, some actors needed convincing, and the government's next mission was to assuage fears. When finally convinced that a majority of domestic interests had been propitiated, the Conservatives introduced enabling legislation (26 Sept.). Most of the provisions in Bill C-24 came into effect as of 12 October, but the retroactive legislation (a form that is permissible in Canadian parliamentary conventions) wended its way through the House until passage on 6 December. The Bloc voted with the government on the bill, which was opposed by the Liberals and NDP.

In its 'Advantage Canada' doctrine released in November, the government signalled its receptivity to foreign business generally. An exception to this was a prohibition of 'state-owned companies' with dubious lineages, a coding for Chinese firms. This came amid growing concern over the possibility of foreign takeovers of key sectors of the economy and American efforts to block extraterritorial takeovers in sensitive sectors. Chinese firms had already taken small stakes in Alberta's tar sands, and the government was uneasy at the prospect of more sales. As reported by the *Globe and Mail* of 26 November, this also reflected a cooling of Sino-Canadian relations over China's human rights record.

Major policy areas

Aboriginal affairs

Whither Kelowna? On 25 November 2005 Ottawa, the provinces, territorial leaders, and representatives of First Nations, Métis, and the Inuit signed a landmark deal aimed at making real improvements in the lives of Aboriginal peoples. Named after the British Columbia city where the pact was concluded, the Kelowna Accord was heralded as a milestone. It was also cast as a symbolic, albeit grand, gesture that might never be fully implemented. The Conservatives essentially walked away from the pact without developing a compelling new vision. Like his predecessor Jean Chrétien, Martin championed Aboriginal causes in the House. He authored Bill c-292, the Kelowna Accord Implementation Act, in an effort, largely symbolic, to hold the Conservative government to account. The bill was approved at second reading on 20 October. All

Conservatives present voted against the measure, a sure sign that the bill was quixotic.

Recognition of the Quebecois

In October, the Quebec wing of the federal Liberal Party passed a resolution calling for the recognition of the Quebecois as a people within Canada. The Liberal leadership contenders, already in a mild tizzy over this proposition (Michael Ignatieff having opened up the conversation in September), danced around the issue. Other parties delighted in this squirming. This opened a space for the Bloc Québécois, and it served notice of motion to recognize the Quebecois as a people to be debated on 23 November. The House had already accepted that Quebec was a 'distinct society.' The BQ hoped that the resolution would take the province another step farther on the path to independence.

Bidding to pre-empt the Bloc, Harper announced a counter-resolution crafted by the Conservatives after extra-party consultations. It read 'that this House recognize that the Québécois form a nation within a united Canada.' The prime minister had early spoken of the inevitability of constitutional change (CBC Radio interview, 1 April), and he had reached an agreement with Premier Jean Charest on an autonomous role for Quebec within UNESCO. The Bloc rejected the Conservatives' variation and sought to amend it by adding the qualified '*currently* within Canada.' Finally the Bloc accepted the inevitable and embraced the moderated text. As BQ leader Gilles Duceppe explained, even the Conservative motion meant that 'the Quebec nation exists now, from now on, and nobody can deny it' (*Globe and Mail*, 25 November). Harper had it the other way around. By entering into the federal arena, the Bloc was at least tacitly acknowledging that Canada had a say in Quebec's future.

Among Liberal leaders, Bob Rae, Ken Dryden, Stéphane Dion, and Joe Volpe expressed doubts about the wisdom of proceeding and worried about substituting symbols for substance. Gerard Kennedy bided time until the day of the vote and came out against, a move on the eve of the leadership convention seen as an effort to cultivate support outside of Quebec. The NDP were content with the resolution, having long since endorsed the notion. The vote was overwhelming, with 266 MPs voting in favour and 16 against. Fifteen Liberals voted no, as did independent Garth Turner. Michael Chong, a Conservative who resigned his Cabinet position in protest, abstained.

What did it mean? Opinion was divided. Susan Riley of the *Ottawa Citizen* pointed out the complications of an 'ambiguous, even dishonest' motion that left unanswered questions such as 'Who is a Qucbccois? Is Quebecois synonymous with 'Quebecer'? Are Quebecois all those who live in Quebec, the 'civic' definition of nationality in vogue in sovereignist circles? Or are they descendants of the original French who first settled Canada? If so, what about franco-Ontarians who come from the same roots? Are they Quebecois, too?' (*Ottawa Citizen*, 27 Nov.). Cerebral constitutional scholars were calm about the consequences, feeling that the wording was too elastic and insubstantial to be of much bother to anyone. There was no impact on the constitution, not least since provinces were uninterested. Sovereigntists were grateful that Ottawa had provided a necessary condition for independence, but this was based on an optimistic reading. Without question, it spared the Liberals having to contend with a divisive issue at its leadership convention.

Crime and punishment

Approaches to the prevention and prosecution of crime blossomed into a major issue during the campaign and remained high on the agenda throughout the year. Anti-crime measures were a pillar of the Conservative campaign, and Harper did not relent upon assuming power. On 3 April he reiterated before the Canadian Professional Police Association that he would repeal the 'faint hope' clause for convicts, substitute earned parole for statutory release, move against gun-toting felons and marijuana growers, retain penalties for possession of small amounts of cannabis, and beef up enforcement. Law-and-order Conservatives sometimes faced off with other parties and groups advocating for action on the underlying causes of crime – racism, poverty, and alienation. The reopening of Parliament on 18 September was dominated by questions on the heels of a tragic shooting spree that claimed one life and left twenty others wounded. The Conservatives stayed the course.

One of the most controversial legislative projects turned on the abolishment of long-gun registry of non-restricted rifles and shotguns used by hunters. Bill C-21, introduced on 19 June, retained the Liberal-era national registry for handguns and blanket prohibition of automatic and assault weapons. The registry instituted by the Chrétien government had been criticized for runaway costs, but the Conservatives were also opposed to mandatory certification for so-called recreational users on principled grounds. It was suspected in some quarters that this was the forerunner to an effort to eliminate all registration. Opposition parties were unimpressed, as was the Canadian Association of Chiefs of Police. Representatives of the chiefs insisted that the registry was an indispensable tool when preparing officers for armed confrontations (*Globe and Mail*, 20 June).

Another significant change was contemplated in Bill C-35 (read for the first time on 23 Nov.). The legislation provided for 'reverse onus' such that crown prosecutors would no longer have to establish why an individual accused of committing a serious offence involving guns should be denied bail. The burden would fall to those charged with crimes (31 Oct.). This was a popular move in many circles, and the mayor of Toronto, a city reeling from gang violence abetted by handguns, was on hand for the announcement. Legal experts were less convinced. Even if 'reverse onus' was constitutionally sound (about which there was some doubt), it was not clear that the provision would have the desired effect. York University professor Alan Young noted that empirical evidence was lacking, and there was little data on 'compliance rates or the recurrence of violence while out on bail' (*Toronto Star*, 1 Nov.). In addition, and although a proportion of those arrested by police were free (on bail, parole, temporary absence, or probation), they may not have been implicated in gun-related crimes. Some opponents thought that a better approach would combine additional policing along with the imposition of minimum mandatory sentences.

Other crime bills included:

- C-9, which ended conditional sentencing for those convicted of a serious wounding offence as in a terrorist or organized crime organization (introduced 14 May, approved 3 Nov.)
- C-10, the purpose of which was to increase mandatory minimum terms of imprisonment for individuals who commit serious or repeat firearm offences while creating new offences of breaking and entering to steal a firearm and robbery to steal a firearm (introduced 4 May but not resolved);
- C-18, which granted the power to issue a warrant for the arrest of persons failing to appear for DNA sampling and relaxing other restrictions on sampling (introduced 8 June but not resolved);
- C-19, which defined street racing – essentially making driving at an excessively high speed a criminal offence – and created new kinds of offences and penalties (introduced 6 June 6, passed 1 Nov.);
- C-22, which raised the age, from 14 to 16, at which a person could consent to sexual activities (introduced 22 June);

- C-27 (sent to the House on 17 Oct.), whereby offenders convicted of a third violent or sexual offence (a 'primary designated offence') could be incarcerated until such time as they no longer posed a risk to society and could be subjected to monitoring, curfew, or treatment when they were released;
- C-32 (introduced 21 Nov.), aimed at driving a vehicle under the influence of illegal, over-the-counter, and prescription drugs by permitting police officers to administer various tests to determine impairment.

Kyoto and greenhouse emissions

Although the Speech from the Throne mentioned climate change, the 2 May budget was bereft of concrete measures apart from a tax credit for transit pass buyers. In contrast to other national parties, the Conservatives swore off the multinational Kyoto Protocols signed by Canada. They preferred what environment minister Rona Ambrose described as a 'made-in-Canada' solution (31 March). The government was also hospitable to the model of the Asia-Pacific Partnership on Clean Development and Climate, a voluntary covenant that included Kyoto-exempted countries such as China and India. Meanwhile, Liberal-era initiatives such as the 'one tonne challenge,' information bureaus, and scientific research programs were slashed.

A new approach emerged in the Clean Air Act unveiled on 19 October. Opposition parties united against Bill C-30, and the government acceded to demands that the legislation be reviewed by a special committee prior to second reading. Review of the bill began on 16 December. In its original form the bill had the following features:

- a reduction of greenhouse gas emissions by half of 2003 levels starting in 2008 and ending in 2050;
- following consultations with industry, the establishment of mandatory reductions tied to intensity – carbon dioxide per unit of economic output – as opposed to absolute targets;
- caps on emissions by major polluters;
- new vehicles and train engines would be required to meet mandatory fuel efficiency standards in 2011 with the expiration of voluntary agreements;
- beginning in 2007, higher engine standards for all-terrain vehicles and watercraft (harmonized with those of the American Environmental Protection Agency), greater efficiency for home

appliances, tougher regulation of volatile compounds of a kind found in cleaning agents, paints, and the like (*Globe and Mail*, 20 Oct.).

Kyoto went unmentioned in the bill. House critics found fault with the delayed start-up date, laggardly roll-out, half-hearted goals, and, especially, the move to intensity-based reductions (meaning emissions could rise in step with production increases).

A Liberal backbencher, Quebec's Pablo Rodriguez, introduced a private member's bill in an effort to hold the government to Kyoto. Bill C-288, the Kyoto Protocol Implementation Act, had as its purpose to 'ensure that Canada takes effective and timely action to meet its obligations under the Kyoto Protocol and help address the problem of global climate change.' Opposition parties united to approve the bill at second reading on 4 October, a vote the prime minister skipped in order to take in a professional hockey game while his Conservative colleagues stood in opposition.

In her report of 28 September, the commissioner of the Environment and Sustainable Development, Johanne Gélinas, stated that Canada could not attain the greenhouse gas emission targets stipulated by Kyoto targets because of a failure of will and imagination. Lambasting the Liberals, she called upon the Conservative government to set realistic targets in a manageable time frame.

Same-Sex marriage reopened ... and closed

All but a few Conservative MPs were unhappy with the passage, in 2005, of legislation to recognize same-sex marriage. Only three Conservatives voted in favour. At the time, Harper vowed to revisit the decision if his party formed the government. True to his word, a resolution was readied for debate in the autumn. If approved, the government would be licensed to draft legislation to restore a traditional definition of marriage without precluding civil unions or nullifying marriages of same-sex couples. Critics argued that the vote was irrelevant (because courts would surely continue to rule an exclusivist definition to be unconstitutional) and needlessly divisive.

As promised, Conservatives were allowed to vote their conscience. Liberals were also freed from party directive. The NDP and Bloc Québécois disciplined their members. The motion was defeated 175–123. This time a dozen Conservatives, including six Cabinet ministers, voted to preserve the new status quo. The number of Liberals opposing same-sex marriages also dropped. Even Joe Comuzzi, who forsook his Cabinet post in 2005 in order to oppose his own government's initiative, voted against the resolution. Harper surrendered. 'We made a promise to have a free vote on this issue; we kept that promise, and obviously the vote was decisive and obviously we'll accept the democratic result of the people's representatives ... I don't see reopening this question in the future' (*Toronto Star*, 7 Dec.).

Extending the Afghanistan mission

Twenty-eight Canadians died in Afghanistan in 2006. The toll included a diplomat assigned to reconstruction efforts, a civilian worker, a medic, a female officer, and a soldier who lost his life as a result of so-called friendly fire from American warplanes. Domestic support for the mission weakened somewhat even though Canadian forces took on a larger role – and assumed a more aggressive posture – in the hostile areas around the second city of Kandahar (24 Feb.). Far from being subdued, Taliban resistance to foreign troops stiffened. Many of the Canadian dead lost their lives to improvised explosive devices (IEDs) or during intense combat with Afghan fighters. Casualties also included many grievously injured soldiers. The Canadian International Development Agency suspended Afghani operations because of the dangerous nature of the situation.

Grim news did not deter the Conservative government. On a quick visit to Kandahar, Prime Minister Harper rallied the troops with a strong reaffirmation of Canada's commitment to stabilizing Afghanistan on 13 March. To shore up the effort, the military agreed to send an extra 200 to 500 troops to join the 2,000 in place, and a squad of Leopard tanks was inserted into the battle zone (15 Sept.). On 19 September Harper boasted that Canada's standing in the community of nations had risen after redeploying out of the capital of Kabul to danger zones.

Despite ruling out a 7 March vote in the House because a debate would demoralize and perhaps jeopardize troops, the government tabled a resolution to extend the mission to at least February 2009. Parties were given just one day's notice and scant time to debate. In a close tally, the resolution passed 149–145. Interim Liberal leader Bill Graham and 29 caucus mates supported the extension. The Bloc and NDP voted against.

The man responsible for authorizing a change in focus, former prime minister Paul Martin, expressed disenchantment with its prosecution for two reasons. First, he felt that military considerations had diminished the '3-D' approach he had approved – diplomacy, defence, and development. He was also distressed that Canada might not be in a position to send peacekeepers to the troubled Sudanese region of Darfur despite assurances from the chief of defence staff, General Rick Hillier, that resources would be available for other actions if the need arose (*Toronto Star* interview, 27 Sept.). Later in the year the Bloc wrapped a motion of confidence in the government around Afghanistan and served notice of its intention to trigger a vote in January 2007.

Notwithstanding the emphasis on military solutions, diplomatic efforts were made to promote wider NATO participation in the difficult assignment in southern Afghanistan. Foreign affairs minister Peter MacKay was public in his pleas for countries such as Italy, Spain, and Germany to deploy their troops in front-line areas (*Toronto Star*, 20 Oct.). Speaking to NATO parliamentarians in Quebec City, defence minister Gordon O'Connor said, 'All NATO allies must prove themselves by sharing the burden in all regions of Afghanistan' (17 Nov.). Although additional naval and air force personnel were added to the rotation, O'Connor and his senior staff admitted that it was difficult to develop a schedule that would limit forces to a single tour of duty (5 Nov.).

Special commissions and inquiries

Gomery Commission and the sponsorship scandal

The official probe of the 1990s sponsorship scandal wrapped up when Justice John Gomery delivered the second volume of his report on 1 February. Release of the first report, with its sensational finding of facts, prefigured the defeat of the Liberal government. The second report was limited to rather less sensational matters, focusing as it did on an analysis of the scandal and recommendations to prevent widescale abuses in the future. Gomery diagnosed the fundamental problem as one of a power imbalance whereby too much control was vested in the executive. 'The most troubling facts were that this aberration originated in the Prime Minister's Office in the first place and was allowed to continue for so long, despite internal audit reports, investigations, warnings and complaints by public servants involved in the actual contracts in question' (*Globe and Mail*, 2 Feb.).

Appalled by the sleaze, Gomery was relieved to return to the decorum of an appeals court bench. Before bidding adieu to Ottawa, he bequeathed a series of 19 remedies ending with a plea for the government of the day to respond to the other suggestions within two years. He called for a public service charter to govern bureaucratic conduct and an emolument for parliamentary committee funding (especially for the Public Accounts Committee). Senior public servants should be appointed in more transparent ways, have stable appointments, and be accountable to House committees. Parliamentarians should have a direct line to deputy ministers rather than relying solely on responsible ministers. Political staff should be specially trained and have opportunities to transform their employment into permanent status. Special funds such as those earmarked for the sponsorship program should fall under the control of the Treasury Board or the Department of Finance, and the government should file annual reports on their status. Gomery would restyle the clerk of the Privy Council as the secretary to the Cabinet, with a primary duty to speak for the public service to Cabinet, and cast the secretary of the Treasury Board as head of the public service. With regard to lobbying, the registrar of lobbyists should be an officer of Parliament, with sufficient funding and power to enforce laws and the capacity to open investigatory files up to five years after a breach had been alleged rather than restricted to a two-year window. Destruction of files would be a punishable offence, and all decisions would have to be committed in writing. Under an amended Financial Administration Act, a bureaucrat could be dismissed for falsely attesting that a contracted service had been fulfilled. Finally, Gomery advised that it would be prudent to depoliticize the appointment of chief executive officers and directors of Crown corporations (*Toronto Star*, 2 Feb.).

Harper's initial reaction was to accept some ideas and study others. Certainly efforts would be made to recoup the $50 million said to be owed to the government (1 Feb.). Although the Federal Accountability Act was approved, Harper rejected some of Gomery's key recommendations (21 Dec.).

Legal proceedings ended for the high-profile individuals facing criminal charges in the scam. Paul Coffin, the first advertising executive convicted in the affair, was marched off to jail after a Quebec Court of Appeals overturned his original sentence of two and one-half years of community service (which involved lecturing on business ethics in university classrooms). Prosecutors challenged the leniency, and Coffin was ordered incarcerated for eighteen months. On 2 March, Groupaction's Jean Brault pled guilty to five counts of fraud. He was sentenced to thirty months' imprisonment on 5 May but was released on full parole after serving five months (7 Oct.). At a low risk for repeat offences and suffering health problems, Brault was allowed to serve the minimum jail time permissible. Chuck Guité, the senior bureaucrat who liaised with the likes of Coffin and Brault, was convicted on five counts on 6 June. Representing himself, Guité was unable to defend charges that he participated in frauds worth in excess of $2 million. The jury also heard that one contact was doubled in value without requiring additional work among other slips. Sentenced to three and a half years, Guité was set free on bail pending appeal (7 July).

The province of Quebec conducted a sidebar inquiry into the sponsorship scandal. Retired Superior Court justice Jean Moisan found that the separatist Parti Québécois received $96,400 from Groupaction during the period from 1995 to 2000. The firm's employees were reimbursed by Brault after making donations. Moisan concluded that party officials, but not its politicians, were aware of the source of the funds. Quebec's provincial party landed some $8,000 from Groupaction. Although technically illegal, these acts were not prosecuted because, said Moisan, they had transpired too far in the past.

Maher Arar inquiry

Justice Dennis O'Connor released the first part of his report on the detention, rendition, confinement, and torture of an innocent Canadian on 18 September. Set up in 2004, the Commission of Inquiry into the Actions of Canadian Officials in Relation to Maher Arar heard testimony up to September 2006. It also released a fact-finding study, written by Professor Stephen Toope, that documented the mistreatment of Arar and three other Canadians at the hands of Syrian authorities.

O'Connor deeded twenty-three recommendations organized around eight themes. Twelve dealt with the RCMP and national security. The other recommendations focused on dealing with countries possessing dubious human rights records, Canadians detained aboard, information sharing and safeguards, profiling by security agencies, and compensation for Arar.

The inquiry caught RCMP commissioner Giuliano Zaccardelli in an uncomfortable and increasingly tenuous position. On release of the report he told members of the Committee on Public Safety and National Security that he accepted O'Connor's recommendations without reservation but then, having scarcely drawn another breath, he began quibbling with the conclusions he claimed to welcome (*Maclean's*, 16 Oct.). Later he confessed that his testimony before the committee on 28 September had been erroneous (4 Dec.). At the time he claimed that he had some knowledge of the affair in 2002 and that the RCMP had tried to steer American authorities the right way. On 5 December he reappeared before a baffled and hostile committee to claim that he had not known of the extent of the Mounties' involvement until the autumn of 2006. Arar's lawyer, Lorne Waldman, argued, 'If he knew, he remained silent and didn't do anything to protect an innocent man for over a year. If he didn't know, then this leads to a whole series of questions. Who is running the RCMP?' (*Toronto Star*, 6 Dec.). Harper expressed his concern over the about-face but refused to rush to judgment. However, with pressure building all around, it took little time for Zaccardelli to hand in his resignation on 6 December. Many commentators hailed his departure as an opportunity for the renewal of an iconic organization that had been tarnished by other incidents in recent years. Opposition leaders insisted that the nominee to replace Zaccardelli should be vetted by an all-party panel before appointment.

O'Connor's second report was issued on 12 December. His thirteen recommendations boiled down to improving independent, empowered oversight of the RCMP. Of principal interest, the Commission for Public Complaints Against the RCMP should be restructured as the Independent Complaints and National Security Review Agency with the authority to initiate reviews. This power should also apply to the Canada Border Services Agency, Citizenship and Immigration Canada, Transport Canada, the Financial Transactions and Reports Analysis Centre of Canada, and Foreign Affairs and International Trade Canada. A new Integrated National Security Review Coordinating Committee would be in place to centralize authority, ensure the effectiveness of independent reviews, coordinate complaints activities, and liaise with other jurisdictions (*Ottawa Citizen*, 13 Dec.).

O'Connor's parting thoughts were shared on the same day that former Supreme Court judge Frank Iacobucci was asked by the government to determine whether or not any federal agencies or officials had a hand in the detention of the three other Canadians: Abdullah Almalki, Ahmad El-Maati, and Muyyed Nurredin (12 Dec.). All had been confined in Syria's notorious military intelligence facilities. This was to be an internal and strictly confidential review, with findings submitted by January 2008.

Air India Bombing Inquiry

On 23 June 1995, an Air India flight from Vancouver exploded in mid-air off the coast of Ireland, claiming the lives of 280 Canadians and 49 others. The cause was a bomb planted on the doomed aircraft.

Investigators pursued a conspiracy, but only one individual was brought to justice. Inderjit Singh Reyat received five years in prison for manslaughter. Two other suspects were acquitted in March 2005 after a trial that began in 2003. Distraught at the outcome, survivors renewed their calls for a public inquiry into the circumstances surrounding the crime and subsequent proceedings.

Bob Rae was asked to advise on the appropriate steps after conducting a thorough review of facts. He recommended an administrative review, a suggestion that was accepted by the then-Liberal government but not acted upon. With safety minister Stockwell Day taking the lead, Harper's government decided on 1 May to hold a full judicial inquiry instead. The terms required the commission to focus on jurisdictional complications that arose during investigations by the RCMP and the Canadian Security Intelligence Service (CSIS), official responses to violent extremism, prosecution of terrorism cases, ways to protect witnesses against intimidation in anti-terrorist probes, 'systemic' barriers to inter-agency cooperation, and possible improvements to security and surveillance systems.

Retired Supreme Court justice John Major agreed to head the commission. He and his lead counsel, Mark Freiman, a former deputy attorney general in Ontario, and Michel Dorval, a prosecutor from Quebec, met with the victims' families before proceedings began with a somber ceremony on 21 June. Evidence was first taken on 25 September. Hearings were to conclude in June 2007, with a report to follow that September.

Among those applying for standing at the inquiry were the federal government, Air India, and representatives of the victims' families in Canada and India. One of those acquitted in 2004, Ripudaman Singh Malik, was granted limited standing and intervener status. Rae testified on 23 October. He observed that passenger and baggage screening seemed to have improved since the bombing. In response to questions about factors that might have impeded investigations, Rae ruled out racism even though cultural differences had led to delays and misunderstandings.

Personalities and controversies

David Emerson and the ethics commissioner

When he leapt from the Liberals to the Conservatives mere weeks after the election, David Emerson insisted he was doing what was best for his Vancouver Kingsway constituents. The Conservative candidate had finished a distant third to Emerson, pulling less than twenty per cent of the vote, and angered Liberal donors demanded Emerson's resignation or their money back. On 11 February, the newly minted minister pointedly refused to bow to pressure to do either and observed that other MPs in the House had changed stripes. He did finally apologize on 1 March. Pressure mounted. On 3 March, ethics commissioner Bernard Shapiro agreed to investigate whether or not the sudden partisan switch was improper. Emerson and the prime minister considered this decision dubious. On 9 March, Harper withheld cooperation, an act that infuriated the opposition. Shapiro's 20 March verdict was that no rule had been broken by Emerson. This came as no surprise to Conservatives but left Opposition parties, democratic reformers, and many Vancouver voters exasperated. Relations between Shapiro and Harper were also irreparably soured.

Wheat Board

Since its inception in 1935, the Canadian Wheat Board (CWB) has operated as the exclusive agent for the sale of wheat and barley. The cooperative marketing system stabilized prices for producers through a 'single desk' system. Over the years attempts had been made to alter the arrangement, especially when commodities were in high demand or free-marketers were in positions of power. The Conservatives were inclined to break up the monopoly, and agriculture minister Chuck Strahl announced plans for a plebiscite to relax the CWB's control in 2007 (31 Oct.). If approved, grain producers would have the choice of selling either to the board or independently. This move, a plank in the Conservatives' election platform, was endorsed by the Western Canadian Wheat Growers and Western Canadian Barley Growers. Washington also voiced approval (*Globe and Mail*, 1 Nov.). As preparations for the plebiscite were being made, new electoral rules were instituted, striking off about one-third of voters. The board was also directed to desist from resisting the government (*Winnipeg Free Press*, 12 Nov.).

CWB president Adrian Measner attacked the proposal, as did most board directors. Organizations such as the National Farmers Union were opposed, as were provincial governments (apart from Alberta). In Ottawa, the Liberals and NDP expressed their displeasure. Measner, an employee for several decades and head of the board since 2003, made his opposition known through rallies, speeches, and press releases. He stood with the new Liberal leader when, on 6 December, Stéphane Dion declared, 'If Prime Minister Harper succeeds in destroying the Canadian Wheat Board by trampling the spirit and the letter of the *Canadian Wheat Board Act*, through gag orders upon and firing of key wheat board officials, through tampering with voters lists – I, as a prime minister, will reinstate the board' (*Toronto Star*, 7 Dec.). Fed up with this defiance, the government fired Measner on 18 December. With the battle still brewing at year's end, both sides were gearing up for a plebiscite limited to providing choice to barley production.

Office of the correctional investigator

Anonymous complaints resulted in a close review of the ombudsperson for inmates in the federal penitentiary system by the auditor general. Details were released on 28 November by the auditor general. Although he had retired, Hall of Fame football player Ron Stewart was found to have been delinquent on numerous grounds, including taking unacceptable absences, expensing junkets unrelated to work, and taking cash in lieu of holidays. Sheila Fraser's team reckoned that taxpayers had been bilked of hundreds of thousands of dollars. Stewart was also found to have given less than full value for time put it. The case was referred to the Royal Canadian Mounted Police for further investigation. Reflecting on yet another potentially poisonous bureaucratic scandal, the *Ottawa Citizen* editorialized that the Accountability Act, although it may be flawed, would 'be a start, however tentative, toward restoring public confidence in a system that is ailing' (29 Nov.).

CHRISTOPHER SPEARIN[1]

Foreign affairs and defence

Upon their federal election win of 23 January, the Conservatives faced a daunting task, as shall be seen, in terms of foreign and defence policy. Not only was their version of the Conservative brand relatively new, having resulted from the merger of the Canadian Alliance and the Progressive Conservative Parties in 2003, but many of the elected members did not have experience in governing. The challenges were complicated by the fact that the Conservatives were able to form only a minority government. Moreover, Stephen Harper and his Conservative candidates had set the bar high during the election campaign, hoping to distinguish themselves from the long-governing Liberals in terms of more respectable, if not closer, relations with the United States and a renewed emphasis upon the Canadian military and Canada's Arctic regions. In addition, upon winning the election they inherited a number of challenges that had confronted the Liberals, not the least of which was the Canadian mission in Afghanistan that was to increase from 650 personnel in early 2006 to 2,300 by year's end. Key, therefore, would be the acumen and abilities of those individuals who would hold important posts with respect to foreign and defence policy.

To serve as foreign affairs minister, Prime Minister Harper chose Peter MacKay. Although MacKay did not have significant foreign policy experience, he was a well-known Conservative, having served in the past as the deputy Opposition leader, the Conservative House leader, and justice critic. What is more, he was the last leader of the Progressive Conservative Party before its merger with the Canadian Alliance led by Stephen Harper.[2] For David Rudd, head of the Canadian Institute

1 The author would like to thank Donald Spearin for his assistance in the preparation of this chapter.

2 Stockwell Day, the former leader of the Reform Party, was also named to the Conservative Cabinet as public safety minister.

of Strategic Studies, MacKay's appointment illustrated his sway in Conservative circles and highlighted some of the tensions that still existed in the relatively new party: 'He's getting a high-profile post in part in recognition for his senior status within the party … I don't think this is necessarily a hatchet-burying exercise between him and Harper' (*Ottawa Citizen*, 7 Feb.).[3]

For the portfolio of international trade, the prime minister made the controversial choice of selecting David Emerson. Before the 2006 election, Emerson had been a Liberal member of Parliament and had served in Prime Minister Paul Martin's Cabinet as industry minister. However, shortly after the election in which he campaigned as a Liberal, Emerson crossed the floor and became a Conservative, thus increasing the minority government's parliamentary backing to 125 seats and reducing the Liberals to 102 seats. On the one hand, Emerson, a former lumber industry executive, brought with him governing experience and knowledge useful for the international trade portfolio. Indeed, he was an individual known more for his interests in policy than in politics. On the other hand, Emerson's decision to become a Conservative was seen as a betrayal, and, for many, the prime minister was seen as hypocritical given that he had campaigned on a platform espousing integrity, honesty, accountability, and sound ethics.

Equally controversial, but for different reasons, was the prime minister's decision to name Gordon O'Connor to the position of minister of national defence. O'Connor, a retired brigadier general with a 30-year career in the Canadian military, had served as the Conservative Party's defence critic after he was first elected to the House of Commons in June 2004. What concerned many was his post-military career as a lobbyist with Hill and Knowlton, during which he worked on the behalf of many firms seeking contracts with the Department of National Defence (e.g., Airbus Military, United Defense, General Dynamics Canada, Raytheon Canada, and BAE Systems). O'Connor made it clear that there would be no conflict of interest, that he would conform with all government guidelines, and, in so doing, that he would not recuse himself: 'I have no shares in any company, I get no remuneration from any company, I don't have any loyalty to any company, so no there was no concern at all' (www.canoe.ca, 5 Feb.). Although the prime minister demanded that ministers, post-government, not profit unduly

3 Prime Minister Harper also named MacKay as the minister of the Atlantic Canada Opportunities Agency.

from their past government experience, he did not wish to set barriers for those in private life seeking public office: 'Having worked in an industry in the past does not constitute a conflict of interest in the present ... We want to prevent people using public service as a way of getting private profit later on. People who have experience in the private sector and wish to serve in government, we don't want to discourage that' (*Ottawa Citizen*, 7 Feb.). When Parliament reconvened in early April, the Liberals, now in Opposition, repeatedly targeted the defence minister during Question Period. Consider, for instance, the words of Liberal defence critic Ujjal Dosanjh: 'The Defence Minister's rap sheet on working for the arms industry is 'as long as your arm,' ... What is worse, the Conservative Platform looks like a tailored wish list for most of his former clients' (*Globe and Mail*, 11 April). Despite these concerns, O'Connor remained in the defence portfolio throughout 2006, although not without some hiccups, as will be seen later.

By naming Michael Wilson as Canada's ambassador to the United States, Prime Minister Harper continued the Liberal tradition of politically appointing the individual for this sensitive post.[4] Wilson, a Bay Street investment banker, held a number of Cabinet posts during the Progressive Conservative governments of the 1980s and early 1990s, including those for finance, international trade, and industry, science, and technology. During the 2006 federal election campaign, he appeared alongside Harper at party events and served as the campaign's co-chairman. His working so closely with the now prime minister was meant to signal to the Americans his potential influence in Ottawa. In this light, even Bill Graham, the interim Liberal leader, agreed with Wilson's appointment: 'Michael Wilson is a highly re-spected person in Toronto, particularly in the business community ... He certainly brings impeccable credentials to the job, and it is in the interest of Canada to have an ambassador who has a close relationship with [Harper]' (*Toronto Star*, 16 Feb.). Similarly, given his wealth of experience, Paul Heinbecker, one of Canada's most recognized past diplomats, said Wilson was an ideal choice: 'He's been involved with Washington off and on for years, and has a very strong international background from his years as finance minister, attending G-7 finance ministers meetings ... He brings both domestic credentials and international credentials' (ibid.). The prime minister named Wilson to the

4 Prime Minister Martin's ambassador to the United States, Frank McKenna, was a prominent Liberal Party member and a former premier of New Brunswick.

ambassadorship on 16 February, and he presented his diplomatic credentials to President George W. Bush in Washington on 13 March.

Foreign affairs

Terrorism and Canada

Prophet Mohammed cartoons. In its first week in office, the new Conservative government had to deal with its first international crisis: the fallout stemming from the publication of cartoons deemed by some to be offensive to the Muslim faith.[5] Danish newspapers had initially printed the cartoons in September 2005, and publications in many other countries, particularly in Europe, followed suit in early 2006.[6] This led to deadly riots in many Muslim countries and the targeting of Western embassies and other institutions.

The government's concerns rested on fears that a backlash could occur against Canadian officials in the Middle East and particularly against Canadian troops serving in Afghanistan. In that country, at least 11 people died in cartoon-related rioting. Defence Minister O'Connor stated, 'It doesn't help. Radicals in Syria and Lebanon, Afghanistan and Iraq, they get people roused up because their religion's being offended … We don't need any more risk in the area than we have' (*Ottawa Citizen*, 14 Feb.). As well, Foreign Affairs Minister MacKay attempted to draw a balance between the respectable exercise of freedom of speech and disapproval of the anti-Western rioting and destruction of property: 'The publication of cartoons of the Prophet Mohammed has caused offence to Muslims and non-Muslims around the world and in Canada … Freedom of expression is a legally enshrined principle in Canada, but it must be exercised responsibly. We commend those Canadians who have acted appropriately … However, we condemn the violent protests that have occurred in some parts of the world, and find the attacks on foreign diplomatic missions particularly deplorable' (DFAIT news release no. 8, 8 Feb.).

Only a handful of publications in Canada reproduced the cartoons. The student newspaper at the University of Prince Edward Island did

5 This was due, in part, to the content of the cartoons, but it was also because of the religious interpretations that forbid illustrations of the Prophet Mohammed.

6 The cartoons were published in Australia, Bulgaria, Croatia, Denmark, Fiji, Germany, Hungary, Italy, Japan, Jordan, Malaysia, the Netherlands, New Zealand, Norway, Poland, South Africa, Spain, Switzerland, the United States, Ukraine, and Yemen.

so, as did a Calgary-based Jewish newspaper. Likely the most prominent publication to reproduce the cartoons was the *Western Standard* with a readership of approximately 240,000. In response, Indigo Books declined to sell that issue in its stores and Air Canada pulled the magazine from its lounges and aircraft. Defence Minister O'Connor hoped that Muslims would respect the fact that the government had not sanctioned the cartoons' publication in Canada: 'I have a bit of concern, but it's freedom of the press. Just like Denmark, we can't control what's in the press ... If people do it, we have to live with the consequences ... I'm hoping that religious groups around the country, around the world will understand that our government does not countenance ridiculing anybody's religion' (*Ottawa Citizen*, 14 Feb.). In the end, no specific Canadian interests were targeted as a result of fallout over the cartoons' publication.

Toronto 18. On 2 June, several police forces in southern Ontario arrested ten men and five youths under the Anti-Terrorism Act. Dubbed the 'Toronto 18'[7] and described by the Canadian Security Intelligence Service (CSIS) as 'adherents of a violent ideology inspired by al-Qaeda,' the individuals were charged with a variety of offences including participation in a terrorist group, receiving terrorist training, and intent to cause an explosion leading to bodily harm and / or destruction of property (Canadian Broadcasting Corporation, 4 June). Over the course of 2006, officials released details of the investigation and the activities of these 'home-grown' terrorists. The investigation, which had been underway for as long as two years, involved CSIS, several Canadian police forces, and foreign security organizations. It used at least two moles on the CSIS payroll. One was an agricultural engineer of Egyptian descent, and another was an official from a Toronto mosque and a relatively well-known advocate for the introduction of sharia law in Canada. The investigation found that the accused had practiced some of their tactics at a camp in Ramara Township in Ontario. Some of the suspects' more grisly objectives included the destruction of the Canadian Broadcasting Corporation's broadcast centre and CSIS's offices in Toronto, the storming of the Parliament Buildings in Ottawa, and even the beheading of Prime Minister Harper.

7 Two suspects were already imprisoned in Kingston at the time of the arrests. Police arrested an additional suspect on 3 August.

The arrests raised a number of thorny issues for Canadian officials. First, with respect to Ottawa's relations with Washington, prominent US officials, such as Secretary of State Condoleezza Rice, were quick to compliment the work of Canadian law enforcement: 'It is obviously a very great success for the Canadian counter-terrorism efforts, which have been very robust' (*Face the Nation*, 4 June). However, for other US officials, the presence of a terrorist cell in Canada simply reinforced their concerns about their northern neighbour's policies towards immigration and border security. These fears were emphasized, for instance, by Peter King, the chairman of the House of Representatives Homeland Security Committee: 'I think it's a disproportionate number of al-Qaeda in Canada because of their very liberal immigration laws, because of how political asylum is granted so easily' (Canadian Broadcasting Corporation, 14 July). Second, with respect to relations between Muslim and non-Muslim Canadians, both Prime Minister Harper and moderate Muslim leaders sought to reduce tensions. Nevertheless, following the arrests, vandals did attack mosques in Canada. Third, with respect to law enforcement, the arrests, as suggested by the University of Toronto's Wesley Wark, would cast a spotlight on the efficacy of Canada's judicial system vis-à-vis terrorism, one that had been found wanting in the wake of the Air India disaster (see next section): 'There's a lot riding on this case because it's going to be the largest terrorism trial in Canadian history ... There are a whole range of issues at stake – national security, the whole question of Canadian-American relations ... Canada's reputation in the world as a partner in the fight against global terror' (*National Post*, 13 June). Over the course of 2006, however, some of the accused were granted bail and prominent civil rights experts suggested that the cases against the Toronto 18 could be subject to challenges under the Canadian Charter of Rights and Freedoms. Finally, with respect to Canada's commitment to Afghanistan (see below), the arrests raised the issue as to whether Canadian participation overseas was enhancing or detracting from security at home.

Air India. During the federal election campaign, the Conservatives announced that, if elected, they would launch a full judicial inquiry into the bombing of the Air India flight on 23 June 1985 that killed 329 people. This election promise came in the wake of the 2005 acquittals of two men charged in the bombing, Ripudaman Singh Malik and Ajaib Singh Bagri. It also came in the context of concerns held by the victims' families that government officials had not yet corrected the mistakes and security lapses that helped to facilitate the terrorist attack and bungled the subsequent criminal investigations at the federal and provincial levels. Although Jean Chrétien, before he became prime minister in 1993, announced that the Liberals would launch an inquiry, none was forthcoming during his tenure. In 2005, although Prime Minister Martin did ask Bob Rae, the former NDP premier of Ontario, to conduct a limited public inquiry, the federal election call stymied his efforts, particularly because the Treasury Board was unwilling to approve the budget for the potential inquiry during this time.

Good to his word, Prime Minister Harper announced in the House of Commons on 1 May that a judicial inquiry would go forth. He charged a retired Supreme Court justice, John Major, with the task of investigating 'the worst mass murder in Canadian history' (Canadian Broadcasting Corporation, 1 May). During the inquiry, which was scheduled to hold hearings from September 2006 until April 2007, Justice Major was to probe a number of issues:

- how seriously the government treated the threat of terrorist attacks by Sikh extremists against Canadians;
- problems in coordination between key government agencies, including CSIS and the RCMP;
- the degree to which Canadian law protected witnesses in terrorism cases against intimidation;
- the efficacy of Canadian laws regarding the financing of terrorism; and
- how terrorism prosecutions should be conducted in Canada.

Prime Minister Harper expressed his confidence that the inquiry would improve the resiliency and effectiveness of Canada's security infrastructure: 'Under Justice Major's guidance, we hope that a focused and efficient inquiry will provide information that will ensure Canada's police agencies and procedures, its airport security system and its anti-terrorism laws are among the most effective in the world' (*Globe and Mail*, 2 May). The government requested Justice Major to submit his report 15 months after the inquiry's launch.

Canadians kidnapped in Iraq. Two kidnapped Canadians working in Iraq for the Chicago-based NGO Christian Peacemaker Teams, Harmeet Singh Sooden and James Loney, were set free in 2006. On 26 November 2005, these two Canadians and two of their colleagues, Briton Norman Kember and American Tom Fox, were taken and accused of spying by a group calling itself the Swords of Righteousness Brigade. In return for the hostages' freedom, the brigade demanded that all Iraqi prisoners held by US and Iraqi authorities be released. The original deadline for this demand to be met was 10 December 2005, but the hostage takers continued to extend their deadlines. This was, in part, due to the intransigence of US and Iraqi authorities and also because of the unprecedented condemnation of the hostage taking by prominent Muslim authorities the world over. Indeed, the NGO was widely known for its efforts in reducing violence around the world and for its helpful endeavours in Iraq specifically. What is more, Christian Peacemaker Teams had publicly condemned the US-led invasion of Iraq in 2003 and linked the foreign presence with the very capture of their personnel: 'We continue to believe that what has happened to our teammates is the result of the actions of the U.S. and U.K. governments in their illegal attack on Iraq and the continuing occupation and oppression of its people. We continue to call for justice and human rights for all who are detained in Iraq ... The innocents should not suffer in the place of those who have done wrong' (Canadian Broadcasting Corporation, 28 Jan.).

In the early months of 2006, the hostage takers released to Al-Jazeera two videotapes of the hostages time-stamped on 21 January and 28 February. The brigade described the 21 January tape as the last warning for their demands to be met. Worrying, therefore, was Tom Fox's absence in the second videotape. His body was found on 10 March.

On 23 March, the three remaining hostages were rescued thanks to a British-led operation orchestrated along with authorities from Canada, the United States, and Iraq. Without a shot being fired, the hostages were found in a house in Mishahda, located 30 kilometres outside of Iraq. The operation was triggered by an intelligence tip garnered earlier in the day. Although it was evident that Canada's Departments of National Defence and Foreign Affairs, along with the Royal Canadian Mounted Police, participated in some way in the operation, less clear was the involvement of Canada's elite Joint Task Force 2. Prime Minister Harper, for national security reasons, was oblique in his response about the role played by Canadian special forces: 'There have been a small number of Canadian military personnel embedded in American and allied units. That's been the case since the beginning of the war. Nothing has changed on that front' (Canadian Broadcasting Corporation, 23 March). On 26 March, Loney arrived in Toronto and Sooden returned to his home in New Zealand.

The Khadrs. The case of Omar Khadr, the second-youngest son of the late Ahmed Said Khadr, the head of Canada's so-called al-Qaeda family, remained in legal limbo during 2006. In the autumn of 2002, the United

States sent Omar to the prison at the US Navy Base in Guantanamo Bay, Cuba, following his capture in Afghanistan. He was accused of throwing a grenade that killed one US soldier and wounded another during a battle at an al-Qaeda compound near Khost, Afghanistan, which took place on 27 July 2002. He was also accused of spying on US forces and planting roadside bombs and landmines which targeted US forces in the summer of 2002.

Omar's case was unique, first, because he was the only Canadian at the prison; other countries had made arrangements with the United States for the transfer of their nationals from the prison. Second, at the time of the incident, Khadr had not yet turned 16 years old (his 16th birthday was 19 Sept. 2002). Although US authorities eventually recognized detainees ages 13 to 15 as 'juvenile enemy combatants' and released them in January 2004, Omar remained in US custody, despite concerns that he might be classified as a child soldier and thus afforded certain protections. What is more, the charges Omar faced – murder by an unprivileged belligerent, attempted murder by an unprivileged belligerent, aiding the enemy, and conspiracy – were not filed until 7 November 2005. At this time, US authorities indicated that they would not be seeking the death penalty in Omar's case.

In 2006 the uncertainty about Omar's detention arose in part because the very constitutionality of the military tribunals for those imprisoned at Guantanamo Bay was in question. Indeed, in April, Omar's attorneys requested that proceedings against their client be halted given the lack of established rules for military trials. Nevertheless, although the 29 July ruling made by the US Supreme Court found that President Bush had overstepped his authority in the creation of the military tribunals, Omar and his fellow inmates remained in US custody. President Bush made it clear that his administration's policy would only be modified, not quashed: 'We will seriously look at the decision, but one thing I am not going to do is jeopardize the safety of the American people. People have got to understand that. I understand we're in a war on terror. These people were picked up on the battlefield. I will protect the people and at the same time conform to the findings of the Supreme Court' (www.CTV.ca, 29 July). The consequent result of the US Supreme Court's decision was the Military Commissions Act of 2006, signed into law by President Bush in October 2006, which was directed at the continuing the incarceration, and eventual prosecution, of inmates such as Omar Khadr.

Other legal ramifications in 2006 stemming from Omar's alleged actions came in the form of a successful wrongful death lawsuit first filed in Federal District Court of Utah on 6 August 2004. The plaintiffs included Tabitha Speer, the widow of the killed US soldier, Sergeant Christopher Speer, and his wounded colleague, Sergeant Layne Morris. The lawsuit's named defendant was Ahmed Said Khadr because of the radical Islamic values he imparted on his children before his death in 2003. For Morris, the lawsuit was one of the many ways in which the war on terror could be prosecuted: 'I hope it sends a message to terrorists everywhere, that we're not just after you militarily, you know, there's financial and there's legal means to make life tough for them' (Canadian Broadcasting Corporation, 6 Aug. 2004). Subsequently, on 20 February, Speer was awarded US$94.5 million and Morris US$8.1 million. The prospects of repayment, however, were slim. Reports indicated that the Khadr family was close to penniless, in large part because the US Office of Foreign Assets Control had not released Khadr family assets it had frozen.

The legal fate of another of Omar's brothers, Abdullah, also remained up in the air in 2006. On 7 December 2005, Abdullah returned to Canada after being released from a 14 month long incarceration in Pakistan. Ten days later, at the request of US authorities, Canadian officials arrested Abdullah in order to facilitate an eventual extradition to the United States. On 8 February, the United States formally charged Abdullah with 'conspiracy to murder a U.S. national outside the U.S., conspiracy to use a weapon of mass destruction, possession of a destructive device and conspiracy to possess a destructive device' (Canadian Broadcasting Corporation, 8 Feb.). In particular, US officials alleged that Abdullah Khadr, during 2003, purchased US$20,000 in weaponry for use by al-Qaeda fighters in Afghanistan. If convicted, Abdullah faced the possibility of life in prison plus 30 years in addition to a US$1 million fine. For US attorney general Alberto Gonzales, the legal actions illustrated the United States' dedication to bring terrorists and their supporters to justice: 'Our efforts to identify and capture alleged terrorists who seek to kill Americans here and abroad transcend all borders ... Today's indictment sends the message to terrorists around the world that we will go to great lengths to bring justice to those who provide al Qaeda and other terrorists with the weapons to carry out their deadly and evil goals' (*Ottawa Sun*, 9 Feb.). Abdullah, however, remained in a Canadian jail for the duration of 2006 as the extradition process went on.

Arar inquiry. The two-year official probe into the unfortunate 'Arar Affair' came to a close in 2006. Prime Minister Martin's government launched the public inquiry in February 2004 in order to investigate the handling of the case of Maher Arar, a Syrian-born Canadian citizen, by Canadian officials. On 26 September 2002, US authorities at New York City's Kennedy Airport detained Arar on his way home to Canada after a vacation in Tunisia. Rather than return Arar to Canada or inform Canadian consular officials of his detention, US authorities sent Arar to Syria under the US extraordinary rendition policy. During his incarceration in Syria, Arar was repeatedly tortured. He was released from Syrian custody on 5 October 2003.

The inquiry's head, Justice Dennis O'Connor, the associate chief justice of Ontario, released his findings in two reports, dated 18 September and 12 December. The first wide-ranging report dealt with the various actions that led to Arar's detention and a smear campaign that continued after his release. The second was more focused on recommendations for civilian oversight and the governing and management of intelligence operations conducted by the RCMP.

At the heart of the first report was this conclusion made by Justice O'Connor: 'I am able to say categorically that there is no evidence to indicate that Mr. Arar has committed any offence or that his activities constitute a threat to the security of Canada' (*Globe and Mail*, 19 Sept.). As a result, O'Connor called for the government to compensate Arar for his suffering, a finding which tangentially reinforced a lawsuit Arar had launched earlier against the Canadian government: 'Psychologically, Mr. Arar's experiences in Syria were devastating ... Mr. Arar went from being a middle-class engineer to having to rely on social assistance to help feed, clothe and house his family' (ibid.). What is more, compensation was merited because of the continued torment Arar faced upon his return to Canada: '[S]ome government officials took it upon themselves to leak information to the media, much of which was unfair to Mr. Arar and damaging to his reputation ... At least one leak sought to downplay the mistreatment and torture Mr. Arar had suffered in Syria. Quite predictably, the leaks had a devastating effect on Mr. Arar's reputation and on him personally ... Mr. Arar, an educated, hard-working engineer, has had great difficulty finding employment. It seems likely that the smear of his reputation by the leakors has taken its toll' (ibid.).

O'Connor's findings on the culpability and diligence of Canadian officials were mixed. On the one hand, O'Connor determined that Canadian authorities were not involved in the US decision-making regarding Arar: 'There is no evidence that Canadian officials participated or acquiesced in the American authorities' decisions to detain Mr. Arar and remove him to Syria' (*Toronto Star*, 19 Sept.). Similarly, he found that foreign affairs officials such as Franco Pillarella, the Canadian ambassador to Syria at the time of Arar's detention, and former consul Leo Martel rightly acted in pursuing Arar's release. O'Connor did suggest, however, that Canadian officials should have assumed Arar was indeed being tortured and that consular officials, as a result, should have improved human rights training.

On the other hand, O'Connor's criticism of the RCMP was damning. Essentially, O'Connor found that the RCMP, through its provision of raw and unanalyzed intelligence to US security officials collected as part of its anti-terror Project A-O Canada investigations, unfairly linked Arar and his wife, Dr Monia Mazigh, to terrorist activities: 'The RCMP had no basis for this description, which had the potential to create serious consequences for Mr. Arar in light of American attitudes and practices' (*Globe and Mail*, 19 Sept.). Indeed, this RCMP intelligence put the two on the US border watch list. He also found that RCMP investigators were insufficiently experienced and supervised in their handling of complex national security probes. In addition, the RCMP did not provide the United States with written conditions on how Canadian-supplied intelligence could be used. In fact, the RCMP, the report claims, downplayed their involvement and potential culpability after the fact when briefing officials from the Privy Council Office. In his comments after the release of the first report, Arar implied that the RCMP needed to be held to account: 'I wanted the people responsible for what happened to me to be held accountable. Justice requires no less. I call on the government of Canada to accept the findings of this report and hold people accountable' (ibid.).

The RCMP, at the highest level, was held to account, although in a somewhat roundabout fashion. At first, the Liberal Opposition was surprised that the head of the RCMP, Commissioner Giuliano Zaccardelli, did not make a comment shortly after the release of the first report. Bill Graham, for instance, wondered aloud if Prime Minister Harper's government was politically interfering with the RCMP: 'This is a funny government. Harper muzzles [public safety minister Stockwell] Day, Day muzzles the RCMP commissioner, and he muzzles everybody down the line. The muzzle starts at the top' (*Toronto Star*, 24 Sept.). When Zaccardelli did comment during testimony on 28 September to the House of Commons Committee on Public Safety and National Security, he indicated that he did not intend to resign, although he did say that the RCMP accepted the inquiry's findings 'without exception' and he offered his apologies: 'Mr. Arar, I wish to take this opportunity to express publicly to you and to your wife and to your children how truly sorry I am for whatever part the actions of the RCMP may have contributed to the terrible injustices you experienced and the pain that you and your family endured' (*Toronto Star*, 28 Sept.).

Zaccardelli's answers to other questioning during this committee meeting ultimately landed him in trouble. In response to questions about his knowledge of the Arar case, the commissioner indicated that he first learned of the RCMP's mistakes back in September 2002. However, during a speech to the Canadian Club in Ottawa on 4 December, Zaccardelli contended that he only became aware of these mistakes earlier in the fall of 2006. Subsequently, the committee called the commissioner back to give further testimony on 5 December, during which he conceded, 'I believe some aspects of my prior testimony could have been more precise and more clearly stated. A number of misconceptions have resulted' (Canadian Broadcasting Corporation, 5 Dec.). Given the sensitivity of the Arar case and now the accusations of perjury, Zaccardelli offered his resignation on 6 December, which Prime Minister Harper accepted.

However, with respect to Canada-US relations and the implications of the Arar case, the matter remained unresolved in 2006. Although Canada took Arar off its border watch list, he remained on the US list. As well, Canada was still concerned that the United States had violated the Vienna Convention on consular access. After a 15-minute phone conversation Prime Minister Harper had with President Bush on 6 October largely dealing with the Arar case, the highest-level bilateral interaction on the issue, the prime minister made it plain that US officials needed to reassess their approach: 'What I would like to see, obviously, is the United States government to come clean with its version of events, to acknowledge, I would hope to acknowledge, the deficiencies and the inappropriate conduct that occurred, particularly vis-à-vis its relationship with the Canadian government' (*Globe and Mail*, 7 Oct.). Although Prime Minister Harper wished for stronger bilateral relations than what existed during previous Liberal governments, he made it plain that Canadian concerns needed to be taken into account: 'We want to help the United States in the war on terrorism … And certainly we share their concerns about security, but at the same time we need to have the assurance that the rules and the agreements between our two governments will be respected in the future' (ibid.). Subsequently, during a joint news conference Secretary of State Condoleezza Rice had with Foreign Affairs Minister MacKay on 21 December, she indicated that she had instructed the US Departments of Homeland Security and Justice to review the Arar case.

Crisis in Lebanon. Although fighting occurred sporadically afterward, the passing of UN Security Council Resolution 1701 on 11 August marked the end of a month-long war between Israel and the terrorist group Hezbollah. The war was sparked on 12 July when Hezbollah militants based in Lebanon conducted a raid into Israel which killed seven Israeli soldiers, wounded an additional eight, and resulted in the capture of two more. The raid, which Israeli prime minister Ehud Olhmert described as 'an act of war,' triggered an Israeli response which, at the fighting's height, featured Israel's navy blockading all of Lebanon's ports, its air force bombing targets in and around Beirut, and the army conducting operations as deep as 30 kilometres into Lebanese territory (Canadian Broadcasting Corporation, 12 July). In response, Hezbollah militants launched rocket attacks against mostly civilian targets in Israel. By the end of the conflict, more than 900 people had died, with both sides claiming victory. Prime Minister Olhmert claimed that Israeli forces had dealt 'a major blow to Hezbollah,' whereas Hezbollah's leader, Sheik Hassan Nasrallah, contended that his group had won a 'strategic victory' against Israel (Canadian Broadcasting Corporation, 14 Aug.).

Throughout the conflict, Canada's stance was strongly pro-Israel, a position in keeping with policy shifts introduced by the new Conservative government.[8] Although several peace rallies in Canada called for an end to the fighting and critics demanded that the federal government denounce Israel's seemingly heavy-handed response, these comments made by Foreign Affairs Minister MacKay were in keeping with the government's approach: 'Canada strongly condemns Hizbollah's attack on Israel, which has included the capture of two Israeli soldiers and the launching of Katyusha rockets and mortar bombs into Israeli towns. These actions only exacerbate tensions in the Middle East, threaten the lives of civilians, and risk a deteriorating humanitarian situation … We urge Hizbollah to immediately and unconditionally release the Israeli soldiers. We call on the Lebanese government to do its utmost to restore order within its border … We also call on Syria and Iran, both long time supporters of Hizbollah, to cease all financial and other assistance to the organization' (DFAIT news release no. 78, 12 July). Although the Liberals pressed the federal government to call for an immediate cease-fire, Prime Minister Harper refused. Whereas Canada deemed Israel's response to be measured given the circumstances, the United Nations undersecretary-general for humanitarian affairs and emergency relief coordinator, Jan Egeland, said the 'disproportionate response by Israel is a violation of international humanitarian law' (Canadian Broadcasting Corporation, 23 July).

During the fighting, one Canadian soldier serving with United Nations Interim Force in Lebanon (UNIFIL) was killed during an Israeli bombardment on 25 July. Kingston-based Major Paeta Hess-von Kruedener, in fact the only Canadian serving in UNIFIL, was working at patrol base Khiyam with three other unarmed colleagues from China, Austria, and Finland. Hezbollah militants had been launching rocket attacks against Israel from sites near the patrol base, perhaps using it as cover. Although the prime minister deemed the death of UN personnel as a 'terrible tragedy,' he doubted whether the Israeli attack was deliberate (ibid., 26 July). However, Kofi Annan, the UN secretary general, was much harsher, describing the Israel attack as 'apparently deliberate' (ibid., 25 July). Indeed, the Israeli attack was not a limited one; it was a sustained bombardment lasting six hours and involving both the air force and the army. During the bombardment, UN peacekeepers called the Israeli military no less than ten times. This included calls from the area UN commander, Lieutenant Colonel John Molloy of Ireland; from the UNIFIL commander, Major General Alain Pellegrini of France; and from UN officials based at UN headquarters in New York City. On 26 July, Prime Minister Olhmert called the UN secretary general to apologize and indicated that a full investigation would be forthcoming.

In terms of helping Canadians abroad, the government's response to the crisis, at first, appeared to be lacklustre. With over 50,000 Canadians in Lebanon, many of them dual citizens, Canada had one of that country's largest foreign communities. Some Canadians, tired of waiting for the government's response and worried about their personal safety, got out of Lebanon via evacuations organized, for example, by the Netherlands and Italy. Other countries, such as France, Greece, Sweden, the United Kingdom, and the United States, had also initiated evacuations shortly after the crisis began. In this regard, interim Liberal leader Bill Graham asked rhetorically, 'What did the British, the French and the Americans do differently?' (Canadian Broadcasting Corporation, 18 July). The government's criticized tardiness, therefore, was put in sharp relief on 16 July when eight Canadians, the holidaying El-Akhras family from Montreal, were killed in an Israeli air strike on the village of Aitaroun. Prime Minister Harper received a phone call

8 For instance, other than Israel, Canada in March was the first country to cut off financial assistance to the Palestinian Authority after Hamas was victorious in legislative elections held in January.

from his Israeli counterpart in which he expressed Israel's condolences for the loss of Canadian life.

On the same day as the bombing of the Canadian family, Foreign Affairs Minister MacKay announced that, with the acquisition of the services of seven ships (which were confirmed on 17 July), the Canadian evacuation would commence later in the week. Evacuees would be ferried to either Cyprus or Turkey and returned to Canada on aircraft chartered by the Canadian government. Criticism and challenges, however, plagued the initial Canadian evacuation efforts. Canadians in Lebanon complained that the Canadian embassy was not providing sufficient assistance and information regarding the departure of ships from Beirut's port. The 19 July departure of the first Canadian chartered ship, the *Blue Dawn*, with 261 evacuees on board was plagued by confusion at the docks, requirements dictated by Lebanese customs and immigration officials, and the Israeli navy's threatening to prevent the *Blue Dawn*'s departure. Indeed, during the *Blue Dawn*'s 15-hour voyage to Cyprus, the Israeli navy stopped the ship twice.

In response to the criticism, the government stressed that it was doing all that was possible. For Prime Minister Harper, he felt that Canada's evacuation was occurring 'extraordinarily quickly' given the challenges: 'Our officials have been in contact with literally thousands of people in Lebanon to prepare this and have lined up resources in several countries to make it possible' (ibid.). Foreign Affairs Minister MacKay indicated that his department had started to look for ships to charter as early as two days after the crisis erupted. Others, such as Kim Girtel, a foreign affairs spokesperson, contended that patience was required given the scale of the challenge: 'It would be nice if we could Star Trek them out, but it's going to take time. Priority goes to people in greatest need' (ibid., 19 July). Canadian officials also indicated that their counterparts in other countries, such as Australia, had contacted them in search of Canadian assistance. As expressed by Foreign Affairs Minister MacKay, 'many like-minded countries find themselves in the same situation as Canada, we are actively discussing and coordinating efforts with them. Officials in Ottawa have been in regular contact with their counterparts in other capitals' (DFAIT news release no. 82, 16 July). In addition, the government sent 100 Canadian Forces personnel to either Cyprus or Lebanon to help with security, logistics, and communications related to the evacuation. Two Canadian navy vessels docked at Halifax were put on 48-hour standby to sail to the region if necessary. To allow for the safe transit, the government arranged for 1,000 Canadians to depart from the Lebanese port of Tyre on 26 July, thus avoiding the dangerous trip to Beirut. By the end of the crisis, the federal government had arranged for the transport of over 13,000 people, what Foreign Affairs Minister MacKay described as the 'largest scale evacuation in Canadian history' (Canadian Broadcasting Corporation, 18 July).

Perhaps the most publicized gesture was the prime minister's decision on 19 July, during an official European tour, to divert his aircraft to Cyprus in order to return some evacuees home to Canada. His aircraft, a military airbus, was stripped down to allow for maximum space. Only a skeleton crew remained, along with a small number of government staff and the prime minister's wife. The press was not allowed on the flight. The aircraft, with 88 evacuees on board from the *Blue Dawn*, departed Cyprus on 20 July and landed in Ottawa during the early hours of 21 July. During the press conference in France in which he made the announcement, the prime minister indicated that his decision was based on necessity, not on tokenism: 'Because of the seriousness of the situation and our relative proximity to Cyprus, we have decided to take the Canadian Forces aircraft we have been travelling on to help airlift evacuees back home ... It's more than a symbolic trip ... There is a need for air support in Cyprus. We believe this is the right thing to do and that's why we are going to do it' (ibid., 19 July).

Major trade issues

World Trade Organization. Some of Canada's efforts related to international trade suffered a setback with the suspension of the Doha Development Round of Negotiations at the World Trade Organization in July 2006. This round, launched in November 2001, was meant to tackle issues such as agricultural subsidies and trade barriers confronting the developing world. The round was both to ensure the spread of the benefits of globalization and, in the wake of the terrorist attacks of 11 September 2001, to bolster the economic progress in poorer parts of the world. The round's success, therefore, as stressed in Canada's 2005 International Policy Statement, was in keeping with both Canada's values and interests. Nevertheless, contentious issues between the developed and developing worlds led the WTO's director-general, Pascal Lamy, to suspend the round. In particular, the so-called G6 – the United States, European Union, Brazil, India, Japan, and Australia – were divided on issues related to agricultural markets and barriers to industrial imports. International Trade Minister Emerson summed up Canada's concerns: 'This is very disappointing for Canada and for all developed and developing countries, given the significant economic benefits that could have been achieved through an ambitious outcome to these negotiations … We are a nation that depends heavily on international commerce, and our government will continue to focus on more liberalized trade, the rules-based multilateral trading system and the objectives behind Doha negotiations' (DFAIT news release no. 84, 24 July).

Softwood lumber. Canada's dispute with the United States regarding softwood lumber exports, ongoing since April 2001 when the US Department of Commerce (DOC) instituted a countervailing duty investigation, finally came to a close with a political solution in 2006. Throughout the dispute, Canadian officials had sought legal redress via the DOC, the United States Court of International Trade, the North American Free Trade Agreement, and the World Trade Organization. In early 2006, for instance, Canada launched a challenge of the US softwood duty rate, it won an appeal at the WTO, and a NAFTA trade panel affirmed that Canada did not subsidize softwood lumber production. On the one hand, Canada did achieve some success with this approach over the years; countervailing and anti-dumping duties initially set at 27 per cent were slowly reduced to less than half this amount. On the other hand, US officials continually conducted administrative reviews and reset different tariff rates which prompted further Canadian challenges. In addition, US officials also failed to comply with rulings made by the NAFTA Extraordinary Challenge Committee.

The political agreement between Canada and the United States, announced on 27 April, contained a number of ingredients. Import duties equating to Can$4 billion that the United States levied against Canadian softwood lumber exporters since 2002 would be returned; the United States would keep the remaining Can$1 billion in levies. The deal would have a seven-year duration with the possibility of a two-year renewal. To protect US softwood lumber producers, Canada's share of the US marketplace would be capped at 34 per cent. Similarly, Canada would implement an export tax should the cost of softwood lumber drop below US$355 per thousand board feet.

For Canadian exporters, a degree of stability returned to this element of bilateral trade which equated to approximately 2 per cent of all Canadian trade to the United States. In this vein, even after the deal's eventual termination, its terms prevent the United States from re-imposing duties for one year. For Ambassador Wilson, the agreement finally put an important component of the bilateral relationship back on an even footing: 'The Agreement will pave the way for a stronger bilateral trade relationship – a relationship upon which so many Canadians depend for jobs and prosperity … It also sets a positive tone that will allow our countries to move forward in collaborating to make North America more competitive on a global scale' (DFAIT news release no. 45, 27 April).

In August, the governing Conservatives announced that it would introduce the agreement to Parliament in order to enact the necessary domestic legislative requirements and that the vote would be considered as a matter of confidence. Although the NDP and the Liberal Party decided not to support the agreement, the Bloc Québécois, on 7 September, provided its endorsement. With the political support now arranged, International Trade Minister Emerson signed the deal in Ottawa on 12 September with his US counterpart, US trade representative Susan Schwab. According to Emerson, 'Canada's New Government today marked another important step toward fulfilling a commitment to resolve the longstanding softwood lumber dispute, signing an agreement with the United States that delivers real results for Canadians' (DFAIT news release no. 99, 12 Sept.).

North American borders. In the wake of the terrorist attacks of 11 September 2001, North American countries continued to struggle in 2006 with achieving the appropriate balance between border security on the one hand and safe, quick, and reliable cross-border commerce on the other hand. In particular, the end of March saw the one-year anniversary of the Security and Prosperity Partnership struck between Canada, the United States, and Mexico. In their trilateral summit marking the occasion and hosted in Cancun, Mexico, the leaders of these three countries announced the creation of a North American Competitiveness Council to provide advice on the smooth integration of key North American industries including the automotive sector, steel production, transportation, manufacturing, and services. They also pushed for further efforts to be made to ensure smart and secure borders on the continent. These efforts included common risk-based screening standards, the electronic management of supply chain security, standards and possibilities for secure documentation, and increased law enforcement exchanges. At the summit's close, Prime Minister Harper stressed that 'Canada, the United States and Mexico are demonstrating a common will to tackle issue that are central to the quality of life of Canadians and all of our continent's citizens. We are making sure that we have smart borders that are both safe and productive' (Prime Minister's Office press release, 31 March).

Complicating the common approach, however, was Washington's decision, announced on 24 November, to implement components of the Western Hemisphere Travel Initiative in the new year. In particular, the initiative, first announced by the US Departments of State and Homeland Security in April 2005, required all people entering the United States by air to present valid passports as of 23 January 2007. The initiative's future requirements called for all Canadians and Americans entering the United States by sea or air to have passports by mid-2009. Given that only 23 per cent of US citizens held valid passports, the initiative presented potential challenges to cross-border trade and the travel of Americans to Canada for either leisure or business.

On the Canadian side of the border, Prime Minister Harper fulfilled an election promise by launching two security initiatives in August. One was to hire more Canada Border Services Agency (CBSA) officers, approximately 400, to ensure that officers at smaller border outposts would not be working alone. The other was to train and equip 4,400 CBSA officers with firearms. In total, the two-year initiative was to cost Can$101 million. With this initiative, Prime Minister Harper was keen to show the Conservative government's activism on the border file, for domestic and American audiences alike: 'Arming CBSA officers and eliminating situations where these officers work alone will allow them to do their job better and more effectively. This continues to show that this Government believes in secure, efficient borders, and is getting things done for Canadian families and taxpayers' (Prime Minister's Office press release, 31 Aug.).

Canada-China relations. Whereas the Liberals, when they were in government, focused somewhat on human rights in China, they placed greater emphasis on growing the Can$35 billion Canada-China trade relationship. In contrast, Prime Minister Harper wanted to illustrate that his new government would be tougher on China and more focused on human rights, governance, and justice within the country: 'I think Canadians want us to promote our trade relations worldwide, and we do that, but I don't think Canadians want us to sell out important Canadian values – our belief in democracy, freedom, human rights' (Canadian Broadcasting Corporation, 19 Nov.). In this regard, during the Conservatives' first year in office, Jason Kenney, the prime minister's parliamentary secretary, met with the exiled Dalai Lama of Tibet. Foreign Affairs Minister MacKay also made public statements about how China was engaged in economic espionage against Canada and how governance and justice within China could be much improved. This approach raised the ire of Liberals such as Michael Ignatieff, who suggested that 'megaphone diplomacy' was not the appropriate way for the government to engage China: 'Mr. Harper, I think, believes you can go to one of the greatest civilizations on earth, a superpower of the 21st century and give them a little lecture on human rights' (ibid., 16 Nov.).

Chinese officials, as well, chafed at the increased Canadian pressure and responded by cancelling a formal bilateral meeting that was to have occurred between the prime minister and Chinese president Hu Jintao during the November Asia Pacific Economic Cooperation (APEC) summit hosted by Vietnam. In particular, the Chinese did not want to discuss the case of Huseyin Celil, a Muslim Chinese Canadian who had been imprisoned for 15 years for alleged linkages to separatist extremist groups. In particular, China had not recognized the man's Canadian citizenship. For the prime minister, the slight was definitely intentional and meant to embarrass: 'This is not the only incident of the Chinese demanding or asking for a meeting and then declining it once it is accepted and it is a pattern that kind of perplexes us' (ibid.). In the end, the meeting between the two leaders was rescheduled, but only as an informal 15-minute chat. Afterwards, whereas the prime minister's aides indicated that human rights issues had been discussed, a Chinese spokesperson said they were not.

International AIDS conference

From 13 to 18 August, Toronto hosted the 16th International AIDS Conference. The conference, which occurs every two years, attracted over 20,000 delegates ranging from researchers to activists to politicians, as well as approximately 3,000 journalists. Participants from 132 countries travelled to Toronto to discuss an array of issues pertaining to HIV / AIDS awareness funding, pharmaceutical developments, and cultural stigmatism. Amongst these participants were former US president Bill Clinton, Bill and Melinda Gates, and Stephen Lewis, the former leader of Ontario's NDP and the United Nations' special envoy on HIV / AIDS in Africa.

Particular media attention was focused on the fact that Prime Minister Harper did not attend the conference. During the conference, the prime minister was on a visit to Canada's three northern territories.[9] Instead,

9 See the later section on the Arctic.

the health minister, Tony Clement, served as the government's official representative. In addition, Canada's governor general, Michaëlle Jean, officially opened the conference at a ceremony held in the Rogers Centre. Nevertheless, during this ceremony, Dr Mark Wainberg, the conference's co-chairman, made it plain that the prime minister's absence was regrettable: 'The role of prime minister includes the responsibility to show leadership on the world stage. Your absence sends the message that you do not consider HIV / AIDS as a critical priority' (Canadian Broadcasting Corporation, 13 Aug.). Dr Julio Montaner, a prominent AIDS researcher at the University of British Columbia, echoed this sentiment: 'We're having in excess of 20,000 people coming to Toronto. We're hosting the largest HIV event ever in the world, and somehow our political leadership is going to look the other way. It's just not acceptable' (ibid., 12 Aug.). However, the prime minister's decision not to attend the conference was not without precedent. Although Prime Minister Brian Mulroney did attend the conference in 1989 when Montreal was the host city, Prime Minister Chrétien did not attend the 1996 conference in Vancouver.

Defence policy

Afghanistan

Mission and debate. When the Conservatives came to power, they inherited a commitment made by the previous Liberal government in May 2005 to increase Canada's presence in Afghanistan. Along with the United Kingdom, Canada would take greater responsibility for operations in the country's south, a move which would free up US soldiers to combat Taliban and al-Qaeda insurgents operating near the Pakistani border. It would also put a more substantial NATO stamp on the international presence in Afghanistan. Because of this promised commitment, Canadians would face greater dangers in Afghanistan than they had in the past. The southern region around the city of Kandahar was at the heart of smuggling routes for both drugs and arms and was strongly pro-Taliban.

Starting in August 2005, the Canadian presence increased to about 600 as the Provincial Reconstruction Team started its work. By the early spring of 2006, the Canadian presence swelled to 2,300 personnel. The collective Canadian presence, dubbed Task Force Afghanistan, was to last for eighteen months and end in February 2007. Canadian efforts would take a multifaceted approach as described by Brigadier General

David Fraser, who was to lead the overall international mission until November: 'We're going to go out there and take the fight to them … But not just from a kinetic point of view. We'll be going out there and helping build governance so the governors can do what they need to do' (Canadian Broadcasting Corporation, 15 Feb.).

Initially, Prime Minister Harper was not keen on having a debate in the House of Commons regarding Canada's ongoing commitment to Afghanistan. He felt that this would undermine military morale and send contrary signals to allies regarding Canada's ability to keep its international commitments. In the end, the prime minister relented, given his party's minority status, but he did so through a take-note debate on 10 April, not an open debate followed by the vote as some Opposition party members had desired. On the one hand, the NDP's defence critic, Dawn Black, provided tentative support: 'I think it does serve a purpose … We are sorry that it's not a full debate in the House, but we will have an opportunity to ask the government a number of questions that we have about our current commitment to Afghanistan which … ends in February' (www.CTV.ca, 10 April). On the other hand, Liberal defence critic Ujjal Dosanjh was more sympathetic towards the government's approach: 'Government has always been able to do that without a vote, and I think it's important sometimes in times of great need and crisis the government can make those decisions without necessarily having a vote in the House of Commons. And I think that power should reside with the government' (ibid.).

Less Opposition sympathy, however, accompanied the prime minister's decision to seek parliamentary approval in May for an extension of Canada's mission through to 2009. Although many Opposition party members during the April take-note debate had called for a full vote in the House of Commons if Canada's mission was to be extended, many regretted the prime minister's decision to seemingly rush the process and bring things to a vote some ten months before the end of the current mandate. For Conservatives such as Foreign Affairs Minister MacKay who had just returned from in-country meetings with Afghan leaders, solidifying Canada's future presence was important given the tasks at hand: 'There is a need for a longer-term plan and commitment … We did not discuss specific time frames or time limits or just how lengthy this mission will be, but I assured the President [Hamid Karzai] that Canada is here and intends to continue to work with our international partners and with the Afghan people to achieve results' (*Globe and Mail*, 16 May). However, for many in the Opposition parties, the vote was a crass political decision meant to remove Afghanistan as a possible election issue and create further strains amongst the Liberal Party, which was in the midst of a leadership campaign. What is more, the prime minister upped the ante by suggesting that even if Parliament voted against the motion, the Canadian mission would still be extended by one year, and he threatened to go to the polls in search of a second-year extension if necessary: 'This government is not in a position to simply walk away or to run away … We cannot walk away quickly. We will proceed with another year' (ibid., 18 May). In the end, the Conservatives won a narrow victory in the vote held on 17 May after a six-hour debate – 149 in favour and 145 against.

Division in the House of Commons towards Canada's Afghan mission was mirrored in the population generally. Around the time of the take-note debate, Decima Research found that only 45 per cent of respondents felt that Canada's deployment was a good idea, whereas 45 per cent thought it was a bad one. In a bid to help boost Canadian support, Afghan president Hamid Karzai travelled to Canada in September in order to praise Canada's commitment. In a speech to the Montreal Council on Foreign Relations, President Karzai linked Canada's work in his country to larger endeavours to fight terrorism and promote international stability and respect for human rights: 'Your contribution as Canadians to Afghanistan stands for a cause bigger than Afghanistan, for a cause that relates to all of us in the world as the fellow citizens of the world' (www.CTV.ca, 24 Sept.). Nevertheless, Canadians were generally not swayed. In a poll released by Decima Research at the start of October, 59 per cent of respondents felt that Canadian military personnel were 'dying for a cause we cannot win' (ibid., 1 Oct.).

Canadian casualties in Afghanistan. Tragically illustrating the increased level of danger associated with Canada's presence in Afghanistan, 2006 was a relatively bloody year in terms of casualties. Whereas eight Canadians died in Afghanistan between 2002 and 2005, 37 died in 2006. Amongst the dead was Captain Nichola Goddard, a 26-year-old forward artillery observer. Her death on 17 May marked the first time a female Canadian combat soldier had died in battle. Also killed in 2006 was Glyn Berry, a 59-year-old senior foreign service officer in Kandahar working as the Provincial Reconstruction Team's political director. He was killed on 15 January when a suicide car bomber targeted the convoy in which he was travelling. Berry and his team were returning to their base after meeting with local Afghan leaders in the village of Tak-the Pol.

In late April, the new Conservative government's handling of Canadian casualties came into question when it changed the policies regarding the honouring of Canada's war dead. No longer would the flag fly at half-mast on Parliament Hill, a policy initiated by the Liberals when they were in government. As well, media coverage was not allowed for the somber repatriation ceremonies that occurred at Canadian Forces Base (CFB) Trenton. A spokesperson for the Department of National Defence indicated that privacy was paramount: 'It is a private and solemn event between the families and the Canadian Forces' (*Toronto Star*, 25 April). Opposition parties, however, were quick to equate the government's policies with those of President Bush. For Ujjal Dosanjh, the Liberal defence critic, 'I can't imagine any other Canadian prime minister trying to manipulate public opinion by hiding the caskets of fallen soldiers … He has borrowed a page from Bush's book … I find it absolutely un-Canadian … He hopes that out of sight is out of mind. Canadians are not going to accept that' (ibid.). Some veterans groups, however, were accepting of the government's policy. The Korea Veterans Association of Canada, for example, wished that honouring Canada's war dead would be restricted to the traditional Remembrance Day ceremonies.

A policy reversal of sorts regarding repatriation did occur, but not without some controversy. During the eulogy he gave for his daughter, Tim Goddard was critical of the government's banning of the media from CFB Trenton: 'I find it troubling that the privacy decision means that we are keeping the press outside the wire … I would like to think Nichola died to protect our freedoms, not to restrict them' (ibid., 27 May). On 26 May, Prime Minister Harper responded by indicating that, in fact, families were always to have had the choice regarding media accessibility for repatriation ceremonies: 'I had given fairly clear instructions that when bodies were to come home that families should be consulted and if all families were agreed on making that particular ceremony public, I thought our government should have no difficulty with that – Obviously I'll look into it and find out if the family's wishes were different than what was done, why that was the case and correct that in the future' (ibid.). Prior to the prime minister's comments, however, Minister O'Connor said this in the House of Commons: 'What we are doing is insisting that at Trenton, when the bodies return, the first time the families meet their fallen members that there be a time of personal grieving' (ibid.). For Liberals such as Ujjal Dosanjh, the prime minister had effectively abandoned one of his ministers: 'I think [Prime Minister Stephen] Harper has clearly undermined him … Whether or not it was intentional, only Mr. Harper would know' (*Globe and Mail*, 2 June).

Prime minister Harper's visit to Kandahar. Shortly after the Conservative government was sworn in on 6 February, speculation arose that Harper, in his first official foreign trip as prime minister, would soon visit Afghanistan. A prime ministerial visit would not only show support to the troops but demonstrate Canada's commitment to the Afghan mission for both a domestic audience wary of the military's combat role and an international audience keen to see the breadth and depth of Canada's leadership on the international stage (*Toronto Star*, 24 Feb.). What is more, officials from the Prime Minister's Office had been seen in the region in February, thus raising further gossip. At the time, Lieutenant Colonel Ian Hope, the Canadian front-line military commander in Afghanistan, recognized the significance of a prime ministerial visit: 'It would be an extremely powerful positive morale effect ... someone of that stature would be great' (ibid.).

For the sake of secrecy and security, news of the actual trip was embargoed until almost 12 hours after the prime minister, along with Defence Minister O'Connor, had landed in Kandahar on 12 March. The delegation from Ottawa arrived in Afghanistan by way of Zagreb, Croatia, and Islamabad, Pakistan. Already in Kandahar was General Rick Hillier, the chief of defence staff (CDS). Upon arrival, the prime minister made it plain that he was there to support equally Canadian military personnel and what the government was doing to promote Canadian domestic security and international stability: 'Canada is not an island, we live in a dangerous world, and we have to show leadership in that world and that's what we're doing and that's what I'm trying to do by going to support our men and women' (www.CTV.ca, 13 March).

Unlike Prime Minister Chrétien's quick visit to Kabul in October 2003, which lasted only a few hours, Prime Minister Harper's visit went overnight and included a speech to 1,000 military personnel from Canada and allied countries at the Kandahar Air Base. During his speech, in part a rallying cry for the troops and in part an international demonstration of his government's dedication, the prime minister claimed that 'cutting and running is not your way. It's not my way. And it's not the Canadian way. We don't make a commitment and then run away at the first sign of trouble. We don't and we won't' (Prime Minister's Office press release, 13 March). The speech also made reference to the humanitarian side of the military's operations and the role the United Nations was playing, two ingredients meant to instil domestic support for the Afghan mission.

Arctic

For the January 2006 federal election, the Conservative Party campaigned for a 'Canada First' defence policy, one that highlighted the increasing importance of the Arctic to Canada. Global warming was likely to make the Northwest Passage traversable for commercial use much earlier than expected. This would likely bring to the fore both the possibility of environmental damage and the long-standing differences between Washington and Ottawa over the passage's status; Canada claimed it as internal waters, whereas the United States defined the passage as an international strait. In addition, Canada had ongoing territorial disputes with the United States over maritime boundaries in the Beaufort Sea, with Denmark over Hans Island, and with Russia over the larger continental shelf. Territorial issues were of growing concern because increased accessibility made it more likely that the region's energy resources, estimated as one-quarter of the world's oil and natural gas deposits, would eventually be harvested. What is more, the Conservative Party's heavy emphasis on the Arctic was meant to distinguish it from the governing Liberals and to offset the perception that the Conservatives had a decidedly pro-American tilt. To this end, during the campaign, Stephen Harper detailed a five-year, Can$5.3 billion plan for increasing Canada's military presence in the north through the construction of three new icebreakers, the creation of a deepwater port, the development of a winter warfare school, the deployment of new aircraft in the north, and the laying of an underwater sensor network.

Shortly after their election win, the Conservatives were able to illustrate their resolve vis-à-vis the Arctic. On 25 January, the US ambassador to Canada, David Wilkins, reiterated US differences about the Northwest Passage and indicated his country's discomfort with some of the northern components of the Conservative's Canada First defence policy. One day later, Stephen Harper, during his first news conference as prime minister designate, focused upon the ambassador's comments: 'The United States defends its sovereignty and the Canadian government will defend our sovereignty ... It is the Canadian people we get our mandate from, not the ambassador of the United States' (Canadian Broadcasting Corporation, 26 Jan.). Later, on 24 February, Defence Minister O'Connor made it clear that the military would play a prominent role in the government's Arctic strategy: 'International law and diplomacy are important instruments in protection of national sovereignty ... However, our claims must be backed by strong military capabilities. This means the capacity for both surveillance and presence over every part of Canada's Arctic territory' (*Globe and Mail*, 24 Feb.).

To bolster Canada's claims in the north, the Canadian Forces conducted Operation Nunalivut (an Inuktitut word meaning 'land that is ours') for 15 days during late March and early April. The operation involved 46 personnel from both the regular force and from the Canadian Rangers and the 1,700 mostly Inuit Reserve working part-time in the Canadian Arctic. However, unlike past Ranger patrols that traversed only 200–300 kilometres from local communities, Operation Nunalivut involved five patrols, some of which met en route in the High Arctic, during an overall 4,500-kilometre trek. The rationale for the operation, as expressed by Colonel Norman Couturier, the commander of military forces in the north, was both symbolic and functional: 'The more military activities we have in that region, the better it is for assertion of sovereignty … Sooner or later, we know there will be emergencies in that region. We have to be ready to operate in that area' (*Globe and Mail*, 10 Feb.).[10] Given the complexity of the operation and the harshness of the climate and geography, Operation Nunalivut cost Can$1.5 million and was a year in the making.

During the rest of 2006, the Arctic's profile in the Conservative government's agenda was uncertain. On the one hand, the prime minister travelled extensively in the Canadian north during August, visiting Iqaluit, Alert, Whitehorse, Yellowknife, and the Jericho diamond mine. On the other hand, the Conservatives' first federal budget did not refer to the purchase of the promised icebreakers, nor were they mentioned in the Can$17 billion worth of military procurement announcements (see next section) or during the prime minister's northern visit.

Defence procurement

In addition to focusing on the Arctic during the election campaign, the Conservatives also made a number of additional promises regarding defence such that annual spending would be at Can$25 billion by 2010–11. Whereas the Liberals had called for an increase of the regular force by 5,000 and of the reserves by 3,000, the Conservatives called for respective increases of 13,000 and 10,000. The Conservatives also indicated that urban army bases, building on reserve infrastructure already in place, would be established in Vancouver, Calgary, Regina,

10 In 2006 approximately 400 commercial flights flew daily over the Arctic.

Winnipeg, Toronto, Quebec City, and Montreal. Also to be created was a 650-member rapid reaction battalion, and the size of Canada's Disaster Area Response Team would be doubled. As for kit, strategic and tactical airlift were all mentioned, as were new replenishment and transport ships.

In late June 2006, in keeping with its election promises (the Arctic capabilities aside), the governing Conservatives rolled out a number of defence procurement announcements costing billions of dollars. For Prime Minister Harper, he was good to his word to 'correct 13 years of Liberal neglect – that we would move forward with major military purchases including new supply ships, new trucks, new helicopters, and strategic and tactical airlift' (*Globe and Mail*, 23 June). With respect to heavy lift helicopters, 15 would be purchased at a cost (including servicing) of Can$4.2 billion. The likely candidate was the Chinook helicopter. For Can$2.1 billion, three new supply ships would be constructed to replace their 40-year-old predecessors. Approximately Can$1.1 billion would go towards buying 2,300 logistics trucks that would replace their 24-year-old predecessors. Three billion dollars would go towards the purchase of four Globemaster C-17s, a strategic lift aircraft produced in the United States. Finally, approximately Can$4.9 billion was to be spent on the purchase of 17 Hercules tactical lift aircraft, the C-130J, to replace Canada's Hercules fleet which, in some cases, had aircraft dating back to the 1960s.

This last decision regarding the Hercules aircraft put to rest some of the concerns about Defence Minister O'Connor's past links to the lobbying industry. While serving as a lobbyist, O'Connor had worked hard for the government to consider the purchase of the A400M produced by Airbus as the Hercules replacement. At the time of the procurement announcement, the senior vice president of Airbus Military, Richard Thompson, contended that the deck was stacked against the A400M: 'We're challenging what we see as being unnecessary, mandatory requirements that we feel exclude a competition. If those things are removed, clearly we have a competition and we'll put our best foot forward and may the best plane win' (ibid., 5 Aug.). The government's stance remained unchanged at the end of 2006.

Ballistic Missile Defence (BMD)

Although the then-governing Liberals decided in February 2005 that Canada would not join the United States in its BMD shield, the issue nevertheless arose on several occasions during 2006. First, during the federal election campaign, Stephen Harper contended that should he become prime minister and should the Americans formally ask that Canada reconsider its stance, he would allow for a national debate and then bring the issue to a free vote in the House of Commons. Once the Conservatives did come to power, O'Connor, during his first major speech as a minister, reiterated this message: 'Our policy is the fact that the Americans would have to approach us to participate in ballistic missile defence, then we would enter into negotiation' (*Toronto Star*, 23 Feb.). On the following day, however, Ambassador Wilkins indicated that he was not aware of any BMD proposal coming from Washington: 'That issue came up and the Canadian officials decided and we move on from that and continue to work together on other issues and in other areas' (*Globe and Mail*, 24 Feb.).

With a US invitation not forthcoming regarding the BMD file, Conservative Party support was left somewhat in limbo. On the one hand, following a meeting with President Bush at the White House on 6 July, Prime Minister Harper indicated that in the face of threats such as a nuclear North Korea, Canada appreciated the US position regarding BMD: 'It should be obvious … why the United States and others would want to have a modern and flexible defence system against this kind of threat … That's something our government at least fully understands' (*National Post*, 7 July). On the other hand, Prime Minister Harper also made it clear at the time that despite worrying challenges that also posed a threat to Canada, 'the government of Canada is not prepared to open the missile defence issue at this time' (ibid.). If the Conservative government did pursue BMD negotiations with the United States, it would demonstrate to Washington the new government's desire for better bilateral relations. However, a number of issues prevented Prime Minister Harper from engaging further: (1) A free vote in a minority Parliament on the issue would likely go down to defeat given the official policies of the Opposition parties; (2) Quebec voters were particularly against Canada supporting BMD, a segment of the electorate key to any eventual Conservative Party majority; and (3) the Afghanistan mission was often seen as being too closely linked to the United States and, as such, BMD would be a step too far.

Also in 2006, the Liberal Party itself did have to re-examine its stance towards BMD. In a discussion paper released in June as part of the Liberals' policy renewal process, Frank McKenna, Canada's former ambassador to Washington and a prominent Liberal Party member, suggested that Canada should reopen the BMD issue with the United States. For McKenna, the strategic context had changed with developments in

North Korea's nuclear weapons programme and with the increasing multilateralization of BMD; Australia, Denmark, Japan, and the United Kingdom had endorsed BMD, and NATO, with Canada's agreement as a treaty member, was discussing the matter too. The issue, however, did not gain much traction in Liberal Party circles; Scott Brison was the only leadership candidate for the federal Liberals who endorsed discussing BMD with the United States. The Liberal Party's stance remained unchanged, although the Senate Committee on National Security and Defence, headed by Liberal senator Colin Kenny, released a report in October contending that '[i]t is in our national interest to co-operate with America to defend the continent ... Supporting [the Ballistic Missile Defence program] would help do that' (ibid., 6 Oct.).

North American Aerospace Defence Command (NORAD)

Although Canada remained outside of BMD in 2006, it did embrace another element of continental defence – NORAD. The bilateral command, in existence since 1958, had been renewed on nine separate occasions and seen its agreement text reworked on three occasions – 1975, 1981, and 1996. In 2006 the text was reworked again to include a maritime warning component alongside NORAD's two other key features of aerospace warning and aerospace control. As for the maritime control function, this was left to the two countries' respective continental commands, Canada Command and US Northern Command. In addition, the revised agreement dropped the requirement for periodic renewal. Now NORAD was to be a permanent organization subject to review every four years with withdrawal permissible with one year's notice. NORAD's permanency was to illustrate the continued solidification of continental defence since the terrorist attacks of 11 September 2001.[11] On 8 May, the House of Commons voted to accept the newly revised NORAD agreement by a substantial margin – 257 votes in favour and only 30 against.

General Rick Hillier

Throughout 2006, General Hillier continued to stand in sharp contrast to his predecessors as Canada's CDS: he was outspoken, willing to directly engage with the Canadian public, and occasionally

11 In this vein, NORAD, as of 2004, started to provide information to US Commands responsible for BMD.

controversial. For some critics, General Hillier had blatantly disrupted the balance of civil military relations by publicly commenting on and at times contradicting government policy. For others, General Hillier's remarks were appropriate given his responsibility to protect the interests of military personnel. Featured then against the prime minister's policy of limiting his ministers' exposure to the media, General Hillier became, by default, one of the main spokespersons and advocates for the mission in Afghanistan. Unsurprisingly, when the Prime Minister's Office seemingly attempted to muzzle the general in April by having him submit his speeches in advance for screening, the Opposition was quick to respond. For Liberal Ujjal Dosanjh, '[t]hat is highly inappropriate … [General Hillier] is not a member of the Cabinet. His role is to be a strong voice for our military and in that sense he's independent, so he can speak about the needs of the military' (*Globe and Mail*, 20 April). In light of the outcry, the PMO moderated its stance, requesting that only the themes, not the text, be produced in advance.

Within the Department of National Defence itself, General Hillier and Defence Minister O'Connor clashed both personally and professionally. As one insider expressed, '[t]hey are polite to each other, they are very courteous, but they don't like each other … They have completely different visions of the Forces' (ibid.). In part, the clash may have come from O'Connor's military background, an anomaly in terms of the experiences of recent Canadian defence ministers.[12] One can consider, for instance, the remarks made by retired lieutenant general Ray Crabbe: 'I've always been somewhat leery about former senior officers becoming ministers of national defence because, I would think, there would be a tendency for him to get involved in the details of running the department simply because of the nature of the individual's background' (*Windsor Star*, 14 Feb.). Other ingredients of the clash speak to the criticism that O'Connor was out of touch with contemporary military requirements. Whereas General Hillier wanted a lighter, more mobile force, O'Connor, for some, was mired in Cold War – era thinking.[13] Finally, the clash may also have come from differences regarding the Canada First Defence Strategy. Whereas General Hillier was keen on prosecuting operations abroad that would, in turn, protect Canadians

12 O'Connor was the first defence minister in twenty years to have previously served in the Canadian military.

13 In fact, in Germany during the 1970s, then-captain Hillier served under O'Connor, then a lieutenant colonel.

at home, O'Connor was keen to acquire assets and capabilities that could be best applied in North America. For some, the government's decision not to mention the promised icebreakers in its first budget and in the subsequent procurement announcements spoke to the CDS having greater sway than the defence minister.[14]

14 Another interpretation is that both men got what they wanted. Whereas General Hillier was keen for the military to acquire Hercules aircraft and helicopters, Defence Minister O'Connor desired the acquisition of C-17 aircraft.

EMMANUEL BRUNET-JAILLY, SERENA KATAOKA, AND WARREN MAGNUSSON

Municipal affairs

The third World Urban Forum was held in Vancouver in June. The theme was 'sustainable cities.' The new federal government co-sponsored the forum with UN-Habitat, thus continuing an initiative of its predecessor. UN-Habitat was formed after the first UN Conference on Human Settlements in Vancouver in 1976. Just as the earlier conference had been held in the wake of the failure of the federal government's urban initiative of the early 1970s, the 2006 event occurred as the 'New Deal for Cities and Communities' promised by the outgoing Martin government began to run out of steam. Although the policy changes that resulted from the change of government in Ottawa in 2006 were relatively limited, it was obvious that new spending initiatives favourable to the municipalities were scarcely to be expected, given the Harper government's fiscal conservatism and its general disinclination to become involved in matters that it thought were under provincial jurisdiction. The same was true with respect to environmental initiatives related to sustainability. For municipalities, the challenge was to deal with problems with the means already at hand. Although Mayor David Miller easily won re-election in Toronto, there were signs of a move to the right politically elsewhere, in tune with the tone set in Ottawa. Cost-cutting measures, rather than expensive new initiatives, were likely to be on the cards.

Cities in the marketplace

The 2006 census confirmed many established trends. The country was becoming more urban by every measure, with 90 per cent of the population growth in 2001–6 occurring in the 33 census metropolitan areas (CMAs). The six largest CMAs (Toronto, Montreal, Vancouver, Ottawa-Gatineau, Calgary, and Edmonton) had grown at double the rate of the other CMAs over the preceding five years and at almost eight times the rate of small towns and rural areas. In fact, the difference was even greater than these measures suggest, given that the small towns and rural areas experiencing growth were rapidly urbanizing. Four of the six new CMAs – which by definition are areas centred on a city of at least 50,000 with a total population of more than 100,000 – were in the Toronto region: Barrie, Guelph, Brantford, and Peterborough. This reflects the trend towards huge urban agglomerations, such as the 'extended Golden Horseshoe' around the western end of Lake Ontario, the cluster about the Island of Montréal, the corridor between Edmonton and Calgary, and the cluster around Vancouver and southern Vancouver Island. More than half the people in Canada live in one of these four areas. Elsewhere, the population is also becoming more urban, as is reflected in the growth of the Moncton and Kelowna areas, which both achieved the status of census metropolitan areas over the years in question.

The westward shift in population was also apparent, as Alberta and British Columbia accounted for about a third of all the new jobs created in 2001–6. Many of the new jobs there were associated with the oil and gas industry, which continued to attract migrants from the rest of the country. Calgary had grown by 13 per cent and Edmonton by 10 per cent, as compared with Toronto (9 per cent), Vancouver (7 per cent), Ottawa-Gatineau (6 per cent), and Montreal (5 per cent) – the latter two cities being near the national average of 5.4 per cent. Job growth was stronger in Vancouver than in Toronto or Montreal, but stronger still in Calgary, at 17 per cent over the five years. That was despite the fact that 2003–5 had been years of slow growth in Calgary – a pause before an expected 7 per cent increase in 2006, according to the Conference Board of Canada. Oil and gas development in Newfoundland was beginning have its effect, as the expected employment increase in St. John's for 2006 was at a rate (2.6 per cent) comparable to Vancouver's (2.4 per cent). Vancouver was beginning to feel the effect of the pre-Olympics construction boom. Elsewhere, the decline in manufacturing was hitting smaller urban centres in Ontario and Quebec quite hard, and Ottawa-Gatineau was suffering from the sudden retrenchment in its high-tech sector. More than half of all foreign immigrants were going to Ontario and most of them to the Toronto area. As the average age of the Canadian worker increased from 39 to 41 over just five years, the workforce as a whole was becoming more diverse in terms of race, gender, and ethnicity, despite differentially high unemployment among recent immigrants and Aboriginal people. Employment rates for the latter groups did improve, although they continued to lag behind the average.

From a municipal perspective, the most obvious effect of these shifts and changes was an uneven distribution of the burdens of adjustment. Some places were faced with high levels of employment and declining population and so were hard-pressed to maintain existing services and facilities. Other places found it hard to keep up with population growth. Still others were coping with shifts and changes that involved different demographics, patterns of movement, and demands for services to both residents and businesses. Thus, the ongoing fiscal crisis of the municipalities took different forms in different places. Although growing cities might be able to take outside investment for granted, that was not the case with places (such as Windsor) that were dealing with the decline of traditional industries or some sort of reversal with respect to the new ones, as occurred in Ottawa. The Ottawa-Gatineau area lost 11,700 jobs in the high-tech sector during the period in question and only sustained a good rate of growth because of expansion in the federal public service. Not surprisingly, anxieties among municipal leaders about the relative position of their communities in the marketplace were intense. Growing demands for public services fell heavily on the municipalities, whose electors were rarely willing to pay higher taxes – especially with respect to their own homes.

For whatever reason, the question of sustainability became more prominent during the year. Some thought of it mainly in terms of sustaining economic (and hence urban) growth in the face of environmental limits; others were more concerned about the environment itself. The tension between these two sets of objectives was apparent in Industry Canada's Sustainable Development Strategy, which 'supports all efforts by partners and stakeholders to implement productivity-enhancing sustainability technologies and processes that can improve their economic, environmental and social performance.'[1] The policy included subsidies for 'competitive industry and sustainable communities' and such performance indicators as the number of firms implementing ISO 14001 (environmental management) standards. All this was in the context of promoting a competitive economy: the question of community sustainability was apparently secondary. In Toronto, in June, the City Council directed staff to develop a Sustainable Energy Plan that would maximize energy efficiency and turn that into an economic advantage. The Conference Board of Canada expressed a similar idea in its October

1 Sustainability Development (2006) Strategy 2006–9, accessed June 2009; www.ic.gc.ca/eic/site/sd-dd.nsf/eng/sd00530.html.

2006 Briefing, 'Sustainability: A Winning Merger of Growth and the Environment.' Although many environmentalists might question the possibility of such a merger, the more prominently expressed view, implicit in the federally supported Green Municipal Fund, was that green technologies could facilitate economic growth while protecting the environment. As the Conference Board put it,

> Within the framework of industrial ecology, a successful industrial ecosystem would effectively manage the energy and material flows linked to industrial activities, such that human needs are met without overwhelming the assimilative capacity of the city, the surrounding area, or indeed the planet. (4)

Clearly municipalities, as the main authorities responsible for land use and waste management, had to deal with the industrial ecosystem. What that would involve was a matter of debate, with some experts such as Dana J. Vanier[2] advocating for basic institutional change – specifically, the creation of broad-based Sustainability Councils at the local level – and others such as Enid Slack[3] focusing on specific policy measures – in her case fees to encourage efficient land use and tax increment financing to encourage brownfield remediation and redevelopment.

Although Calgary was often singled out as an example of unsustainable sprawl (in fact, its ecological footprint is the biggest of any Canadian city, on a per capita basis), the council there could point to a number of sustainability initiatives, especially with regard to energy.

> Calgary was the first municipality in North America to implement an environmental management system and achieve ISO 14001 certification. The initial phase of its corporate climate change plan included the first wind-powered light rail transit system [2001], the installation of systems to capture methane gas at its landfills and wastewater treatment plant, and a building retrofit program. These measures have already [2006] cut the city's greenhouse gas emissions by more than 80,000 tonnes. (Federation of Canadian Municipalities, *Our Communities, Our Future, Annual Report 2005–2006*, 18)

In a July the City of Calgary issued its new Climate Change Action Plan, which involved a 50 per cent reduction in greenhouse gas emissions

2 'Process for Implementing a Municipal Sustainability Plan,' in Institute for Research on Construction, National Research Council of Canada, *Handbook on Urban Sustainability*, 743–66.

3 'Fiscal Imbalance: The Case for Cities,' Institute on Municipal Finance and Governance, University of Toronto, 1 June.

from 1990 levels on the part of the city itself and a more modest community goal of a 20 per cent reduction in per capita emissions from 2005 levels by 2020. Crucial to the municipality's capacity in this regard was its wholly owned subsidiary, ENMAX, which was generating power from extensive wind farms for the light-rail transit (LRT) and other municipal purposes.

The Calgary report carefully skirted the issue of climate change denial. Although questions of sustainability might be conceived primarily in economic or environmental terms, it was obvious that deeper cultural issues were also involved. How were people to inhabit their cities? What was involved in living in a way appropriate to the twenty-first century?

The culture of cities

If sustainability was as much a cultural as an economic issue, so too was the question of wireless communications. Would a forward-looking city not make Wi-Fi available to everyone, for both business and personal use? Wasn't it a matter of bringing everyone across the digital divide so that everyone could participate in the new economy and contribute to its productivity? That, at least, was a theme that Jim Green had articulated during his unsuccessful campaign for the mayoralty in Vancouver in 2005. An issue posed there and elsewhere was whether municipalities should get involved in developing Wi-Fi systems as a public utility (as Fredericton has done) or just leave the matter to private enterprise. So-called 'community wireless networking,' developed on a non-profit basis, was another alternative being developed by digital activists in various cities, including Ottawa, Montreal, Toronto, and Vancouver. The questions raised were similar to the ones debated a century ago or more, in the context of the then new hard-wired electricity and telephone services. What Henri Lefebvre called 'the right to the city'[4] was evidently at issue, as was the culture or cultures the city might enable. On the whole, consumer culture and the culture of capitalism remained predominant, perhaps even more obviously in 2006 than in 1906.

Another cultural issue of sorts was pesticide use. Although municipalities had little or no role in the regulation of agricultural pesticides, they had become prominent with respect to the control of pesticides used to maintain lawns and gardens in urban areas. The Supreme Court of Canada's 2001 ruling in the *Spraytech* case had opened the door to

4 *Writing on Cities* (Oxford: Blackwell, 1996).

municipal regulation and encouraged anti-pesticide activists across the country to press their municipal councils to ban pesticide and herbicide use for purely ornamental purposes.[5] By 2005 no less than 36 per cent of the country, in population terms, was covered by such bans. This was an indication of the occasional effectiveness of political campaigns that link activists in different communities but are locally rather than nationally or provincially focused. It also is an interesting instance of the 'precautionary principle' at work because the bans are justified in terms of the uncertainties around the health and environmental effects of the chemicals concerned, rather in relation to hard scientific evidence. Is openness to the precautionary principle a matter of cultural sensibilities, or does everything turn on attitudes towards pristine lawns and the wild plants and animals that thrive in cities?

A symbolic setback for environmental activists was the closure of Guelph's pioneering municipal composting facility, which had been in existence since 1995. Many other cities, including Edmonton and Toronto, had followed suit in the interim, but Guelph was unable to find the money to renew its facility when the time came. Everywhere issues of waste management, water supply, and water quality were at issue. In the Victoria area, the Capital Regional District was finally ordered by the province to develop a sewage treatment system, in the face of longstanding complaints about the practice of putting untreated effluent into the Strait of Juan de Fuca. There was an ongoing scientific dispute about this, connected to differing evaluations of the effects of treatment and the environmental impact of the effluent. For many, the scientific issues were secondary to questions of public image: how could a place that promoted itself as a pretty tourist destination and retirement centre be anything other than scrupulous in the way that it deals with its liquid waste?

Quite a different cultural issue was posed by the ongoing demand for improved or different sports facilities. Such facilities are not usually considered as part of the infrastructure of a community, but they clearly are, and their renewal is part of the fiscal burden facing municipalities. This is a field of activity in which complex questions arise about fee for service, access for the disadvantaged or disabled, provision for the old and the young, and so on. As one set of consultants reported,

5 Sarah Pralle, 'The 'Mouse that Roared': Agenda Setting in Canadian Pesticide Politics,' *Policy Studies Journal* 34, no. 2 (2006): 171–94.

While there is no comprehensive assessment of outstanding or emerging demand it is clear that existing infrastructure, much of which was built in response to the post-war baby boom and nascent sport and recreation profession, cannot meet the needs of today's multi-ethnic, multi-generational, multi-abled, and multi-interest, sport and recreation participants and competitors.[6]

A bewildering array of funding and management options have been tested in various communities, as befits the complexity of public needs and demands. The relationship between public and commercial facilities for leisure and recreation is an ongoing issue, hidden within demands for public-private partnership. What should be provided as a public service? What should be subsidized? What should be available on a non-profit basis? What should be purely commercial? And what role do the municipalities have in reaching out to the marginalized and the disadvantaged, including cultural communities that are struggling in this country? Big issues of this sort are often obscured by the latest photo-op for a federal or provincial minister announcing a grant for some local facility.

That said, there could hardly be a more moving picture than the one of Vancouver mayor Sam Sullivan receiving the Olympic flag at Turin on behalf of the next host city. Sullivan is quadriplegic. Other moves by Sullivan, such as Project Civil City, were much more controversial. Project Civil City was oriented at street behaviour. It resonated with many of the ideas of the Harper government about tougher attitudes towards crime and antisocial behaviour. It also blurred the line between public and private policing in a way that was becoming more common in Canadian cities. The implications for inclusion of the disadvantaged were at best uncertain.

Regional governance

Some of the obvious regional government issues were played out in Ontario, where the new Greenbelt Act put some of the municipalities in the outer Toronto area at odds with the provincial government because of the municipalities' interest in continued growth. This conflict was

6 A Planning and Management Service, *Innovative Sources of Funding for Development and Rehabilitation of Sport and Recreation Infrastructure*, Final Report for the Federal-Provincial/Territorial Sport Committee (October 2006).

most apparent in Durham, the regional municipality immediately east of Toronto, which insisted on designating certain protected lands for future development, despite provincial policies to the contrary. Obviously, the pro-development forces wanted to be ready in case there was a change of government in the province. The conflict was complicated because the mayor of Ajax, one of the local municipalities in Durham, was a strong supporter of the Greenbelt and a critic of the regional municipality.

Another key move on the part of the Ontario government was to create a Greater Toronto Transportation Authority (GTTA) with responsibility for integrated planning of rail and road services in and around Canada's biggest city. One aim was to provide for a single fare card that would allow for easy transfer between different modes of public transportation, whoever might be operating them. The new authority would have four representatives from Toronto proper, four from the outer suburbs and satellite cities, one from Hamilton, and two from the province. This weighting towards the area surrounding Toronto – more or less reflective of the population balance – raised questions about the relationship between the new authority and the Toronto Transit Commission (TTC), responsible for buses, subways, and streetcars within Toronto proper. The TTC was struggling with the financial implications of proposals to expand the rapid transit system in the east and the subway system in the northwest: neither initiative seemed viable without support from the senior governments; it was doubtful whether both initiatives could be pursued simultaneously. Demands from the outer suburbs – which, incidentally, were crucial to the electoral fortunes of both the federal and provincial governments – further complicated the issue. Institutions to plan for the greater Toronto region had never been very successful in the past, and there was reason to suppose that the new GTTA would face similar difficulties.

Regional transportation issues were equally fraught in greater Vancouver, where the relevant transportation authority, TransLink, faced fierce opposition to its latest fundraising scheme, a special tax on commercial parking spaces. The province commissioned a study of the organization, which was less than a decade old. One of the issues was the question of boundaries. TransLink's responsibilities did not extend as far up the Fraser Valley as did the connected urban settlements. Meeting the needs of these outer communities would complicate the already fraught politics of the authority, which were marked by fierce disagreements about the location, character, and financing of fixed rail lines, the relative priority of bus services, and provision for private automobiles. Pressure to extend SkyTrain services to the airport in time for the Olympics had already resulted in a change of priorities, and the Pacific Gateway program agreed upon between the federal and provincial governments in 2006 promised new investments in roads and bridges to facilitate freight traffic through the Port of Vancouver. It wasn't clear that TransLink, any more than the GTTA, could really control the evolution of a regional transportation system that was being developed in large measure by senior governments in response to a variety of pressures.

In Ottawa there were similar controversies, although they were contained within the bounds of the city, which had been greatly extended in 2001. The big issue was a much discussed plan for a north – south LRT line intended to shape development in the southern suburbs. Opponents claimed that the most pressing needs were along the east – west corridor (a familiar refrain to anyone in Toronto or Vancouver) and the proposed system was too expensive and unnecessarily disruptive (also familiar refrains). John Baird, the federal Treasury Board president and a local MP, intervened by delaying federal funding until after the November elections. The scheme then collapsed because of voter hostility to expected tax increases.

The Canadian Public Transit Association deplored the fact that Canada is the only Organization for Economic Cooperation and Development (OECD) member country that does not have a 'long term, predictable federal transit-investment policy' (*Public Transit and the Role of the Federal Government*). Although organizations such as the Canadian Chamber of Commerce kept drawing attention to the issues, and the new federal government continued its predecessor's commitment to sharing proceeds of the gas tax, funding remained a huge issue for the responsible authorities. When there is so little to go around, it is not surprising that local politicians fight so hard over route location and local voters remain sceptical about the financial implications for them.

Local democracy

There were municipal elections in four provinces – Ontario, Manitoba, Saskatchewan, and PEI – as well as the northern territories. David Miller, the centre-left mayor of Toronto, cruised to victory, and the council there retained its colouring. If there was a trend elsewhere, it was towards the right, as Sam Katz won another term as mayor of Winnipeg, Hazel McCallion won in Mississauga, and a newcomer, Larry O'Brien, easily defeated incumbent Bob Chiarelli and long-time progressive councillor Alex Munter in a three-way race in Ottawa. O'Brien's campaign centred on the promise of a tax freeze: his come-from-behind victory was very decisive and was widely perceived as a rebuke to the outgoing council as a whole.

The Ontario elections were the first to be conducted in that province on a four-year term, introduced by the provincial government in May against significant opposition. There was also more use of alternative voting methods, such as postal balloting and electronic voting. Such methods had been an option available to municipalities since 1996. Their use in Ontario came in the wake of controversies in Quebec in 2005, which were the subject of a damning report by the province's chief electoral officer in 2006. In Quebec, the difficulties had been with respect to electronic voting, but it was postal balloting that caused the greatest controversy in Ontario. Particularly in the Kawartha Lakes area, the number of ballots disqualified because of voter error – putting the voter declaration in the wrong envelope or not including it at all – was unacceptably large. A bit less than a third of all Ontario municipalities had allowed postal balloting, and half of them reported serious difficulties with voter disqualification. In Markham, there was a campaign to increase voter turnout by encouraging electronic voting. Although organizers claimed some success, overall participation was still just 26.5 per cent. Evidently these new voting methods do not overcome all the problems with voter participation.

One issue, raised by Mayor Miller and others in Toronto, was the possible extension of the municipal franchise to resident aliens. Such an arrangement is common in Europe. The case for it in Toronto seems particularly strong, given that there are so many recent immigrants and the rate of participation in municipal elections on the part of newcomers is low. The provincial government stuck to the traditional view, however, and insisted that voting should remain a privilege of citizenship.

As usual, most incumbents won, but there were some upsets. Hamilton, Oakville, and Waterloo all chose new mayors, whereas in London Anne Marie DeCicco-Best turned back a challenge from former Liberal MP Joe Fontana. It is difficult to identify a pattern because local issues – including ones of personality – are so conspicuous, but questions about the pace and character of development, urban sprawl, and downtown regeneration are everywhere prominent. In the outer municipalities of the Toronto region, issues of urban containment were particularly vexed, whereas in such places as Hamilton and Windsor concerns about economic revitalization were necessarily more pronounced.

The Canadian Labour Congress (CLC) made a bigger than usual effort to identify and support favoured candidates across Ontario. It made a similar effort in BC in 2005. In Ontario 217 of the 438 Labour-endorsed candidates were successful – although it is difficult to say how much of a difference the endorsements made. The greatest apparent success was in Guelph, where the mayor and the majority of councillors were backed by the Labour movement in conjunction with a left-leaning local party, the Guelph Civic League.[7]

Although the election did not produce much change in the composition of the Toronto City Council, it was the first to be held after the province passed the Stronger City of Toronto for a Stronger Ontario Act, a measure that met many of Mayor Miller's demands for more power for himself and the city. Miller was able to appoint an executive committee of his own liking, and the city got the authority to act within its own areas of jurisdiction without specific leave from the province. Although Toronto had long made the case that it was different from other municipalities because of its size, the province was under pressure to extend similar powers – including the right to decide on the exact form of the local council and its executive – to other municipalities. Legislation along those lines was introduced in June, but the relevant provisions would not take effect until 2007. The newly elected municipal councils could look forward to having greater flexibility than their predecessors.

In Winnipeg, Sam Katz's decisive victory – along with the election of more conservatives to the council – confirmed the ongoing popularity of a style of municipal leadership that emphasized low taxes, civic boosterism, and support for the police, as opposed to bold new social or environmental policies. In Regina, Pat Fiacco – a rather different figure in certain respects but equally successful in securing re-election as mayor – also emphasized his support for the police, commitment to low taxes, and fervent dedication to the city. His flagship policy was 'I love Regina.' Substitute the name of the city, and one could have a slogan for many municipal election campaigns. Fiacco had national prominence as chair of the Big City Mayors' Caucus of the Federation of Canadian Municipalities (FCM).

7 Larry Savage, 'Organized Labour and Local Politics: Ontario's 2006 Municipal Elections,' *Labour/Le Travail* 62 (Fall 2008): 171–84.

Cities in the confederation

Whatever their ideological bent, municipal politicians were concerned about the implications of the change of government at the federal level. While in opposition, the Conservatives had been sceptical about Liberal initiatives in relation to the municipalities because the Conservatives took a stricter view than the Liberals of the division of responsibilities between Ottawa and the provinces and in any case wanted to focus their attention on what they regarded as the 'core' responsibilities of the federal government. The latter did not include local infrastructure, but it was hard to ignore the ongoing pressure for federal funding or the political advantages of matching Liberal commitments. The Harper government came to office promising to deal with the 'fiscal imbalance' about which the provinces – especially Quebec – had been complaining. The municipalities wanted to be included in that commitment and had some success. When the first Conservative budget came down in May, the municipalities were pleased to find that previous promises about sharing the gas tax had been maintained and that there was new money for the Canada Strategic Infrastructure Fund and the Municipal Rural Infrastructure Fund. Lawrence Cannon, the new minister for transport, infrastructure, and communities, had been a municipal councillor in Gatineau, and FCM leaders regarded him as a friendly face within the new Cabinet.

In its June report entitled *Our Cities, Our Future*, the Big City Mayors' Caucus called again for 'a permanent share of growth-responsive taxes' (37), such as those on incomes, corporate profits, and sales. Even a 1 per cent share would yield significant revenue, although the cities were evidently hoping for 5 per cent. They also wanted a National Transit Program to meet the $23 billion investment requirement over the next few years. David Miller, mayor of Toronto, repeated these demands when he was re-elected in November. It was an old song, now delivered to a governing Conservative party that had failed to win any seats in Toronto, Montreal, and Vancouver in the election in January. What were the implications for cities of *that* imbalance?

KRISTIN BURNETT

First Nations

Federal developments

Uncertain times – the federal election

The Liberal government under Paul Martin ended 2005 on an optimistic note regarding Aboriginal issues. In late November a First Ministers' Summit on Aboriginal Issues, the first meeting of its kind, was held in Kelowna, British Columbia. The Kelowna Accord was the product of this summit and the result of more than two years of negotiations. The agreement promises $5.1 billion in spending on health care, housing, and education for Aboriginal communities in Canada over the next five years (*Globe and Mail*, 12 Jan.).

Unfortunately, the impending federal election in late January left the Kelowna agreement in limbo. The platform of the Conservative Party did not clarify its stance on the Kelowna agreement or the party's position on Aboriginal issues (*Conservative Party of Canada Federal Election Platform, 2006*). This uncertainty was exacerbated following comments made by Conservative MP Monte Solberg in early January: '[T]he Kelowna agreement is something that the Liberals crafted at the last moment on the back of a napkin on the eve of an election. We're not going to honour that. We will have our own plan that will help natives a lot more than the Liberals' (*Globe and Mail*, 11 Jan.).

Stephen Harper, leader of the Conservative Party, wrote a letter to the national chief of the Assembly of First Nations (AFN), Phil Fontaine, on 6 January responding to Solberg's comments. In the letter Harper indicated that he was committed to the five- and ten-year targets established in Kelowna to address Aboriginal poverty but had reservations about the $5.1 billion pledge made by the Liberal government. The letter confirmed the Tories' commitment to honouring the $2 billion settlement package for former residential school students negotiated by the Liberals (ibid., 12 Jan.).

Fontaine and other AFN leaders had serious reservations regarding the Conservatives' commitment to Aboriginal issues. When the Conservatives formed a minority government on 23 January, Prime Minister Harper did not speak to Fontaine, the national chief of the AFN, for over a month (*Windspeaker*, Feb.). During the ceremony inducting the new Cabinet at Rideau Hall, for the first time in many years, no elder was present to smudge the government (ibid., March). Nor did the new government's throne speech mention First Nations people (ibid., April). Jim Prentice was appointed Indian affairs minister and Rod Bruinooge was named Prentice's parliamentary secretary (ibid., March).

The Congress of Aboriginal Peoples (CAP)

CAP is one of five federally recognized Aboriginal organizations and is designed to represent the interests of urban Aboriginal peoples. As an umbrella organization CAP does not have individual memberships; rather it represents the interests of provincial and territorial Aboriginal organizations at the national level. Patrick Brazeau, age 31, replaced long-time incumbent Dwight Dorey on 23 February as national chief (ibid., May).

CAP had its funding frozen in February after an audit revealed irregularities in the spending of money the organization had received in order to pursue Métis hunting and fishing rights (*Globe and Mail*, 16 June). The audit found that $163,245 used by the Ontario Métis Aboriginal Association (OMAA), CAP's Ontario affiliate, had to be repaid. In addition, the OMAA was unable to explain payments to the Native Trading House, a company run by the former vice-chief of CAP, Frank Palmeter.

CAP then suspended the OMAA in August (ibid., 31 Aug.). Brazeau stated that he believed that the funding freeze was an attempt by public servants loyal to the Liberals to destroy the Congress. CAP was the only Aboriginal organization to endorse the Conservative party during the election (ibid., 16 June).

In contrast to the AFN, CAP was optimistic in 2006 about its relationship with the new government. CAP's national chief, Patrick Brazeau, said his 'relationship [with Harper] is a good one and hopefully we can elaborate on that. I have met him about four or five times since the election and I've spoken with him on several occasions' (*Windspeaker*, Dec.). In the fall Prentice announced a $1.3 million increase in CAP's funding (ibid.).

Realignment of federal spending

Shortly after the federal election in late January, the new Conservative government announced a plan to realign federal spending on Aboriginal people to reflect the shift from rural to urban in Canada's Aboriginal population (*Globe and Mail*, 11 March). Peter Dinsdale, the executive director of the National Association of Friendship Centres, worried that discussions about a realignment in federal spending would cause a rift between on- and off-reserve people: '[W]e have to be careful about that. They seem to be kind of pitting us against each other' (ibid.).

Dinsdale's biggest concern was that the $16 million in federal funding for the 117 friendship centres across the country was set to expire at the end of the March and yet no new funding commitment had been announced. Friendship centres began in the 1950s in response to the growing number of Aboriginal people migrating to cities. The centres provide essential services and community to individuals who have not only entered a new environment but are also at risk of 'falling through the cracks' in terms of services provided by the provincial and federal governments. The centres offer referrals and counselling on matters of employment, housing, education, and health and liaise with other community organizations.[1] Dinsdale says, '[T]he most dispossessed and the most economically depressed people of this country rely on friendship centres every day for bread and butter issues like a warm spot to go. The kind of attention that's been paid over the 12 years under the Liberals to this issues has resulted in almost a culture of crisis among friendship centres across the country' (ibid.).

The statistics regarding the geographical distribution of Aboriginal people are unreliable: the centres estimate that 49 per cent of Aboriginal people live in urban centres; the AFN says 40 per cent; and the Congress of Aboriginal People (CAP) says 79 per cent (ibid.). Nor do these statistics account for people who divide their time between reserve communities and cities or towns.

The budget

The federal budget was announced 2 May. None of the financial commitments outlined in the Kelowna Accord were met. Critics charged that

1 http://nafc.ca/en/content/our-history (accessed 5 August 2010).

the $3 billion in Aboriginal spending trumpeted by the Conservatives over the next fiscal year was misleading. Of the $3 billion promised, $2.2 billion was to go towards payments for residential school survivors, a financial commitment made by the previous Liberal government. Instead, the Conservatives committed just $450 million in funding for Aboriginal initiatives over the next two years, while cuts were made in several areas; programs geared towards preserving Aboriginal languages and cultures were decreased by $160 million and the budget for Indian and Northern Affairs Canada (INAC) was reduced by $500 million over the next two years (*Windspeaker*, Dec.). The Conservatives' budget suffered in comparison to the $800 million pledged by the Liberals for 2006 under the Kelowna agreement. Clement Chartier, president of the Métis National Council, was disappointed at the Conservatives' failure to uphold the Kelowna Accord: '[W]hat was the point of doing a lot of work if governments aren't prepared to live up to the commitments of a previous government?' (*Globe and Mail*, 3 May).

Aboriginal Affairs Committee

Maurice Vellacott was elected chair of the House of Common's Aboriginal Affairs Committee. Vellacott was Harper's choice for the position. Other members of the Committee tried to block Vellacott's election because of his 2004 comments in defence of the police officers who had abandoned an Aboriginal man to freeze to death on the outskirts of Saskatoon (ibid., 2 May). In an interview at the time, Vellacott blamed the media for spreading false accusations about Ken Munson and Dan Hatchen, the two police officers later convicted for their actions. Instead Vellacott said the reason that Native people were found outside the city was that there was 'a shack outside of town where natives would gather to drink' (*StarPhoenix*, 21 April). Vellacott resigned from the position on 10 May. New MP Colin Mayes was quickly elected to the post. Mayes is well known for writing an editorial in defence of the Harper government suggesting that reporters should be jailed for writing misleading skewed stories (*Globe and Mail*, 11 May).

The First Nations Governance Act

The Conservative government vowed to make accountability its top priority by forcing Aboriginal communities to take on more responsibility. Harper announced his decision to revise and reintroduce the First Nations Governance Act that had been introduced under the former

Liberal government in 2003 (ibid., 27 March). The Liberals withdrew the First Nations Governance Act after significant opposition from the Aboriginal community.

Human Rights Act

Prentice introduced Bill C-44 in the House of Commons on 13 December to repeal the section of Canada's Human Rights Act that shielded the actions and decisions of band councils and elected chiefs from human rights complaints (ibid., 14 Dec.). Under section 67 of the 1977 Human Rights Act, the administrative structures created by the Indian Act were exempted. This exemption was intended to be a temporary measure in order to allow the federal government and First Nations people time to bring the two pieces of legislation into line.

Bill C-44 would allow band members to bring complaints against councils and chiefs to the Canadian Human Rights Commission. At the moment, Aboriginal people living on reserves do not have the right to challenge decisions made by their band councils about who gets access to housing, land, and children's transportation to school (ibid.).

The First Nations community was divided on this legislation. On the one hand, individuals such as Grand Chief Stan Beardy of the Nishnawbe Aski Nation (NAN), a political group that represents 49 nations in Treaties 9 and 5, thinks the bill 'may ultimately bring relief to people living in the kind of squalor most Canadians can only imagine. I think they'll demand that they have access to universal rights like everybody else' (ibid.). On the other hand, people such as Aboriginal rights lawyer Murray Klippenstein voiced concern about the lack of consultation with Aboriginal people and the failure to address the balance of individual rights and collective interests (ibid., 16 Dec.). The Native Women's Association of Canada opposed the bill because they were not consulted before it was tabled.

Indian residential school settlement

An agreement-in-principle (AIP) on compensation for survivors of abuse suffered in residential schools was signed by the AFN, church organizations, former students, over 70 lawyers, and the federal government on 20 November 2005, pending Cabinet and court approval (*Windspeaker*, Dec. 2005). Included in the AIP were early payments for residential school survivors who were over the age of 65 by 30 May 2005 (ibid., Jan.). Unfortunately, the early payments for elderly residential schools survivors were delayed following the election of the Conservative party on 23 January (ibid., March).

Although early payments were expected to begin in January, they were deferred until a new deal was reached with the Conservative government in late April. The main points of the AIP remained in place: a common experience payment of $10,000 to each former residential school survivor with an additional $3,000 for each year spent in school (*Globe and Mail*, 26 April).

Problems with the early payment system persisted. As many as 500 residential school survivors across Canada received a letter from the federal government rejecting their application. In some of these cases records of attendance no longer existed as a result of fire or managerial incompetence. Sharon Thira, executive director of the Indian Residential School Survivors Society (IRSSS) sent a letter to Jim Prentice asking for clarification, pointing out that 'until recently the federal government has assured IRSSS that in instances where records could not be found for a former student, an affidavit from fellow classmates would be accepted as confirmation of attendance.' Prentice replied that these affidavits would no longer be accepted because 'in going through the approvals process with my Cabinet colleagues, it was decided that the previous government was not performing adequate due diligence in verifying claims and the verification process was strengthened' (*Windspeaker*, October). Under the Liberals only 5 per cent of the claims were being investigated to verify attendance; under the Conservatives all claims are being reviewed.

Among those who received letters rejecting their compensation claims from Indian Residential Schools Resolution Canada, the organization established to handle the claims process, were people in possession of records that prove their provincial government sent them to residential schools and one person who had already secured a judgement for physical abuse at a school in court. Thira offered an example of a '96 year old Elder who had no age peers. He went to residential schools, you can tell that just by talking to him. He's able to tell you what his number is; he's able to tell you what the hallways looked like; he's able to tell you what bed he slept on in the dorm. So you know he went to residential school but he's got a letter saying 'we don't have records for you,' and he feels like he's not believed' (ibid., Oct.). Thira elaborated on the emotional cost of these rejections, stating that you 'have to remember too many people haven't talked about residential school before. Then, when they put in this application form, they feel,

Wow, I'm finally being recognized. And then they get the rejection letter. They read that someone is telling them that they're lying' (ibid.).

Luc Dumont, director general of Indian Residential Schools Resolution Canada, said that the rejection letters were 'part of the growing pains associated with starting up the early payment process' (ibid.). Dumont also admitted that in some cases the rejection letters were just mistakes.

In addition to concerns surrounding appropriate records, the issue of government taxation of these payments remains a problem. In Manitoba social services was requiring people on assistance (including people who received Old Age Pensions) to pay back a portion of their settlement money. The AFN intervened and Manitoba passed legislation excluding settlement payments for residential school survivors from taxation and clarifying that they would not be counted as income in determining people's right to social benefits (ibid., Jan.).

United Nations Declaration on the Rights of Indigenous Peoples

On 29 June the Human Rights Council of the United Nations voted on the Declaration on the Rights of Indigenous Peoples. Of 47 members, 30 voted in favour and 2 against while there were 12 deliberate abstentions, and 3 countries that did not attend the session. Canada and Russia were the two countries that voted against the declaration. Alex Neve, secretary general of Amnesty International Canada, commented on the vote: '[W]e are outraged that Canada would demonstrate such bad faith in opposing a text that it helped write. It is even more astounding that Canada would then try to persuade other states that another round of negotiations is needed. It was fortunate, although embarrassing for all Canadians, that Canada quickly found itself isolated on the council that was prepared to move forward with a principled defense of indigenous people's human rights.' After over a decade the United Nations Declaration on the Rights of Indigenous Peoples would finally go before the General Assembly for ratification (ibid., Aug.).

AFN election

Two candidates ran for national chief of the AFN in July at the annual General Assembly: Bill Wilson, a hereditary Kwawkgewlth chief from British Columbia, and Phil Fontaine, the incumbent. Wilson was seen as a controversial figure for his comments regarding non-Aboriginals including the following: '[Y]ou [Euro-Canadians] were nothing but a bunch of dirty, smelly white people on boats and if we'd known what you were going to do, we should have killed you all' (ibid., July). On 12 July Fontaine was re-elected leader of the AFN at the twenty-seventh annual General Assembly (ibid., Aug.).

In spite of strong support for Fontaine, a number of treaty chiefs present at the assembly declared their intention to form a separate organization. Chief Bryan LaForme of the Mississaugas of the New Credit First Nation said his council and others in Ontario were seriously considering leaving the AFN (ibid.).

Provincial and territorial developments

British Columbia

Government spending. In late March Premier Gordon Campbell promised to increase funding by $1 million to preserve First Nations' languages through increasing programs and technology. Of the 53 Aboriginal languages in Canada, British Columbia has 32. Of those 32, five are already extinct (*Globe and Mail*, 1 April).

The Aboriginal Pilot Sales Program. On 8 June the British Columbia Court of Appeal ruled that the Aboriginal Pilot Sales Program does not breach the *Charter* rights of non-Aboriginal fishermen (ibid., 9 June). The Pilot Sales Program is administered by the Department of Fisheries and Oceans and allows certain First Nations to sell all, or part of, the fish they catch under their communal fishing licences. Under this program three First Nations are allowed to fish for salmon commercially in the lower Fraser River region. The Fraser River supports one of the largest salmon runs in the world and is considered an extremely important and valuable resource. Salmon are extreme sensitive to pollution and are increasingly disappearing from many major rivers.

In 1998 several non-Aboriginal commercial fishermen were arrested during a protest of the Pilot Sales Program. The fishermen argued that this government policy authorized 'exclusive commercial fishing by an organization whose membership is based on race and this violates the charter' (ibid.). In 2003 Judge William Kitchen of the Provincial Court of British Columbia concurred, ruling that the Charter rights of the non-Aboriginal fishermen had been violated. The Crown appealed to the

Supreme Court of British Columbia, who ruled in 2004 that the program did not violate the fishermen's charter rights (*First Nations Drum*, July 2008). The non-Aboriginal fishermen appealed to the BC Court of Appeal, which upheld the decision.

Elaborating on the ruling, Madam Justice Pamela Kirkpatrick writes, '[E]ven if the policy were discriminatory, it should be allowed because of fundamental Aboriginal rights enshrined in the constitution.' Of the annual catch about 20 per cent is caught by fishers with Aboriginal licences, whereas 80 per cent is harvested by those with commercial licences. Chief John, spokesman for the BC First Nations Summit, said, '[I]t is not a non native-only fishery. It is about an equitable allocation of resources' (*Globe and Mail*, 9 June).

Prime Minister Harper published a letter to the editor in the *Calgary Herald* in early July outlining his position: '[L]et me be clear – in the coming months, we will strike a judicial inquiry into the collapse of the Fraser River salmon fishery and oppose racially divided fisheries programs' (*Calgary Herald*, 11 July). Prentice echoed Harper, saying that the Conservatives would not support a 'racially segregated commercial fishery' (*Globe and Mail*, 14 July). Aboriginal fishers receive their quotas based on where the river flows through their nation's territory.

Treaty firsts. After thirteen years of negotiation the Lheidli T'enneh First Nation, a small band near Prince George, became the first nation to reach a final treaty agreement under the British Columbia treaty process. Some of the elements of the deal included self-government, $27 million in one-time-only funding, over 4,000 hectares of land, revenue sharing for fifty years, access to a long-term wood supply, and an allocation of sockeye salmon. Mark Stevenson, chief negotiator for the band, was excited about the deal: '[I]t is an agreement that I believe is good for the Lheidli T'enneh, good for the province of BC, and good for Canada' (ibid., 2 Aug.).

The only other nation to establish a treaty with the provincial government is the Nisga'a, which was finalized in 2000, and this was done outside of the treaty process through the courts. This is because BC's treaty process is extremely slow. It has six steps. It starts with a statement of intent and ends with the development of long-term implementation plans. Since 1993 no group has reached the sixth stage and only six nations have reached the fifth stage. Steven Point, head of the BC Treaty Commission, says the problem lies in staffing: '[T]here needs to be more seats for chief negotiators.' The commission only has 6 seats for chief negotiators. The BC Treaty Commission, the independent body that oversees the treaty process in the province, was established in 1993 (ibid., 28 Sept.).

Over the past thirteen years, treaty negotiations in BC have cost over $1 billion. In order to participate in the treaty-making process First Nations groups have had to borrow over $289 million. Auditor General Sheila Fraser accuses INAC of poor time management and squandering the resources needed for treaty making: '[A]ll but one of its target dates for concluding agreements-in-principle have been missed. Nor did we find any reliable estimates as to when INAC believes negotiations with all First Nations groups currently in the treaty process will be completed, and at what cost' (ibid., 29 Nov.).

The West

The Gateway Pipeline. Enbridge has proposed the creation of a pipeline that will connect Alberta's oil sands with international markets via the West Coast (ibid., 13 March). Aboriginal groups in Alberta and BC located along the proposed pipeline threatened legal action because they had not been consulted (ibid., 14 March). A 2004 ruling by the Supreme Court of Canada requires the federal government to undertake meaningful consultation with First Nations groups for industrial projects on their traditional land, even if legal title has not been officially decided (ibid., 21 March).

Enbridge hopes to have the pipeline up and running by 2010 and responded to Aboriginal concerns by announcing plans to donate $200,000 over the next two years to the University of Victoria to create a national chair in Aboriginal Economic Development (ibid., 28 June).

The United Nations. In early May the Alberta and federal governments were censured by the UN's Committee on Economic, Social, and Cultural Rights for their treatment of the Lubicon Lake First Nation, which is located in northern Alberta (*Windspeaker*, July). This was the third time that Alberta and Canada had been cited by the UN for violating the human rights of the Cree.

When the federal government negotiated Treaty 8 in 1899 the Lubicon Cree were overlooked. This neglect and oversight continued until rich oil, gas, and forest resources were discovered on Lubicon land. In the last four decades over 2,600 oil and gas wells have been established on Lubicon land without the band's permission. This has had tragic consequences for the Lubicon community. Until 1979 the Lubicon were largely self-sufficient through the pursuance of hunting, trapping, and other traditional activities. This is no longer the case because of environmental degradation.

Governance. On 17 February, Federal Court justice Pierre Blais ruled on the first of four applications filed for judicial review by Marcel Balfour, a band councillor for Norway House Cree Nation (ibid., March). Balfour made these applications in response to the actions of Chief Ron Evans and several band councillors after he raised concerns regarding band governance. In the application Blais ruled that Chief Evans participated in the 'usurpation of power and that a sub-group of councillors held numerous secret meetings and had engaged in deplorable blackmail and influence peddling' (ibid.). The other applications involved orders for full access to band financial records and council meetings and an order to quash the band council's decision not to hold a by-election as required under the band's Election Procedures Act following Evans's resignation. Evans left Norway House to become grand chief of the Assembly of Manitoba Chiefs. Balfour was successful in his applications and an election was held in mid-March. He beat acting chief Fred Muskego (ibid., April).

As band councillor, Balfour had requested access to the band's financial records and been subjected to harassment and intimidation by the chief and other members of the council. They reduced Balfour's salary, tried to evict him from his apartment, confiscated his computer, denied him access to band council offices, held secret meetings, and did not allow him access to band records and documents (ibid.).

Balfour reserved his harshest criticism for the federal government: '[T]he chief guilty party in all of this, in my view, is also the department of Indian Affairs. Its officials are totally complicit in these kinds of goings-on wherever they may occur across Canada. I asked them a long time ago to take corrective action in Norway House, but they simply refused to do so, and I was forced to go to court' (ibid., March).

Ontario

Caledonia and the Haudensaunee. Douglas Creek Estates (DCE), a subdivision on the southern edge of Caledonia, a small riverside community located in Haldimand County in southern Ontario, was occupied by members of the Six Nations (Haudensaunee) in late

February as a result of a long-standing land dispute (*Globe and Mail*, 15 April). The subdivision is under construction by Henco Industries.

The land, also known as the Haldimand Tract, was granted by the Crown to the Haudensaunee for settlement in 1784. Henco Industries claims the Six Nations surrendered the land in 1841, and the Haudensaunee maintain that they never relinquished their rights to the Haldimand Tract. In 1987 the Haudensaunee filed a land claim regarding the land. Before the issue was resolved the Crown sold 40 acres of the tract to Henco Industries in 1992.

In March Henco Industries acquired several court orders to evict the protesters from DCE (ibid.). The Ontario Provincial Police (OPP) failed to enforce the court orders and the protesters remained. On 20 April the OPP raided DCE at 4:30 a.m. and arrested sixteen people (ibid., 21 April). By carrying out the raid the OPP violated its own protocol, which calls for avoiding force in conflicts with Aboriginal communities. The sixteen individuals were later released without charges.

Roadblocks were set up by Six Nations supporters on Argyle Street, a main thoroughfare running through the middle of Caledonia, in response to the raid. The next day talks among the Haudensaunee, the elected band council and confederacy chiefs, Ottawa, and Ontario began (ibid., 22 April). This was the first time traditional chiefs had been included in land negotiations.

On 24 April residents of Caledonia who did not support the Haudensaunee held a rally. Later that day about 500 people from the rally approached the police barricades at the DCE, demanding that the protesters be made to leave and yelling racial epithets (ibid., 25 April). The situation remained extremely volatile for several hours.

In August Superior Court judge David Marshall ordered a halt to all talks between the Six Nations and the federal and provincial governments because the 'barricades must come down, the rule of law return, and the police begin to enforce the law on the property' (ibid., 9 Aug.). The Ontario Court of Appeals later found Marshall made this ruling in error.

The provincial government finally declared a moratorium on construction on all disputed land in the region in late May (ibid., 20 May). DCE was purchased from Henco Industries by the provincial government for $12.3 million (ibid., 23 June). The provincial government also agreed to compensate residents of Caledonia who had suffered during the Haudensaunee occupation of DCE (ibid., 20 Dec.). At the end of the year the land dispute remained unresolved and the Haudensaunee had not been compensated.

Ongoing water crises. For the third time in twelve months, a spring flood forced the evacuation of Kashechewan (ibid., 24 April). Kashechewan is a Cree community located 450 kilometres north of Timmins, Ontario. Minister Prentice announced that the agreement the community had reached with the federal government the previous fall to relocate the reserve nearby, fix the water supply, increase the number of nurses, build new houses, and renovate the school would not be honoured (ibid., 2 June). Prentice cited lack of money as the reason for this decision (*Wawatay News*, 9 Nov.). Instead, the Conservatives appointed Alan Pope, former Ontario Cabinet minister, to investigate the community's problems and suggest solutions. Pope's solution was to create a new reserve for the community outside Timmins. According to Pope, this resolution will offer Kashechewan greater access to health care and job opportunities (*Toronto Star*, 13 Nov.).

The Pikangikum First Nation, a fly-in reserve located 200 kilometres north of Kenora, also faced severe water problems in 2006. A report carried out by the chief executive officer of the Northwestern Health Unit in Kenora, Dr Peter Sarsfield, found the community to be suffering a drinking water crisis (*Globe and Mail*, 23 Oct.). The report reveals that all but 20 homes on the reserve did not have access to basic water and sewage services. Residents were using wooden outhouses and carrying their untreated drinking water by pail from the lake. Those houses that did have water and sewage services relied on tanks that were filled by trucks on a weekly basis.

A modern water treatment plant was built in 1995, but none of the homes on the reserve were hooked up to it (ibid., 6 Nov.). As a result Pikangikum has a higher incidence of gastrointestinal, skin, and urinary tract infections than any other First Nations community. Sarsfield says he was 'shocked at the extent of the neglect that almost appeared purposeful' (*Intertribal Times*, 26 Oct.). All infrastructure projects in Pikangikum were halted in 2000 after Ottawa placed the First Nation under outside management. This remained the situation at the end of 2006 even after a federal court ruling in 2002 declared the government's decision was 'patently unreasonable' (*Globe and Mail*, 6 Nov.).

Pikangikum was not placed on the list of Aboriginal communities identified by Ottawa as having high-risk water problems. Tony Prudori, an INAC spokesman, said this was because Pikangikum's water treatment plant was considered a medium risk and only those plants considered to be a high risk were placed on the list (ibid., 24 Oct.). The list was generated according to the existence and condition of water plants in Aboriginal communities and not the infrastructure that connected those services to residents' homes.

Pikangikum was not the only reserve in northern Ontario experiencing a severe water crisis. Nineteen of the 49 nations in NAN were under a boil water advisory (*Wawatay News*, 3 Nov.).

Kitchenuhmaykoosib Inninuwug (KI). Formerly known as Big Trout Lake First Nation, KI, an Ojibwa / Cree First Nation in northern Ontario, is fighting to prevent the Toronto-based mining company Platinex from beginning mineral exploration in its traditional territory located near their present-day reserve (*MiningWatch* Canada, 15 Sept.). Under Ontario's mining laws the free entry system grants access to all Crown lands for mineral exploration unless specified otherwise. Under these mining laws there is no requirement that the provincial government consult with Aboriginal people or other land users prior to opening up Crown lands for mineral exploration and there is no system in place to establish which lands are environmentally significant or vulnerable (ibid., 29 Jan. 2004). Ontario's mining laws are in direct conflict with recent Supreme Court decisions which require the Crown to conduct meaningful consultations with First Nations people before allowing development on disputed lands.

In 2000 KI filed a Treaty Land Entitlement Claim (TLE) with the federal and provincial governments. In February 2001, KI and nine other First Nations in the region issued a moratorium on all development without proper consultation. In 2006 Inco Ltd. sold its mining leases to Platinex Inc. for $300,000 (*Toronto Star*, 20 June). Platinex failed to consult with KI and in October 2005 publicly announced its mining application on the TSX Venture Exchange and said that KI had verbally consented to 'low impact exploration' (*MiningWatch Canada*, 15 Sept.). This is after KI wrote a letter to Platinex explicitly stating that Platinex did not have the community's permission to conduct exploration and that KI would block all mining activities in the region.

Platinex tried to begin operations in February, and the KI set up a roadblock on the winter road to stop the drilling team from reaching the site (*Globe and Mail*, 22 Feb.). To circumvent the roadblock Platinex flew a two-man drilling team directly to the exploration site. Members of the KI community protested at the site and the crew was withdrawn (*Toronto Star*, 20 June).

In April Platinex sued KI for $10 billion in damages and sought a permanent injunction against the community to prevent future protests at the drilling site, alleging violence and intimidation (*Globe and Mail*, 1 Aug.). KI responded by countersuing the company for damages and requesting an injunction against future exploration. KI was awarded the injunction and drilling was halted (*Toronto Star*, 20 June). Platinex was prohibited from drilling for five months while negotiations were undertaken. The company returned to court on 12 October to appeal the injunction (*Wawatay News*, 26 Sept.).

The KI are also seeking to use the courts to force the Ontario government to revise the free entry system, claiming it is a violation of the Charter of Rights and Freedoms because it lets 'prospectors seek mineral riches almost wherever they please' (*Toronto Star*, 20 June) without being forced to consult with or deal with local communities.

Quebec

Lawsuit. The Pessamit First Nation is relaunching a lawsuit against Hydro-Québec (HQ). The Innu community, located along the north shore of the Saint Lawrence River, is seeking $11 billion in damages for 'total devastation of culture and way of life.' Over the last five decades more than twelve hydroelectric dams have been built on their traditional territory (*Nation*, 21 July). In 1998 the Pessamit filed a $500 million lawsuit with the Quebec Superior Court contending that the dams were built on Innu land without their consent. The First Nation agreed to put their lawsuit on hold in order to undertake negotiations with the Quebec government. Chief Raphael Picard says, '[T]here is no progress at the table,' and the Innu have returned to court to resolve their concerns (*Globe and Mail*, 7 July).

Rupert River Diversion Project (RRDP). HQ received the green light from Stephen Harper on 18 December for the RRDP (*Water Chronicles*, 19 Dec.). The RRDP will expand the James Bay complex by flooding 600 square kilometres of pristine wilderness and building four dams, 75 dikes, and a three-kilometre tunnel. The Rupert River Diversion Project will redirect the headwaters of the Rupert River north to the Eastmain River and into the La Grande Hydroelectric watershed. This will be the largest hydroelectric project undertaken in Quebec in over a decade and will cost the province one of the world's last great untouched rivers (*Globe and Mail*, 19 Dec.).

The RRDP is a result of an agreement, La Paix des Braves, signed between the Grand Council of the Crees / Eeyou Istchee (GCC) and the Quebec government. In exchange for the RRDP, HQ renounced its right to dam and divert the NBR complex (Nottaway, Broadback, and Rupert Rivers). The NBR complex was originally part of the James Bay project.

This project will create 5,500 jobs and provide millions of dollars in revenue for the Cree of northern Quebec (ibid.). Bill Namagoose, executive director of the GCC, spoke to the divisions in the Cree and First Nations community over the agreement: '[S]ome people see the Paix des Braves as a concession of the Waskaganish Sibi while others see it as the rescue of two rivers and thousands of square miles of land … others see the loss of Cree autonomy, while some see the new agreement with Quebec as the restoration of Cree consent in many areas' (*Eeyou Eenou*, summer 2006).

Quebec Native Alliance (QNA). The QNA is an organization that represents Aboriginal people living off reserves and is the Quebec affiliate of CAP. The former grand chief of the QNA, Guillaume Carle, filed an $835,000 lawsuit in Quebec Superior Court against QNA for allegedly slandering his name (*Nation*, 4 Aug.). Carle said his problems with QNA began when he raised concerns about the organization's mismanagement and in particular of the company, Corporation Waskahegen, used to deliver social housing programs (*Globe and Mail*, 8 July).

Carle was recently elected the grand chief of a new national Aboriginal organization in early July called the Confederation of Aboriginal People. He hopes it will lead to the collapse of CAP. Patrick Brazeau, grand chief of CAP, accused Carle of 'appealing to people with questionable native lineage who simply want a card that may let them hunt and fish without licence' (ibid., 10 July).

Allegations of misspending forced INAC to suspend CAP's funding for five months while an audit of the national office was conducted (ibid., 8 July). At the end of the year the provincial affiliates of the Congress were in the process of being audited.

Maritimes: treaty rights

On 7 December the Supreme Court upheld a ruling by the New Brunswick court regarding the rights of Aboriginal people to cut and use timber for domestic use such as the construction of houses, furniture, or watercraft (ibid., 8 Dec.). On 9 December 1999 Darrell Gray, a Mi'kmaq from the Pabineau First Nation, was charged with illegally taking maple trees from Crown land. Two years later in a separate but related incident, two Maliseet men – Dale Sappier and Clark Polchies, members of the Woodstock First Nation – were arrested for the unlawful possession of timber from Crown lands (*CBC News*, 7 Dec.). The men defended their right to harvest timber by saying that they planned to use the wood for firewood, Cabinets, tables, and flooring (*Globe and Mail*, 8 Dec.). All three men were found not guilty of illegally harvesting wood by New Brunswick courts because the trees were for domestic use (*Aboriginal and Forestry Law Update*, Dec.). The New Brunswick government disagreed and appealed the decision, taking the position that no such rights existed.

Commenting on the unanimous decision, Supreme Court justice Michel Bastarache said, '[I]f aboriginal rights are not permitted to evolve and take modern forms, then they will become utterly useless. The cultures of aboriginal peoples who occupied the lands now forming Canada prior to the arrival of Europeans – and who did so while living in organized societies with their own distinctive ways of life – cannot be reduced to wigwams, baskets, and canoes.' The court did place limits on 'domestic use,' however, by limiting harvesting to lands traditionally used by bands and ensuring that harvesting did not extend to any form of commercial enterprise (*Globe and Mail*, 8 Dec.). This decision elaborates on the court's 2005 ruling in the Bernard and Marshall cases which stated that an Aboriginal right to harvest trees commercially did not exist (*Canadian Press*, 20 July 2005).

Aboriginal leaders described the judgment as very important with the potential to substantively ameliorate the lives of their communities. Jeff Tomah, chief of the Woodstock First Nation, commented that 'housing has been an issue for quite some time and this case here will help' (*CBC News*, 7 Dec.). AFN national chief Phil Fontaine called the decision 'a step towards the eradication of poverty in First Nations communities' (*National Post*, 7 Dec.).

The North

Mackenzie Valley Pipeline Project. This project remained stalled at year's end because the Deh Cho First Nation refuses to settle with the federal government regarding the construction of the pipeline across their territory. Prentice has offered the Deh Cho control over 15 per cent of the claim, a cash settlement, and the right to negotiate self-government. Forty per cent of the pipeline will potentially be built on

Deh Cho territory (*Toronto Star*, 11 Nov.). Other nations in the region have settled in exchange for a share of the pipeline revenues (*Globe and Mail*, 28 June).

A Joint Review Panel (JRP) began public hearings on the Mackenzie Valley Pipeline Project in February. The hearings are expected to last into mid-April 2007, well past the previously extended deadline, because of a recent Supreme Court decision (*Toronto Star*, 11 Nov.). The Dene Tha, a Cree community located in northern Alberta, took the federal government to court over the JRP because they had serious reservations regarding the pipeline's impact and maintain that Ottawa did not properly consult with them about the review. The Supreme Court ruled on 10 November that the federal government 'breached its duty to consult' with the Dene Tha First Nation (*Globe and Mail*, 11 Nov.). As a result, the JRP cannot file its final report until it holds further hearings.

The JRP consists of seven members selected by the Mackenzie Valley Environmental Impact Review Board (MVEIRB), the Inuvialuit Game Council, and the federal minister of the environment and is expected to assess the project's environmental impact and the potential effect on the social, cultural, and economic well-being of the local residents and communities.[2] The proposed 1,200-kilometre natural gas pipeline will run through the Northwest Territories' Mackenzie Valley, from the Beaufort Sea to a hub in northern Alberta.

The Nunavut Project. On 1 June 2005 Thomas Berger was appointed as conciliator by the federal minister of Indian affairs and northern development, the premier of Nunavut, and the president of Nunavut Tunngavik Incorporated (NTI)[3] to resolve the impasse over negotiations to renew the Implementation Contract and amend and update the Nunavut Land Claims Agreement (NLCA). Berger's interim report issued 31 August 2005 dealt with the funding arrangements for those boards responsible for the management of land and resources

2 http://www.mackenziegasproject.com/theProject/regulatoryProcess/ (accessed 22 August 2010).

3 'NTI ensures that promises made under the NLCA are carried out. Inuit exchanged Aboriginal title to all their traditional land in the Nunavut Settlement Area for the rights and benefits set out in the NLCA. The management of land, water, and wildlife is very important to Inuit. NTI coordinates and manages Inuit responsibilities set out in the NLCA and ensures that the federal and territorial governments fulfill their obligations.' http://www.tunngavik.com/about/ (accessed 22 August 2010).

in Nunavut.[4] Berger's final report entitled 'The Nunavut Project' was released 1 March and dealt specifically with Article 23 of the NLCA, which according to Berger 'lies at the heart of the promise of Nunavut' and the breakdown of the NLCA (Berger, 1 March).

Article 23 deals with representative Inuit employment in the public service. Given that 85 per cent of the Nunavut population is Inuit, this should be reflected in the public service (ibid.). According to Berger's report 'only 45 percent of the employees of the Government of Nunavut are Inuit. This figure was more or less achieved early on, as Inuit took up mainly lower level (e.g. administrative support) positions in government' (ibid.). As a result, the majority of higher-level public service jobs are held by people who are not Inuit, and a significant portion (15 per cent) are occupied by Nunavut residents who are not locals (ibid.).

Berger believes that education is at the root of the failure to implement Article 23, which 'cannot be discussed intelligently without discussing education.' According to Berger, '[T]he schools are failing. They are not producing graduates truly competent in Inuktitut; moreover, the Inuit of Nunavut have the lowest rate of literacy in English in the country' (*Whitehorse Star*, 13 April). According to statistics released by NTI, 76 per cent of Inuit students drop out before they finish grade twelve, compared to 25 per cent of students in the rest of Canada.[5] NTI launched a $1 billion lawsuit against the federal government for failing to live up to its commitments outlined in the NLCA on 6 December.

4 Thomas Berger, 'Conciliator's Final Report: Nunavut Land Claims Agreement Implementation Planning Contract Negotiations for the Second Planning Period,' 1 March 2006; http://www.ainc-inac.gc.ca/al/ldc/ccl/fagr/nuna/lca/nlc-eng.asp#ft3b.

5 http://www.tunngavik.com/blog/2006/04/05/berger-calls-for-bilingual-education-system-in-nunavut/ (accessed 22 August 2010).

CAREY HILL

British Columbia

The year 2006 was one for David Emerson to remember (or perhaps forget). He was elected in the British Columbia riding of Vancouver-Kingsway as a federal Liberal. Because the Liberals did not win enough seats to form the government, he crossed the floor to sit as a Conservative and was appointed to Cabinet as international trade minister, minister for the Pacific Gateway, and minister for the Vancouver-Whistler Olympics. This created much controversy. More controversial perhaps was the softwood lumber agreement Emerson forged with the United States in his new role. Finally, a deal on softwood – but one unsatisfactory to the BC lumber industry and provincial government.

While Emerson bounced from controversy to controversy, the BC economy bounced back. A surplus was forecast in the budget and the economy was expected to grow beyond 3 per cent. Finance minister Carole Taylor reversed the direction of the government from cuts and restraint to new spending on schools, hospitals, and roads as the new credit rating of the government reflected the efforts of the BC Liberals to reduce the provincial debt.

The year was also marked by marathon labour negotiations in which 30 public-sector unions representing over 130,000 workers inked new contracts with the BC government to ensure labour peace during the 2010 Olympics. BC's teachers, too, built on the success of these public-sector unions and reached a deal that before had been elusive.

BC also demonstrated leadership during the year on the Aboriginal file as Premier Campbell committed to implement the Kelowna Accord in British Columbia even though it would not be executed in the rest of the country. The Kelowna Accord was a last-minute commitment of the Martin Liberals that Stephen Harper's Conservatives chose not to follow.

In addition, the year included a focus on BC's children, first in the budget and then by Judge Ted Hughes in his report on reforming the province's child protection system.

Federal election

The year began with a federal election after Paul Martin's Liberals had been defeated in the House of Commons as 2005 ended. British Columbia was considered to be a wild card in the federal election because its 36 seats were in play in several ridings.

Vancouver Centre was a riding to watch as the NDP's Svend Robinson marked his comeback in a fight with Conservative Tony Fogarassy and Liberal Hedy Fry. Formerly the Tory riding of Canada's first woman prime minister, Kim Campbell, Vancouver Centre was home to incumbent Hedy Fry. In addition to her years of experience in politics, Hedy Fry was a physician and had served as president of the BC Medical Association. She emerged victorious in the Vancouver Centre race with 43.8 per cent of the vote. Svend Robinson came in second with 28.67 per cent and Tory Tony Fogarassy was third with 20.46 per cent. This was to be long-serving NDPer Svend Robinson's comeback after he was charged with theft and did not participate in the 2004 election race.

In an effort to woo voters in British Columbia, the Liberals released a package of programs aimed at BC at a news conference in early January. Among its elements, the package included support for Vancouver's four-pillars drug strategy, which the Conservatives had suggested they would discontinue (*Canadian Press Newswire*, 6 Jan.). It also included federal aid for the mountain pine beetle outbreak in the BC interior, more gasoline-tax money for urban transit, and programs for green infrastructure.

When the election campaign was over, the Conservatives took the lead in BC, garnering over 37 per cent of the vote and winning 17 seats, none of which were in the city of Vancouver. The Liberals achieved over 28 per cent of the vote and won 10 seats while the NDP managed to win a total of 9 seats accounting for just over 27 per cent of the vote.

Emerson fallout after the election

On 6 February David Emerson, Liberal MP for Vancouver-Kingsway, crossed the floor and joined the Conservatives. He was appointed to the Conservative Cabinet and named minister of international trade and minister for the Pacific Gateway as well as for the Vancouver-Whistler Olympics. Prior to his election, Emerson had an illustrious career including as CEO at Canfor Corporation. In addition to serving in the federal government, he had experience as a deputy minister within the

Federal election: BC seats

Party	Number of seats	Vote count	Vote share
Conservative	17	682,109	37.33%
Liberal	10	521,473	28.54%
NDP	9	504,738	27.62%

Source: CBC Canada Votes 2006

BC government. His academic credentials included a PhD in economics from Queen's University.

Although he was arguably qualified to serve within Cabinet, British Columbians did not approve of Emerson's defection. In a poll conducted after he crossed the floor, he had the support of only 28 per cent of British Columbians, with 6 in 10 disapproving of his actions (*National Post*, 14 Feb.). For his part, Emerson referred to those who didn't support him as 'partisan zealots' (ibid.). The case for his membership in Cabinet was that Vancouver had been shut out because it had not elected any Conservatives. Through service in the Cabinet, Emerson could use his vast knowledge to represent Vancouver especially in light of its needs around the 2010 Olympics and he could also offer his expertise to Cabinet on the softwood lumber file.

In April, a Vancouver voter hired a plane to carry a banner over Parliament Hill protesting the decision by Emerson to cross the floor and join the Conservatives (*Ottawa Citizen*, 26 March). Even within Tory ranks, Emerson's decision was controversial to some. MP Garth Turner criticized his own government for allowing the move and said Emerson should resign and run as a Conservative before he be allowed to join Cabinet (*Kimberley Daily Bulletin*, 13 Feb.). For his part, Premier Gordon Campbell weighed into the debate, suggesting that David Emerson's appointment was good for BC:

> [David Emerson] probably knows more about that softwood file than anyone else that's ever been in charge of it. I was certainly surprised but I think it's great for British Columbia. David has always said that his major goal was to strengthen Canada and strengthen the province and clearly in that portfolio, he's got some significant British Columbia files. (*Canadian Press Newswire*, 6 Feb.)

Federal cabinet includes four B.C. ministers

In addition to David Emerson, the federal Cabinet included three other ministers from British Columbia. Another seasoned veteran was Stockwell Day representing Okanagan-Coquihalla. He was appointed minister of public safety. He was first elected to Parliament in 2000 as leader of the Canadian Alliance after having served many years in the Alberta Legislature as minister of labour, social services, and finance. Another British Columbian, Jay Hill, was appointed chief government whip. He represented the British Columbia riding of Prince George Peace River and was first elected in 1993. James Moore, member of Parliament for Port Moody – Coquitlam – Port Coquitlam, was also appointed to Cabinet as parliamentary secretary to the minister of public works and government services. He also served as parliamentary secretary to David Emerson, specifically on the Vancouver-Whistler Olympics file.

Throne speech

The provincial throne speech was delivered soon after the federal election on 14 February and focused on efforts to transform British Columbia in four key areas. Lieutenant Governor Iona Campagnolo read,

> British Columbia's great transformation has just begun. The strength of our province has always been the strength of its people – as leaders, builders, innovators, risk-takers, and pioneers of opportunity. These are exciting times of monumental potential. Let us reach for the great promise of British Columbia and fashion our golden decade together.

There were four key themes: (1) the Transformational Force of Our Aging Population; (2) Harnessing the Power of New Knowledge and Creativity; (3) Building on the Transformational Force of Canada's Pacific Gateway; and (4) Transforming British Columbians' Quality of Life. The theme of transforming the aging population included activities such as defining and enshrining the five principles of the Canada Health Act plus adding a sixth, sustainability. It also included a focus on nurses – attracting and retaining them and expanding the BC Nurseline. In terms of aging, there was the aim of working with the Pacific Alzheimer Research Foundation to establish a national research collaborative to help find a cure for dementia. This first theme was really about the provincial health system, investigating other health systems to improve it, and modifications to enhance it.

The second theme focused on reforming the public school system including modernizing the curriculum, improving broadband access, and expanding apprenticeships and trades training. This theme also included investments in research in Genome BC, the Rick Hansen Man in Motion Foundation, and the Canadian Cancer Society as well as the development of a new B.C. Foundation for Natural Resources and Engineering Research.

The Pacific Gateway theme, the throne speech's third element, built on efforts already underway such as the opening up of the Port of Prince Rupert, as well as on BC's connection to the Asia-Pacific countries. The government expressed a desire to work with BC's tourism associations to help British Columbia become the destination of choice for Asian tourists. Moreover, universities, colleges, and institutes across BC would aim to develop and offer new Pacific studies programs, and training in Mandarin, Japanese, Punjabi, and Korean would be expanded. There were many other initiatives under this theme, including making the BC Spirit Bear BC's official provincial animal.

The fourth theme, 'Transforming British Columbians' Quality of Life,' focused on efforts to improve social policy, in particular, for Aboriginal peoples. Regionalization of Aboriginal child and family service delivery was to continue. The Kelowna Accord, although not implemented nationally, was to be realized in BC to close the gaps in health status.

Other social policy activities included changing employment programs to help people on income assistance and implementing a new housing strategy. There was also a crime focus, such as pushing the federal government for tough new minimum sentences for drug traffickers, as well as for immediate extradition of foreign traffickers and the use of new technology to help improve law enforcement and integrate policing.

During the year, the Campbell Liberals took two legislative measures that appeared to be somewhat contradictory; one offered transparency whereas the other was seen by the Opposition to limit debate. Mid-year, the Liberals issued a tender for a contractor for 'planning, facilitating and providing television coverage of open Cabinet meetings at locations throughout the province of British Columbia' (*Times-Colonist*, 30 May). The contract was expected to be valid until 31 March 2007. The open Cabinet meetings were to be held in various locations throughout BC including Vancouver and Kelowna.

Second, the Liberals announced in September that they were cancelling the fall legislative sessions and would only hold sittings for reasons of important business. Some Opposition members of the Legislative Assembly (MLAs) such as Maurine Karagianis of Esquimalt-Metchosin suggested this was contrary to the spirit of fixed legislative sessions that the same Campbell Liberals had introduced in 2001 (*Parksville-Qualicum News*, 22 Sept.). The Liberal MLA for Maple Ridge – Mission, Randy Hawes, and former NDP MLA Moe Sihota clarified that fall sessions were generally only used to address business left over from the spring session. Sihota explained that there had also been little need to have many fall sessions when the New Democrats had been in power (*Victoria News*, 15 Sept.).

Budget

Soon after the throne speech, finance minister Carole Taylor delivered the BC budget speech. BC's economy was projected to grow by 3.3 per cent in 2006 according to the Ministry of Finance. There was a forecast surplus of $1.45 billion (*Trail Times*, 22 Feb.). The focus of Minister Taylor's budget speech was BC's children, with $421 million to enhance services, better support caregivers, and ensure the well-being of vulnerable children. Taylor explained, 'To highlight just a few of the improvements, this means an additional three thousand children will benefit from infant development programs, another 5,200 will see improved access to therapy programs, and another 1,100 children with special needs will receive support services in regular childcare settings' (ibid.). The funds would also be used to hire additional social workers.

Other expenditures included $400 million for training and skills development, including $90 million for a new tax credit program. Property tax reductions would be allocated $309 million. A major expenditure and theme of the year was public-sector compensation. Carole Taylor outlined that $6 billion would be available including $1 billion for incentives. In addition tourism, sport, and arts spending would be increased by 12.7 per cent, focusing on Olympic opportunities (ibid.).

Labour issues: marathon public-sector bargaining

In order to achieve labour peace during the upcoming 2010 Olympics, the provincial government devised a 31 March deadline to complete all public-sector bargaining and offered unions bonuses for meeting the deadline. Over 130,000 public servants were affected by the negotiations and the settlements. These contracts covered 90 per cent of public-sector workers and all expired at the end of March. The previous agreements under the Campbell Liberals had often involved wage freezes or rollbacks as well as settlements imposed by the legislature. For example, in Campbell's first year in office both transit workers and nurses were legislated back to work. That same year, labour legislation was amended making it illegal for teachers to strike. The Liberals' tenure had been seen by many on the Left as one of opposition to unions, leading to considerable labour strife and a near-general strike in 2004. A bold move by the finance minister Carole Taylor to buy labour peace was considered a gamble by some (*Vancouver Sun*, 22 March), but it paid off handily in the end. By 16 March eleven deals had already been reached. One deal was described by Carole Taylor as including general job security and a signing bonus of $3,300 for each and every employee that worked out to an 8 per cent lift before the wage increases took effect (*Canadian Press*, 16 March).

BC's doctors were among those who achieved deals by 11 March. Their contract included up to $1 billion in incentives to reach agreements before current contracts expired, $4.7 billion over four years for wage increases, and an additional amount of $300 million for agreements that extend to April 2010 if the government's surplus that year exceeded $150 million (*Canadian Press*, 11 March).

The thirty public-sector unions that achieved agreements by 31 March included several in the universities sector as well as BC Transit, BC Hydro / International Brotherhood of Electrical Workers (IBEW), many British Columbia Government Employees Union workers, Canadian Union of Public Employees (CUPE), Insurance Corporation of British Columbia (ICBC) workers, BC Housing, and many others. The largest union to negotiate a contract by the deadline was the Health Employers Association of British Columbia (HEABC, hospital workers) numbering 44,700, with the second-largest being provincial public servants (BC Government and Service Employees' Union, or BCGEU) numbering 24,470. The smallest union involved was the Legal Services Society / Professional Employees Association (27 people). In total, 130,866 unionized employees received deals by this date; benefits of the negotiations were also extended to 42,000 non-union employees in the public sector.

Labour issues: teachers bargaining

Whereas other public-sector unions gained from a new approach by the Campbell Liberals with most public-sector contracts signed by April, teachers remained without a contract into July. However, the deal that was eventually reached was deemed 'historic.'

The relationship between BC's teachers and the provincial government's bargaining agent, the British Columbia Public Schools Employers' Association (BCPSEA), had been stormy since the first year the Campbell Liberals were elected as they modified labour legislation to forbid teachers from striking. In 2005 the teachers went on an illegal strike and were supported by wildcat strikes from other unions including CUPE. Their contract dispute remained unsettled well into 2006.

In June, teachers voted 85.2 per cent in favour of illegal strike action once again (*Canadian Press*, 9 June). During the negotiations that same month, the government purchased ads detailing wage increases for teachers over 10 years depending on their level of experience. The British Columbia Teachers' Federation (BCTF), the union for BC's 36,000 teachers, also featured an ad campaign with the following message: 'Our kids deserve the best education possible. They need teachers who are paid fairly and treated with respect. Kids matter; teachers care. A message from BC teachers' (*Victoria News*, 30 June).

The BCPSEA was optimistic a deal could be reached. Hugh Finlayson noted that it was not 'a question of finding the middle ground, it's getting within the zone of settlement, which is within the pattern that's already set' (*Canadian Press*, 9 June). The labour negotiations that had already occurred during the year, especially those ostensibly to buy labour peace for the Olympics, would set the tone for this negotiation and the outcome.

One of the arguments made by the BCTF during the negotiations was that a recent trade agreement between Alberta and British Columbia made it easier for teachers to leave the province, especially because wages are 20 per cent higher in Alberta (*Peace River Block Daily News*, 12 June). Finlayson of the BCPSEA disputed that BC teachers were leaving to go to Alberta and suggested that as many teachers were leaving Alberta to come to BC.

A deal was finally reached late on 30 June. The contract provided teachers with a 16 per cent pay increase and a signing bonus of $4,000, higher than most bonuses during the 'March madness' negotiations. Jenny Sims, president of the BCTF, explained, 'We had assured parents that we were going to work around the clock and that we were going to pull out all the stops to ensure that parents and students and our teachers had stability going into the fall and we are pleased today that are able to live up to that' (*Daily Townsman*, 4 July). The five-year contract was ratified by teachers on 8 September.

Other labour news during the year included a decision by the labour board to block a union from organizing staff in the auto department at a Wal-Mart. The United Food and Commercial Workers attempted to organize 10 employees in the Tire Lube Express department of a Cranbrook Wal-Mart (*National Post*, 5 July).

Ferry sinking

Early in the morning of 22 March, the ferry the *Queen of the North* sank in Wright Sound 135 kilometres south of Prince Rupert after hitting Gil Island while travelling from Prince Rupert to Port Hardy. All but 2 of the 101 people onboard managed to get to safety. Two people remained missing as the year closed. The vessel was approximately one kilometre off-course at the time of the collision (*CBC News*, 26 March). The sinking of the ferry affected communities served by it because it was a source of supplies. David Hahn, BC Ferries president, and Premier Gordon Campbell worked to address delivery of supplies to the islands served by the *Queen of the North* after the tragic accident (*Nelson Daily News*, 24 March).

Ironically, the government approved spending on three new ferries for the northern waters the same day the *Queen of the North* sank. The premier denied that his government had not acted quickly enough to approve the funding (*Prince George Citizen*, 23 March).

Highway of Tears

In April, RCMP members and Aboriginal groups including tribal leaders and family members participated in informal workshops on BC's Highway of Tears (*Moncton Times-Transcript*, 1 April). Along remote northern Highway 16 which runs from Prince George to Prince Rupert, 35 women and girls have gone missing or been murdered since 1988, many of them Aboriginal. Police are stumped and continue to look for clues while victims' families call for more to be done.

Interprovincial cooperation

Also in April, BC signed a trade agreement with Alberta. The deal had been in the works since October 2003 when Alberta premier Ralph Klein and BC premier Gordon Campbell signed a protocol of cooperation (*National Post*, 29 April). In addition to the trade agreement,

15 other agreements have been signed between the two provinces during the past three years. Worker mobility was a focus of some of these agreements, allowing operators of charter buses to have easier access to both provincial markets. There were also cooperative efforts in the areas of energy research and development, post-secondary education, and management of interprovincial parks.

In the fall, the two provinces announced that they expected other provinces to join the deal, specifically citing Saskatchewan and suggesting at least three other jurisdictions were considering it. The deal eliminated barriers to labour and investment mobility between the two provinces, 'creating one economy,' according to BC economic development minister Colin Hansen (*Edmonton Journal*, 26 Sept.). Alberta's Gary Mar and BC's Colin Hansen contrasted their agreement with failed attempts by the federal government to get a similar agreement in 1995. They explained that the failed agreement had required provinces to actively open areas to reciprocity whereas the BC-Alberta agreement includes everything unless an exemption is asked for and accepted (ibid.).

Kelowna Accord

During the year, the federal Harper Conservatives made it clear that they would not implement the Kelowna Accord. Provincial premiers, in particular BC's Gordon Campbell, made efforts to put pressure on the federal government to implement the historic accord. The Kelowna Accord was a historic moment wherein the provinces, the federal government, and national Aboriginal leaders came together and agreed to close the gap in quality of life, including in life expectancy between Aboriginal peoples and the average Canadian. The accord was concluded on 25 November 2005. It comprised $5.1 billion in spending over five years, including $1.8 billion for education, to create school systems, train more Aboriginal teachers, and identify children with special needs; $1.6 billion for housing with $400 million to address the need for clean water in remote communities; $200 million for economic development; and $1.3 billion for health services. This agreement stipulated funding for both on- and off-reserve First Nations, the Métis, and Inuit. The National Aboriginal Organizations (NAO) that participated in the accord included the Assembly of First Nations, the Métis National Council, the Inuit Tapiriit Kanatami, the Native Women's Association of Canada, and the Congress of Aboriginal Peoples (*Canadian Annual Review 2005*).

At the time of the agreement, Gordon Campbell had likened it to a 'seat at the Table of Confederation' for Aboriginal peoples (*Canadian Intergovernmental Conference Secretariat* 2005). During the election, Jim Prentice stated that the terms of the Kelowna Accord would be followed if the Conservatives won (*CBC News*, 11 Jan.). Another Conservative Cabinet minister, Monte Solberg, suggested the commitments would not be kept because they were crafted at the last minute on the back of a napkin (ibid.). By spring, the Conservatives had not followed through on the Liberal commitment and argued that it did not constitute a 'national consensus' given that Aboriginal leaders from Quebec did not take part (*CBC News*, 2 June).

In May, Gordon Campbell delivered a special statement to the legislature about the importance of the Kelowna Accord. He explained,

> I characterized [the Kelowna Accord] as Canada's 'moment of truth.' ... It was our chance to end the disparities in health, education, housing and economic opportunity. All first ministers rose to that moment of truth alongside Canada's Aboriginal leaders to undertake that challenge. Having made that extraordinary national commitment, any unilateral reversal will invite consequences that only make us poorer as a nation. (*Office of the BC Premier*, 4 May)

Moreover, he noted,

> The honour of the Crown is at stake as I said, all of the premiers committed to that. I am encouraged that the federal government has said that they are going to close those gaps. They may want to fashion that plan in their own way. I think in British Columbia we're going to live up to the commitments we made in Kelowna. (*Chilliwack Progress*, 5 May)

In June, the western premiers also expressed their support for the accord.

One of the concerns about the Kelowna Accord was that it was not formatted for signatures. However, one of Kelowna's subsequent trilateral agreements has been concluded, between the federal government, the British Columbia government, and the B.C. First Nations Leadership Council representing all 203 First Nations in BC. Immediately following the Kelowna Accord's negotiation, these parties signed the Transformative Change Accord (TC Accord). The purpose of the TC Accord is 'to bring together the Government of British Columbia, First Nations and the Government of Canada to achieve the goals of closing the social and economic gap between First Nations and other British

Columbians over the next ten years.' Furthermore, 'this Accord respects the agreement reached on November 25th and sets out how the parties intend to implement it in British Columbia.' Unlike Kelowna, the TC Accord was formatted for signatures and was signed by executive delegates of the three levels of government, including the prime minister and premier. Although Kelowna may not be implemented nationally, it will be implemented in British Columbia, according to the premier and to commitments made at and after Kelowna.

It is of note that the approach of the Campbell government to a new relationship with Aboriginal peoples has been considered 'ironic' or certainly a reversal (*Nelson Daily News*, 9 May). In 1999 Campbell led the Opposition Liberals to vote against the Nisga'a Treaty and it only narrowly passed the legislature in a 39–32 vote.

In addition to efforts to save the Kelowna Accord, the BC government also continued its work to develop a new relationship with Aboriginal peoples through agreements such as the 'relationship accord' reached by Aboriginal relations minister Tom Christensen with the Métis Nation of British Columbia, representing an estimated 40,000 Métis in BC (*Campbell River Mirror*, 24 May).

Social services: the Hughes Report

The relationship with Aboriginal peoples was considered by Judge Ted Hughes in his report on child protection in BC. He specifically recommended that Aboriginal people see themselves in the ministry. Judge Ted Hughes made 62 recommendations in his report, which was released in April. Hughes was appointed in 2005 to review the child protection system in the province after the death of an Aboriginal girl, 19-month-old Sherry Charlie. The child had been killed by a caregiver after placement through a local Aboriginal social services agency (*Parksville-Qualicum News*, 11 April). Hughes drew attention to the ministry's decision to restructure while at the same time taking budget cuts. The ministry had undertaken a process to consolidate 11 regions into 5 and appoint 5 regional directors to replace a single provincial director while at the same time cutting its budget. In addition, restructuring involved efforts to keep more children at home.

Hughes had served in the past as deputy attorney general of BC and had also led several inquiries, including one into the role of the RCMP during the APEC protests.

Hughes painted a picture of a child welfare system in flux between 2002 and 2003. He noted how amidst budget cuts there were efforts to introduce new programs to keep children at home but that social workers were never trained to implement these programs. The Community Living Authority was also created at this time to provide services and support to children and adults with developmental disabilities. Moreover, in addition to the reduction in the number of regions, a joint Aboriginal management committee began planning for the eventual establishment of five Aboriginal authorities. Budget cuts included an almost 12 per cent cut to services for children and families and a 55 per cent cut in executive and support services (since 2001) including quality assurance.

Among Hughes's recommendations, he advocated for a representative for children and youth that would maintain some of the current responsibilities of the Office for Children and Youth, but it would have independent status similar to that of the advocate as well as perform some functions carried out by the commission. Hughes suggested that the representative be an independent officer of the legislature with the same standing as the ombudsman or the auditor general. In 1995 the child and youth advocate was created as an independent officer to advocate on behalf of children and youth. The Gove Inquiry soon reported and recommended the development of a Children's Commission to review deaths and serious injuries of children in care and to investigate complaints. Hughes noted that he expected these would have been one body if the advocate had not already existed at the time of the Gove recommendations. A review found that there were overlaps and duplications between the two offices and in 2002 a single Office for Children and Youth was created. There were to be fewer reviews of children's deaths with the bulk of this responsibility going to the coroner's office. The office was placed within the Ministry of the Attorney General to give it some independence from the Ministry of Child and Family Development.

In addition to recommending the establishment of a new representative, Hughes suggested that a new standing committee of the legislature be struck to which the representative would report at least annually. Hughes saw the representative as having two roles: one focused on children and families and helping them manoeuvre through the child welfare system as well as make complaints, if needed, and the second on monitoring, reviewing, auditing, and investigating the performance of the child welfare system. The representative would also have responsibility for investigating deaths in care; Hughes considered whether this responsibility should reside with the coroner and determined it should not because the coroner did not have expertise in child welfare. Moreover, the coroner's focus is on the death itself whereas the representative is intended to focus on the child's life in relation to the child welfare system.

Hughes included a chapter specific to the child welfare system for Aboriginal children. Half of children in care in BC are Aboriginal. Aboriginal children are 9.5 times more likely to be in care than non-Aboriginal children. Hughes recommended that of the representative and two deputies at least one of them be Aboriginal. Moreover, he recommended a strategy to recruit and retain more Aboriginal people to work in the ministry.

Health systems issues

In a year when BC's Speech from the Throne identified defining and enshrining the principles of the Canada Health Act as well as adding a sixth, sustainability, it was the only province to be fined in 2006 by the federal government for extra billing at private diagnostic and surgical facilities. It was, however, fined a small amount of money compared to the costs of the health care system: $29,019 was deducted from transfer payments compared with BC's $11.5 billion health care budget (*National Post*, 5 April).

Concerns with rising health care costs were flagged by the finance ministry during the year. Finance minister Carole Taylor said she would appoint a special investigator to examine the financial pressures being experienced by the regional health authorities. She explained that estimates suggested that by 2017, some 71 per cent of the BC government's budget would be devoted to health care costs.

Mining accident

In May, a terrible mining accident claimed the lives of four people in Kimberley, including two paramedics who were trying to rescue the Teck Cominco workers. An investigation of the deaths determined that an oxygen-deprived atmosphere seeped out of a waste-rock dump through a covered ditch and into a pipe that fed a water-sampling station inside a shed (*Times-Colonist*, 31 Oct.). The four people who died were Douglas Lloyd Erickson, Bob Newcombe, Kim Weitzel, and Shawn Currier (*Ottawa Citizen*, 19 May).

Softwood lumber

The softwood lumber saga continued in 2006 with David Emerson playing a leading role. The previous August saw a NAFTA panel reject a US commerce department appeal on a decision that Canada did not subsidize lumber producers. As a result of the ruling, Canada had expected the United States would stop collecting duties and would refund the duties it had collected (*Canadian Annual Review 2005*). As the year closed, the United States continued to argue that Canada's four major lumber-producing provinces (BC, Ontario, Alberta, and Quebec) were subsidizing timber rights to get a third of the US market (ibid.). BC accounts for more than half of the softwood lumber exported to the United States.

The year 2006 was a monumental one for softwood lumber as a Canada-US deal was finally reached. However, the deal was a disappointment to the BC lumber industry and the provincial government. By April, a deal that BC supported was in the works. A framework was under discussion that capped Canada's share of the US lumber market and removed duties on Canadian softwood (*Trail Times*, 28 April). The seven-year agreement would include the refund of about $4 billion of duties collected by the United States over the past few years but would also limit Canadian shipments to the US market if US lumber prices began to fall (*Nelson Daily News*, 28 April). In July, an agreement was reached between international trade minister David Emerson and US trade representative Susan Schwab.

The seven-year agreement was renewable for two additional years and ended US duties in place since May 2002. Exporters had the choice of triggering a significant export tax when US lumber prices fell below US$355 per thousand board feet, starting at 5 per cent and ramping up to 15 per cent, or shipping under a quota based on Canada's 34 per cent share of the US market plus a small tax ranging from 2.5 to 5 per cent (*North Bay Nugget*, 20 May). BC initially offered qualified support for the deal with the caveat that there would need to be acceptance by the United States of its market-oriented timber pricing reforms that have been being implemented since 2002.

In June, BC premier Gordon Campbell explained BC's position on the softwood deal, particularly noting BC's market-oriented reforms:

> We are going to say clearly and unequivocally: 'These are our forests. We are going to operate them. We are going to compete and this deal is going to be good for British Columbia as well as Canada or it's not going to be a deal.' (*Leader Post*, 6 June)

The market reforms were important to BC because the value of BC lumber was declining as a result of the pine beetle infestation and the deal would require BC to pay higher US stumpage fees. BC forests minister Rich Coleman asked the federal government to make amendments to the deal but it went ahead in July. David Emerson said that the industry could not veto the deal and refused to modify the agreement.

Forest fires

By July, the number of forest fires had already surpassed the previous year's total of 964. There was an average of 100 new forest fires a day reported. The reason for the sharp increase was a province-wide dry spell and almost daily lightning strikes according to the Forests Ministry fire information officer (*Daily Townsman*, 7 July).

Marc Emery

Marc Emery, the self-styled Prince of Pot, was arrested on 'drug kingpin' charges in 2005 and was to be in court in 2006 to hear whether he would be extradited to the United States. Emery owned a marijuana paraphernalia shop and bookstore in downtown Vancouver. In announcing the extradition request in 2005 the US Drug Enforcement Agency (DEA) explained that Emery was 'one of the attorney general's most wanted international drug trafficking targets' and that his arrest was a 'significant blow' to the marijuana legalization movement (*Hamilton Spectator*, 24 March). Emery's arrest was the result of his marijuana seed sales across North America. Emery said that until his July 2005 arrest only two people been had ever been prosecuted for selling seeds and they had only received fines (ibid.). In June, Emery appeared before the BC Supreme Court and stated, 'I am a menace to the establishment' (*Canadian Press Newswire*, 21 June). He noted that neither the Liberals nor the Conservatives were in favour of ending prohibition. He claimed that in the last 12 years his work in British Columbia and that of his colleagues had made considerable strides towards legalization.

Looking forward to the Olympics

News about the Olympics became a common occurrence in 2006 as residents, policymakers, and industry looked forward to Vancouver-Whistler 2010. The provincial government pressed the federal government for more money. The BC auditor general released a controversial report suggesting the estimated costs of the Olympics were considerably lower than the reality. An anti-Olympics group got the attention of the press.

In August, Prime Minister Stephen Harper, BC premier Gordon Campbell, BC minister of international trade and the Vancouver-Whistler Olympics David Emerson, the mayor of Vancouver Sam Sullivan, and members of the Olympic committee announced that the Vancouver Olympics would get an additional $110 million, $55 million from the federal government and $55 million from the provincial government.

Anti-Olympics protesters, known as 2010 Watch, pointed to the auditor general's report as rationale for boycotting the Olympics (*Prince George Citizen*, 28 Sept.). The auditor general, Arn van Iersel, released his report suggesting that British Columbians would be on the hook for $1.5 billion as a result of the games in contrast to provincial government projections of $600 million.

Critics suggested the auditor general included expenses within his report that were not directly related to the Olympic Games.

Spirit Bear: environmental protection

In line with the Speech from the Throne, BC premier Gordon Campbell declared the Spirit Bear to be protected as he established 1.2 million hectares of new parks along a 400-kilometre area of BC's wild coastal forests. This area has been called the Great Bear Rainforest by environmentalists. A large section of the protected land is the 103,000-hectare Kitasoo Spirit Bear Conservancy on Princess Royal Island. Some 200,000 hectares of the land was dedicated to protect the Kermode bear, or Spirit Bear, because of its white fur (*Vancouver Sun*, 8 Feb.). This bear is only found on the BC coast.

Salmon farming

BC's largest agricultural export is farmed salmon. However, in recent years environmentalists and some scientists have raised concerns that farmed salmon are infecting wild salmon with sea lice. A Department of Fisheries and Oceans study was released during the year suggesting that farmed and wild salmon can coexist. Environmentalists and the well-known biologist Alexandra Morton argued that the only way to have them both is to protect the wild salmon by separating the farmed salmon in closed containers that will not allow them to escape (*Canadian Press Newswire*, 2 Aug.).

To highlight the controversy, in May a new salmon farm licence gave rise to accusations and concerns. Grieg Seafood BC Ltd received a licence to farm fish on the BC coast in the Broughton Archipelago (*Business Examiner*, 1 May). The senior regulatory affairs manager for the company, Tim Davies, suggested there was no need for accusations, explaining, 'We want to see a vibrant wild fishery and a vibrant farm fishery. This is not an either-or situation. Both can happen on the BC coast' (ibid.).

Air India

In June, the Air India inquiry began. A bomb exploded on Air India Flight 182 on 23 June 1985 and all 329 people on board were killed. The Air India inquiry was meant to investigate what has been termed the largest mass murder in Canadian history. The Honourable John C. Major, QC, was appointed commissioner. The inquiry was to consider if there were deficiencies in Canadian government officials' assessment of the threat of Sikh terrorism at the time of the bombing, if there were problems in effective cooperation among government agencies and departments including the RCMP and the Canadian Security Intelligence Service, how the government should address the challenge, and what changes in practice or legislation might be required, particularly those relating to the screening of passengers and their baggage. The first action of the commissioner was to meet privately with about 80 members of the families who lost loved ones (*Kitchener Record*, 21 June). A BC link to the Air India bombing was that the only person ever charged in the bombing, Inderjit Singh Reyat, was tried in BC court and convicted.

Pickton trial

The trial of Robert Pickton began on 30 January. Pickton was charged with 27 counts of first-degree murder involving women sex-trade workers from Vancouver's Downtown Eastside. In March, the judge ruled that Pickton could not be charged with the murder of an unidentified victim. Thus the number of charges against him was reduced from 27 to 26. In August, the judge ruled that trying all 26 charges in one case would be too onerous for the jury, so he split the case in two with initially 6 murder counts to be tried and the remaining 20 to be tried at a later date (*CBC News*, 5 Dec.). In December, jury selection began with over 600 potential candidates told to show up at the courthouse in New Westminster (ibid.).

New president at UBC

A new president was named to the University of British Columbia in 2006. Stephen Toope, president of the Pierre Elliot Trudeau Foundation and a former dean of McGill Law School, took the reins from Martha Piper (*Gazette*, 25 March). Piper presided over considerable residential development on the UBC campus, and she was also successful in lobbying the federal government to provide more funding for post-secondary education, in particular, research. Under her leadership, the international profile of UBC was increased.

To underscore the success of UBC in terms of its profile in recent years, a report that tracked 35 business and economic climate indicators for BC found that UBC led the top Canadian research universities in terms of gross income from technology licences. It was also a leader in the number of US patents it had been awarded (*Vancouver Sun*, 14 March).

CMA chooses British Columbian

The Canadian Medical Association chose its president in August. They selected a British Columbian, Brian Day, who owned a private surgical clinic in Vancouver. The choice was controversial and underscored the debate within the association between public and private medicine.

Boil water advisory

In November, a huge storm knocked out power in Greater Vancouver to over 200,000 homes and ended in a massive boil water advisory, the largest in Canadian history (*CTV News*, 19 Nov.). The boil water advisory lasted several days with residents being told not to drink or wash food with the water. The advisory led to bottled water shortages as well as a lack of coffee beverages because most espresso machines are hooked directly into the city's water supply. About 900,000 people living in Vancouver, Burnaby, and the North Shore were advised to boil their water. These residents get their water from the Capilano and Seymour watersheds, which experienced mudslides during the storm. Mudslides can increase the turbidity of the water and potentially make it unsafe to drink. The storm had overwhelmed the water treatment system, and water coming out of the taps was brown and cloudy. The particulates in the water can make it more difficult to disinfect, increasing the risk of gastrointestinal illness. In 2002 the Greater Vancouver Water District approved the construction of the Seymour-Capilano Water Filtration Plant in part to address turbidity events such as this one in the Greater Vancouver region. The plant is slated for completion in 2009.

Economy

BC's economy continued to be hot in 2006. One side effect of this was labour shortages. Statistics Canada's Ivan Fellegi told the Vancouver Board of Trade that job growth was three times the rate of growth in the rest of Canada on average. BC manufacturers have reported labour shortages; 12 to 14 per cent reported trouble filling skilled labour positions, with 6 per cent noting a shortage of skilled workers (*Vancouver Sun*, 28 April).

In April, as further evidence of the hot economy, Standard and Poor's Ratings Services upgraded BC's rating to AA+. That same day finance minister Carole Taylor held a press conference and discussed the investments the BC government would make in schools, hospitals, roads, and transit in contrast to Alberta's approach to use surplus or targeted funds to pay down the debt.

Construction of commercial, industrial, and institutional buildings is another indicator of economic performance. Since 2002 this construction across Canada has increased by 8.8 per cent. Two metropolitan areas – Vancouver and Calgary – accounted for nearly one-quarter of the jump in investment in office buildings. Investment in Vancouver office towers increased 45.1 per cent to $458 million as a result of the Asia-Pacific transactions and likely investments by firms serving the 2010 Olympics (*Gazette*, 24 May).

While Vancouver and Calgary shared office tower investment successes, BC and Alberta also led the country in house price increases over the previous five years. For example, the highest price increase was in Vernon, in BC's Okanagan Valley, where prices increased 129 per cent. The survey was undertaken by Century 21 and examined a selection of markets across the country (*Canadian Press Newswire*, 17 May).

BC Stats reported that BC has the biggest gap between rich and poor among Canadian provinces (*Canadian Press Newswire*, 11 May). This contrasts with Alberta, where benefits are more widely spread. The report suggested that the income level of Alberta's poor was 17 per cent above the level of the average income of the poor in BC. The average family income in BC in 2004 was $64,100, basically unchanged since 1990.

As the year closed, an internal provincial government document was obtained by the *Vancouver Sun* that discussed the 'Asia-Pacific Initiative: British Columbia's Vision' (*Times-Colonist*, 26 Dec.). The BC strategy offers a plan to more than triple Canada's current $100 billion in annual trade with the Asia-Pacific by 2010. The document suggests that the country's governments should 'unite to build up West Coast ports, promote Asian trade and foster cultural ties with the Asia Pacific' because this will offer significant economic benefits (ibid.).

HAROLD JANSEN

Alberta

On the surface, it would be hard to imagine that 2006 would have brought Albertans much to complain about. The province was absolutely booming, with rapid economic growth, large wage increases, low unemployment, and strong consumer spend ing. People were flocking to Alberta from across Canada and around the world to share in the province's good fortunes. The problem was, however, that Alberta's boom was creating a number of problems for the people and the government of the province. The theme of the year was dealing with the consequences of the boom. By the end of the year, the question of how the province would manage growth had resulted in an unexpected and significant change at the highest level of political power in Alberta.

The boom

Alberta's economy had been growing rapidly for a few years, but the growth kicked into a higher gear in 2006. The source of this growth was the record high price of oil. In the peak of summer driving season, when demand for oil is at its highest, the price of West Texas intermediate crude oil reached a record US$77 a barrel. This had two important consequences. First, there was increased interest in exploration and development in Alberta's conventional oil industry. Although conventional oil's share of Alberta's production was decreasing over time as the reserves of easily accessible oil in the province dwindled, the high prices made less-accessible oil potentially profitable. Furthermore, the high prices also made it worthwhile for companies to try to squeeze the remaining oil out of older oil fields. The second significant consequence was that potential investors in capital-intensive oil sands development saw the possibility of profits at high prices that were not there in a lower-price environment. Natural gas prices, in contrast, declined through the year, which dampened gas exploration and development in Alberta. The net result of these developments was an astonishing

6.9 per cent increase in economic growth in 2006, one of the highest annual increases in Alberta's history.

Managing the consequences of growth

One of the main beneficiaries of the torrid pace of economic growth was the provincial treasury. When the provincial budget was brought down in March, the government was projecting that it had run a $10 billion surplus for the 2005–6 fiscal year. The provincial government's November fiscal update reported that the province was running a $5.4 billion surplus for the 2006–7 fiscal year. It was no exaggeration to say that the provincial government had more money than it knew what do with. The provincial budget was evidence of that. Spending increased by 8 per cent over the previous year. The government increased funding for almost every program, picked up the tab for tuition increases at Alberta's public post-secondary institutions, provided rebates to protect Albertans from high natural gas prices, and spent $13.3 billion on roads, buildings, and other infrastructure. The province cut its corporate tax rate, already the lowest in Canada at 11.5 per cent, to 10 per cent. There was little in the way of individual tax cuts, other than a small increase to the personal tax exemption and an increase to the income level at which Albertans had to pay health care premiums, a benefit directed primarily at lower-income earners. Even with the large spending increases and tax cuts, payments to the province's Sustainability Fund and the Heritage Savings and Trust Fund, the government still did not seem to know what to do with all of the money.

The best evidence of this came early in the year as the provincial government began to issue a 'prosperity dividend' of $400 to every man, woman, and child in the province. The program – quickly dubbed 'Ralph bucks' after Premier Ralph Klein – was, not surprisingly, popular with the average voter, who did not mind receiving a minor windfall to start the year. It was also popular with retailers in the province, who ran sales trying to entice Albertans to spend their cheques. Critics, however, argued that the move revealed a lack of vision and direction in the provincial government. Instead of investing money either in long-term savings or in pursuing a particular policy goal, such as creating a system of world-class universities, the provincial government just cut cheques to people. The policy obviously reflected Klein's populist inclinations but led to grumbling among many Progressive Conservatives, who sensed a lack of focus and direction in their government.

As Alberta's economy grew, businesses had difficulty attracting and retaining labour in the province. During 2006, unemployment in Alberta fell to 3.4 per cent, its lowest level in three decades. 'Help wanted' signs were seen in store windows everywhere. Albertans endured long waits for service at restaurants, which had trouble retaining staff. The problem was particularly acute in building trades. Skilled labourers such as electricians and plumbers were in particularly high demand. Alberta's businesses worked hard to recruit workers from elsewhere in Canada and abroad. People flocked to Alberta from across Canada. Between the beginning of July 2005 and the end of June 2006, a full 57,000 more people moved to Alberta from elsewhere in Canada than left. This was the equivalent of adding a city the size of Medicine Hat to Alberta's population in a twelve-month period.

As predicted by the law of supply and demand, the combination of high demand for labour and a relatively low supply drove up wages. This in turn drove up consumer spending, which increased by an astounding one-sixth during the year. This strong demand had the expected impact on the rate of inflation, which neared 4 per cent for the year. Most of the increase in prices came from increased housing prices. The average house price rose almost 40 per cent in Alberta in 2006. This fueled a housing boom, as builders sought to capitalize on the high prices. Nearly 50,000 new homes were started in Alberta, a new record. In tandem with a shortage of skilled labourer, the housing boom caused building costs to soar in 2006, increasing the costs of expansion for businesses and, in particular, the oil industry. It also drove up the capital costs for the provincial government as it sought to build infrastructure to keep pace with the torrid pace of growth. The building boom only created even greater demand for skilled labour, driving the cycle even more.

Alberta's increasing economic might raised questions about the economic balance of the federation. The rapid pace of economic growth in Alberta and, to a lesser extent, in neighbouring British Columbia and Saskatchewan meant that money and population were shifting westward. The sight of the Alberta government distributing $400 cheques to its citizens while Ontario was running a budget deficit was a dramatic demonstration of the way the economy had evolved. As is almost inevitably the case in Canadian politics, the issue got dragged into federal-provincial conflict, triggered in this case by Prime Minister Stephen Harper's commitment to examine the 'fiscal imbalance' between Ottawa and the provinces. The premiers and the federal government were examining how to rework the system of transfers from the federal government to the provinces.

Central to these discussions was the equalization program, a system that saw the federal government transfer money to so-called 'have not' provinces. In recent years, the program had gone from being based on a formula to one that was increasingly driven by exceptions and ad hoc side agreements. Almost everyone agreed that a formula approach was preferable; the problem was identifying a formula that would work. Central to the dispute was the issue of how to deal with Alberta's windfall resource revenue. Including them in a formula would drive up the overall value of the program, increasing the payments to poorer provinces. Alberta staunchly opposed such a move and was an ally of Ontario premier Dalton McGuinty, whose province was the other main contributor to the equalization program. It was McGuinty, however, who took the lead on this. Like Alberta, Ontario would not benefit from increased equalization payments, but unlike Alberta, Ontario was not awash in resource dollars. Klein's primary contribution was the not particularly well-informed threat that Alberta would withdraw from the equalization program. After a year that saw lots of negotiation between premiers and two expert reports, it appeared that the chasm between the provinces was too wide to be bridged and that the federal government would be taking the leadership on this file in 2007. The question of the impact of Alberta's resource wealth on Canadian federalism remained to be resolved.

Another sign of the westward shift of economic power came on 28 April, when Premier Klein and British Columbia premier Gordon Campbell signed the Trade, Investment and Labour Mobility Agreement (TILMA) between the two provinces. The agreement focused on harmonizing regulatory standards between the two provinces, allowed for licensed tradespeople and professionals in one province to work in another, and required open competition in government procurement between the two provinces. TILMA represented a solution to the frustration some provincial governments felt in the slow progress towards eliminating interprovincial trade barriers. It also, however, symbolized a new economic powerhouse in western Canada. Together, Alberta and British Columbia's population nearly matched that of Quebec and was the second-largest economy in the country, after Ontario. Furthermore, the TILMA region was growing faster than its counterparts in central Canada, suggesting that the economic weight of the West was only going to increase.

The question of how to distribute the benefits of Alberta's oil and gas industry were not limited to national politics but was also relevant within the province. Although the provincial treasury was overflowing, Albertans were increasingly asking questions about whether the province was deriving its fair share of the oil and gas resources they owned. Alberta's oil and gas royalties were not increasing as quickly as energy prices. Furthermore, the provincial government budget projected a drop in total oil and gas royalties over time, even if prices remained high. At the heart of the royalty problem was the changing composition of Alberta's energy industry. Alberta's natural gas reserves, the source of most of the province's royalty revenues, were depleting fairly quickly. Although the rate of decline was less steep than with gas, conventional oil was also in decline. As more of Alberta's oil production came in the form of bitumen produced from the oil sands, the province was facing the consequence of its flat 1 per cent royalty rate on bitumen production until oil sands developments amortized their capital costs. Although the oil sands royalty regime was defended as necessary to encourage the kind of capital-intensive development needed to exploit the resource, it became more difficult to defend as prices climbed.

Besides the more direct economic consequences of the almost unchecked economic growth in the province, more and more questions were raised about the environmental impact of the rapid development of the oil sands in northern Alberta. Partly fueled by the questions raised by Al Gore in the popular documentary *An Inconvenient Truth*, one of the concerns was the impact of oil sands development on climate change. Not only did the oil sands produce a carbon-intensive product, but the means used to produce bitumen was itself carbon-intensive. Developing bitumen requires large amounts of energy. Critics pointed out that the province's oil sands industry was using relatively clean-burning natural gas to develop a relatively dirty source of energy in bitumen. The other resource being used to develop the oil sands was water. The in situ method of oil sands development relied on injecting steam deep into the group to force the oil to the surface. In a province that does not have abundant water, the use of so much water to develop Alberta's oil sands also raised critical scrutiny.

Although it was relatively easy for many Albertans to dismiss the concerns of people such as Al Gore and other environmentalists, former premier Peter Lougheed's increasingly vocal criticisms of the impact of unchecked oil sands development was less easy to dismiss. In interviews and speeches throughout the year, Lougheed questioned not only the environmental impacts of the development but also the social and economic costs of the rapid pace of growth, the use of natural gas in the oil sands, and the royalties being charged by Alberta (see, for example,

Policy Options, September 2006). Lougheed called for a moratorium on new oil sands projects and developments until the province could sort these things out. Coming from the elder statesman of Alberta politics, these criticisms could not be dismissed easily.

A new premier

Lougheed's interventions into the public debate over the pace of growth in Alberta helped to highlight the question of political leadership in Alberta. Given that the provincial government had seemingly unlimited money to spend on any project or problem it faced, it would have been hard to predict that the boom would have caused significant political upheaval in the government. So deep was the discontent over the government's perceived lack of direction that it led to Ralph Klein having to step aside as Conservative leader and premier and to Ed Stelmach taking the reins of the Conservative dynasty.

Progressive Conservatives increasingly expressed concerns among themselves over what they saw as a lack of fiscal discipline in the government. They saw a government content to merely throw money at problems rather than come up with a coherent plan or direction for the province's future. To these critics, the 'Ralph bucks' plan seemed only to confirm that the premier had no vision for the future of the province. Combined with Klein's lackluster performance in the 2004 provincial election and the resulting decline in popular votes and seats, the premier's critics had no shortage of ammunition to use against the man who had led the party to four consecutive election victories.

Those critics within the Conservative party had a prime opportunity to express their discontent with the direction of the government at a party convention scheduled for the end of March in Calgary. On the agenda for that convention was a leadership review vote mandated by the party's constitution. The trigger for the revolt against Klein was the timetable of his departure. During the 2004 election campaign, Premier Klein had made it clear that it would be his last election. In the weeks leading up to the convention, Klein firmed up his resignation plans and timetable. He announced that he would resign in October 2007 and remain on as leader after that until the party selected a new leader. The extended resignation timetable did not sit well with Klein's critics, who felt that this would merely extend the rudderless drift seen in the government.

A few days after announcing his timetable for resigning, Klein ruled that any Cabinet minister seeking to succeed him would have to resign from Cabinet by 1 June. The premier's justification for this was to prevent those in Cabinet from using their positions and perks to advance their leadership bids. This move angered infrastructure and transportation minister Lyle Oberg, who was a leadership aspirant. He told his Brooks constituency association that he would not ask them to vote in favour of Klein at the leadership review. Oberg later said he regretted his words (*Calgary Herald*, 23 March). The party caucus voted to suspend Oberg from the caucus and from Cabinet for his remarks. Despite having been removed from the caucus, Oberg announced that he would continue his quest to become party leader.

This drama from within the normally quiet Conservative caucus only served to heighten the spectacle surrounding the leadership review. The vote was held on the evening of 31 March. In a stunning rebuke to Klein, only 55.4 per cent of the delegates supported his leadership. Although he met the minimum threshold to continue as leader, it was clear that Klein's support in the party was too tepid to continue. On 4 April Klein announced that a leadership contest would start in September and that he would step down by the end of 2006.

Several candidates emerged to seek the position as Conservative Party leader. Intergovernmental affairs minister Ed Stelmach had announced his leadership intentions even before the leadership review, having resigned from Cabinet shortly after Klein announced the rules. Oberg stayed in the contest. Advanced education minister Dave Hancock resigned from Cabinet in April and announced his intention to seek the leadership. Over the summer, Victor Doerksen, the minister for science and innovation, resigned from Cabinet and announced his leadership bid. Two backbench MLAs also announced their intention to seek the leadership. Former University of Calgary political scientist Ted Morton announced his intention to seek the leadership. Alana DeLong declared her leadership intentions but withdrew shortly thereafter. Former Edmonton MLA Mark Norris, who lost his seat to the Liberals in 2004, had long been rumoured as a possible successor to Klein, and he threw his hat into the ring as well. Gary McPherson, an advocate for people with disabilities, also ran. The widely acknowledged front runner, however, was former provincial treasurer Jim Dinning, who had been eyeing the leadership for years and had an organization in place.

The leadership contest was conducted under the same rules as were used to elect Klein in 1992. The race was a universal membership ballot, which meant that all party members directly voted for the leader. The first ballot was a straight vote among all of the candidates. If no candidate earned a majority on the first ballot, then the top three candidates would advance to a second round of voting one week later. The second ballot was a preferential ballot, meaning that if none of those three candidates had a majority, the third-place candidate would be eliminated and his or her votes would be distributed according to the second preferences indicated on them. The vote was wide open to any Albertan who bought a $5 Conservative membership, even if they bought it on the day of either ballot.

Dinning's front-runner status was seen in the large number of endorsements he enjoyed from within the Conservative caucus. Furthermore, Rod Love, who had masterminded Ralph Klein's run for the leadership in 1992, backed Dinning. Although the candidates did not have to disclose their donors and spending, it appeared that Dinning had ample financial resources, given that he ran a slick and well-financed campaign. Morton represented one of the more visible challenges to Dinning. His ties to the federal Conservative Party and, in particular, its Reform / Canadian Alliance roots, helped to buoy his candidacy. He appealed to those who supported a more independent position for Alberta within Canada, as he supported an Alberta pension plan and the creation of a provincial police force. In fact, Paul Hinman, leader of the small conservative Alberta Alliance party, endorsed Morton and encouraged party members to take out Conservative Party memberships and support him. Morton also staked out a position as the social conservative candidate, which further distinguished him from the more moderate Dinning.

There was also a regional dimension to the candidacies. As a former mayor of Calgary and an MLA from that city, Klein had been understandably more attuned to that city than to other parts of the province. As another Calgary candidate, Dinning also faced the problem that he represented Calgary's continued dominance of the party structure. There was a feeling among some that it was time for other parts of the province to have their turn. This aided the candidacies of northern Alberta candidates such as Hancock, Norris, and Stelmach.

Despite all these putative differences between the candidates, universal membership votes are often decided largely by organizational muscle. What mattered for the candidates is how many party memberships they could sell and how effectively they could turn out their vote. No public opinion poll could truly capture what was happening on the ground. Consequently, there was real suspense on 25 November, voting day. Nearly 100,000 people voted in the first round and, as expected, Jim Dinning was in first place with 29,470 votes. His lead over Morton, however, was relatively small as Morton took 25,614 votes. In third place was Stelmach, whose 14,967 votes were well behind the two front runners but enough to beat out Oberg, who finished fourth, and the rest of the field.

Under the rules, Dinning, Morton, and Stelmach all proceeded to the second-round preferential ballot on 2 December. Oberg, Hancock, and Norris all endorsed Stelmach. McPherson endorsed Dinning, whereas Doerksen did not endorse any of the three remaining candidates. The vote seemed polarized between the more moderate and establishment Dinning and the more conservative outsider candidacy of Morton. Both men were from Calgary, which left Stelmach as the only candidate from outside that city. More than 140,000 people voted on the second ballot, and after the first count, Stelmach was in first place with 51,764 votes, just ahead of Dinning's 51,282 votes. Morton's 41,243 votes put him in third place. He was eliminated and the ballots of his supporters were distributed to the other candidates according to their second preferences. Not surprisingly, given the polarization between Dinning and Morton, 25,813 of Morton's supporters had indicated that Stelmach was their second choice, compared to only 4,227 who supported Dinning. Stelmach emerged as the winner of the leadership contest.

Because so much attention had been focused on the two Calgary front runners, Stelmach's victory came as a surprise. Relatively little was known about the former farmer from northern Alberta. On 15 December Stelmach took the oath and became Alberta's new premier. Stelmach's first order of business was to appoint a Cabinet. The 18-member Cabinet was dominated by rural Alberta. Only 4 of the 18 ministers represented districts in Edmonton and Calgary, despite the fact the two cities made up over half of the province's population. Only two women – Iris Evans and Janis Tarchuk – made it into Cabinet. Critics seized upon the lack of urban and female representation as evidence that Stelmach and the Conservatives were out of touch with the realities of modern Alberta. One thing Stelmach did was reward his supporters in the leadership contest, most prominently Lloyd Snelgrove, who became president of the Treasury Board and was second in precedence behind the premier. Oberg and Hancock, whose support after the first ballot likely contributed to Stelmach's election, were rewarded with the high-profile finance and health portfolios, respectively. Morton, an avid hunter, was given the position of minister of sustainable resource development.

It is difficult to overstate how significant a shift this was in the province's politics. In 2006 the Progressive Conservatives celebrated the thirty-fifth anniversary of their 1971 election victory. The party had governed continuously since then. Other than the 1993 provincial election, the party's grip on power had never been seriously challenged. A change at the top was tantamount to a change in government. This was particularly true because, for better or for worse, Klein dominated Alberta politics in a way that few premiers have during their tenures. His Cabinet ministers had relatively little public profile; he was the face and voice of the government.

The contrast with Stelmach could not have been starker. Where Klein was charismatic and flamboyant, Stelmach was quiet and a much less effective communicator. For those tired of the bombast of the Klein years, it was a welcome change. It remained to be seen whether Stelmach would be able to reinvigorate the party and government as Klein had done when he became leader in 1992 or whether he would preside over a decline in its support as former leader Don Getty had done when he took over in 1985. Still others wondered whether Stelmach might prove to be the new Harry Strom, the last sitting Alberta premier to lose an election, when he led Social Credit to defeat in 1971. How Stelmach and his team would rise to the challenge of maintaining the party's grip on power in Alberta looked to be the story of Alberta politics into the next year.

2006 federal election

The story of another Albertan ascending to a position of political prominence also made headlines in Alberta. On 6 February Calgary's Stephen Harper was sworn in as Canada's twenty-second prime minister and became the third Albertan to assume this position in Canadian history. Harper assumed the position after the 23 January election in which he led his Conservative Party of Canada to a minority government.

Although at the national level the election was a close one, the outcome in almost all of Alberta's 28 seats was never really in doubt. In 2004 the Conservatives had won all but 2 seats in Alberta. David Kilgour, who had been elected in Edmonton Beaumont for the Liberals in 2004, had left the party in 2005 and was not running for re-election. This meant all of the focus was on Edmonton Centre, the only seat held by a Liberal incumbent. Anne McLellan, the minister of public safety and emergency preparedness, was seeking a fifth term. The Conservatives again nominated Laurie Hawn, who had lost to McLellan by fewer than 750 votes in 2004. This time, Hawn won the seat. The Conservatives also took Kilgour's old seat, completing a sweep of the province. For the first time since 1988, the Conservatives held every seat in Alberta. Overall, the Conservatives enjoyed the support of 65 per cent of the province's voters, up from the 62 per cent the party received in 2004. The scandal-ridden Liberals earned just 15 per cent of the vote, down from 22 per cent in 2004. The NDP had its best showing since 1988, winning almost 12 per cent of the vote. The Greens did better in Alberta than in any other province in Canada, with 6.5 per cent of the popular vote.

For the first time since the dramatic 1993 election, Alberta had substantial representation in the government caucus. Despite this, the essential logic of Canadian electoral politics remained in place. For the Conservatives to win a majority government, it would have to do better elsewhere in Canada, particularly in seat-rich Ontario and Quebec. There were no more seats left for the Conservatives to win in Alberta. This focus became clear in Harper's Cabinet appointments. Despite having a large cadre of long-serving members of Parliament with long histories of service to the Conservatives' predecessors, Alberta earned only three spots in the 26-minister Cabinet. Calgary's Jim Prentice became minister of Indian affairs, Medicine Hat's Monte Solberg was appointed as minister of citizenship and immigration, and Spruce Grove's Rona Ambrose was handed the tricky environment portfolio. Although Alberta's representation in Cabinet was certainly in proportion to its share of the population, the exclusion of long-serving MPs such as Jason Kenney and Diane Ablonczy stung even more considering Harper went outside his party to appoint David Emerson to Cabinet and even used the Senate to appoint Michael Fortier. The most startling omission from Alberta was Ablonczy, who had been elected for the Reform Party in 1993 and distinguished herself in Parliament. This was particularly noteworthy given that another criticism of the Harper Cabinet was the relative lack of women.

The Cabinet appointments set the tone for the federal government as the Harper government sought to convert its minority into a majority. The challenge for Harper was to manage to reach out and appeal to Quebec without alienating his Alberta support base as Brian Mulroney had done two decades earlier. For the most part, it appeared through 2006 that Albertans were willing to give Harper the benefit of the doubt. The federal Conservative government remained popular in Alberta throughout the year.

Another health care reform founders

The political drama over leadership in Alberta and the change in government had an impact on one of the pressing public policy issues in the province: dealing with the rising costs of health care. One of Ralph Klein's failures as premier had been his repeated attempts to change the delivery and administration of health care in Alberta in a bid to contain costs. Throughout his tenure as premier, he had made repeated attempts to bring in reforms, only to have them stalled either because of public opposition or because of the impermeability of the public health care system.

Shortly after Harper's election victory, Klein announced that his caucus had voted unanimously to proceed with what he called the 'Third Way' health care reforms. There were two major components to the reforms. First, Albertans would be allowed to purchase private health care to cover certain provisions, thus giving them speedier access to particular procedures. Second, doctors would be able to work in the public system and provide private health care simultaneously, a significant shift from the existing system that required doctors to be either wholly public or private. Klein warned that these reforms might put the province at odds with the Canada Health Act.

The timing of the announcement was not mere coincidence. Past Liberal federal governments – with few seats in Alberta and bleak prospects of improvement – had been only too happy to threaten Alberta's government with reprisals for proposed reforms. This time, however, the Alberta government sensed an opening. Harper's government could be seen as more receptive to a potentially larger role for private health care on ideological grounds. Furthermore, the domination of the government caucus by Albertans could also be seen as making the federal government more reluctant to beat up on Alberta.

The proposals, due to be introduced in the legislature in April, unleashed a firestorm of opposition in the province. The provincial government received thousands of letters and phone calls about the proposed reforms, mostly from people concerned about what they saw as a shift to a two-tier health care system. Most critically, however, both Prime Minister Harper and federal health minister Tony Clement warned that the reforms might violate the Canada Health Act, something that could jeopardize health care transfers from the federal government to Alberta. The Alberta government had provided an opportunity for a federal government desperate to show that it was capable of governing within the political mainstream to demonstrate its commitment to the popular publicly funded health care system.

In mid-April, a few weeks after the tumultuous leadership review and Klein's resignation announcement, the provincial government announced that it would not be pursuing its 'Third Way' reforms.

Instead, the province would focus on recruiting health care professionals to work in Alberta in an effort to reduce wait times. The retreat partly reflected the opposition both within the province and from the federal government. Some of this retreat also likely reflected Klein's weakened position as a 'lame duck' premier. Simply put, Klein did not have the political capital left to push the reforms through against both a federal government determined to show its moderation and a reluctant public. The job of reforming Alberta's health care system would be a task that Stelmach would inherit. The failure to meaningfully reform Alberta's health care system would be part of Ralph Klein's legacy in his fourteen years as premier of Alberta.

The legislature

Given the strong support for public health care in Alberta, it is not surprising that the Third Way proposals dominated debate in the legislature. Sensing the government was out of step with public opinion on health care, both the Liberals and the New Democrats sought to press the issue during Question Period. Premier Klein's leadership woes also cast a shadow over the legislature. A bizarre incident in the legislature 1 March brought both of these issues together. During debate over the Third Way idea, a Liberal MLA asked a legislature page to take a copy of the party's position paper on health care to Premier Klein. Klein described the report as 'crap' and threw it at the page. Despite an apology from the premier, the incident raised even more questions about Klein's erratic behaviour, his arrogance, and his fitness to govern. With Klein already in trouble on other fronts, the situation did little to help the premier's grip on power.

After the government retreated on the Third Way proposals, the legislature's attention focused on other bills. Three bills were particularly contentious and noteworthy. Bill 20 amended the Freedom of Information and Protection of Privacy Act to exempt government briefing documents from both access to information requests and internal audits. Despite the meagre opposition size, the government invoked closure to pass that bill. Bill 40, known as the Post-Secondary Learning Amendment Act, allowed Cabinet to change tuition at post-secondary institutions, rather than the legislature. Together, the two bills seemed to indicate a move to greater government secrecy and less transparency.

The third contentious piece of proposed legislation was a private member's bill. Morton introduced Bill 208, a bill that would have allowed any minister or marriage commissioner to refuse to perform same-sex marriages without sanction. It would also have allowed teachers to refuse to teach any part of school curriculum that talked about same-sex marriage. Furthermore, schools would have been required to inform parents if same-sex marriage was being taught in the school curriculum and students would be allowed not to attend. The bill passed second reading in the legislature, but delaying tactics by the Liberals and New Democrats prevented the bill from coming to a vote for third reading. Besides being an incident where the Opposition parties stopped something from happening, the bill revealed the split between social conservatives and liberals in the Conservative caucus. Both international and intergovernmental affairs minister Gary Mar and Conservative leadership contender Dave Hancock voiced their opposition to Bill 208.

When the legislature wrapped up in late May, most observers thought it was done for the year. The Conservative leadership selection process would consume the government's attention in the fall. The government, however, recalled the legislature for a week at the end of August, primarily to allow the government to get authorization to spend an addition $1.2 billion on various projects. Morton's Bill 208 was scheduled to come up for debate again, but an Opposition filibuster prevented a vote. Given that this marked the end of the session of the legislature, the bill was dead, unless Morton decided to try again it in the 2007 legislature session.

Other news

A police task force that had been investigating the deaths of Edmonton-area sex-trade workers made an arrest after police found the body of Theresa Innes in a Fort Saskatchewan home. Project KARE arrested Thomas Svekla and charged him with murder. There was no word from police about whether he was connected to the other murders. Svekla was due to go to court in January.

In happier news, the Edmonton Oilers had a banner year, making it all the way to the Stanley Cup finals, where they lost a heartbreaking seventh game to the Carolina Hurricanes. The Oilers' improbable Stanley Cup run, including upset after upset over higher ranked opponents, united the city and featured capacity crowds singing 'O Canada' at the top of their lungs during the national anthems. Much as was the case in 2004, when the Oilers' arch-rivals, the Calgary Flames, made it to the final, the Oilers' success put Flames fans into a conflicted position. Even in Calgary, however, some people could be seen cheering for the Oilers.

JOSEPH GARCEA

Saskatchewan

The year 2006 was one of those interesting years for Saskatchewan in which elections, debates in the legislature, changes to the composition of Cabinet, surprising improvements in the performance of the provincial economy, intergovernmental relations, and Aboriginal issues all provided their share of materials for media reports and the daily conversations of what Saskatchewanians like to refer to as 'coffee row.'

Elections

The 2006 federal election, which produced a minority Conservative government led by Stephen Harper, did not change Saskatchewan's partisan political landscape very much. The Conservatives won 12 of the 14 seats in the province. The other 2 seats were won by Liberal candidates. One of those was the prominent Liberal candidate in Regina, Ralph Goodale, who had served as finance minister in Prime Minister Paul Martin's government. The other was Gary Merasty, a young Aboriginal candidate who defeated Conservative incumbent Jeremy Harrison by only 67 votes in the large northern constituency of Desnethe – Missinippi – Churchill River (*Saskatoon StarPhoenix*, 24 Jan. and 8 Feb.). As in the previous federal election, the NDP was unable to win any seats despite coming close in a few.

At the provincial level there was one by-election that received substantial attention because the outcome was important for all three major parties. The by-election resulted from the resignation of the incumbent Saskatchewan Party MLA, Brenda Bakken-Lackey, who cited frustrations and differences within the party caucus as one of the factors that led her to resign. The Saskatchewan Party candidate, Dustin Duncan, managed to hold on to the seat with approximately 49 per cent of the vote, compared to 27 per cent for Liberal Party leader David Karwacki and 24 per cent for NDP candidate Graham Mickleborough (*Saskatoon StarPhoenix*, 17 June). The results of the by-election underscored that the NDP was becoming increasingly vulnerable to losing the next election unless it found ways to increase its electoral support (ibid.).

This was also election year for urban and northern municipalities as well as for reeves and half of the councillors of rural municipalities. The trends of low voter turnout in a substantial number of municipalities, high re-election success rates among incumbents, and substantial numbers of wins by acclamation persisted in these elections.

Political parties

The year 2006 was not a particularly good one for any of the political parties. The governing NDP lost some of its popularity, some respected and long-serving MLAs, and a by-election. With the next provincial election looming on the horizon, the NDP was not well poised to capture a fifth term in office. Part of the reason for this is that at least four long-serving NDP MLAs, some of whom were high-profile Cabinet ministers, announced that they would not be running in the next election and others were pondering the possibility that they would do the same. Premier Lorne Calvert indicated that the resignations were occurring because he had asked all caucus members to make their intentions known on whether they planned to leave or stay (ibid., 26 Dec.). The resignations resulted from a combination of political battle fatigue among long-serving MLAs and also a growing concern that it would be very difficult to win the next general election. Indeed, it was that concern regarding a potential electoral loss that allegedly led a young Cabinet minister, Kevin Yates, to question among caucus members the merits of the continuance of Premier Lorne Calvert as party leader. Allegedly, such questioning resulted in being constrained to resign from Cabinet only seven months after being appointed to it (ibid., 19 Sept.).

For the Liberal Party 2006 was also a difficult year that ended with its future in serious doubt. Its two major setbacks happened within a few days in June when the party leader was unable to win a by-election that would have provided him with a seat in the legislature, and a potentially strong candidate from Saskatoon, Rob Norris, defected to the Saskatchewan Party (ibid., 30 June).

The year was not particularly good for the Saskatchewan Party either (ibid., 30 Dec.). Despite the hope and hubris that was being felt among Saskatchewan Party members as a result of what was clearly a difficult year for the NDP and the Liberal Party, it was facing some problems of its own, stemming from a retirement, a death, a court case, and the prospects of the re-emergence of the Progressive Conservative Party. At the end of the spring sitting of the legislature, former party leader Elwin Hermanson, who had almost won the previous election, announced that he would not be a candidate in the next provincial election (ibid., 24 June). Two months later one of the longest serving and most influential caucus members, Ben Heppner, died (ibid., 27 Dec.). During the year the Saskatchewan Party also had to deal with the prospect that the Conservative Party, which had been in a hiatus for nine years, would start becoming politically active and field candidates in the next provincial election. Ultimately, it decided that it would not (ibid., 29 May), largely because it was embroiled in a lawsuit against trustees of the $2.8 million fund who were not providing it with requisite operating funds allegedly because they were supporters of the Saskatchewan Party (ibid., 26 May). By the end of the year the Conservative Party had opened an office in Saskatoon, but all else remained either undecided or in limbo (ibid., 8 Dec.). Another troublesome distraction was a court case brought against it by a former Progressive Conservative Cabinet minister, Grant Schmidt, who was seeking compensation for the expenses he had incurred in winning the Saskatchewan Party nomination for the Melville-Saltcoats constituency in 2003 that was subsequently revoked by the leader of the Saskatchewan Party (ibid., 9 Feb.).

Legislature

With only 2 seats separating the government and the official Opposition (30 seats to 28 seats), each legislative sitting was important for both parties particularly because they were gearing up for a general election that would likely be held within one year. This was clearly evident in the first few days of the spring legislative session and particularly during the budget debate shortly thereafter. Many of the Question Periods during the session entailed debates regarding whether the province was gaining or losing ground in terms of economic performance, job creation, and population growth (ibid., 15 March).

In its effort to enhance its electoral support, the provincial government started criticizing the federal government on several issues. Towards that end the government triggered an emergency debate calling on the federal government to increase contributions to agricultural income stabilization programs by approximately $200 million (ibid., 16 March). Similarly, the provincial government criticized the federal government for abandoning the commitment to produce a better early learning and child care policies (ibid., 17 March).

During the spring legislative session thirty-six bills were enacted, most of which were of relatively minor consequence. One of the bills of significant consequence was the Municipal Revenue Sharing Amendment Act, which provided the statutory basis for adding $12.2 million to the revenue sharing pool for all municipalities as had been promised in the budget. That increase brought the total for the revenue sharing pool to $97 million for the year.

The dynamics in the fall session were no better than they had been in the spring as both parties continued their efforts to improve their political positioning and standing in the polls in anticipation of the election that would be held the following year. This was evident in the debates related to the throne speech, the budget update, and some key pieces of legislation that were introduced.

The throne speech delivered at the start of the fall session articulated the following objectives: increasing public infrastructure renewal; reducing wait times within the health care system; working with urban municipalities in developing an 'urban development agenda'; partnering with Aboriginal governments to host a national summit on Aboriginal economic development; improving the investment climate for northern Saskatchewan; advancing the anti-crime and the anti-racism strategies; building on the Voluntary Sector Initiative; improving the national farm insurance program; pressing the federal government to make a statutory commitment for an open and fair plebiscite on the future of the Canadian Wheat Board; and pressing the federal government to honour its commitment to produce and use a fair and equitable equalization formula. The throne speech also included the announcement that the province would enact legislation for an annual Family Day statutory holiday in February (ibid., 27 Oct.).

Two notable pieces of legislation were introduced by the government in the fall session, one to establish the Family Day statutory holiday and one to cut provincial sales tax by 2 per cent (ibid., 30 Dec.). The most notable private member's bill was the one introduced by an official Opposition MLA calling for fixed provincial election dates. The bill was designed for the dual purpose of pressuring the government to call an election sooner rather than later and profiling the Saskatchewan Party as the most committed champion for democratic reforms. If it had been enacted, Saskatchewan would have joined British Columbia, Ontario, and Newfoundland as provinces with fixed election dates (ibid., 28 Dec.).

Executive

In 2006 there was a change in both the lieutenant governor and Cabinet. Gordon Barnhart, who had served as clerk in the provincial legislature and in the Senate, was appointed by Prime Minister Stephen Harper to replace Lynda Haverstock as lieutenant governor (ibid., 2 Aug.). Lynda Haverstock, who was originally appointed for a five-year term in 2000, served a six-year term because she was given a one-year extension by Prime Minister Paul Martin to remain in that position during Saskatchewan's centennial year.

In February Premier Lorne Calvert announced a major Cabinet shuffle, the first since the November 2003 provincial election (ibid., 3 Feb.). The shuffle entailed dropping two ministers from the 18-member Cabinet, adding two new ones, and transferring five others to new portfolios. The two ministers who were dropped from Cabinet had both indicated that they would not run in the next election. One of these was Joanne Crofford, who served as minister of community resources, and the other was Peter Prebble, who served as minister of corrections and public safety.

Another change in the composition of Cabinet occurred in the fall of that year when Kevin Yates was allegedly forced to resign as minister of corrections and public safety after only seven months in Cabinet because he had raised concerns regarding Premier Lorne Calvert's ability lead the party to another election victory. He was replaced by Warren McCall, a young MLA from Regina (ibid., 19 Sept.). Although he resigned from Cabinet, Yates continued to serve as an MLA and maintained his position in the NDP caucus. The NDP government was fortunate that he decided to stay because it could not afford to lose any of its members either through defections or by-elections in a legislative context in which it held a slim majority of 2 seats (30–28).

Budget

The 2006 budget was produced in an improved economic context resulting from two years of exceptional revenue growth largely owing to increased revenues from oil, gas, and mineral royalties as well as some growth in the rest of the economy. In delivering the budget speech the minister of finance noted that this was the thirteenth balanced budget in a row. What he did not mention was that most of those budgets were balanced by drawing revenues from the Crown corporation sector. He also noted that this budget entailed paying down the $7.3 billion debt by an additional $101.9 million, thereby lowering it to $7.2 billion, the lowest amount in fifteen years. The government also pointed out that the projected debt-to-GDP ratio was 16.7 per cent for 2006 and 15.8 per cent for 2007, compared to 41.6 per cent in 1993, two years after the NDP returned to power (www.gov.sk.ca/finance/budget).

The budget had some benefits for several major sectors. This included tax cuts for the business sector and the elimination of the capital tax on any new investment in the province. This reduction made the province more competitive in relation to Alberta's tax regime (*Saskatoon StarPhoenix*, 7 April). It included increased transfers and capital project funding for education boards, post-secondary education, municipalities, health regions, agricultural income, and insurance support programs. It also included added funding for social programs, Aboriginal educational institutions, and educational training and career development opportunities for Aboriginal people. The budget contained provisions to reduce education property tax on agricultural land and the continuation of an 8 per cent education property tax credit program for residential, commercial, and industrial property. The MLAs voted along party lines and the budget passed with the 29 NDP members voting for it and the 27 Saskatchewan Party members voting against it (ibid., 15 April).

One of the most significant budgetary decisions of the year was made in the fall when the minister of finance surprised everyone by announcing a reduction both in the sales tax and in the small corporate tax, which cost the provincial treasury $500 million in lost revenues (ibid., 7 Nov.). The provincial sales tax was cut from 7 per cent to 5 per cent at a cost of lost revenues of approximately $325 million, and the small business corporate tax was cut from 5 per cent to 4.5 per cent for a cost of $175 million. The minister explained that the tax cuts were made in light of increased revenues from other sources and projections that the tax cuts were sustainable for the foreseeable future (ibid., 28 Oct.). These tax cuts were welcome news for taxpayers in a province with the second-highest tax rate in the country (ibid., 17 June).

Economy

During 2006 the provincial economy started improving to the point where it was much stronger than it had been for nearly two decades. The improvements were the result of increased revenues from natural resources and agriculture. The improvement was evident in an economic growth rate of approximately 3.8 per cent that was 0.6 per cent better than the previous year and overall salary increases of approximately 3.5 per cent (ibid., 1 Sept.). In an attempt to improve Saskatchewan's economic performance the provincial government had implemented many of the recommendations of the Action Committee on the Rural Economy (ACRE) (ibid., 14 Oct.).

Not only did Saskatchewan's economy continue to improve during 2006, it also continued to change from one that was primarily agriculture-based to one that was becoming increasingly resource-based. Whereas jobs in the agricultural sector dropped by approximately 25 per cent during the previous five years, those in the natural resources sector increased by 35 per cent during the same time (ibid., 20 Oct.). The mining sector was doing particular well, and the provincial government along with the Greater Saskatoon Chamber of Commerce started considering the merits of establishing a uranium refinery to maximize benefits locally in that sector (ibid., 13 May, 10 May, and 22 June).

Despite the relatively good economic performance, job creation was still fairly modest at 2.1 per cent, compared to 5.1 per cent for Manitoba, 10.3 per cent for BC, and 12.7 per cent for Alberta (ibid., 2 Dec.). Despite the low rate of job growth the provincial government continued increasing immigration flows to the province to fill specialized jobs and to increase the population (ibid., 8 Dec.).

Judiciary

Two issues created some intrigue in the judicial sector in Saskatchewan. The first was the legislation enacted by the NDP to reduce the number of judges on the Saskatchewan Court of Appeal from nine to seven. The rationale provided by the provincial government was that there were not sufficient appeal cases to warrant maintaining a court of nine judges. The provincial government's decision was viewed as curious because only minor administrative savings accrued from it; the judges' wages were paid by the federal government (ibid., 4 Dec.).

The second issue was the speculation that the president of the University of Saskatchewan, Peter MacKinnon, had been shortlisted as one of three potential candidates to fill a Supreme Court vacancy. Although he was not appointed to the court, it raised his profile within and beyond the province and reminded everyone that no Supreme Court judges had been appointed from Saskatchewan since the appointment of Emmett Hall in 1963 (ibid., 21 Feb.).

Intergovernmental relations

In 2006 federal-provincial relations were strained much more than usual. The strain was caused by disagreements between the newly elected Conservative federal government led by Prime Minister Stephen Harper and the NDP provincial government on several key issues (ibid., 16 Jan.). The most notable disagreement involved equalization payments. At issue was the federal government's decision not to eliminate revenues from non-renewable natural resources from the formula used for calculating equalization payments. It was estimated that the decision was costing the provincial government approximately $800 million annually. The battle raged for the entire year, with the provincial government and its MLAs criticizing the Conservative federal government and its MPs for being hypocritical in criticizing the Liberal federal government's position on this issue prior to the election and then adopting the same position after the election (ibid., 28 Jan. and 12 Dec.). The federal Conservative government and its MPs responded by accusing the NDP government and its MLAs of trying to score political points against Ottawa as a means of improving their standing in the polls. The debate intensified substantially during the last quarter of the year (ibid., 12 Oct.). Part of the challenge the provincial government faced in its lobbying effort was that the provincial economy was much stronger than it had been for many years. In 2006 it started becoming a 'have province' that had sufficient revenues to cut its provincial sales tax by 2 per cent for a total of $300 million (ibid., 13 Dec.). In lobbying Ottawa, Premier Calvert joined forces with Newfoundland and Labrador premier Danny Williams, who also wanted resource revenues eliminated from the equalization formula. By the end of the year neither of them was able to achieve his objective (ibid., 19 Dec.). All they were able to do was get the federal government to promise that some funds would be transferred to those provinces in the future to offset the loss in revenues through the equalization system (ibid., 29 Dec.). The amount of revenues promised through other means was far less than the amount that they claimed they were owed through the equalization system.

Other issues that strained federal-provincial relations included the Harper government's decision to scrap the child care agreements signed by the previous government and the province, which would have provided Saskatchewan with $146 million in funding over five years (ibid., 18 March); the cutting of approximately one-third of federal funding to the Saskatchewan Forest Centre; the federal government's softwood lumber deal with the United States; the scrapping of the deal to sell grain hopper rail cars to a farmer's coalition; and ongoing uncertainty over whether future agricultural programs would continue to be split 60 / 40 per cent between the federal and provincial governments (ibid., 15 May). Other controversial issues that emerged during the year were the delays in providing income support for farm families adversely affected by the massive spring floods (ibid., June 30) and the refusal of the federal government to abandon plans for shifting from the single-desk wheat marketing system involving the CWB, to a dual marketing system (ibid., 11 Nov. and 2 Dec.). Despite their differences on the CWB, the provincial government and the official Opposition agreed that the restructuring of the Canadian Agricultural Income Stabilization program and an immediate $200 million emergency payout from the federal government were absolutely essential (ibid., 16 March).

One of the major decisions related to intergovernmental relations was made by the Saskatchewan government not to join its Alberta and British Columbia counterparts in signing the Trade, Investment and Labour Mobility Agreement (ibid., 30 April). Its decision was based largely on concerns that although social services, health care, and labour laws were exempt from the agreement, there were no clear exemptions for the contracting practices of Crown corporations and municipalities.

Provincial-municipal relations focused primarily on financial issues. The increase in the revenue sharing pool was seen as a step in the right direction by municipal associations, but by no means a sufficient step. The Saskatchewan Urban Municipalities Association (SUMA) complained that the revenue sharing was still woefully inadequate in light of how much it collected in taxes from ratepayers in communities (ibid., 7 Dec.). Similarly, despite the $53 million in property tax relief offered to rural property ratepayers, the Saskatchewan Association of Rural Municipalities (SARM) complained that the level of relief was insufficient (ibid., 31 Oct.). Both municipal associations were trying to soften up the provincial government to get more benefits in the budget that was being produced for approval the following spring. In their efforts to advance their particular case for reducing the level of education tax even more than the 30 per cent that had been implemented in the 2006 budget, approximately 100 municipalities started to withhold the education portion of the property taxes that were to be transferred to school boards. This prompted the provincial government to introduce legislation that would authorize it not only to withhold some provincial grants from municipalities that were not transferring tax revenue but also to charge them interest for the amounts not transferred (ibid., 7 Nov.). A positive development in the municipal sector was SARM's effort to facilitate inter-municipal collaboration. Towards that end SARM launched its 'Clearing the Path' initiative (ibid., 1 March). Despite some limited fledgling efforts in that direction, no major progress was made by the end of the year.

Aboriginal affairs

The Federation of Saskatchewan Indian Nations (FSIN) elected Lawrence Joseph as its new chief. The provincial government was unsure what effect his election would have on FSIN-provincial relations, especially because in his capacity as vice chief responsible for the justice portfolio, Chief Joseph had been an outspoken critic of the province's justice system (ibid., 27 Oct.). The federal government had reason to be concerned too as the FSIN vice-chief, Guy Lonechild, called on the scrapping of the Indian Act (ibid., 27 Sept.), and other FSIN members criticized the Harper government for not implementing the Kelowna Accord (ibid., 16 June).

Despite many successes in the Aboriginal sector, one of the disappointments was the problems facing the First Nations University of Canada (FNUC). To rectify the governance and management problems that were having an adverse effect on faculty retention and program delivery, a task force was appointed to make recommendations for reform. The task force made some constructive recommendations, but the board and the FSIN were not willing to implement many of the most important reforms (ibid., 21 March). Given the compensation that had to be paid to many employees for violations of labour relations regulations, several lawsuits and grievances pending, and the paucity of leadership and will for reforming the FNUC, questions were raised as to whether the problems would or could be solved (ibid., 9 June and 10 Nov.).

Another major issue in the Aboriginal sector was the dispute between the provincial government and FSIN regarding whether the Gaming Framework Agreement that they signed in 2002 should be reviewed and revised. The FSIN chief indicated that if the revenue sharing formula was not changed to make it more favourable to First Nations he would not support the extension of the agreement (ibid., 30 Nov. and 1 Dec.).

A couple of notable interrelated events also occurred within the Métis governance system. The first was the charges laid against two Métis people for allegedly tampering with election materials in the 2004 Métis Nation Saskatchewan (MNS) election (ibid., 22 April), and the second was the decision of the federal and provincial governments to suspend funding to the MNS because its executive refused to hold another election that would be conducted by an independent agency, as demanded by many of the Métis people in the province and recommended by the Métis Electoral Consultation Panel in 2005 (http://www.fnmr.gov.sk.ca/documents/metis/ElectoralConsultRpt.pdf).

GEOFFREY LAMBERT

Manitoba

Even normally laconic Manitobans were moved to say of 2006, 'It's not too bad, eh?' For the year brought a taste of economic well-being the province had not enjoyed for some time.

There was a steady, if not spectacular, growth in the economy. Work was available for most people who wanted it, and at good wages. It was still possible to buy a house in a prestigious neighbourhood without having to hold up a bank. And there was a detectable air of optimism. Manitobans seemed ready to believe that they were at last in the queue for permanent prosperity.

The governing New Democratic Party kept a low profile, allowing its leader, Gary Doer, to take a lot of the credit for this auspicious set of circumstances. This he did with his customary gusto.

Some polls named him the most popular politician in the country. It seemed as if he might be in power forever. Certainly, there were few who expected that he would quickly be replaced by his new Progressive Conservative (PC) counterpart Hugh McFadyen, former mayoralty aide and one-time world junior curling champion.

Economic developments

It is a cliché by now (it has been mentioned by this contributor frequently over the long years of his authorship of this section, for instance) that the economy of the province is diverse and, hence, virtually impregnable. One of the pillars of the structure may crack, but the whole will be saved by a major improvement in another area.

There was, for example, a substantial rate of growth in some sectors in 2006, namely those which benefited from expansion in areas linked to housing construction. It was indeed a good year for furniture and appliances as the housing boom continued. This was the product of cheap money policies introduced by financial institutions, but these were to lead to chaos by 2008.

Further, although agriculture on the face of it did not do so well, this outcome was largely a result of decreased grain incomes and the continuing drag on the cattle market. Offsetting that were increases in some products, such as oil grains, and, particularly, the growth of the burgeoning hog industry. That extremely malodorous industry was well capable of (pardon me) bringing home the bacon.

Of the other major sectors, mining and utilities did about as well as trade analysts said they would. It was vitally important that in the not too distant future the province's massive hydro potential be developed. The government did in fact announce that it would go ahead with the construction of the Conawapa dam, for a major surge in Manitoba's hydro income might (politicians always said 'would') propel the province towards 'have' status.

It is extremely interesting to briefly revisit the employment statistics. Manitoba's estimated population at the back end of this year was around 1.232 million. The unemployment rate averaged 4.6 per cent. This placed the province in second spot, behind Alberta.

Natural increase did much to boost the population. A significant determinant here was the well-above-average birth rate among First Nations communities.

Offsetting that in most years is the drift of younger Manitobans to the glittering fleshpots of British Columbia, Alberta, and (although less so now) Ontario. This exodus was the subject of much debate in the province, producing the usual round of rhetoric and unlikely choices (like bringing back the Jets to Winnipeg).

What had an enormous impact on the Manitoba statistics and everything that could be inferred from them was the large body of persons who came to Manitoba in 2006 or the years immediately preceding it. The net figure, the excess of those who came over those who departed, was about 6,000. They came from all 'the three corners of the world' as Shakespeare put it, although in a different context.

The major sources were the Philippines, China, and India. Traditional sources, such as the United Kingdom, were no longer important in the scheme of things. Immigrants came to take on all manner of jobs, although a significant cadre were destined for the home care or hospital areas. Many came as sponsored immigrants (normally family), whereas others were promoted by the government or particular groups in the community.

And they were not all destined for Winnipeg. Some of the smart, vigorous towns (such as Steinbach and Winkler) within easy reach of the provincial capital worked hard to attract a share of the immigrants and were rewarded.

Many of the implications of this trend are obvious. Manitoba, like Canada as a whole, gets more and more diverse. Manitoba is the least Anglo-Saxon province, aside from Quebec. There is a ready assumption of the importance of compromise, the glory of individual liberty, and so forth, but there is a risk of conflict and lack of consensus.

The budget

One thing people can be sure of is that the taxman will call, like a thief in the night. In 2006, Budget Day was June 13, and the big taxman was London School of Economics PhD Greg Selinger, Manitoba's minister of finance.

As he had done on all his previous appearances, Selinger liked to pinpoint theoretical nuances, points of principle which emphasized the differences between the NDP and their opponents. In their six and a half years in office, he believed, his government had been motivated by a desire for accessibility and accountability, balance between industrial and 'green' alternatives, and housing needs (especially for young families); by the overriding necessity of remedial legislation for the Aboriginal people; and by the goal of achieving an appropriate fiscal mix, in which the up-and-coming middle classes are not taxed to death.

For 2006–7, Selinger promised to emphasize the needs of the 'big three' (health care, education, and the debt) while keeping a promise to lighten personal and direct taxation. Estimated revenue was set at $8.764 billion, with $3.113 billion coming from the federal government.

As was commonly the case with governments at both levels at this particular juncture of Canadian history, the Manitoba New Democrats promised to deliver a fiscal surplus. Moreover, for such are the ways of men when their heads are turned by office or its prospect, they are expected to bring in a surplus well in excess of that originally promised.

Leading the field in expenditure (which was initially set at $8.622 billion) was health care, which now consumed 42 per cent of the provincial government's spending. The problems in this area are immense and likely to have a chance at resolution only when the individual political parties stop pretending they are the only ones who care about this issue. Still, it was gratifying to see a couple of local hospitals noted for quality in national magazine reviews.

Education – primary, secondary, and post-secondary – had also over the years been studied to the point of exhaustion. Experienced, skilled professionals in the school system confessed to being burned out in trying to cope with the mediocrity of leadership in their field. And at the college and university level, administrators suffered a high degree of frustration at the government's frozen tuition fee policy. However, there were hints that it might be dropped, although how anybody can retreat with grace from a position so blatantly wrong-headed was not explained.

Government's role in the life of the economy has become more varied as time has gone by. Three government agencies were in the news this year, two of them making the administration look rather good. One was Manitoba Hydro, which was by this time well along with its project of building a new head office downtown, in fact a couple of blocks from the MTS Arena, the fabulously successful edifice built on the site of the old, historic Eaton store.

The government also benefited from the cool and effective management of the Manitoba Public Insurance Commission (MPIC or Autopac for short). It had withstood so many changes and done its job so well that, despite attempts to privatize it, it had become a landmark.

Less well thought of was the Crocus Fund, the squalid story of which had been circulating for a number of years. In brief, it was a venture capital fund which had made some dubious investments before ceasing trading. There were questions in the assembly and resignations from the fund. The government stonewalled with rare skill and the issue never achieved much status in the public eye. In the light of the province's storied history with public scandals, perhaps the average citizen only takes cash scandals seriously if they occur when the Tories are in power.

The legislative session

For a number of years now, the Legislative Assembly of Manitoba has held two sessions. One, in the fall, is to allow for the introduction and generally restrained consideration of legislation. The real fireworks take place in the spring, a time when legislative schoolboys could chuck thick, leather-bound volumes at each other. Before the switch, legislators had only the spring to air their views in, and bangs on the head with thick books were not unheard of.

The legislative sessions of 2006 were in this mode. The two throne speeches (13 June and 15 Nov.) again spoke to the principles of the NDP and took great pride in the accomplishments of the ruling party.

The NDP clearly held the whip hand during the sessions, and it was clear that the PCs, even six to seven years down the road, had not yet come to terms with their being ousted from power. It was not as if the New Democrats had such great men and great measures at their disposal. In reality, their legislative agenda seemed based on the principle of doing as little damage as possible to protect the legislative majority the government expected in the anticipated 2007 general election.

Generally, legislation in the provincial parliaments of Canada consists of financial legislation, the incorporation of new entities, the revision of statutes already on the books, and the consideration of reports from a variety of sources. In 2006, for example, perhaps the most significant pieces of legislation concerned some changes in the administration of workers' compensation, attempts to protect seniors from being defrauded by confidence tricksters, and the first attempts by a legislature in this country to regulate the activity referred to as 'payday loans.'

Quite apart from its legislative functions, however, parliaments serve a number of other purposes. They check and control government; they enable members to establish reputations which carry them into higher office; and they articulate the interests of numerous societal groups.

Developing an image of contemporary legislative bodies is not easy. So much of it is in the hands of the media. For example, the asserted weakness of the legislative opposition was commented on frequently by the two local papers and by the numerous electronic media. However, some groups were effective in getting attention to their views but at some cost to their legitimacy.

Perhaps the training of backbenchers and their possible recruitment through the system is a visible function of each new generation of parliamentarians attempting to find its place in the sun.

And the glittering prizes did find their way to some backbenchers this year as the premier held a Cabinet reshuffle in September. Three new women Cabinet members were sworn in, an event of great symbolic importance. Indeed, there was a story going around to the effect that because four female NDP MLAs now serving in the Doer Cabinet were from seats in Southwest Winnipeg, they ought to be collectively referred to as the 'Southern Belles.'

That day was the last in Cabinet for the Reverend Tim Sale, who had handled a number of social service portfolios. A product of Upper Canada College and the University of Toronto, he had been a social worker and Anglican priest. When first elected, he was expected to behave like a leftist lout. In fact, he became a widely liked and respected member. He had chosen to retire at that time to provide his successor with the time to get used to his portfolio before the next election.

Politics and political parties

To all intents and purposes, the NDP was unchallenged. The hackneyed phrase 'the natural governing party' came back into use. It was not, actually, a description which fits Manitoba especially well. There have been so many parties and combinations of parties holding office since 1870. In fact, if there has been a natural governing party in the half century since 1958, it has most likely been the Tories, but the fact remains that the NDP had won six of the last ten elections and was in a good position to win a seventh. In 1988 they were reduced to 12 seats, and the Liberals enjoyed a temporary vogue. Why had the New Democrats been able to recover and restore their status as one of the leading ND parties in the country?

It is perhaps fitting to start with their choice of leader in 1988. An astonishing 18 years before, they selected Gary Doer immediately following that 1988 debacle. As suggested earlier, he has frequently been named 'the most popular premier in the country.' Clearly, his rather engaging, down-to-earth personality was of immense political value to his party.

Further, he took the party from the left to the centre. It was his skill that enabled him to successfully construct a government of what a prominent Victorian historian might have described as one of 'Tory men and Whig measures.' Doer seemed free of any dint of ideological purity, preferring the more raffish turf of pragmatism.

Yet he had been able to construct a Cabinet with a wide range of opinion. For example, both the Reverend Tim Sales and Steve Ashton were regarded as on the Left but had no obvious difficulties in functioning in Cabinet.

In being a moderate, Doer was in the grand tradition of Manitoba politics, of which John Bracken was arguably the deftest exponent. Also, the prospects of any 'out party' never do seem prime following an unsuccessful election.

The Tories still appeared shell-shocked and rudderless. Their performance in the 2003 election had actually been quite creditable, and their leader, Stuart Murray, showed a refreshing candour on the issues. But a genteel and cultured man was not what the electors wanted. So, at a party annual general meeting in the fall of 2005, the Tories called for a leadership review, which quickly became a leadership selection.

The method of selecting the leader was to be one member, one vote, the process adopted by most parties in this country over the last twenty-five years. The difference is that the Manitoba PCs changed their minds several times. On this occasion, the successful candidate was the choice of the modified system in use by the federal Conservatives.

There was a noticeable lack of interest in the campaign, at least outside the party. The issues raised were the usual boring list of right-wing clichés, and there was a lack of any significant personal appeal among the candidates. The old faithful party dreadnoughts were not around this election.

The three candidates who finally decided to throw their hats into the ring were Hugh McFadyen, a lawyer, one-time curling champion, aide to Winnipeg mayor Sam Katz, and former staffer to Gary Filmon; MLA Ron Schuler, plain-spoken populist and able parliamentarian; and largely unknown Ken Waddell, who represented, or claimed to, those in the party who felt some unease about the choice.

McFadyen won quite easily on the only ballot. He headed into a legislative session which some thought might be interrupted by an election call, with Doer enjoying a huge lead in the polls. But the voters were to be spared that excitement until 2007.

Meanwhile, the Liberals soldiered on with their 2 seats. Their leader, Dr John Gerrard, appeared safe, however, and continued to wait for a miracle. Polls conducted by Probe Research for the *Winnipeg Free Press* suggested that that would be a long time in coming.

The federal election of 2006

As proof that majorities both come and go, the Liberals resumed the lack of success that had plagued them in previous elections. The Liberals lost ground, and the NDP improved somewhat. The big winners were the PCs. The Liberals and the NDP both won 3 seats in the province, the Tories 8.

In the new Cabinet, three Manitobans played a role. One was Rod Bruinooge, the Aboriginal member from Winnipeg South, who played the role of giant killer by narrowly defeating Reg Alcock. He was appointed secretary of state for Aboriginal affairs. Vic Toews, member for Provencher, was appointed to Cabinet as attorney general and also served as provincial minister. The other appointee was Steven Fletcher, the first quadriplegic ever to serve in the House of Commons and who represented Charleswood-Assiniboia in the House of Commons. He was to be secretary of state in the health ministry.

The absence of Brian Pallister, a former leadership candidate, was a surprise. Another high-profile candidate, but one who lost, was Ed Schreyer, former premier of Manitoba and governor general of Canada.

Other events

The character of a community is marked by many features. One is how it bears its pain. Every Winnipeger of decent instinct was disgusted at news of the cruel torture and death of a cute little girl called Phoenix Sinclair, aged five. Left to die on the basement floor of the slum her family occupied, her body was flung onto the rubbish dump. Her mother and her stepfather were charged with murder. What concerned many was the fact that she had many times been in the care of Child and Family Services, who had apparently not noticed the evidence of abuse.

One might also wish to see how a community displays itself. For a great many years, Winnipeg has been the butt of jokes by places such as Toronto. The name 'Manitoba' meant nothing, a situation it shared only with New Brunswick. It was decided to spice the old place up. A Madison Avenue advertising agency was hired. It did extensive research for a seven-figure sum. It was to select a slogan for the ages and set those snobbish Eastern buffoons on their ear.

The agency came up with 'spirited energy,' a slogan with neither charm nor roots. Somebody else would have to try again.

And finally, this was municipal election year. Sam Katz was re-elected in Winnipeg, although by a narrower margin than originally expected. He led a loose pro-development coalition which was in favour of turning Fort Garry Gate – the oldest part of the city, across the road from the Forks – into a condominium development. He took the same position with the parking lot at the Assiniboine Park zoo.

KEN COATES AND GREG POELZER

The Territories

After a lengthy period of slow evolution and limited national attention, the North found itself in the forefront of national and international affairs in 2006. The combination of territorial and federal elections, intense debate about international territorial politics, and passionate debates about Arctic sovereignty and climate change ensured that the North remained in the public eye throughout the year. In addition, a period of comparative prosperity and enthusiasm about Arctic resources provided the North with a new level of economic promise and opportunity.

The North in national politics

In 2006, the Canadian North burst into a prominence not known in Canada since the time of John Diefenbaker's 'Northern Vision' campaigns of the 1950s and the Mackenzie Valley Pipeline inquiry in the 1970s. The region experienced a unique conjunction of events and processes: growing concern about global warming and the impact on the Arctic, the strengthening of Indigenous governments, increased territorial assertiveness, and a major international furor over Arctic sovereignty and northern resources. After decades of struggling for national and international attention, the North found itself in the middle of an intense debate about the future and the control of the region.

The Conservative minority government, elected in January 2006, placed a very high priority on Arctic sovereignty. The Tory administration had incorporated northern issues into its 2006 election campaign, promising to strengthen northern military defenses and to assert Canadian sovereignty over the North. The commitment to spend more than $3 billion on building Arctic-capable ice-breakers and on investing heavily in northern defence infrastructure was the most substantial and focused policy pronouncement on the region in decades. Arctic debates focused in part on questions of control over the Northwest Passage: Canada claimed the waterway as inland waters; the United States asserted the right of passage to an international route. Growing Russian militarization of the Arctic, highlighted by the assertion of rights to the continental shelf towards the North Pole, raised the spectre of another Cold War. That the High Arctic contained large reserves of oil and gas, perhaps as much as a quarter of the world's undiscovered resources, gave northern issues added urgency and fueled the potential for international competition.

Prime Minister Stephen Harper visited the North to highlight his government's commitment to the region. An August 2006 trip to Ellesmere Island provided an excellent backdrop for the prime minister's call for the United States to ratify the UN Convention on the Law of the Sea and to therefore recognize Canada's claim to Maritime sovereignty. Declaring in another speech that 'you can't defend Arctic sovereignty with words alone,'[1] Harper committed the Canadian government to the improvement of the country's year-round military capabilities, providing front-line northern infrastructure and a significant investment in the Canadian Rangers, the Inuit-dominated civil defence force that assisted with military surveillance in the far North. Although the Canadian military appreciated the newfound attention to their Arctic roles and needs, other political parties urged the government to focus resources on social and economic conditions and to complete its commitments to the settlement of Indigenous claims and agreements.

Arctic sovereignty gained additional poignancy as a result of escalating concern about climate change, global warming, and the stunningly fast retreat of the Arctic ice cap. The 2006 release of Al Gore's documentary *An Inconvenient Truth*, with dramatic claims about the imminent disappearance of Arctic ice, drew international attention to the region. Scientific reports emerged at the front lines of public debate about the Arctic environment, including the *Arctic Climate Impact Assessment*, a report of the Arctic Council, largely funded by the US government. The reports documented that Arctic sea ice had fallen to an all-time low. The combination of the global threat (climate change would result in rising water levels and widespread coastal damage) and the local dislocations (with the prospect of undermining Inuit lifestyles) drew international attention to the Arctic. Aboriginal leaders, particularly Sheila Watt and Mary Simon, assumed prominent roles in the

1 Prime Minister Stephen Harper, 'Securing Canadian Sovereignty in the Arctic,' speech given in Iqaluit, Nunavut, 12 August 2006.

global political debate. Arctic temperatures seemingly rose faster than anywhere on earth, and the fragile northern ecosystem changed quickly in response to the shifting climate. Northern residents expressed strong concerns about the environment and pushed the federal government, with little success, into action.

Debate and concern about the Mackenzie Valley Pipeline continued through 2006. The long-touted project, now supported by Indigenous groups in the region who had an ownership stake in the pipeline, ran into new difficulties. Rapidly escalating costs, estimated in 2006 to be in excess of $7.5 billion, coming on the heels of a lengthy review by the National Energy Board, imperiled the undertaking, which seemed trapped in interminable delays, assessments, and public debates. With companies focusing on oil sands projects and development of the natural gas shale projects in the south, the economic viability of the undertaking seemed in doubt. The corporate sponsors, led by Imperial Oil, lobbied for government subsidies', whereas community groups, including Alternatives North, argued against using government funds to support a potentially profitable enterprise. Importantly, 2006 saw a continuation of the trend towards local engagement with the pipeline project. First Nations in the Dehcho region, including the communities of Fort Simpson and Fort Liard, considered joining the Aboriginal Pipeline Group, slated to be a substantial owner of the planned pipeline initiative.

The protracted 2006 election, following on the collapse of the minority government of Prime Minister Paul Martin, included a substantial northern component. The campaign occurred in the middle of the Canadian winter, giving a decidedly Arctic cast to the whole experience. In this instance, however, the northern flavour came from the substantial focus on issues of Arctic sovereignty, Arctic defence, Indigenous rights and aspirations, and competing strategies for the promotion of northern resource development. All three parties' leaders – Stéphane Dion, Stephen Harper, and Jack Layton – visited the North during the campaign, never a given in the south-focused realities of Canadian federal politics. The New Democratic Party focused its policy proposals on social and economic conditions in northern communities. Martin and the Liberals, building on the 2005 Kelowna Accord on Aboriginal issues, promised a substantial commitment to Indigenous self-government, education, housing, and economic development, capped by the promise of substantial increases in federal funding for Indigenous affairs. Stephen Harper and the Conservatives emphasized military investments and Arctic sovereignty, tapping into a long-standing national concern about Canada's seemingly weak hold on the Far North.

The federal election in the Yukon focused on a contest between the incumbent, popular constituency politician Larry Bagnell, long-time NDP party activist Pam Boyde, and Conservative candidate Sue Greetham. Neither the Tories nor the NDP expected to make inroads against Bagnell, who enjoyed strong support across the territory. The campaign was unremarkable and attracted little attention on the national stage, and there was no surprise when Bagnell was returned with almost 50 per cent of the total vote. Yukoners turned out in substantial numbers, with 66 per cent of eligible voters turning out to cast their ballots.

The Northwest Territories saw a dramatic turn in political fortunes. Liberal MP Ethel Blondin-Andrews had represented the riding through five successful campaigns and had risen to a minor Cabinet post as minister of state for children and youth in the Martin government. Blondin-Andrews had experienced difficult political times over the previous years, including high-profile domestic problems, but seemed a reasonable bet to hold her seat despite a very narrow victory in the previous campaign. The election was unusual in that both the Conservatives and Liberals ran Aboriginal candidates, with only the NDP running a non-Aboriginal representative. Commentators felt that Blondin-Andrews and Richard Edjericon of the Conservatives would split the Aboriginal vote, leaving the NDP to benefit from the saw-off. Dennis Bevington of the NDP ran a solid campaign, focusing in part on the incumbent's inability to deliver strong returns for the Mackenzie Valley. Richard Edjericon of the Conservatives attracted a respectable 20 per cent of the votes. However, Bevington won the seat for the NDP with more than 42 per cent of the ballots, with Blondin-Andrews well behind the winner. Blondin-Andrews was devastated by the results, clearly expecting to be returned to office and surprised by the outcome.

In Nunavut, incumbent Liberal Nancy Karetak-Lindell had a relatively easy time securing re-election for the fourth time. The territory had the lowest voter turnout in the North – only 54 per cent – but Karetak-Lindell was returned easily, gaining over 40 per cent of the total vote. David Aglukark Sr of the Conservatives polled well, attracting almost 30 per cent of the ballots, with NDP candidate Bill Riddell lagging well behind at 17 per cent. Karetak-Lindell declared that the 2006 election would be her final campaign, capping off her political career with a solid victory. The success was bittersweet for her, however, as she had to switch from the government to the Opposition benches, with Karetak-Lindell worrying that the Liberal work on the resources for the Kelowna Accord would disappear in the new government. At the end of 2006, Nancy Karetak-Lindell announced that she was stepping down at the next election.

The 2006 election, which produced a Conservative minority government after a bitter and highly personal campaign, ended with an ironic twist. The Harper Conservatives had run one of the most North-centred campaigns in recent political history and seemed genuinely committed to major and sustained investments in the North. Although the Conservative Party focused primarily on military and strategic issues, the party program called for renewed commitment to resource development and the improvement of social conditions. Now, somewhat tenuously in office, the Conservatives faced the odd challenge of implementing an aggressive northern policy program without a Conservative seat in the region. Indeed, with two Liberals and a New Democratic Party representative from the territorial North, the North seemed poised in opposition to the Conservative agenda. More than anything, the federal election of 2006 ensured that northern issues would remain prominently on the national agenda and that the diversity of northern and national perspectives on northern concerns would be well represented in the coming years.

The North remained politically engaged throughout 2006. Continuing a pattern of territorial meetings, the three northern premiers – Dennis Fentie of the Yukon, Joe Handley of the Northwest Territories (NWT), and Paul Okalik of Nunavut – met in November 2006 to continue their discussions about a northern accord. The meeting produced a substantial meeting of the minds across the North, with a strong emphasis on federal-territorial funding formulas, funding for health care, and northern perspectives on the Arctic sovereignty debate. The North attracted steady federal attention throughout the year, headed by visits from the prime minister, including a controversial stop during an International AIDS Conference in Toronto and close attention by the new Conservative minister of Indian affairs and northern development, Jim Prentice. Prentice, with long-standing experience on Aboriginal issues, turned his attention to negotiating a devolution deal with Nunavut, following on the heels of an earlier accord with the Northwest Territories. Northerners were active in the 2006 federal Liberal leadership campaign. Larry Bagnell, one of the last members of Parliament to declare a preference, threw his support behind Michael Ignatieff, and some 70 per cent of Yukon delegates followed him, only to see the political neophyte lose to Stéphane Dion.

Territorial politics

The Yukon went to the polls on 10 October 2006. Dennis Fentie, premier and leader of the Yukon Party, called the election after four years in office. The lead-up to the election had proven unusually tumultuous, even for a territory that had a track record for rejecting governments after one term. The Yukon Party lost its majority, dropping from 12 of 18 seats to 9 of 18 by 2006. NDP leader Todd Hardy learned that two of his members were in discussions about joining the Liberals. He kicked them out of the caucus, which in turn allowed the Liberals to assume the NDP's role as the official Opposition. Just before the election, John Edzerza left the Yukon Party and sat as an independent. The NDP pushed legislation to stop individuals from crossing to another political party, sparking one of the nastiest legislative debates in years. The complications facing the NDP increased when Hardy announced that he had leukemia and had to be absent from the territory for most of the election. Hardy and Fentie discussed holding back on the election until the NDP leader's treatments had finished, but the Yukon Party decided to call the election while Hardy was still under care in southern British Columbia.

With the Yukon economy doing well, even the Opposition parties recognized that they faced a formidable challenge in the effort to dislodge the government. Liberal leader Arthur Mitchell declared that his party would focus on political ethics and government accountability, only to find that their chosen campaign theme did not resonate with voters. The Liberals, NDP, and Yukon Party all ran full slates of candidates, with fourteen Aboriginal candidates contesting the election. Four independents also contested the campaign but did not play a significant role. The campaign itself followed familiar themes, with the Yukon Party favouring resource development and attracting criticism from the Liberals and NDP, as well as from environmental groups. The standard issues of health and child care, federal-territorial funding arrangements, and service delivery remained prominent in the election. Considerable attention focused on land claims or, more precisely, on the implementation of the 11 agreements signed in the territory. Small-town mayors urged parties to pay more attention to development opportunities outside of Whitehorse, but the issue did not gain much traction. The results surprised most observers, who thought the Fentie administration had alienated voters. The Yukon Party, capitalizing on their 'open for business' message, secured another majority when they won 10 of 18 seats and pulled in 40 per cent of the territorial vote. The Liberals finished second with 35 per cent of the vote and 5 seats. The NDP, led by Todd Hardy, who fought the campaign while coping with cancer, gained only 3 seats and 24 per cent of the vote. Two of the contests ended up with less than a 10-vote differential, requiring official recounts, but neither result changed.

The Yukon Party government maintained an active agenda throughout 2006. The territorial government re-established elected government in Dawson City, giving the scandal-plagued community a new chance to run their affairs, as well as providing the municipality substantial debt relief. The government spent extensively through the year, tabling a $600 million budget and then requesting another $100 million near the end of the year. The budget, in turn, reflected substantial improvements in the federal government's allocation to the territory. The government, meeting with First Nations at the innovative Yukon Forum, debated how best to allocate the new funding. The Yukon Forum allocated much of the money to housing projects, mostly on First Nations lands, and a series of other major initiatives. The government also kept alive the potential Alaska – Canada rail link, a long-discussed project designed to stimulate economic development throughout the territory, and opened a climate change research centre at Yukon College.

Public affairs in the Northwest Territories lacked the turmoil and excitement of the Yukon. Much of the political attention focused on municipal elections. October elections brought substantial changes. Yellowknife mayor Gordon Van Tighem returned by acclamation. Two mayors – Anne Marie Tout of Norman Wells, Diana Ehman of Hay River – lost their seats. More generally, officials were concerned about the very poor turnout for the municipal and local participation rates. Communities that had formerly attracted up to 80 per cent of voters to the polls fell to around 30 per cent in 2006.

Aboriginal land claims remained a prominent issue, particularly because of the continued difficulties securing an agreement with the strategically located Dehcho First Nation. This group, whose traditional territories included 40 per cent of the Mackenzie Valley Pipeline corridor and who had been reluctant to agree to the pipeline project, once again were unable to agree to terms with the government of Canada, turning down an offer for 39,000 square kilometres and $104 million in cash. The strength of the territorial diamond mining sector – up to the third-largest in the world in 2006 – kept the NWT economy on a positive trajectory. Diamond exports reached $1.7 billion by 2005, with production surging but returns from the resource declining. The success of diamond mining ensured a steadily increasing territorial GDP at almost three times the national rate, sparking a solid and continued increase – 21 per cent in 2006 – in housing prices, almost double the national rate, and leaving the territory with the second-highest housing prices in Canada.

Political affairs in Nunavut focused on a uniquely northern balance between the intensely local and the increasingly international. Inuit leaders such as Paul Okalik participated actively in climate change debates, arguing that the excesses of southern, industrial societies had placed the Arctic at risk. Inuit leaders also devoted a great deal of effort to contesting European attempts to shut down the seal trade and to further control the polar bear. At the opposite extreme, some residents complained about the re-election of James Arvaluk from Pond Inlet in an October 2006 by-election, pointing out that he had twice been convicted of violent offences. There were other changes in the territorial assembly, with Peter Kilabuk (Pangnirtung) leaving Cabinet and Tununiq MLA Jobie Nutarak, the Speaker, dying in a snowmobile accident and being replaced by Patterk Netster of the Nanulik constituency. The Nunavut self-government initiative, seven years old in 2006, was proceeding unevenly, with the high costs amplified by serious problems with program delivery. Indeed, the Canadian auditor general, Sheila Fraser, argued for the recentralization of Nunavut services in order to bring costs under control. Negotiations on devolution restarted late in 2006, providing some reason for hope that the structural and financial challenges in the territory would be addressed.

The political affairs of the Inuit Tapiriit Kanatami (ITK), the organization charged with coordinating the work of the Inuit land claims organizations, remained of critical importance in Nunavut. Jose Kusugak resigned the presidency in 2006. At the annual general meeting, the ITK selected Mary Simon to assume the post. Already a prominent northern leader, Mary Simon used the presidency of the ITK to promote Inuit concerns on a national and international scale and to solidify the gains made through the land claims settlements. Simon launched several outspoken critiques of the Conservative government, criticizing them for abandoning the Kelowna Accord and not paying sufficient attention to Indigenous issues. That a great deal of work remained to be done was revealed late in the year when the Nunabut Tunngavik Inc. sued the government of Canada, claiming that the government had not followed through on its commitments to implementing the land claims agreement.

Economy

Economically, the territorial North enjoyed one of its most successful years in decades. In the Northwest Territories, the development and operations of the diamond mines, heavy investment in mineral explorations, and the continual prospect of the development of the Mackenzie Valley Pipeline sparked a territory-wide boom. The Yukon experienced comparable opportunities, with a strong tourism sector combining with high commodity prices to produce a very strong economy. Nunavut remained the economically weakest of the territories, although mineral and diamond properties held some promise. High levels of unemployment remained endemic, with local Inuit residents experiencing continued difficulties finding work and maintaining decent incomes.

In the Yukon, public-sector employment continued to dominate and the territory enjoyed a solid year in terms of employment, with most of the improvement coming from the resource field. The Yukon had the second-highest employment rate in Canada (behind Alberta), in large part because of the comparative youthfulness of the population. However, the territory had an unemployment rate of 9.4 per cent, the sixth-highest rate in Canada, which in turn represented a sharp decline from the previous year. Despite a higher-than-Canadian-average unemployment rate, the Yukon faced a labour shortage, particularly in skilled trades. Overall, the economy was reasonably strong but with a slight dip in 2006. The territory's GDP exceeded $1.5 billion, an increase of 4.8 per cent over the previous year. The growth rate of 2.9 per cent paralleled that of Canada as a whole. A decline in non-residential construction was the primary factor in the territory's slowing expansion.

NWT residents had the highest per capita income in the county, with an average income of over $44,000. Individuals with a bachelor's degree earned over $94,000 on average. The community of Norman Wells, a key oil centre in the central Mackenzie Valley, had an average family income of over $130,000. Families in the regional centres of Inuvik, Fort Simpson, and Hay River exceeded $90,000 per year. As in the Yukon, public administration remained the dominant sector, with almost 22 per cent of all employees; close to 10 per cent were on social assistance. Unemployment, at 10.4 per cent, was fourth highest in Canada. Territorial GDP grew at a rate of 2.9 per cent and topped out at over $4 billion, largely on the basis of a surge in non-residential construction related to the resource sector. This produced a per capita GDP of over $98,000, a full $28,000 more than Alberta and more than double the Canadian average. Mining declined slightly in 2006, as did government spending. DeBeer's Snap Lake diamond mine was expected to come into production in 2007, promising another surge in territorial economic activity.

Nunavut struggled to keep up with the Yukon, not to mention the increasingly prosperous Northwest Territories. The territory's GDP jumped 3.4 per cent, largely on the basis of the opening of Tahera's new Jericho diamond mine and development of the Meadowbank and Doris North gold properties. The opening of the mines included a commitment to training positions for 60 Kivalliq Inuit. Promising reports related to the Baffinland Iron Mines Corporation's Mary River property pointed to a potentially profitable mine with major investments in infrastructure needed to bring the order to the coast at Milne Bay.

Outside of the mining sector, however, business interest in the territory remained stagnant, continuing a half-decade-long pattern of limited investment. Unemployment remained very high, at more than 14 per cent, although that number left out the large number of residents who had ceased looking for work. Indeed, the employment rate in the territory – at only 60 per cent – ran well behind the comparable figures in the other territories. Educational attainment, a key differentiator on income, remained the lowest in Canada, with the government of Nunavut investing substantial resources in adult upgrading and technical training. High school, college, and university graduates in Nunavut had the highest average income of any comparable group in the country. (The high incomes, of course, were offset by the highest food and subsistence costs in Canada.)

Social issues

Social conditions continued to shift slowly through the North. One of the most promising developments was a sharp decline in northern and national crime rates in 2006. The national rate fell by 3 per cent to the lowest point in a quarter century. The decline in the North was even greater, with the Yukon recording a drop of 9 per cent, Nunavut down a full 11 per cent, and the Northwest Territories falling 5 per cent. Given the continual debate about endemic and high crime rates across the North, the news was certainly welcome.

The Yukon remained a unique society. Over half of all Yukoners over 15 years old had post-secondary training, the highest rate in the country.

Over 20 per cent had a university degree, but only the same number of Yukoners with post-secondary education had actually completed their studies in the territory, many of whom came from other parts of Canada. The nature of NWT society continued to change through 2006. The level of educational attainment improved steadily, with some 67 per cent of territorial residences holding a certificate, diploma, or degree. Not surprisingly, there were substantial regional variations in educational background. In Yellowknife, 81 per cent of residents over 15 years had such a qualification; in the smaller communities, over 45 per cent of residents did not have a certificate, diploma, or degree.

Nunavut residents struggled with serious social conditions. Housing shortages plagued all the communities in the territory. Indeed, almost 40 per cent of the people lived in crowded conditions, 13 times higher than the national average. (If there was a silver lining in the housing crisis, it was the fact that many youth had extended family members with them, able to assist with language and cultural learning.) The new Conservative federal government responded to the crisis, allocating $300 million to the three territories for housing, providing Nunavut with sufficient funds to add 725 units. The same percentage – 40 per cent – experienced food shortage with some regularity. These statistics covered only one part of the sociopathology of Nunavut, however, for the territory's residents continued to struggle with ill health, criminal behaviour, alcohol-related crises, and rampant teenage pregnancy. Youth suicide, with most victims between ages 14 and 24, remained a serious issue.

Language proved equally controversial in 2006. Thomas Berger, who had a long association with major initiatives in the North, released a key report on language and education in Nunavut, pointing out the fundamental challenges of combining Inuktituk teaching with job-ready skills and arguing $20 million a year was required to address the problem. Nunavut faced a formidable balancing act as they sought to protect their threatened language while ensuring that youth had reasonable career possibilities. The Berger Report also pointed out how crucial education was to the future of the territory. Although Inuit people constituted four-fifths of the population of the territory, they made up only about half of the civil service, by far the largest employer. Moreover, among those positions with the civil service, most were at lower levels. The lack of skilled personnel also created another problem. Most Inuit residents with university education came through teacher education programs. Instead of going into the teaching profession, many were 'poached' by government and other employers, thus exacerbating the problem with providing Inuit education at the K – 12 system. These challenges, common to all three territories, were particularly acute in Nunavut.

The North found itself in the national and international spotlight throughout 2006. The combination of the Arctic sovereignty and security debate, diamond mining, the unrealized oil and gas potential of the High Arctic, and the complexities of Indigenous politics created both controversy and a growing sense of opportunity in the North. All three territories experienced significant political challenges in 2006, in part because of the changes associated with the federal election and growing international concern about climate change and Indigenous rights. Internally, the long-standing struggles of economic instability, social and cultural challenges, and administrative change left the North with a sense of perpetual transition and undercut what should have been a profound sense of accomplishment. Although the growing attention being given to northern affairs helped Indigenous and territorial leaders gain access to the global media, another potentially disruptive process emerged in this period. The Arctic had become an international battleground, with national governments, including many outside the circumpolar region, taking an active interest in the region. Rather significantly, 2006 represented a possible turning point in northern affairs with the territories potentially losing control of the political agenda and with international priorities replacing Northern concerns.

ROBERT DRUMMOND

Ontario

In 2006 the Ontario government continued to face challenges in the areas of education and health – its two most expensive (and arguably most important) portfolios – and it persisted in attempts to address questions of supply and demand in the market for electricity. While the inquiry continued into the 1995 events during a First Nations occupation of the provincial park at Ipperwash, a new occupation by members of an Aboriginal community – this time of a residential building site – began in Caledonia, near Hamilton. Other issues involving First Nations communities and land claims also surfaced during the year, with the constitutional issue of responsibility – federal or provincial – complicating any resolution. Although the government again found itself with a lower-than-expected shortfall in its accounts, it was reluctant to predict an earlier end to deficit budgets, and it faced demands for assistance from troubled industries – most notably the forestry sector in northwestern Ontario. It also carried on – with little success – its campaign to persuade Ottawa and the other provinces that Ontario deserved more resources from the federal government. Diverse issues of environment, justice, and social services expanded the range of political concerns making news during the year, with considerable attention being paid to the certainty that the next provincial election would occur in the fall of 2007. Provincial politics was conducted through most of the year against the backdrop of a federal Liberal Party leadership race. One of the candidates, Gerard Kennedy, began the year as a Cabinet minister in the McGuinty government, and another was former Ontario NDP premier Bob Rae, who had crossed the floor to join the federal Liberals.

The Thirty-Eighth Provincial Parliament continued its second session when it resumed sitting on 13 February. During the calendar year, the legislature passed 36 public bills, including significant changes to the Ontario Human Rights Commission, extension of Occupational Health and Safety legislation to farm workers, consumer protection legislation in several areas, lengthening of normal terms for municipal councils, and changes to the taxing authority of the city of Toronto. One of the potentially most interesting actions taken was the creation of a Citizens' Assembly with a mandate to review the electoral system of the province and make recommendations for possible revisions of that system. Such recommendations were expected to be made in time to be put before the electorate in a referendum accompanying the 2007 provincial election.

In the course of the year, there were some departures from the House and some new faces coming into play. In March by-elections were held to replace members who had left to run federal office; there were no changes in party control of Ottawa-Nepean and Whitby-Ajax, which remained in Conservative hands, or Toronto-Danforth, which stayed with the NDP. A by-election to replace Gerard Kennedy in Parkdale – High Park moved the seat from the Liberal to the NDP column. In September Joe Cordiano resigned for personal reasons and Cam Jackson and Tony Wong gave up their seats to run for municipal office. Finally Greg Sorbara, who had left Cabinet in 2005 because of being named in a search warrant, returned to the finance portfolio in May after Justice Ian Nordheimer concluded that there were insufficient grounds for his inclusion in the warrant. His return led to a mini-shuffle as Dwight Duncan returned to energy, Donna Cansfield went to transportation, and Harinder Takhar (who had been reprimanded by the ethics commissioner for what Takhar called an honest mistake) was given a new portfolio of small business and entrepreneurship, carved out of economic development and trade. In the area of trade, the premier had taken an unusual step in April when he appointed former Conservative premier Ernie Eves to head a new Investment and Trade Council to promote investment in the province.

The provincial auditor general took early retirement in April, in order not to suffer a pension penalty, but the new auditor general ended the year with a similar list of concerns about wasteful spending, including charges without receipts, questionable expenditures by teachers and school board staff, and hundreds of thousands of unaccounted for OHIP cards in circulation.

Near the end of the year, it was announced that the long-serving president of the Ontario Public Service Employees Union, Leah Casselman, would not stand for election to another term. Her experience and dedication would be missed – almost certainly on both sides of the table.

Health

The government and Opposition seemed to agree on the use of 'wait times' as a means of assessing improvements in health care delivery, and in mid-January the government committed $19.8 million to improving waiting time for access to cancer treatment and a further $2 million to improve access to hip and knee replacement surgery. By 27 April Cancer Care Ontario was reporting that wait times for radiation had been decreasing while those for chemotherapy remained stable, in spite of increasing demand for both. The following day, health minister George Smitherman announced that Ontario would spend a further $222.5 million to reduce patient wait times for cataract and cancer surgeries, hip and knee replacements, cardiac procedures, and MRI exams. He observed that wait times for cancer surgery and cardiac procedures were now within national guidelines and that wait times for cataract surgery and hip and knee replacements were decreasing when they had previously been on the rise. Nearer the end of the year (8 Dec.) the government announced it would commission an independent audit of the way in which wait times for diagnostic tests (such as MRI exams) were being calculated. They named Liberal senator Michael Kirby as the person to conduct the audit; however, Opposition critics questioned Kirby's independence and suggested that his Liberal ties meant his report would lack credibility. The report was expected in early 2007.

In mid-April, the government introduced legislation that would significantly affect the provision of prescription pharmaceuticals in the province. The first concern of the legislation was to press the drug companies to provide the government with discounted drugs for its Drug Benefit plan for seniors and persons on social assistance. A second issue was the intention to allow pharmacists to substitute generic drugs for brand-name drugs when filling prescriptions. The legislation would also establish a new drug program CEO who would make decisions more quickly about which drugs the province would fund. He / she would also have the responsibility of advising the public why the province had elected *not* to fund a particular drug. A citizens' council would be created to advise the government on drug policy.

A controversial element of the bill was a provision that would end the system of rebates paid to local pharmacists by generic drug companies. However, the health minister sought to soften that blow by providing funds to pay pharmacists for counseling patients about chronic diseases. The preference for generic drugs was a concern to several patient groups, while the manufacturers and distributors of brand-name drugs made the usual observation that the preference for generics would reduce incentives for brand-name companies to spend on research and development of new medications. The health minister first chided the drug companies, urging them to tone down the rhetoric in opposition to the bill. (One CEO had compared the proposed legislation to the cancellation of the AVRO Arrow in the 1950s.) He then dismissed patient concerns, saying the generic products were deemed to be the same as the brand-name counterparts. By mid-May the local pharmacists, who had been pleased by the prospect of funds to counsel patients, were objecting to the loss of rebates from the generic drug firms, on the grounds that their fees and business plans were based in the expectation of those rebates. In response, the government moved in early June to amend the bill and include the possibility of 'professional allowances' of up to 20 per cent of the value of drugs purchased from a generic producer.

A number of matters related to the organization of health care delivery were issues during 2006. In early January the province announced the creation of an independent, not-for-profit cataract surgery clinic, licensed by the government and with funding provided by the health insurance plan, to consolidate surgeries from four area hospitals in one location, which could also serve as a teaching site for the ophthalmology residents in the University of Toronto's Faculty of Medicine.

In mid-January a coalition of health care workers represented by several different unions expressed their view that the newly designed Local Health Integration Networks might result in reduced services to patients. The report had little traction and the province proceeded with those networks.

In late January the province was given the go-ahead to close the three remaining institutions for the care of developmentally disabled adults. Residents would, with their consent, be relocated either to group homes or to the homes of relatives.

On 30 January the government announced it was starting a pilot project in four Toronto hospitals intended to test a means of reducing the burden on emergency rooms. At three of the hospitals there would be special emergency care centres established. At the fourth, pre-admission and pre-discharge lounges would be established for patients to be seen and admitted (or discharged) more quickly. In other hospitals, the province also undertook to establish emergency care for in-patients to prevent complications that would prolong their hospital stays.

In an area where action was called for but not rapidly pursued, the province had scrapped the system in place for auditing bills of physicians, following the recommendations of former Supreme Court Justice Peter Cory, but by October they still had not moved to replace the system with an improved version. In December, it was announced that a new audit system had finally been designed in consultation with the Ontario Medical Association. In general the system had the approval of physicians and was set to be implemented in 2007.

Movement had been somewhat quicker in the area of home health care. The province accepted 68 of 70 recommendations in a report on home care by Eleanor Caplan, former provincial and federal Cabinet minister; they allocated some $30 million to implement the recommendations as part of an overall commitment of $117.8 for home care and community support. The NDP in opposition remained critical of the competitive bidding process – for home care providers seeking contracts with Community Care Access Centres – introduced by the Harris government and retained after the Liberals took office. The system, in their view, increased the proportion of for-profit care in the system, which they saw as involving extra costs that did not contribute to quality of care. They also saw the bidding system as destabilizing, in that long-term home care patients might have developed relationships with caregivers who were replaced when their firms lost contracts. The changes did not do away with the competitive bidding, whose proponents argued it facilitated cost containment.

In May there were complaints from nurses that the province was not keeping a promise to hire 8,000 more nurses as soon as possible. The Ontario Nurses Association (ONA) sent 8,000 signed postcards from their members to highlight the issue. The health minister asserted that 4,000 additional nurses had been hired since the Liberal takeover, with more to come, but the ONA and the NDP disputed the number, saying that there were nurses being laid off in some jurisdictions. Shelley Martel, the NDP health critic, was quoted as saying that at least 1,000 recent hires had been for short-term (three- or six-month) positions rather than for permanent employment (*Canadian Press*, 1 May). On 3 May it was reported that Ontario was seeking medical professionals abroad, which led the Registered Nurses Association to observe that such recruiting sent a negative signal to those currently employed (as well as qualified local personnel seeking work).

On 2 May the province announced a tentative collective agreement between the Ontario Hospital Association (OHA), representing 43 hospitals, and the union representing 6,500 technical personnel. However, the nurses and the OHA declared an impasse in contract negotiations at the end of May, inviting the health minister to intervene. Earlier in the month, the minister had offered a full-time job guarantee to all new nursing graduates, but that did not lead to a resolution of contract issues for those currently employed. On 15 July CUPE and the OHA reached a three-year agreement covering non-medical hospital staff which was ratified four days later. It was 3 November, however, before any deal involving nurses was settled, and then it was only for some 1,200 nurses employed in long-term care facilities. By December, the contract for some 50,000 hospital nurses had been submitted to arbitration, but on the thirteenth of the month the arbitrator announced his decision would be held over until 2007.

In late January a Vancouver company announced plans to open three clinics in Ontario at which they would charge patients a registration fee of $1,200 and a further membership fee of $2,300 per year. The fee was considered by critics to be a means of giving people with money a chance of jumping the queue for health care. The clinics promised patients proper access to medical expertise and more time with their doctors. A lobby group on health care, the Ontario Health Coalition, secured a legal opinion that the clinics could be in violation of the Canada Health Act and Ontario's Commitment to the Future of Medicare Act. CEO Don Copeman argued that because he would bill OHIP for medically necessary services, he was within the Canada Health Act; however, Health Minister Smitherman warned that fines were possible if the additional fee for patients was seen as extra-billing for insured services. The firm planned to open the clinics by the end of the summer, but a revised timetable in late August suggested the Toronto clinic would open in late December or early January and the London and Ottawa locations by May 2007. At that point it was also announced that two additional Ontario locations were under consideration – one in Windsor and the other in Kitchener – to be opened in early 2008. On 6 October Matthew Sylvain reported in the *Medical Post* that Copeman was having difficulty opening because of problems finding suitable real estate, as well as the concerns of the health ministry that his business plan comply with the law. The main concern of the ministry was the annual fee to be charged to patients. Copeman said the money was to help support annual salaries physicians in the clinic would receive over and above the billings for insured services they would be obliged to charge OHIP. The fees, he argued, were legal because 'we are mostly focused on primary prevention and inter-professional care of chronic diseases but in the noninsured areas.' He further asserted that he would not be attracting physicians to leave the public system but rather bringing a net addition of comprehensive family physicians to the community. The health minister remained skeptical and at year end was bemoaning the proliferation of private clinics and insisting that there was no acceptance by the Ontario government of private fees for insured services.

The ban on smoking in public places and work sites, passed in 2005, required support during 2006, and the government committed $3.8 million in May to combat teen smoking and a further $5.5 million to local public health units for costs of enforcing the ban. Then in September, movie actor Sean Penn lit up a cigarette while being interviewed by the press in the Sutton Place Hotel during the Toronto International Film Festival. The hotel was fined for failing to stop him, and Toronto medical officer of health David McKeown undertook to write a letter of reprimand to Mr Penn. No one was under any illusion that the letter would alter the actor's behaviour, but at least the city and the province would send the message that no one was exempt from the law.

On 17 January provincial medical officer of health Sheela Basrur issued her first report to the Ontario Legislature. In her report she called on the province to deal with the shortage of public health workers and the paucity of appropriate technology to ensure that the province would be able to cope with an outbreak of infectious disease. She acknowledged that the province was better prepared than it had been in 2003 when SARS hit, but she insisted more needed to be done. In March a Task Force on Agency Implementation issued the last part of its report to Basrur. It called for the creation of an arm's-length public health agency that would function as a hub allowing multiple government departments to tap into a single database for scientific data and research. As described by Lauren la Rose of *Canadian Press*, the agency would provide laboratory services and technical support to local public health units and would 'specialize in infectious diseases, health promotion, chronic diseases, injury prevention and environmental health' (20 March). The report also called for modernizing the Ontario public health laboratories, which task force co-chair Dr Terry Sullivan called 'the invisible workhorses' of the province's surveillance system. He recommended the labs be transferred to the new agency's jurisdiction in a phased process by the end of 2008. On 10 December Ontario announced the creation of the Agency for Health Protection and Promotion modelled on the Centers for Disease Control in the United States. This agency was intended to satisfy many of the recommendations of the task force report.

On 6 December the province's much-respected chief medical officer of health, Dr Sheela Basrur, stepped down from her position in order to begin treatment for a rare form of cancer. Sympathy for her personal situation was compounded by concerns about the effect of her absence on the future of public health in the province.

Education

Much of the attention to education in 2006 was in the post-secondary system, as the government announced new tuition fees for universities and colleges and the faculty at the Colleges of Applied Arts and Technology went on strike in the early part of the year. Issues in the primary and secondary systems were more diverse, with only substitute teachers being involved in labour contract matters.

In mid-January the education minister, Gerard Kennedy, indicated he would be allowing local school boards to set salaries for their members (trustees). The compensation had been set at a maximum of $5,000 by the Harris government, and it was suggested that it might go up to between $18,000 and $20,000 in some jurisdictions. The move to a low fixed rate had been intended to emphasize the part-time nature of the role and to have boards seen as more akin to advisory bodies than governance councils. In large municipalities, however, the responsibilities of the boards were such that a higher remuneration was thought necessary to attract good candidates. When a wide-ranging education bill was passed in June, one of its provisions was the right of school boards to set trustee remuneration, provided they had first conducted public consultations.

On 31 January the Elementary Teachers Federation of Ontario asked substitute teachers not to accept employment with the Lambton-Kent District board. They promised similar requests were forthcoming for Toronto District and Simcoe County boards. Contracts for 'occasional' teachers had expired on 31 August 2004. At issue were better daily schedules, improved pay, and better access to full-time jobs, but behind those issues, according to the union, was a desire to see substitute teachers treated as professionals, equal to those holding full-time positions. The union took out a series of radio advertisements with the message, 'There's no substitute for a substitute teacher.' By 24 April all but three boards had reached settlements, and on 9 May the last remaining local without a contract (Near North, representing some 275 'occasional' teachers) began rotating strikes. After some breakdowns in negotiations a settlement was finally achieved on 29 May.

Therapy for autistic children, identified as an educational access issue, continued as a concern in 2006. According to NDP critic Shelley

Martel, quoted by Angela Pacienza, the government had budgeted $89 million in 2003–4 and had not used some $32 million, whereas in 2004–5, they had budgeted $89 million but had diverted $21 million to other children's programmes in the Ministry of Children and Youth Services (*Canadian Press*, 26 May). According to Martel, the waiting lists for children needing autism treatment continued to grow during those years. According to the government, wait times for assessment had been reduced by close to 70 per cent and the 2005–6 budget for autism intervention had been fully spent – indeed overspent by some $6 million. Ministry spokesperson James Ip was quoted as saying the government was making progress and that the current budget was over $100 million, covering assessments, speech programmes, therapy, and other services. On 16 June the government announced a further $13.1 million for autism therapy.

The issue continued to get attention through the summer, and in late August, Shelley Martel again assailed the government for its record in addressing autism. Quoted by Keith Leslie she asserted that some $67.2 million promised for autism programming since 2003 had been spent elsewhere, while the number of children waiting for treatment had gone from 76 to 753 since the Liberals had come into office (*Canadian Press*, 29 Aug.). The government argued that past under-spending had been, in part, due to the lack of qualified therapists and that some the current budget of over $112 million was being devoted to training such personnel. The promise to ensure that all autistic children got the treatment they required had been a pre-election commitment of the premier in 2003.

In late June a task force formed to review the Safe Schools policy initially introduced by the Harris government reported, calling for changes in the 'zero tolerance' act, which they said was not working. Education minister Sandra Pupatello (who had replaced Gerard Kennedy when he stepped down to run for the federal Liberal leadership) said the report would be considered over the summer and changes would be forthcoming in the fall. Further action on the report was somewhat delayed when Pupatello moved to economic development and trade in mid-September to replace Joe Cordiano, and Kathleen Wynne – not previously in Cabinet – became the new education minister.

Post-secondary students had been warned that the tuition freeze established in 2004 would not continue in 2006–7, and on 7 March Chris Bentley, minister of training, colleges, and universities, indicated that the tuition announcement would be forthcoming the following day. When the tuition announcement came, it included differential increases for new students and continuing students, as well as different maxima for regulated programs (such as arts and sciences) and partially deregulated programs (such as law and graduate business). The overall annual increases in any institution were to be limited to 5 per cent, but most upper-year undergraduates would see increases of 4 per cent per annum. Universities were required to guarantee through bursaries that qualified students would not be denied access because of financial need, and the province increased the availability of grants under the Ontario Student Assistance Programme (OSAP) by capping its debt at $7,000 per year. They promised $1.5 billion in student aid over five years and increased book and supply allowances in the program.

Predictably student groups opposed the increases and regretted the end of the tuition freeze, whereas post-secondary institutions indicated they would necessarily take advantage of the maximum permitted increase because of rising costs. The province required institutions to sign accountability agreements showing how the additional fees would improve quality, accessibility, and affordability. They also announced the creation of a Higher Education Quality Council to monitor quality and access. On 15 May they announced the council would be headed by former Supreme Court of Canada justice Frank Iacobucci.

On the day before the tuition announcement, faculty in the Colleges of Applied Arts and Technology (CAAT) went out on strike, calling for smaller classes and more full-time appointments. Approximately 150,000 students across the province were affected. The parties agreed to resume talks on 20 March to seek an end to the strike, but talks broke off two days later. The union called for binding arbitration, for which the college employers suggested final offer selection. Eventually the parties agreed instead to a mediation-arbitration process and the striking faculty returned to work. On 28 June the arbitrator announced a settlement with wage increases of 15.3 per cent over four years, with a task force being struck to consider workload issues.

In early September, it was observed that the students in the 'double cohort' (created by the abolition of grade 13) were now approaching graduate school. (Indeed, the double cohort was partly responsible for the fact that CAAT and university enrolment in the province was at a record high in September.) The question was raised whether there would be sufficient space in graduate programmes for all who qualified. On 20 September the province announced plans to add $240 million in new post-secondary funding to provide 12,000 additional graduate school spaces over a two-year period.

Energy

An almost constant concern during the year was the question of electricity supply. Efforts to replace coal-fired generating capacity through the development of renewable sources such as wind, water, and solar power were challenged by the relatively small amount of energy that could be so produced. On the other hand, nuclear power, which could be produced plentifully, required significant capital investment and created substantial and long-dangerous residue.

In January the government promised that there would be public hearings before any further investment in nuclear power was undertaken. Critics of the nuclear option expressed the fear that consultation would be rushed and that the decision had already been made.

In early February the government announced plans to pay consumers to create solar energy of up to ten megawatts, surplus to their own requirements, and to convey the extra to the provincial power grid. The same day, the Independent Electricity System Operator (IESO) urged that the coal-fired plants at Lambton and Nanticoke remain available in case of peak demand, and the energy minister indicated that might be done. The plants at Thunder Bay, Lambton, and Atikokan were to close by 2007 and Nanticoke in 2009. Around the same time, the government announced plans to build a natural gas electricity plant in downtown Toronto, despite opposition from the mayor.

Some of the challenges of developing new supply were highlighted in early April when Stephen Snyder, CEO of the Calgary-based Trans-Alta Corporation, urged Ontario to scrap price caps on electricity. Only by doing so, he said, could Ontario encourage the investment needed to refurbish or replace 80 per cent of generating capacity over the next fifteen years. Energy minister Donna Cansfield indicated the hybrid market would remain and said that the supply situation was in hand. She cited recent investment of $3 billion in renewable energy sources alone. Trans-Alta, however, had suspended further investment in Ontario until the province's long-term regulatory plan was clear.

On 10 April the Association of Major Power Consumers urged the province to keep coal-fired generators open, arguing that natural gas was more expensive and nuclear was slow to come on line and that if rates increased, jobs would be lost. But later in the month the premier expressed his view that nuclear power might be the province's best option, again leading critics to wonder if the decision to pursue nuclear had already been made. Shortly after the premier's musing, the Power Workers Union added their voice to the call for maintaining coal-fired plants, suggesting that blackouts could be expected if the plans to close all the plants proceeded on schedule. In June, the *Toronto Star* was still speculating that the premier was 'poised' to announce plans to continue with the development of nuclear power plants. If the province was to follow the Ontario Power Authority (OPA) recommendation to rely on nuclear power for 50 per cent of its electricity, some existing plants would need to be refurbished and at least one further plant with two reactors created. It was reported that six sites were under consideration, with environmental assessments to be requested for more than one. The government was said to favour an expansion at Darlington, where land was available and community authorities were favourably disposed.

On 12 April the Ontario Energy Board announced electricity rate increases to take effect 1 May. Depending on local utility charges, consumers might face increases of between 3 and 15 per cent.

In early June, Dwight Duncan (who had returned to the energy portfolio) reaffirmed the province's plan to close all coal-fired plants. Furthermore, he responded to questions of nuclear power by saying that he would 'soon' provide a response to the December 2005 report of the OPA concerning the proportion of electricity generation that could be expected from various sources. He also suggested there might be some 'streamlining' of the environmental assessment process for some generating facilities, leading environmentalists to be concerned that the law was being watered down for these projects. A couple of days later, after *Canadian Press* reported unnamed sources said the IESO had overestimated supply and underestimated demand, Duncan indicated that the closure of the Lambton and Nanticoke coal-fired plants might have to be postponed – Lambton beyond 2007 and Nanticoke beyond 2009.

There was of course a relationship between supply and aspects of demand, including the cost of power and efforts to conserve electricity. On 16 January the IESO reported that between 12 April and 31 December 2005 Ontario consumers had been charged some $384 million less for electricity than it had cost to produce and supply it – a difference of about $60 in a typical household. The rates that the OEB established to take effect 1 May 2006 were to reflect the shortfall. However, on 9 February, the province extended the price caps that had resulted in rebates to households to cover large consumers (mainly firms) as well.

In late September, the IESO announced that electricity demand had reached a record level on 1 August but had fallen so low during the Labour Day weekend that for one hour the price of electricity had actually been negative. (Large industrial consumers would receive a credit for that hour.) On a more general note, the *Globe and Mail* reported December 15 that the four agencies that had been created on the break-up of Ontario Hydro had cost 50 per cent more than Ontario Hydro since 1998.

First Nations

In January hearings resumed before Justice Linden's Commission of Inquiry into the 1995 events at Ipperwash Provincial Park. Robert Runciman, former Cabinet member in the Harris government, testified early in the month concerning the meeting that had been held among political officials, police representatives, and civil servants just prior to the night on which Dudley George had been killed. He denied that Premier Harris had used an obscenity in urging the removal of the Indians from the park, and he testified that the sense of urgency that earlier witnesses had described was a result of fears that the situation might drag on for some time and deteriorate into a more violent and / or intractable dispute. Chris Hodgson, another former Harris Cabinet member, testified later that week and denied that either he or the premier had used the obscenity earlier witnesses had attributed to one or another of them. He went on to testify that he had not wanted to be the government's spokesperson on the file and that he had followed a 'script' in delivering his messages. He described the occupation of the park as illegal and did not qualify the statement by noting that was the government's legal opinion rather than an agreed fact. Crown prosecutors had dropped charges against the occupiers of the park on the grounds that they had a sincere belief that their actions were not illegal and that the park contained burial grounds that should be returned to the Indian band. Federal documents later sustained the position that the park included burial sites.

OPP superintendent Tony Parkin testified in early February that there had been considerable misinformation prior to the OPP's entry to the park. It was reported that a car had been attacked by men wielding baseball bats; it turned out to be a case of one man having thrown a stone at a car. The occupiers were reported to be armed; they were not. Women and children were reported to be leaving the park, suggesting the occupiers were planning violent action. No such evacuation had taken place.

On 14 February former premier Harris began his testimony before the inquiry. He began by denying that he had used an obscenity in urging the Indians' removal. And he suggested that the police official who had described the government's approach as 'redneck' had it all wrong. He denied taking a hard line or in any way influencing police. On the final day of his testimony it was reported he would face a 'truth ceremony' mounted by Aboriginal observers on his entry to the inquiry site. The implication was that his testimony was not believed by the First Nations group. When he left the building after his testimony, he faced catcalls and accusations of lying from assembled protesters. In his testimony he again denied that he had tried to influence police, and his lawyer observed that no one had challenged that claim in cross-examination. He insisted that he had wanted the 'illegal' occupation ended quickly but that he had known he had no authority to direct police operations. He asserted that he would not change a thing about his handling of the situation. Speaking to reporters after the hearing, he stated that he had appreciated the opportunity to give testimony on his and his government's side of the story and that he hoped the George family would get the information they wanted.

In early June Premier McGuinty accused the Conservatives of not having learned the lesson of Ipperwash as they counselled strong action against a new group of native protesters. Conservative leader John Tory accused the premier of prejudging the results of the inquiry, and former premier Harris's lawyer issued an open letter to the premier asserting that his remarks had been defamatory and that if he made them outside the legislature he could expect legal action.

On 24 August the inquiry came to the end of its hearings and Mr Justice Linden retired to prepare his report. It was expected not to be issued until sometime in 2007.

Well before the Ipperwash inquiry came to an end, the government was faced with its own occupation of disputed lands by native protesters. On 28 February a group of Six Nations protesters occupied a housing construction site in Caledonia, near Hamilton. They alleged that the land in question was theirs, whereas the province said it had been sold (not leased) for a transportation corridor in the 1830s. Perhaps mindful of the Ipperwash example, the provincial government had not moved quickly to evict the protesters.

On 12 April the government announced it was considering compensation for contractors and builders who had been affected by the occupation of the construction site. Then on 18 April talks between the government and the protesters broke down, and on 20 April the OPP conducted a predawn raid intended to evict the occupiers. Police were overwhelmed when additional protesters were quickly summoned, and they withdrew. Talks resumed, and by 22 April they were reported to be progressing fruitfully. However, by that time the protesters had extended their occupation to create a roadblock on one of the roads into the town; they later blockaded a second road.

On 29 April the government announced the appointment of former Liberal premier David Peterson to represent the province in talks at Caledonia. Neither he nor the government was prepared to discuss possible timelines for resolving the dispute. On 2 May representatives of the Six Nations met with UN officials in Geneva and asked the Committee on Economic, Social, and Cultural Rights to mediate the talks. The action was largely symbolic and the talks continued without UN intervention.

On 3 May the hate crimes unit of the OPP was called upon to investigate a poster that had appeared in Caledonia inviting people to a meeting to discuss the 'final solution to the Indian problem' with pictures of Ku Klux Klan figures in the background. Given that the poster contained no date, time, or place for the meeting, it was suspected by many to be a hoax. On the same day, the federal government appointed former federal Cabinet minister Barbara McDougall to represent it in land claims talks concerning Caledonia. For its part, Ontario appointed Jane Stewart (former federal Indian and northern affairs minister) to represent the province in the land claims discussions.

On 16 May protesters began to allow traffic to flow past one road barrier. On 19 May the province moved to ban construction 'indefinitely' at the Caledonia site in the hopes of persuading protesters to withdraw the road barriers, although the protesters denied they had yet agreed to do so. The developer, Henco Industries, was 'outraged' at the decision and called on the government to buy the land from them at 'fair market value' (*Canadian Press*, 19 May). It did appear that removal of the barrier on Highway 6 was imminent, though it was delayed by the mounting of a 'counter-blockade' of Aboriginal traffic by the Caledonia residents on 21 May. On 22 May the barrier was removed. On 24 May the government indicated it would provide approximately half a million dollars to assist business in Caledonia who had been adversely affected by the protests.

On 12 June by the premier's order, talks at Caledonia were suspended after two violent incidents – the swarming of an elderly couple in a car and assaults on a news crew – were reported at the remaining road barrier. Talks would resume, the premier said, when the final barricades came down and the Aboriginal community cooperated with police investigations of the weekend complaints.

On 22 June the government proposed to extend financial assistance to homeowners as well as businesses affected by the stand-off. The following day the province announced it was buying the Caledonia housing site for some $12.3 million and that it was considering whether additional compensation should be provided to Henco for lost profits.

On 8 July the *Toronto Star* reported that a petition was circulating to demand the dismissal of OPP commissioner Gwen Boniface for her handling of the Caledonia dispute. No action against her was ultimately pursued, but before the end of the summer she had resigned to take up a position in Ireland. In October the government appointed Julian Fantino – former chief of police in York Region; London, Ontario; and Toronto – to the post.

Meanwhile Justice David Marshall called for police and government officials to appear before him to show why an order he had issued in March calling on the protesters to leave the housing site had not been enforced. By early August, he had found the failure to enforce his order was contempt of court and he ordered negotiations on Caledonia to cease until natives ended their occupation. Attorney General Bryant said he would go to court arguing that Marshall had no authority to order an end to negotiations. On 25 August the Ontario Court of Appeal ruled that the contempt of court order against the occupiers of the site ran out on 5 July when the province purchased the land from the developer. Because the province did not claim the protesters were on its property unlawfully, the court said, the protesters could remain. A full appeal of Marshall's order was scheduled to be heard 25 and 26 September.

On 29 August protesters occupying the building site asked for donations of food and building supplies so that they could complete the houses that were under construction and remain on the site over the winter. Residents of Caledonia – who alleged continuing harassment and taunting of neighbours by the protesters – were reportedly 'horrified' at the prospect that the occupation could continue through the winter.

At the end of October the constitutional issue of responsibility for the land claims issue led to a certain amount of political posturing by representatives of the federal and provincial governments. David Ramsay, the minister then responsible for Aboriginal affairs, travelled to Ottawa for the purpose of presenting the federal Indian affairs minister a bill for some of the costs of the Caledonia land dispute and to urge a larger federal role in negotiating an end to the stand-off. Prentice, calling the actions of Ramsay and the premier 'grandstanding,' elected to pursue a little grandstanding of his own and canceled the meeting after Ramsay had arrived in Ottawa. The federal government denied any responsibility for costs, arguing that the province was constitutionally responsible for property and civil rights and the administration of justice. The province argued the dispute arose from an Indian land claim and that such issues were a matter of federal jurisdiction. Meanwhile, the occupation continued. By November 14 tempers had cooled and Premier McGuinty was pleased to see the federal government showing a commitment to resolving the Caledonia dispute. Minister Ramsay said the federal authorities were looking at reimbursing Ontario for some of its costs.

At year end the occupation of the Caledonia site continued and no resolution had yet been reached of the land claim that had given rise to the protest in the first place.

Another troubling issue involving First Nations concerned the Kashechewan reserve on the shore of James Bay. In late April, residents of the reserve experienced a mass evacuation because of flooding caused by spring run-off. This evacuation came less than a year after a similar removal because of contamination of the reserve's water supply. In early May the province raised the possibility of moving the reserve some 30 kilometres up-river and 55 metres above sea level. The move would require the federal government to designate the new location as a reserve. Before that plan could proceed, however, the federal government appointed former Ontario Cabinet minister Alan Pope to review the alternatives and recommend a solution. When he reported in November, his recommendation was to move the residents of Kashechewan to the outskirts of Timmins. The reserve would then have readier access to emergency services and employment possibilities and would be safe from further flooding. The move would take a number of years to complete.

Social, labour, and legal issues

On Boxing Day in 2005 a midday shoot-out in Toronto's downtown shopping district led to the death of a young bystander. The province promised early in 2006 to commit $51 million in a battle against gun crime, including more police, prosecutors, and judges, special training for police, and more victim support staff.

In early April, black jail guards in a provincial facility reported they had received threatening letters with racist content from people with whom they worked. Minister Monte Kwinter declared such letters unacceptable and indicated that his office was working with the Ontario Public Service Employees Union (OPSEU) to ensure a safe working environment. The problem appeared to persist given that OPSEU called in October for a public inquiry into the threatening letters.

In early June police arrested seventeen young men in southern Ontario and charged that they had been part of a radical Islamist terrorist plot targeting numerous facilities and persons in the province. They were alleged, in some cases, to have received training in overseas camps and to have held further training sessions in rural areas close to Toronto. Trials were expected in 2007.

The province has been considering the possibility of extending religiously based arbitration in family law matters to tribunals that would apply the principles of Islamic law. Such tribunals already existed for the Jewish community and some Christian sects. In 2006 the province decided, rather than extending the practice, to put an end to such tribunals altogether.

In January the province proposed a series of changes to the Ontario Municipal Employees Retirement System which would allow emergency workers to negotiate supplementary benefits including earlier retirement. CUPE threatened a province-wide strike if the bill was pursued, but the strike was averted by the government's promise to conduct a review of the legislation in six years. The Association of Municipalities of Ontario (AMO) also opposed the bill, saying it would impose additional costs on local governments. However, municipal affairs minister John Gerretsen disputed the AMO's conclusion, noting that any supplementary benefits would be negotiated along with other items, and there could be trade-offs, so it was difficult to estimate the specific cost of the one item.

The legislature raised the minimum wage in Ontario to $7.75 per hour effective 1 February, but pressure for more increases continued. The Ontario Coalition for Social Justice (made up of unions and anti-poverty groups) rallied at Queen's Park on 17 October calling for an increase to $10 an hour, and NDP member Cheri Di Novo tabled a private member's bill with that provision. The bill passed second reading in early November but, like most such bills, did not proceed further.

In light of reports that people had lost their homes through identity theft when someone had taken out a mortgage on their property without their knowledge and then taken off with the money, the government included amendments to the Land Titles Act in an omnibus consumer protection bill passed in December. The changes would make it impossible for someone to lose their home because of a falsified mortgage or fraudulent power of attorney.

In March, following the introduction of a private member's bill by Conservative Tim Hudak that would have limited property assessment increases to 5 per cent per annum, the ombudsman undertook to make recommendations for improvement in the assessment system. He made twenty recommendations of which the assessment body undertook to implement seventeen. In late April the premier acknowledged some problems in the assessment system but denied that Hudak's cap was a satisfactory solution. On 29 June the government announced a two-year freeze of the assessment system so that a revamp could be planned. Critics observed that this hot-button issue was now effectively off the table until after the next election.

As the year ended, the campaign for that next election was pretty clearly already underway.

DANIEL SALÉE AND RICHARD BISAILLON

Quebec

Quebecers entered 2006 waiting, in both the economic and political sense, for the other shoe to drop. The Quebec economy continued a slow decline into increasing stagnation, with economic growth for the year at only 1.6 per cent, down from 2.0 per cent in 2005 and continuing a decline from the level of 2.6 per cent two years earlier in 2004. The unemployment rate in the first quarter was at 8.4 per cent for the province as a whole and at 9.4 per cent for Montreal. The rest of the year did not offer much improvement with a cumulative unemployment rate of 8.0 per cent for the province compared to 6.3 per cent for the country as a whole. Late in the previous year, former premier Lucien Bouchard and a list of supporting signatories – most with strong ties to the private sector, identified as 'les Lucides' – had released their collective opinion on the economic malaise that continued to mark Quebec's economy: a continuing lack of performance that saw the province lag behind the rest of Canada and delay the full economic, social, and political conditions that could lead to a sovereign Quebec. Their position, heavily critical of the Quebecois work ethic and voiced fairly strongly from the political Right, invited a rapid response from the opposite end of the ideological spectrum. The 'Solidaires,' a loose coalition of individuals drawn from Quebec's fragmented political Left, riposted to the overt criticism and operative assumptions contained within the 'Lucides' document.[1] This accelerated a series of mergers between fractional parties started several years earlier that produced a new political party – Québec Solidaire – in early February 2006.

On the federal front, the initial release of the Gomery Commission's Phase 1 report on the Liberal sponsorship scandal late in the previous

1 For details on the debate between Lucides and Solidaires, see the chapter on Quebec in the *Canadian Annual Review of Politics and Public Affairs 2005*.

year had set the stage for a political response by Quebecers as whole. The report had prompted a vote of non-confidence in the minority government headed by Paul Martin and a call for a federal election on 23 January, early in the new year. The electoral response clearly showed the sense of affront amongst the Quebec electorate. The Liberals lost 23 seats in Quebec alone, dropping from 36 in the 2000 election to 13. The province typically becomes more supportive of sovereignty, and its political proponents, when external events touch a collective nerve, and as a result, the Bloc Québécois saw a corresponding increase of 13 seats, up from 38 in the previous election to 51. A newly united political Right under the Conservative Party of Canada led by Stephen Harper picked up 10 seats in the province, up from a single seat held under the Progressive Conservatives in the last election.

Consensus on rejection, but not on direction

Jean Charest and the provincial Liberals might well have thanked their federal counterparts for a brief respite from the focused dissatisfaction offered by a broad spectrum of Quebecers over the previous three years of their current mandate. Hard on the heels of the first phase of the Gomery Commission's report and the rare call for a midwinter federal election, Premier Jean Charest and the provincial Liberals pushed through the National Assembly another highly contentious piece of labour legislation that imposed collective agreements on the public-sector unions by decree. Bill 142, passed late in 2005 on 15 December, retroactively applied a wage freeze of 33 months and held public-sector increases to 2 per cent per annum for the remaining four years of contracts that spanned seven years in application. And this in a province whose labour code had until recently limited the term of negotiated agreements to three years by way of compelling the parties back to the negotiating table on a regular basis.

The law was but the most recent example of negotiation by decree that had marked the relationship between the provincial Liberals and the unionized public sector over a series of mandates stretching back to the early 1990s, a pattern set decades earlier under the Liberal government of Robert Bourassa during the Common Front labour conflicts of the 1970s. Organized labour's collective threat to remember the affront during the next provincial election generally fell on deaf ears. Notwithstanding a very public campaign sporting bumper stickers that parodied the provincial motto of 'Je me souviens' (I remember) as carried on Quebec licence plates, along with 'LOI 142' as a plate number, everyone knew that organized labour had traditionally supported the overtly sovereigntist and avowedly 'labour friendly' Parti Québécois (PQ) throughout much of recent electoral history. However, that party too had indulged in similar practices early in the 1980s and had shown such an inclination well into the mid-1990s. Add to that the fact that Lucien Bouchard, head of the PQ from 1996 to 2001 and one of the party's most popular leaders, was the lead signatory of the 'Lucides' neo-liberal position statement, and organized labour found itself suspended between a traditional enmity of the Liberals and a declining affinity or resonance with the Parti Québécois.

The criticism and threatened electoral rejection of the Quebec provincial Liberals found a broader foundation than just that offered by organized labour generally or the public-sector unions in particular. Across Quebec there was an ongoing and increasing perception that the party was leading the province towards a more corporatist and neo-liberal vision of the Quebec 'state.' There were, in addition, certain rumblings from within the party itself, as given evidence by a contentious Cabinet shuffle early in 2006. Running for the Liberals, Raymond Bachand had won a by-election in the riding of Outremont in mid-December 2005 and was quickly parachuted into the position of minister of economic development, thereby displacing Claude Béchard, who in turn bumped Thomas Mulcair as minister of the environment and sustainable development. That the newly appointed Minister Bachand had of late come from a major private-sector management consultation firm had caught the attention of many. Add to this the fact that one of the first acts of Claude Béchard as minister of the environment and sustainable development in March 2006 was the privatization of a large parcel of land held in public trust since 1938 in a park centred around Mount Orford, and the increasing social perception became one of the Liberals deconstructing the social democratic foundation of Quebec along with its historical patrimony.

The broad rejection of the Liberals – federally for the presumption that Quebecers could be 'bought,' as demonstrated by the sponsorship scandal, and provincially through what was seen by many as an unmistakable neo-liberal and corporatist agenda under the leadership of Jean Charest – should not be construed as an endorsement for any of the political alternatives. As noted earlier, a similar tendency towards the ideological Right had become manifest in the Parti Québécois over at least the previous decade and certainly since the ascendancy of Lucien Bouchard to the leadership of the party in 1996. Dissatisfaction with both the Liberals and the PQ had in fact sparked the success of the Action

Démocratique du Québec (ADQ) in provincial by-elections during 2002–3. By the end of 2004, they held 5 seats in the National Assembly. Although always hard to pin down as to its own platforms, positions, and policies, most particularly on Quebec sovereignty, the party was significantly to the right of the Liberals and clearly far removed from the original ideological position of the PQ. In fact, ADQ's success provincially, and through its provision of candidates previously associated with the party, helped fuel in part the Conservative Party of Canada's inroads into Quebec in the 2006 federal election.

The rightward shift in the ideological tendency amongst the province's two mainstream provincial political parties and a similar drift in that of contemporary alternatives at both the federal and provincial levels may have serendipitously combined with a centralizing movement amongst a diversity of fractional parties on the political left that gave birth to Québec Solidaire in early February. Still, as a political alternative – and given evidence by the results of one provincial by-election win in mid-December 2005, one in April 2006, and two in August – Quebecers continued to manifest their dissatisfaction with the provincial Liberals by supporting the Parti Québécois. André Boisclair had ascended to the leadership of the PQ in mid-November 2005 and won in the provincial riding of Pointe-aux-Trembles in August 2006; this came along with the victory of Marie Malavoy for the PQ in the riding of Taillon. Federally, the seats that Quebecers awarded to the Bloc and Conservatives in 2006 constituted a backlash against the Liberals at both levels of government. However, a consensus of rejection on political alternatives within Quebec also gave evidence of a lack of similar consensus on political direction. Electoral victories for the PQ in three by-elections in 2006 were again more an expression of dissatisfaction with the ruling Liberals, and this notwithstanding the leadership of André Boisclair, whose mandate was never a strong one. The creation of a political alternative on the ideological left came as an invitation to which Quebecers did not respond in any marked fashion.

Questioning state bureaucracy

On 30 September a major highway overpass collapsed in Laval just north of Montreal, killing five people and injuring another six. Chunks of concrete had been falling from the structure and an inspector was sent to pick up the debris at least an hour before the collapse. Sadly, the official chose not to close the overpass. The provincial government immediately struck an inquiry on 3 October and asked former premier

Pierre Marc Johnson to lead it. The main causes of the disaster were eventually identified as poor construction and materials along with some serious design flaws. The overpass, built in the 1970s, had been extensively repaired in 1992, but in fact that repair actually contributed to the ultimate failure of the structure. An examination of all similar structures was immediately ordered, and a second overpass constructed nearby and at the same time as the one that collapsed was closed and ultimately torn down and replaced.

This tragic event underscored long-standing concerns over Quebec's aging physical infrastructure. The Canadian Council of Professional Engineers had been calling for better monitoring, inspection, and maintenance programs and accelerated renewal of aging infrastructure. Yet the issue of maintenance is really but a part of the problem insofar as issues related to poor design and shoddy materials contribute greatly to the rate of failure of Quebec's transportation infrastructure. Maintaining shoddy workmanship and construction is pointless and, as noted, can actually contribute to failure down the road. Recalling the collapse of another nearby overpass in 2000, also in Laval, this one under construction and crossing Quebec's busy Highway 15, issues of poor construction were the cause there as well. The main supporting beams were too short and precariously placed. The collapse saw one man killed and two others injured.

Lack of funds and cutting of corners has become inevitably endemic in a province that has a huge and growing public debt (notwithstanding the fact that the government proposed a balanced budget in March 2006). Not surprisingly Quebec's sizable bureaucracy is increasingly held responsible for the seeming inability of the state to respond to the institutional needs of Quebecers.

The inability of Quebec's health care system to cater to patients' needs in a timely fashion is a case in point. In the famous Chaoulli decision rendered by the Supreme Court of Canada in 2005, the court ruled that Quebec's prohibition against private health insurance in the face of inordinately long waiting lists for surgeries constituted a violation of patients' rights under the Quebec Charter of Human Rights and Freedoms, specifically Quebecers' right to life and security of the person. A minority of the deciding judges also felt that Quebecers' rights under section seven of the Canadian Charter were also being violated. Throughout the decision there is a sense that although the court acknowledges the government's right to manage its own affairs, the situation had been problematic for so long a time that efforts to improve it were too few and changed little. As Judge Deschamps wrote in the decision, 'For many years, the government has failed to act; the situation continues to deteriorate … Under the Québec plan, the government can control its human resources in various ways … While the government has the power to decide what measures to adopt, it cannot choose to do nothing in the face of the violation of Québecers' right to security. The government has not given reasons for its failure to act. Inertia cannot be used as an argument to justify deference.'[2]

This bureaucratic 'inertia,' this seeming inability to respond to the needs of the citizenry, plagues both the state and the institutions under its direction. Neither of Montreal's two super-hospitals, in the planning stage since 1991, had seen the beginning of construction by 2006, yet five Montreal hospitals were closed in 1995. The impact on health care and hospital access has been profound on every front, most particularly with crowded emergency waiting rooms, as well as the wait for surgery that prompted the Chaoulli case. Having acknowledged the right of government to manage its affairs, yet insisting that it act, the Supreme Court decision gave the Quebec government one year to rectify the situation.

By way of a response the provincial government launched a public consultation process and produced the document *Garantir l'accès: un défi d'équité, d'efficience et de qualité* (*Guaranteeing Access: A Challenge of Fairness, Efficiency and Quality*) on 16 February. This was followed by the introduction in June of Bill 33, '[a]n Act to amend the Act respecting health services and social services and other legislative provisions,' which came into law on 13 December 2006. The act puts into place a centralized system for managing waiting lists for surgery that is administered through individual hospitals as well as laying out the framework for 'specialized medical centres' that may be either within or completely outside the public health care system. No hybridized centres are allowed; that is, doctors working in any one centre must all be either in the public system or all be outside the system. Regulations conceived for the ownership and administration of these specialized health centres demand that majority ownership and control fall to the medical doctors operating the centre. Regardless of the side of the health care debate one supports – that the creation of private health clinics are the thin edge of the wedge leading to the end of public health care or that they

2 *In Passim*, Chaoulli v. Quebec (Attorney General), [2005] S.C.R. 791 2005 SCC 35, p. 63.

represent a needed and inevitable solution to the problem at hand – one observation that can be made is that much of Bill 33 represents an attempt at solving the problem of a bloated and inefficient health care bureaucracy with more bureaucracy. The creation of specialized private health care centres may well alleviate the worst examples of painful, even fatal delays in the public system. However, proposing a bureaucratic regulatory solution to the situation in the public sector, when that same bureaucracy has, in fact, been a significant part of the problem itself, seems counter-intuitive at best.

Premier Charest and the provincial Liberal Party may have been 'forced' into allowing the creation of specialized health centres – public and private – by the Supreme Court decision in the Chaoulli case. But given the party's neo-liberal bent, one may well wonder to what extent Premier Charest and the Liberals were pushed or whether they jumped. Bill 33 is in a way a middle-of-the-road solution, neither fish nor fowl. It continues to abide by a fairly deep-seated popular commitment to public health but nonetheless responds to market pressures to privatize the system. In the end, letting the system slowly slide into a state where privatization appears as a serious way out of its inefficiencies may well prove to be the surest path back to the dominance of private medicine. Why else had some genuine attempt not been previously made to remedy the fundamental problems in the public health care system? That question will probably continue to preoccupy public policy analysts for many years to come.

Dealing with public disapproval over policy

Although the passing of Bill 33 seemed an inevitable consequence of the Supreme Court decision, on other policy decisions, acting in ways contrary to the expressed wishes of the electorate is not without its political toll, as the government discovered over the uproar triggered by its proposed sale of part of Mount Orford Provincial Park to private developers. The public perception of the situation was caught best by Montreal's *Gazette* in its coverage of a huge protest led against the proposed sale held on Earth Day, 22 April 2006, when it led off its article with the words, 'Something about a government selling off 'protected' parklands to a condo developer seems to have touched a nerve with the Québec public.'[3] Ten days earlier, a PQ member of the

3 *Gazette*, 23 April 2006.

National Assembly had deposited a petition in the house with 171,445 signatures demanding the protection of forested lands in the Pascagama and Vallée des montagnes blanches regions of Quebec. The Earth Day protest was no small thing. In a city that rarely sees large numbers of protester over any substantive issue anymore, the *Gazette* reported approximately 7,500 protesters in one location and a further 12,000 at a second location in the city. Less than two months later, on 12 June, Premier Charest and the Liberals invoked closure to pass four bills, including Bill 23, on the privatization of 649 hectares of the site including the ski hill, golf course, and 85 hectares of adjacent property slated for the construction of condos. By way of mollifying those opposed to the sale, it was announced that the government would in turn purchase new lands adjacent to the existing park to compensate for the parcel lost to privatization. Critics noted that it was the unique ecology of the mountain itself that had prompted the original purchase of the lands in 1938 by 27 municipalities. The property, originally comprising 58 square miles, was transferred in trust to the government. By year's end, a class action suit had been launched on behalf of the original contributors of money and property. Again, the invocation of closure seems the hallmark of a government that solves its problems by closing off discussion and debate. The dissent within the Liberal Party itself was manifest when Pierre Paradis, member of the National Assembly for Brome-Missisiquoi, broke with party discipline and voted against the bill while voting with the government on the other three bills passed at the same time and in the same manner.

Of the other three bills passed, one, Bill 31, was over the privatization of government-owned racecourses, and one was reminiscent of Bill 142, legislating settlements by decree in the public sector and passed late in December of the previous year. Bill 37 imposed working conditions and legislated compensation for Quebec's medical specialists until 2010. Part of the problems plaguing Quebec's public health care system is illustrated by the impact of the bill on the medical specialists. Although it holds increases for each of the four years covered by the bill to 2 per cent per annum, in line with increases for other public-sector employees, the percentages are applied against salaries that are around $100,000 lower than the Canadian average for specialists in other provinces. In September, three months after forcing the bill through the National Assembly, the Québec Association of Medical Specialists announced its intention of questioning the constitutionality of the law before the courts. The particularly hard line taken against the medical specialists is further illustrated by the fact that the government, by way of 'punishing' the specialists for not accepting a package worth $593 million in June just before the passage of the law, imposed a settlement that reduced the offer by $125 million, with further reductions of $50 million for fines and penalties. The doctors were threatened with further severe financial penalties should they engage in any active form of protest against the law.

The labour front: jobs lost and added, old conflicts resolved

On 27 April a deal was announced between Canada and the United States on the long-standing softwood lumber dispute. The dispute, in one form or another, had been running since the early 1980s, with American companies complaining that the Canadian government was subsidizing the industry here. Essentially, insofar as provincial governments generally 'own' Canada's forests and set the cost of cutting lumber on these lands through stumpage fees that are administratively set rather than set price as a function of supply and demand in the market, American producers alleged that this subsidized Canadian production. Notwithstanding a series of decisions by international panels set through the World Trade Organization and under NAFTA that were generally in favour of the Canadian position, the United States remained steadfast in applying compensatory tariffs against Canadian softwood imports. Prime Minister Stephen Harper manoeuvred the deal through Parliament without losing the confidence of the House with the support of Gilles Duceppe and the Bloc Québécois. The Liberals came out against the deal and voted against it, with a few Liberal members voting for its passage.

Notwithstanding the fact that British Columbia is the largest exporter of softwood to the US market, Quebec's softwood and pulp-and-paper industry was less than positively affected by the resolution of the conflict. There is a certain irony in the way events unfolded in 2006, particularly as to the relation of Quebec's producers to the larger conflict. Later in the year, on 23 August, it was announced that Domtar, a Quebec-based company since 1914, was merging with the giant American pulp-and-paper company Weyerhaeuser. Although the initial announcement sought to reassure all that the merger would not result in job losses in Quebec, barely six weeks later on 11 October, Domtar announced the closing of four mills, three of which were in Quebec. The closures were expected to result in the loss of 900 jobs. Mills in Matagami and Val d'Or were to be closed as well as in Lebel-sur-Quévillon, all located in northern Quebec. With the decline of mining in this area, the hit to the region's remaining resource extraction industry was hard felt. Whatever motivated the Bloc to support the softwood lumber agreement, it did not benefit Quebec's producers after the fact.

Economic news for other parts of Quebec was both bad and good. In late October, Norsk Hydro announced the closing of its magnesium plant in Becancour, around 150 kilometres northeast of Montreal. The closure would result in the loss of around 380 jobs. Reasons for the closure were assigned to the strong Canadian dollar and stiff competition from China. On the other hand, Alcan announced that they were investing $2 billion over the next ten years into new and existing facilities in the Saguenay region of Quebec. Approximately 700 jobs are tied to Alcan's new and existing production there, with spin-off effect producing many more to be generated by the planned new construction of a factory.

Another long-standing conflict was settled in Québec, this time to the general benefit of many Quebec workers. On 20 June the government announced that it had reached an agreement with Quebec's big unions and organizing bodies on pay equity. The initial agreement would see retroactive adjustments to the salaries of approximately 326,000 workers, mostly women, over the space of the next two years. With a value announced at approximately $4 billion, the agreement has its greatest impact in the public-sector areas of education and health care. A supplementary agreement including day-care workers was announced in September. From the point of view of the unions, the deal was less than perfect, insofar as salary comparisons between what are identified as predominantly 'male' and 'female' types of employment are held within institutions and not across sectors. Still, as a victory for the struggle for 'equal pay for work of equal value' the agreement went far in correcting local inequalities.

Ethnicity and difference: sensitivities over Quebec's national identity

A little before one o'clock in the afternoon on 13 September, a heavily armed 25-year-old man named Kimveer Gill entered Montreal's Dawson College on a shooting rampage. Within half an hour Gill had shot and killed one student and wounded another nineteen before killing himself. Quebec had seen two similar previous events. First, there was the 6 December 1989 killing of 14 young women by Marc Lepine, also 25 years of age. Lepine wounded an additional 14 male and female students before also committing suicide. Then, in August 1992, a Concordia University engineering professor, Valery Fabrikant, shot and killed four colleagues on the downtown campus of that institution and wounded a co-worker. Events of 13 September 2006 caught Quebecers by surprise, as well they would have under any circumstances, and sparked a renewed debate over the issue of gun control, the long-gun registry, and violence in Quebec's public institutions. Premier Jean Charest immediately made a plea to the Conservative government in Ottawa to cancel its intention to remove the long-gun registry. He acknowledged that the registry was not perfect, and that it had indeed cost more than projected, but claimed that once in place, it was a useful tool in preventing most of those who would seek to obtain firearms with murderous intent from getting legal access to weapons.

Other, less measured reactions included an article by Jan Wong in the *Globe and Mail* published on 16 September, three days after the shootings, offering the thesis that there may be a link between the three aforementioned events that could be traced to 'how alienating the decades long linguistic struggle has been' in Montreal, and that 'it hasn't just taken a toll on long-time anglophones, it's affected immigrants, too.'[4] Wong linked Gill's cultural origins with the fact that Marc Lepine was 'half Algerian, a Muslim, and his name was Gamil Gharbi,'[5] having changed his name seven years before the 1989 shootings to Marc Lepine. She also noted that Valery Fabrikant 'was an immigrant from Russia.'[6] While acknowledging the unique characteristics of each of the actors, Wong noted that 'all of them had been marginalized in a society that valued *pure laine*.'[7] Reactions were swift and decisive, most particularly within Quebec. Federalists and sovereigntists alike rejected the thesis out of hand and expressed a range of responses from simple disappointment to outrage. The *Globe* distanced itself from Wong's article towards the end of the month, but only to indicate that it was an opinion piece as opposed to reportage. Wong turned down invitations to defend her position, specifically one high-profile offer by talk show host Guy A. Lepage to appear on the popular television show *Tout le monde en parle*. Wong ultimately maintained her position.

The justifiable umbrage taken by Quebecers in reaction to Jan Wong's article cannot deny the fact that many have become more vocal in their

4 Jan Wong, 'Get Under the Desk,' *Globe and Mail*, September 16, 2006, p. A8.

5 Ibid.

6 Ibid.

7 Ibid.

criticism of new Quebecers' demands for reasonable accommodation. On 6 March the Supreme Court of Canada put the final decision to an issue of religious freedom and reasonable accommodation that had arisen five years earlier over the right of a young Sikh, Gurbaj Singh Multani, to wear his ceremonial kirpan to school. The issue arose when Gurbaj, a grade 7 student, was playing with friends in the schoolyard, and his ceremonial dagger fell out of his clothes onto the ground. On the basis that the kirpan was in fact a weapon, and as such banned from the school's property, the student was told that he could not return to school with the kirpan. The local school authority initially struck an agreement with the Singh family as to permit their son to wear the kirpan so long as it was secured by sewing the dagger shut in its cloth sheath. The governing committee of the larger school board, however, overturned that decision. The family went to court, and the Superior Court agreed that the outright prohibition of the kirpan was excessive, stating that the young man could wear it to school so long as certain security provisions were satisfied rendering it safe from accidental or intentional exposure. The school board went to appeal, where the lower court decision was overturned.

The unanimous Supreme Court decision stated that outright prohibition was a violation of Gurbaj Singh Multani's rights under the *Charter of Rights and Freedoms*. However, the school did have the right to place certain conditions on the student to ensure the safety of others and outlined a set of conditions somewhat similar to those offered in the Superior Court decision. That the issue touched a broader nerve was shown by the reaction of many of the parents of students in Multani's school when the lower court decision was made and Multani was permitted to return to school. Public protests and manifestations of dissatisfaction were such that Multani ultimately moved to a private school. The intensity of the public reaction seemed somewhat out of balance with the real or potential threat posed by a Sikh student carrying a securely fastened and hidden kirpan. As the Supreme Court decision noted regarding the ability of Multani or another student to employ or obtain the weapon with violent intent, 'there are many objects in schools that could be used to commit violent acts and that are much more easily obtained by students, such as scissors, pencils and baseball bats.'[8] The backlash is more easily attributable both to the religious nature of the accommodation and the

8 Multani v. Commission scolaire Marguerite-Bourgeoys, [2006] 1 S.C.R. 256, 2006 SCC 6, 2 March 2006.

visibility of the petitioner. Quebec has become one of the most secular societies in the half-century since the Quiet Revolution, and a certain sensitivity to outward manifestations of religious belief increasingly becomes tied to the fact that many new and visible Quebecers are far more adherent in their beliefs than those born here.

Be that as it may, both the Wong article and the Supreme Court's ruling on the Multani case demonstrated once more that questions of national identity remain a central part of the political landscape in Quebec and a highly delicate issue that cannot be easily solved, as the Harper government, like others before, found out. In a bid to appease die-hard sensibilities and favour a rapprochement with Quebec, Prime Minister Harper introduced a motion to the House of Commons on 27 November, recognizing that 'the Québécois form a nation within a united Canada.' The motion carried 266–16 and the initiative was generally well received in Quebec, in spite of the fact that the prime minister took care to qualify the use of the term *nation* in relation to Quebec as 'cultural-sociological' rather than in any legal sense of the word.

Notwithstanding this almost unanimous parliamentary support, some were quick in their criticism of the motion and the motives that prompted it. Liberal Party of Canada leadership candidate Gerard Kennedy called the motion 'politically inspired,' while minister of intergovernmental affairs Michael Chong resigned his office and announced his intention to abstain from the vote 'because it implies the recognition of ethnicity.'[9] Chong's comments, and the assumptions inherent therein, do beg the question: Who are the Quebecois? Does membership still necessarily imply that one must be an old-stock francophone? After the last referendum even the Parti Québécois addressed the issue to demand only two criteria: that one live in Quebec and speak French. So when the former minister stated that he cannot accept the motion of recognition of the Quebecois as a nation within Canada because it implies the recognition of ethnicity, he likely echoed the view of many, both inside and outside of Quebec, that the Quebecois are an ethnically defined nation.

What is clear is that when Gerard Kennedy stated the motion was 'politically inspired' he was essentially correct. In fact, the entire issue had become a hot potato during the Liberal Party of Canada leadership

9 See CBC news report for 27 November 2006, http://www.cbc.ca/canada/story/2006/11/27/nation-vote.html.

race that autumn. On 21 October the Quebec wing of the party passed a resolution recognizing Quebec as a nation. Most vocal amongst the leadership candidates in his support for that motion, at least at certain times, was Michael Ignatieff. Amongst the rest of the candidates, as given evidence by the words of Gerard Kennedy, there was a distinct range of positions. Not that one gets the sense that many were against the idea in principle, only that – like Kennedy – they saw the entire issue as a political land mine at a time when the party was least ready for such a hot-button topic. Clearly, the Liberals as a group had some fence mending to do in Quebec. If anyone did not believe that after the first Gomery Commission report, then the results of the federal election earlier in the year must have driven home the point. Perhaps Ignatieff's position was somewhat tactical. His coming out on Quebecois language, culture, and geographic history as qualifications for recognition as a separate nation certainly put the ball in the court of Stéphane Dion as a Quebecer, if not precisely as a *Quebecois*. Both Dion and Bob Rae came out against the position.

Nevertheless, by the end of November it became clear that the motion was going to be placed before the House in some form, by some party. The Bloc was ready to present its own motion, and it was left to the prime minister to try and steer the process in such a way as to indicate that he and the Conservatives were offering a long-deserved olive branch to Quebec. Dion as well was ready with a counter-proposal. Ultimately, it was the modified motion, as crafted by the Harper Conservatives, that carried the House. The addendum to the first half of the motion recognizing the national status of the Quebecois; those reading 'within a united Canada' were acceptable to the Bloc, at least for now. If half a loaf is better than none, then a nation within a nation will serve. Of the 16 votes against the motion, 15 were Liberals. Last-minute attempts at arriving at a consensus amongst the leadership contenders failed. Discretion in politics being, as elsewhere, the better part of valour, there were 3 abstentions and 21 MPs absent from the House. And Stéphane Dion won the leadership race and became the head of the Liberal Party of Canada.

What was Quebecers' collective perception of the House motion recognising that the 'Québécois' form a nation within a united Canada? From the point of view of a nationalist, the forbidden word had been spoken. Being acknowledged as a nation in any sense begs the question: a sovereign and autonomous nation or not? 'Within a united Canada' is moot, in the true sense of the word. And it will be discussed and argued. What was given less attention was the question posed earlier: 'Who are the Quebecois?' From the point of view of those who are not overt nationalists, the acknowledgment came as a long anticipated and widely demanded admission of the unique language, culture, and history of Quebec, although it may have been received as a begrudging admission, one awkwardly timed and somewhat politically suspect. But what of the perception of anglophones, allophones, Quebec's First Peoples, and new Quebecers?

Many died-in-the-wool Anglos took offence at the admission, just as many *pure laine* Quebecois found it woefully inadequate. Perhaps 'old stock' Quebecois might be a more acceptable semantic label these days, but many older francophones whose heritage is firmly rooted in the soil of Quebec will smile, nod, and quietly accept the admission. Many others – steadfastly nationalist as they may be – will want still more. Canada and Quebec's First Nations quickly responded to the motion by first acknowledging the right of the Quebecois to formal recognition but wondering why a similar admission had not been offered regarding their own status. The national chief of the Assembly of First Nations, Phil Fontaine, noted that '[w]e have this [Québec motion] on one hand and on the other we have Canada opposing the Declaration of Indigenous Peoples at the UN.'[10] At the Socioeconomic Forum of the First Nations held in late October, Ghislain Picard, the chief of the AFN of Quebec and Labrador, made it quite clear in his opening speech where Indigenous peoples stood: they compose nations in their own right and they will never be assimilated to the Quebecois nation.[11] As for many other Quebecers, those born elsewhere or who by virtue of their personal circumstances do not neatly fall into the Quebecois category, they simply wondered where this motion placed them in the grand scheme of things. But then, most of them have been wondering that for quite a while and did not get a clearer answer in 2006 than at any other time before.

Quebec in Canada: committing to federalism

The recognition of Quebec as a nation by the House of Commons pleased the Charest government, who welcomed the initiative as an encouraging sign that Canadian federalism can indeed be the open and

10 See http://www.ctv.ca/CTVNews/TopStories/20061123/quebec_reaction_061124/.

11 *Rapport final du forum socioéconomique des Premières Nations*, annexe 2, http://www.autochtones.gouv.qc.ca/publications_documentation/publications/forum-francais.pdf.

pluralist institutional framework the Quebec Liberals have worked hard to foster since they came back to power in 2003. A few months earlier, in May, Prime Minister Harper and Premier Charest had signed a historic agreement that established a formal role for Quebec at UNESCO. With this agreement the Harper government had implicitly signified its openness to the idea that Quebec can be seen as a semi-autonomous political entity. At least this is certainly how the agreement was perceived by the Quebec government as Premier Charest declared, 'The signing of this Agreement, based on asymmetrical federalism, ushers in a new era of partnership between our two governments. Our presence in UNESCO will give us a say in sectors that are important for Québec's identity, such as culture, science and education. The federal government is formally recognizing Québec's capacity to act on the international front.'[12]

Still, despite the apparent goodwill of federal politicians and institutions towards Quebec's historical claims, the relations between Quebec and Ottawa in 2006 continued to be soured as in previous years by the issue of fiscal imbalance. Quebec remained adamant that Ottawa should stop interfering in areas of provincial jurisdiction and increase equalization and transfer payments. On this score, though, Quebec is no longer alone complaining about the unfairness of the Canadian federal system. Virtually all the other provincial governments have several bones of contention with their federal counterpart. In April all the premiers endorsed the conclusions and recommendations of the Council of the Federation's Advisory Panel on Fiscal Imbalance. Set up a year earlier, the panel was mandated to look at the underlying causes of fiscal imbalance, review possible mechanisms to address the problem, and make recommendations to restore fiscal balance. While everyone seemed to agree that fiscal imbalance is a reality and that the existing equalization formula fails to ensure that all Canadian citizens enjoy the same level and quality of services, building a consensus around the proper ways to achieve fair equalization was another matter altogether. The July conference of premiers in St. John's concluded on a disappointing note as Ontario, Alberta, and British Columbia refused to embark on a common front with the other provinces if this was to imply that they reach deeper into their respective constituents'

12 Press release, Prime Minister's Office, 5 May 2006, http://www.pm.gc.ca/eng/media.asp?id=1151.

pockets so that other members of the federation meet their financial obligations.

In the absence of this much needed consensus, Quebec seems condemned to press its case for fiscal redress and additional transfer payments with Ottawa on its own. Although it is used to it, a little support from the other provincial governments would have been nice. All the more so given that detractors of Quebec's claims for a reviewed equalization formula readily portray the province as a spoiled brat deeply ensconced in its own culture of entitlement. *Globe and Mail* columnist Jeffrey Simpson, for example, argued that fiscal imbalance is a myth that Quebec cultivates only to make up for its unwillingness to raise taxes further. Simpson noted that Quebec's social-democratic policies are fine, but they are expensive. If Quebecers want them, it is their choice, but they should not expect the rest of Canada to pick up the tab.[13]

As Quebec sovereigntists would have it, Simpson's argument is just one more proof that English Canada completely misunderstands Quebec and its particular needs. Jean Charest's government prefers instead to think that Quebec can continue to operate productively within the Canadian federation. Fiscal imbalance aside, it brought to fruition in 2006 a few initiatives that bore witness to its unflinching belief in the virtues of Canadian federalism. Notable among such initiatives is the reciprocity agreement signed with Ontario in June over labour mobility and the recognition of the professional qualifications of tradespeople in the construction industry. The agreement now allows Quebec entrepreneurs to bid for construction contracts tendered by Ontario municipalities and governmental organizations and adds to the list of Ontario trades eligible for professional certification in Quebec. Benoît Pelletier, the minister responsible for Canadian intergovernmental affairs, hailed the agreement as further demonstration of Quebec's leadership in intergovernmental relations in the Canadian context.

Quebec's new policy on Canadian francophonie released in November is another initiative the government put forward as a proud sign of its commitment to Canadian federalism. Contrary to previous governments that have tended historically to neglect *le fait français* outside Quebec, the Charest government had indicated in 2004 at the forum on Canadian francophonie it held in Quebec City that it intended to rekindle Quebec's role as promoter of francophone culture in Canada. The

13 Jeffrey Simpson, 'Le mythe du déséquilibre fiscal,' *La Presse*, 16 April 2006.

new policy is the result of this initial declaration of intent. It is based on two guiding principles: first, that francophones all over Canada must reinforce and consolidate their links in order to increase their presence and influence everywhere in the country; and second, that Quebec must play a leadership role in fostering closer ties between all francophone communities and helping their development. To these ends, the Quebec government has pledged to initiate and support a number of actions in key sectors such as culture, communication, education, economic development, and health and had the National Assembly adopt a law in December that created the Centre de la francophonie des Amériques, a new institution designed specifically to facilitate interaction between francophone communities in all their diversity.

Although it asserts the centrality of francophone culture and is not without nationalistic overtones, this new policy has very little in common with the sovereigntist creed. In fact, it stands miles apart from it in that it downplays the sociological and political specificity of Quebec and insists instead on Quebecers' cultural proximity with all the other French-speaking Canadians – as if to say we are French and different from the English-speaking majority; that is worth protecting, but in the end we are also Canadian. By investing Quebec with the mission of reaching out to francophone minorities outside the province, the Charest government ultimately implies that without Quebec as the hub of the French fact in Canada – without Quebec, that is, as a full-fledged, central participant in the Canadian federation – they are inevitably at risk. Behind the paternalism of the policy's spirit, one finds a deep-seated act of faith in Canadian federalism. The Charest government may well have found a way to abide by Canadian federalism all the while defending, at least rhetorically, Quebec's cultural primacy – and be the 'nation within a united Canada' that Harper called for.

Bracing up

If many Quebecers, by whatever definition, entered 2006 waiting for the other shoe to drop, they closed the year in a state of somewhat shocked disequilibrium. The year had seen painful events, surprising reactions, and somewhat less than candid admissions. They had reacted to the affront of the sponsorship scandal and the first phase of the Gomery Commission report as Quebecers and Canadians often do, they turned the offending party out of office. In so doing there seemed to be little consensus or outright endorsement of the political alternatives. They had confronted Canada's and some particular Canadians' perception of Quebec, Quebecers, and perhaps the Quebecois – if the last seems not always to include all of the former – and been puzzled, profoundly offended, and in at least the one instance, somewhat pleasantly surprised. Quebecers had expressed concern at the erosion of their historical patrimony to the benefit of private interests; they had been vexed by the continued inability of the government to safely manage and maintain its institutions and physical infrastructure and concerned by changes in the fabric of their society emanating from what many saw as external influences and the collective, but internal, 'other.' Quebecers' famed ability to weather change and continue under duress was put to the test in 2006. They closed the year hoping the road ahead would be less bumpy.

RICHARD WILBUR

New Brunswick

The old adage 'the smaller the pit the fiercer the rats' certainly applied to New Brunswick's political scene in 2006, especially when one views the confusing events that dominated the spring session of the legislature. One would be hard put not to be sympathetic towards Tory premier Bernard Lord as he struggled to keep his government afloat amid backbench dissension which finally wiped out a bare one-seat majority. Few were surprised when he called a fall election. The fact that the Liberals managed a 3-seat majority yet won fewer votes than the Conservatives was less a tribute to the new premier Shawn Graham and more a sign that the electorate remained both confused and disenchanted at New Brunswick's brand of politics.

Premier Lord's last session

The year began on a positive note for the Tories when the veteran Liberal MLA Frank Branch resigned from his party to sit as an independent, a move that came as police in his home constituency of Bathurst began an investigation into the North Shore Forest Marketing Board, where he had been manager for several years. His decision left the Liberals with 26 seats compared to 28 for the Conservatives. On 17 February, Michael (Tanker) Malley from Miramichi quit the Tories after being passed over in Premier Lord's major Cabinet shuffle announced three days earlier. The government was now in a minority position with the balance of power in the hands of the two independents. On 28 March Malley rejoined the Tories and was then named Speaker of the House, a move that brought loud but futile criticism from the Opposition as well from a former Tory Cabinet minister and current backbencher. Tony Huntjens had expected to be chosen Speaker if it came to vote and publicly accused Malley of using blackmail tactics to get the position. On 10 April Premier Lord revealed that Branch would accompany him when he attended a first ministers' meeting the next day in Montreal, a decision that protected the government's tenuous hold in the House. On 30 May, Malley narrowly survived a non-confidence motion that would have removed him as Speaker. Branch was absent during the intense two-hour debate preceding the vote, which the government won 27–25.

On 27 March, the day before Malley took the speaker's chair and twenty-four hours before the 2006–7 budget was to be tabled, Premier Lord announced a $100 million energy relief plan containing 14 measures to address skyrocketing energy costs. Electricity rates would be capped at 8 per cent; the prices of gasoline and home heating oil would be regulated; NB Power's management bonus program would be cancelled; the facility's practice of estimating metre readings would be discontinued; and a feasibility study would be conducted into a second nuclear reactor at Point Lepreau.

The next day, finance minister Jeannot Volpe in his budget address predicted a surplus of $22 million and expenses totaling $6.029 billion. Education topped the priority list with promises of 240 more teaching positions, but a start on a province-wide kindergarten program was delayed until the fall of 2008. In 2005 the federal Liberal government signed a deal with the Lord administration to spend $31 million on such a program, and even though Stephen Harper cancelled this arrangement, the new budget said $23 million of this amount would be spent by the end of the 2006–7 fiscal year. The remaining $8 million would be used to establish a trust fund from which existing child-care operators could apply to upgrade their facilities. Personal income tax rates would remain the same, but re-indexing would mean those in the lower brackets would be exempt as of 1 January 2007. The general corporate income tax would be lowered from 13 to 12 per cent. Addressing a widely publicized issue, the budget promised that as of 1 April 2006, seniors entering nursing homes would no longer have to sell their homes to pay for such care. Neither would couples be separated before moving to such facilities.

The much-anticipated budget vote on 7 April went as expected after Speaker Malley dropped broad hints a few days earlier that he planned to support his former colleagues. The standing vote was 27 for the government, 26 for the Liberals, who also received the support of former Tory Branch. By casting the tie vote, Malley said he was guided by the principle that a Speaker generally voted with the government on confidence issues. The remainder of the spring session dragged on for several more weeks. The Liberals were able to reject departmental estimates in committee of supply when they created a deadlock after the Tories threatened to change committee rules, which would have given their committee chair 2 votes. A compromise was reached whereby the Opposition would get enough support for two bills, one protecting rural schools from closures and another that would shorten the time for a by-election to six months rather than the present year after a seat becomes vacant. As well, the Liberals would get to chair standing committees on health and education. As a result, the government was able to pass several key bills, including one giving graduating university students tax breaks up to $10,000 each if they settle in the province for up to five years, another requiring budgets to be balanced, and one permitting the government to sue tobacco companies for tobacco-related health damages. These measures subsequently received royal assent when the House finally rose on 22 June.

Other major acts passed into law included the Petroleum Products Pricing Act regulating gasoline and home heating oil as of 1 July. Another replaced the Public Utilities Board with the Energy and Public Utilities Board, which would be responsible for setting regulated gasoline and home heating oil prices once every two weeks. The Liberal Opposition voted against the bill but four MLAs were absent, which required Speaker Malley to cast the deciding vote in favour. Eleven days into the new price regulation regime, more than 120 gas retailers across the province had closed off their pumps in protest, but by the year's end, the system was still in place and the retailers seemed resigned to accept the change.

The general election

Former Cabinet minister Peter Mesheau's decision not to run again, which he announced to a caucus meeting on 9 August, once again placed the government in a minority position and prompted Premier Lord's long-expected announcement the following day. New Brunswickers would go to the polls on 18 September. As one Fredericton academic, Professor Joseph Masciulli of St Thomas University, put it, 'If [Lord] loses, he's practicing law for the rest of his life … For Graham it's do or die. He either wins this one or he's out' (*Telegraph-Journal*, 11 Aug.). The results would prove him correct.

Lord's opening salvo before a partisan Fredericton crowd a few hours after the writs were issued said voters could choose between the Tories' promise to cut gas prices by two cents within a month after the election compared to the Liberals' approach of 3.8-cent cut within 120 days. Fluctuating gas prices and another unresolved issue from the 2003 election, high car insurance premiums, made the headlines early in the rather quiet campaign, but so did another familiar problem, the Orimulsion fiasco that had resulted in a $2.2 billion lawsuit brought by NB Power against the Venezuelan supplier of the high-sulphur fuel. On 6 September Lord told a Moncton audience it was the power commission's fault rather than the Tory Cabinet that the deal fell through. Knowing this, he said, NB Power nevertheless went ahead and authorized the $750 million cost to refurbish the Coleson Cove facility outside Saint John so it could use the fuel. A few days earlier Liberal leader Shawn Graham promised that if he formed the government he would launch a public inquiry. This had been urged earlier by the former NDP leader and long-time MLA for Saint John Elizabeth Weir before she retired in 2005 to accept a new post as chair of a commission promoting energy efficiency. During the now traditional party leaders' televised debate on 7 September, Orimulsion was the main topic, and even though Graham was considered by pundits to have been the most aggressive, there were 'no knockout blows' (*Telegraph-Journal*, 8 Sept.). Meanwhile, an opinion poll conducted by Corporate Research Associates between 17 and 30 August reported that three quarters of New Brunswick motorists believed gasoline prices would be higher or unchanged under the price regulations that took effect 1 July. On the other hand, support for and opposition to price regulation was nearly evenly split.

Ten days before Election Day, the leaders of the two main parties, along with the NDP candidate, outlined their plans to voters on another long-standing issue, health care. Premier Lord defended his government's efforts to reduce waiting times by increasing spending 'by more than $1 billion more per year on health and senior care since we were first elected' (*Telegraph-Journal*, 9 Sept.). He said this increase resulted in 224 more physicians practicing in the province and 931 full-time nurses. If re-elected, his government would introduce a new Fitness and Culture Participation Tax Credit allowing families to receive up to $50 credit on expenditures related to sport and culture programs. New resources totaling $6.1 million would be made available to aid nearly 40,000 citizens suffering from diabetes plus an equal number who have yet to be diagnosed. More doctors would receive training 'here at home,' and the per diem rate for special care homes would be increased. He touted the new regional hospital nearing completion in the upper Saint John River valley, a move that raised a storm of protest especially among Woodstock residents. He also praised the creation of seven new community health centres but understandably ignored the fact that at least three of them in predominantly Acadian communities in the northeast had been downgraded from regional hospital status, again a move that was fiercely opposed.

Shawn Graham said a new Liberal government would create bursaries for medical students who agreed to practice in their home province and would give income tax credits for recent graduates already working in New Brunswick. Medical training 'opportunities' would be established in Moncton and Saint John. 'Certain services would be restored to specific areas including the Acadian peninsula,' and a single provincial ambulance service would be established replacing the current privately operated system. An online Prescription Drug Monitoring Program would be 'the first component of an Electronic Patient Record,' while a Liberal government would 'partner with Regional Health Authorities, service providers and community organizations to develop a Provincial Addictions Strategy including increased access to addictions services and treatment.'

The statement from NDP leader Allison Brewer, which occupied the lower third of the full-page commentary, dealt with a totally different theme, auto insurance. She completely endorsed a public auto insurance plan recommended in 2004 by a legislative select committee chaired by her predecessor, Elizabeth Weir. She stated, 'Sadly for drivers in New Brunswick, both the Liberals and the Conservatives ignored the recommendations … The result was predictable, drivers are still penalized by the insurance companies on the basis of where they live, not just the vehicle they drive or their driving record.' A week earlier, Graham, who favoured a public system during the 2003 general election campaign, promised that if he formed the government this time, he would give auto insurance companies sixty days to improve their coverage policies 'or a public auto insurance system will be launched in New Brunswick' (*Telegraph-Journal*, 2 Sept.). Don Forgeron, vice president of Atlantic for the Insurance Bureau of Canada, refused to comment on Graham's ultimatum but promised his industry would work with whomever was in power. The same day the Liberal leader put forward his party's stand, the New Brunswick Insurance Board, which is the insurance regulator, said the average premiums should be reduced by 11.6 per cent this year. Premier Lord told reporters that the Liberal approach might produce higher rates and would cost taxpayers millions.

As the four-week campaign dragged onward to voting day on 19 September, the steadily diminishing crowds turning up to greet Lord indicated the likely outcome. The 38-year-old Graham and his fellow Liberals took 29 of the 55 seats at stake, just 3 seats more than the

Conservatives, who took 47.7 per cent of the votes compared to the Liberals' 46.9 per cent.

Once again the NDP were shut out, taking only 5 per cent of the ballots cast. Two Tory ministers, Brad Green of Fredericton in health and Brenda Fowlie of Saint John in energy, were defeated, as was Michael (Tanker) Malley in Miramichi – Bay du Vin, the riding once firmly held by Frank McKenna. The Liberals took 2 more seats to consolidate their hold on the Saint John area but elsewhere the electoral map looked much the same as three years earlier. The Tories held all but one of the six Moncton-area seats and also kept most of those in the southeast and along the Saint John River around Fredericton and over to the Maine border, plus the solidly francophone northwest corner know as le Republique de Madawaska. The Liberals retained their hold in the northeast as well as the least populated ridings across the centre. All in all, it was a narrow win, leaving Graham with the same two problems that plagued Lord over the previous three years: how to control the legislature and how to find the money to maintain the level of services 720,000 people have come to expect.

The ever-challenging public sector

NB Power

Much media ink and electronic air time during the year was devoted to the trials and tribulations of NB Power, perhaps the single most important public institution affecting the daily lives of all New Brunswickers. 'NB Power had too many bosses,' ran the headline in the 11 January issue of the *Telegraph Journal*. The annual report of the auditor general, Michael Ferguson, also noted that though there had been improvements in the debt-ridden utility, at various times it was taking direction from the premier's office, the Department of Energy, and the NB Electric Finance Corporation, which, he believed, 'could cause some confusion.' He had not looked specifically into the Orimulsion contract, but his comments strongly suggested this issue could have been resolved or perhaps avoided under a more unified management. The utility's image was not enhanced a few days later when it defended the large retirement packages to senior executives involved in recent restructuring – packages that saw the former vice president of corporative strategic planning take away $316,836, making him the highest-paid provincial official in 2004–5. Provincial public accounts figures, made public annually to show all those civil servants earning over $40,000, revealed that NB Power officials held five of the first ten spots. On 24 January, NB Power officials appeared before the Public Utilities Board (PUB) requesting a 13 per cent rate increase for residential users and 12.9 per cent for large industrial customers such as pulp mills. On 9 February, the utility's distribution company filed a revised profit forecast, at the PUB's request, predicting a $22.6 million profit for the fiscal year ending 31 March, compared to a budgeted figure of $4.4 million. The five-fold increase was the result of higher than usual rainfall through the previous autumn, which reduced costs through a greater reliance on the cheaper hydro from the dams on the Saint John River. On 19 June, after a lengthy public review process, the PUB recommended a 13 per cent residential increase and 15 per cent for large users, but ordinary ratepayers could escape the effects if the Lord government carried out its promise to cap all increases at 8 per cent. When the Liberals assumed power in September, they gave the PUB a three-month reprieve before deciding whether it should be replaced by a new energy and utilities board as planned by the Tory government. A subsequent and lengthy rate hearing before the PUB reduced the residential increase to an average 9.6 per cent. Meanwhile, in mid-December the new energy minister, Jack Keir, said the Graham government would not launch an independent inquiry into the Orimulsion deal until NB Power had concluded its $2 billion lawsuit against Venezuela's state-owned oil company (*Telegraph-Journal*, 28 Dec.). A few days earlier, he said the government was considering fast-tracking its feasibility study on a second reactor at the Point Lepreau nuclear facility, currently undergoing a costly refurbishing of Canada's first-ever Candu reactor (ibid., 19 Dec.).

Meanwhile, in the private energy-generating sector, Irving Oil Ltd announced it was proceeding with its $750 million project to build a liquefied gas (LNG) plant near the present Canaport facility in Saint John. By mid-May, the terminal site had been cleared and levelled and the two partners, Irving Oil Ltd. and the Spanish firm Repsol YPF SA, had awarded contracts for the engineering, procurement, and construction for the giant project expected to be completed by late 2008. In October, Irving officials said they were considering building a second oil refinery at Canaport at a cost of between $5 billion and $7 billion. The present facility, the largest oil refinery in Canada, which was upgraded in 2000 at a cost of $1.5 billion, produces 300,000 barrels a day and employs 1,500. A second refinery would add another 1,000 full-time jobs. Farther down the coast, opposition was growing among citizens on both sides of the border against plans by American promoters to build two

LNG facilities in Maine only five kilometres across the Saint Croix estuary from the resort town of Saint Andrews. It would see huge tankers passing almost daily through Head Harbour Passage, a narrow body of water containing massive whirlpools and totally within Canadian territory. Saint Andrews mayor John Craig got the verbal assurance of Greg Thompson, the local MP and federal veterans' affairs minister, that Canada would take every legal means to prevent LNG tankers from using Canadian waters. The American proponents have argued that Canada cannot block commercial ships because of the 'innocent passage' provision of international marine treaties.

Health

Judging by statistical evidence, New Brunswickers' general state of health matched the shortcomings of the provincial delivery system. A report released in mid-January by the Canadian Institute of Health Information (CIHI) said that the province had the lowest number of physicians per capita in Canada, and a month later this same institute revealed that New Brunswickers, both adults and children, were among the most obese. In February during an editorial meeting with the *Telegraph-Journal*, Premier Lord defended his government's decision to close 280 beds: 'I agree it was fast, but it was the solution that was needed.' He argued that the savings meant investments in other areas such as PET / CT scanners and satellite dialysis units (ibid., 16 Feb.). Two days later his newly named health minister, Brad Green, who succeeded the retiring Elvy Robichaud, said the province would not be following Quebec's example by allowing the private sector to deliver some services. In April an official for the University of New Brunswick's nurse-practitioners' MA program revealed that only one was expected to graduate this year, which posed problems for the government's previously announced target of adding 10 nurse practitioners a year until there were a total of 40. In 2005 there were 21 nurse-practitioners working in the province (*Daily Gleaner*, 15 April).

In mid-October, two days before Premier Graham was to chair a two-day wellness conference in Fredericton, a report from the Fraser Institute said New Brunswickers face 31.9 weeks' or almost eight months' waiting time for any major treatment, about twice as long as in Ontario and nine weeks longer than in Nova Scotia. It predicted there would be no improvements as result of increased spending. 'The problem is the design of the health care program itself' (*Telegraph Journal*, 17 Nov.). Three weeks later Premier Graham announced that the new

Liberal government would be spending an additional $7.2 million annually to hire 190 more staff members for nursing homes. On 22 November, health minister Mike Murphy confirmed a statement made two days earlier by Dr Larry Kennedy, a practicing family doctor and a long-time MLA for Victoria-Tobique. The new government would not follow its predecessor' plan for the upper Saint John River valley, which would have drastically reduced the services offered by hospitals in Plaster Rock and Perth-Andover in favour of consolidating services at a new facility nearing completion at Waterville, a tiny community near Hartland. Murphy said this change had been promised during the Liberals' election campaign, but he added that there would no reopening of full services at the Caraquet hospital because no similar promise had been made (*Telegraph-Journal*, 23 Nov.).

Education

In 2003 Premier Lord unveiled his Quality Learning Agenda aimed at placing the public school system within the Canadian top three in terms of academic performance within a decade. Three years later, in yet another in-depth examination of that system, former university president and law professor Dr Wayne MacKay called Lord's goal 'a challenging objective … Things need to happen quickly. If you don't pay now, you're going to pay later' (*Telegraph-Journal*, 16 March). Among his ninety-five main recommendations: increase per-student funding to bring New Brunswick from the bottom to the middle of the pack among Canadian provinces; more training for teachers and school support staff on inclusion policies and classroom management; explore the possibility of inclusive day-care and preschool settings for children; make the French immersion program more inclusive and reduce the concentration of students with learning challenges in the core English program; and develop a learning disabilities strategy to help caregivers identify and respond to needs faster. The education minister, Claude Williams, said the report 'won't get put on the shelf' and, though making no specific promises, he would host a provincial forum 28–29 May to give teachers, parents, and experts the opportunity to comment on MacKay's report, which had taken a year to complete (ibid.).

For the remainder of Lord's administration, little more was done to address the concerns raised by MacKay except for an attempt to address the concern for more vocational training. In May the minister of post-secondary education and training, Jody Carr, in presenting his estimates, pointed to the addition of 140 seats to be made available in the trade courses. He also noted that the Tory budget included $800,000 for a commission on the future of post-secondary education (*Times Transcript*, 11 May). Considering the near total absence of movement on the education file once the new Liberal administration assumed office in September, it is safe to assume that education and the MacKay report's recommendations did not rank near the top of Premier Graham's priority list.

Natural resources sectors continue their decline

The year opened on a slightly positive note with news that the new owners of the former Saint Anne – Nackawic paper mill, closed since September 2004, would begin operations on 16 January with a workforce of 275. About 80 former unionized employees were not rehired. The new company, formed jointly by the Aditya Birla group from India and Tembec Inc. of Canada, paid about $20 million to buy the bankrupt firm's private land holdings and secured $67 million in direct loans and guarantees from the New Brunswick government. For the next eighteen months the mill will produce kraft pulp while it moves part of the production to dissolve pulp for use in the manufacture of rayon – a diversification plan the new owners hope will protect the company from changing marketing forces that caused the bankruptcy two years earlier (*Daily Gleaner*, 13 Jan.). In December 2005 the Lord government had introduced a $250 million aid package to help the ailing forest industry – still the province's biggest single industry with 17,000 wage earners directly and many thousands more indirectly employed. Since 2004, some 1,200 jobs in the pulp and paper sector alone have been lost, and this does not include layoffs from closed mills scattered across the province. The Nackawic package included tax concessions, wood supply guarantees, and a reduction in Crown land stumpage fees.

Shortly after announcing the aid program Premier Lord and his natural resources minister, Keith Ashfield, visited Finland to meet with directors of UPM Kymmene, a forestry conglomerate whose extensive holdings include a ground wood mill and a pulp mill in Miramichi. More than 450 workers were given three-month layoff notices in late 2005 and many wondered when, if ever, they would return to work. In March, the natural resources department announced it was cutting the number of provincial forest rangers, from 160 to 80. It was also ending mandatory inspections of all logging activities on Crown lands in favour of a new forest audit system. Tom Mann, spokesperson for the public-sector union representing the forest rangers, questioned the timing of the decision, which followed stalled contract negotiations and a strike vote taken by the members a month earlier (*Telegraph-Journal*, 21 March). David Coon of the New Brunswick Conservation Council released two internal government reports obtained under the NB Right to Information Act which stated that 'the public may perceive this as a significant decrease in the number of enforcement staff, no matter what spin is put on it' (ibid.). It added that 120 rangers should be assigned to this role.

In December, following a lengthy process stretching back six years, the Supreme Court of Canada ruled unanimously that native band members had the right to harvest timber within their traditional territory for such purposes as firewood or for building furniture or a home. They did not have the right to harvest wood for commercial sale, and the Supreme Court added that their ruling was subject to provincial regulation (ibid., 8 Dec.). An earlier court turned down a native request to harvest logs from Crown land for commercial purposes.

The future of another traditional staple, commercial fishery, clearly hinged on two bottom feeders, lobster and crab. Scientists believe the warmer water in the normally frigidly cold Bay of Fundy is responsible for the sharp increase in that area's lobster catches – up in 2004 by roughly four times what was seen in 1981 – and the upward trend continued in 2006. Conversely, lobster fishermen working the Northumberland Strait and the Gulf of Saint Lawrence reported another poor year with catches dropping to half of what they were in 2000. Some fishermen blamed the Confederation Bridge. A new report on the health of the strait noted increased sediment around the bridge piers, which when added to runoffs from farm pesticides and road salt could be contributing factors to the deteriorating water conditions and lower lobster catches (ibid., 21 June). Incomplete landing figures released at the end of the fall lobster season in District 25, encompassing southeastern New Brunswick, indicated the decline was continuing, although fishermen in the northeastern areas reported catches about the same as in 2005 – fair but nowhere near what they had been a decade earlier. Snow crab fishermen in the Acadian peninsula, some of whom had become millionaires after this fishery began in the 1970s, were hard hit by lower prices and a Department of Fisheries and Oceans (DFO) decision to cut quotas as a conservation measure. At the close of this spring fishery, concern was expressed by both provincial and federal politicians for the plight of 2,700 fish plant workers, most of them women, some of whom received only three weeks' employment because of lower catches. This was not enough to qualify them for employment insurance benefits. A special federal pilot program giving them an extra five weeks in benefits expired at the end of the fishing season and was not renewed.

Underscoring the old adage that no news is good news, the province's agriculture sector had little to report during the year except that according to a report released in November by Farm Credit Canada, a good market and an equally good potato crop increased New Brunswick's farm values by 1.1 per cent in the first half of the year. By contrast, values remained unchanged for dairy and beef operations (*Times Transcript*, 10 Oct.).

Other stories that caught public attention

The Miramichi Hospital fraud case

In February Judge Drew Stymiest became the first judge in the history of New Brunswick to face criminal charges when he and three other directors of the Miramichi Hospital Corporation were found guilty of defrauding the institution of close to $1 million between 1994 and 2000. The 56-year-old judge, who as a Crown prosecutor had been involved in a number of high-profile cases including the murder trial of boxer Yvon Durelle in 1977, had been suspended from the bench with pay ($140,000 a year) since the police investigation began in 2001. At the end of four months hearing evidence, the jury found the group guilty of 40 out of the 47 counts, which included setting up a shell company to hide the stolen funds, kickbacks, double-billing, and fake invoices. Stymiest had been a hospital board member for 20 years and its chairman during the time the crimes were committed (*Telegraph-Journal*, 8 Feb.). The day after the court decision, he faxed a four-line letter of resignation to the justice minister, and on 31 March he was sentenced to five years in prison and ordered to make restitution of $218,000 while the other three received sentences ranging from one to four and a half years. Each was given four months' credit for the time they spent on remand in the provincial jail since their conviction.

The case of the Grand Manan Five

On 22 July local frustration with an alleged crack dealer on Grand Manan Island, a prosperous fishing community two hours' ferry ride from the mainland, spilled over into a four-hour riot on Saturday night. When it ended, a house was a smoldering ruin and fifteen people – including the alleged dealer, Ronald Ross – suffered only minor injuries despite the use of shotguns, knives, and baseball bats. Three members of the local RCMP detachment could only stand by as a mob, estimated at over 40 participants, threw rocks at volunteer firefighters trying to put out the fire. Five men ranging in age from 25 to 31 were subsequently charged, and in a jury trial held in the historic old courthouse in Saint Andrews, two were convicted of arson and two of weapons charges; the fifth was acquitted. All five expressed remorse for their role in the riot and each of the convicted received a one-year conditional sentence of house confinement except for work (all were fishermen). Each was ordered to pay Ross $5,000 in restitution. Ross would stand trial at a later date on charges of threatening to kill one of the accused and burn his house (ibid., 25 July, 3 Nov. and 20 Nov.). The case got national media coverage.

The fight over Lord Beaverbrook's art gifts

A very different court case, which began four years earlier and went to arbitration on 3 October before retired Supreme Court judge Peter Cory, was watched with intense interest by officials of art galleries and museums across North America. On 30 August, the Saint John *Telegraph-Journal* repeated a story carried earlier by the London *Sunday Times* outlining the latest efforts by Maxwell Aitken III, grandson of Lord Beaverbrook and director of the London-based Beaverbrook Foundation, to claim ownership of scores of paintings originally bequeathed to Fredericton's Beaverbrook Gallery. Readers learned that Maxwell Aitken III had been forced to sell the family estate and that his creditors, which included several banks and Britain's Inland Revenue, had been unable to recover significant assets held by a Panama-based company. The peer was now chairman of CheekyMoon, an online gambling company featuring games such as CheekyPoker and Naughty Netball. Such tidbits would undoubtedly increase the interest of many New Brunswickers who had never set foot in any gallery. Taking advantage of the mountain of publicity, officials at the Beaverbrook Gallery launched two exhibits during the year which drew over 30,000 paid visitors – a gallery record. The first was entitled *Arts in Dispute*. The other was organized by a Los Angeles foundation, holder of the world's largest private collection of the sculptor Rodin; together the exhibits proved to be the most successful efforts in the gallery's forty-seven-year history (ibid., 14 Feb.). In December Marty Klinkenberg, the Saint John journalist who had been covering the trial since it began, reported that Judge Cory had 'challenged key portions' of the closing statement of the Beaverbrook Foundation's chief lawyer, claiming that some of the counsel's evidence suggested 'concealment, not disclosure.' This left a general impression that when the judge handed down his verdict in several weeks' time, it would result in most of the disputed paintings remaining in Fredericton (ibid., 6 Dec.).

Agent Orange fallout at Camp Gagetown

The key events took place thirty years earlier, but more than 1,500 people were seeking compensation in 2006 for health problems they claim were caused in 1966 and 1967. That was when the US military forces, training at Camp Gagetown, tested concentrated defoliants. In 2005, three of the nine suspected sites were tested by scientists and were found to have high dioxin levels. These were subsequently barricaded by CFB Gagetown officials, but a Health Canada spokesperson said the department was waiting for the results of a health study before taking further action. In the meantime, she stressed there was no evidence that soldiers who passed through the area were put at risk (ibid., 2 June). The head of that study, Dr Dennis Furlong, a Dalhousie physician and a former provincial health minister, said it was too early to draw conclusions about the soil samples that had high dioxin levels. In December, he released the second of a three-installment report which concluded there was no risk of long-term illness for most of those who had been living near or working at the base. So far, the Veterans' Affairs department had received 1,100 claims from veterans who believe their health was put at risk by the military spray program and twenty have received disability pensions based on their exposure to Agent Orange. Despite promises made in October by local MP Greg Thompson, the Veterans Affairs minister, that he hoped 'this fall' to present Cabinet with a compensation package worth about $20,000 for each claimant, by the year's end hundreds of aging claimants were still waiting.

Liberal Premier Graham's cautious approach to governing

It took Shawn Graham little more than two weeks after his party's election victory to achieve one of his most challenging jobs – choosing a Cabinet. Among the twelve anglophones and seven francophones were two of the three women in his caucus. Five of the new ministers were from Saint John compared to only two from the Moncton area, but the latter duo held key portfolios, Mike Murphy in health and Victor Boudreau in finance. Fredericton would be represented by Kelly

Lamrock in education, Greg Byrne in Business New Brunswick, and T.J. Burke, the first Aboriginal MLA, the new attorney general, and justice minister. Graham also announced that the provincial gasoline excise tax would be cut by 3.8 cents a litre, starting immediately, and the auto insurance industry was given until 2 December to give drivers a better deal or else he would introduce a public insurance system. First-year university students attending provincial institutions would see their tuition fees reduced by $1,000 this semester and another $1,000 after Christmas (ibid., 4 Oct.). Honouring his campaign promise to act within twenty-four hours after being sworn into office on the long-delayed project to clean up Saint John Harbour, Graham met the following day with Mayor Norm McFarlane and pledged $26.6 million, representing the one-third provincial share of the $80 million project. By the year's end, neither the City of Saint John nor the Harper government had come through with the remaining two-thirds and open sewage continued to flow into the harbour as it had done for the past several generations.

Despite calls from the Conservative Opposition for a fall legislative session, as Graham had agreed to during a spring budget debate, the new Liberal House leader, Stuart Jamieson, declining on the grounds the new government needed time to review programs and draft a new budget, said the House would be convened on 6 February 2007, five months after it had prorogued for the general election (ibid., 19 Oct.). Over the next few weeks, after the usual replacement of former Conservative deputy ministers with Liberals, Premier Graham took to the road, heading first to Toronto to meet CEOs of some of Canada's largest firms at a meeting arranged by former Liberal premier Frank McKenna, now a busy corporate director himself (ibid., 16 Nov.). A week later Graham was the opening speaker in Montreal at the national Liberal leadership convention. He made no speeches or major public appearances for the rest of the year, leaving it to two Cabinet ministers to make significant announcements. On 28 November the public safety minister, John Foran, said after a caucus meeting in Saint John that new legislation would be introduced restricting the use of all-terrain vehicles and snowmobiles to drivers over sixteen. Within the previous 16 days two children, one 13 years old and the other 16 years old, died as a result of separate accidents involving such vehicles. A week later, Burke, the justice minister, announced the new government had successfully negotiated a 13.5 per cent reduction in auto insurance rates and got the industry's agreement to remove the driver's gender as a pricing determinant. He was not able to change the boundary differential which penalized drivers in the northern areas. Industry officials were conspicuously absent when Burke met the media but two of the largest insurers issued statements noting that rates in the province had decreased by 33.7 per cent over the past thirty months, one adding that it was 'unfortunate' the government 'felt compelled to circumvent the province's own existing independent rate review board.' Ronald Godin, chair of the Consumer Advocate for Insurance, said he was pleased at the rate reduction but noted that 'a lot of people in the north were convinced we were going public' (ibid., 5 Dec.).

On 13 December Bernard Lord announced his resignation as party leader and as the MLA for Moncton, saying it was the best thing for 'our family, for myself and for our party.' He dismissed rumours that he would become the next French ambassador or that he would enter the federal field: 'They're just not true. My desire is to work in the private sector' (ibid., 14 Dec.). The resignation would take effect 31 January, just prior to the opening of the next legislative session. His departure follows that of Allison Brewer, who quit the leadership of the NDP in October after the party's poor electoral results. A week after his announcement, he defended his government's fiscal record, claiming, despite two auditors' reports to the contrary, that 'when we left office we were still heading for a surplus' (*Times Transcript*, 21 Dec.). A week earlier a report by the provincial auditor general Michael Ferguson said the Lord government accelerated the $60 million grant payments to universities to avoid posting a projected deficit for the 2006–7 fiscal year, a move that allowed the government to produce a $38 million surplus instead of a $22 million deficit. A report released a week later by the accounting firm Grant Thornton, commissioned by the new Liberal government, underscored the province's challenging financial state. It warned that if current and projected spending continued, there would be a deficit of $17.6 million this year, one that did not include over $60 million in campaign promises the Liberals said would receive funding during this period. The new finance minister Victor Boudreau's response was immediate: he cancelled the promised harmonized sales tax (HST) rebate on home heating costs to low-income earners. Instead, they would receive a one-time home energy cheque for $100, a move that would save the province $35 million. Clearly, the new government faced the same challenge that haunted its predecessor: how to pay for essential services without adding to the already huge provincial debt.

PETER E. BUKER

Prince Edward Island

PEI had stable economic activity and mild growth in 2006. There were numerous provincial initiatives in the realms of energy and the environment and much infrastructure investment. Politically there were municipal elections and one provincial by-election, the four incumbent federal MPs were returned to office, and the provincial electoral boundaries map was redrawn amid great controversy.

Economy

In 2006 PEI's economy expanded by 2.0 per cent and the provincial GDP at market prices was estimated to be $4,332 million. Personal income grew by an estimated 3.7 per cent to $3,729 million. The *All-Items Consumer Price Index* rose 2.2 per cent. Total employment was 68,600 people, and the average unemployment rate was 11.0 per cent. The population was estimated by Statistics Canada as 137,920 (and 135,851 by the 2006 Canadian Census). In 2005–6 PEI had 232 immigrants – the largest net international migration since 1973. In terms of annual changes by major economic measures, total investment in PEI increased 2.8 per cent to $788 million; tourist expenditures increased 3 per cent to $334.1 million; total fish landings rose an estimated 1.5 per cent with a value of $166.6 million; retail trade was up 4.1 per cent to $1,486 million; total farm cash receipts were 3.2 per cent higher at $379.8 million; island manufacturing rose to $1,349.4 million, an increase of 3.9 per cent; and exports rose 1.7 per cent to $772.8 million. The public sector – education, health and social services, and public administration – accounted for 33.1 per cent of total island employment.

PEI received $1,170 million in total revenue in the fiscal year 2005–6, which was almost 5.0 per cent higher than the previous fiscal year. Provincial tax revenues increased 7.9 per cent to $711.1 million, while total federal transfers accounted for 38 per cent of the total revenue.

Total expenditures rose 1.7 per cent to $1,169.3 million, and there was a surplus in the operating fund of $680,000. As of 31 March the provincial net debt was up 1.3 per cent to $1,292 million.

Fiscal events

In April the Department of Agriculture, Fisheries, and Aquaculture was reorganized to better identify and manage value-added opportunities in organic, environmentally responsible production. In May government began an Aquaculture and Fisheries Research Initiative mandated to research the impact of vase tunicate on the mussel industry in the Montague / Brudenell, Saint Mary's Bay, and Cardigan River systems. In June a PEI government-commissioned report examining the financial condition of Northumberland Strait fishers recommended reducing lobster licence numbers and establishing a debt-review board, government-sponsored low-interest loans, and a lobster habitat restoration program. The recreational cod fishery, closed since 2003, was reopened for PEI's Southern Gulf of Saint Lawrence.

In February Garden Province Meats was offered a $1 million loan by the province, and in April the provincial government created a new loan program for financially struggling hog producers. On 29 August the Quebec City – based Natural and Organic Food Group Inc., along with PEI Pork Plus, purchased the Garden Province Meats facility.

The year 2006 was the final year of the Canada-PEI Infrastructure Program involving 81 projects valued at more than $38 million. The Municipal Rural Infrastructure Fund (MRIF) had thirty-six projects in varying states of approval, with an estimated value of more than $20 million. The Strategic Infrastructure Fund was financing sewerage and water upgrades in Charlottetown, Summerside, and Stratford. Government had committed a total of $8 million to the 2009 Canada Summer Games, with $3.6 million already allocated. In October $12 million in public investment was announced under the second round of the Canada – Prince Edward Island MRIF for 40 projects. Community capital upgrade funding also continued to be available under the federal Gas Tax Agreement.

In October the government announced a ten-year provincial corporate tax rebate program for bioscience companies. The government introduced the PEI Energy Savings Bonds program, starting 11 December, for islanders to invest in the Eastern Kings Wind Farm, which was expected to supply 7.5 per cent of PEI's electricity needs.

On 11 October the Wind Energy Institute of Canada, an independent, non-profit facility funded by the federal and provincial governments and designed to propel growth and development in wind energy, was officially opened in North Cape. The PEI Energy Corporation requested tenders for the Prince Edward Island Wind-Hydrogen Village Project, which would demonstrate how wind and hydrogen technologies could work together.

In June Moody's Investors Service upgraded the province's credit rating on long-term borrowing from A2 to A1; the improved rating reflected the province's reduced debt-to-GDP ratio to 31.4 per cent and a decline in the debt-to-revenue ratio to 116.0 per cent.

Effective 1 April 2006, the minimum wage in Prince Edward Island increased from $6.80 per hour to $7.15 per hour.

Politics and the legislature

The Canadian federal election was held 23 January; all four incumbent Liberal MPs were returned in PEI. The provincial voter turnout was 73.2 per cent, the highest in Canada.

The spring 2006 sitting of PEI's Third Session of the 62nd General Assembly began on 30 March, adjourned 24 May, and sat for 27 and 28 June before being prorogued. The Fourth Session of PEI's 62nd General Assembly began on 16 November and ended 15 December.

On 7 February the provincial government announced the Immigrant Connections Program offered through the Provincial Nominee Program (PNP). The Immigrant Connections Program was designed to compete for international immigrants and thereby avoid the anticipated decline in population in PEI. The PNP was a five-year federal-PEI pilot partnership agreement between the province and Citizenship and Immigration Canada.

In early April, the Department of Community and Cultural Affairs created the new Division of Public Safety to encompass the fire marshal office, the Emergency Measures Organization, the administration of the 911 program, and a new section for joint emergency preparedness projects. Enhanced PEI driver's licences, part of an initiative among the Atlantic provinces, were introduced to make licences consistent in design, improve security features, and save money.

On 13 March a provincial government proposal to incorporate areas surrounding the three municipalities of Mount Stewart, Morell, and Saint Peters was overwhelmingly rejected in votes taken at public meetings. A provincial by-election was called 20 March for District No. 2, Morell – Fortune Bay, following February's resignation of agriculture and fisheries minister Kevin MacAdam, who quit to join the staff of Peter MacKay – the federal foreign affairs minister, Atlantic Canada Opportunities Agency (ACOA) minister, and minister responsible for PEI. Progressive Conservative Olive Crane won by a slim margin. Montague-Kilmur MLA Jim Bagnall was sworn in as minister for the Department of Agriculture, Fisheries, and Aquaculture on 27 March. The island New Democratic Party selected 26-year-old Charlottetown native Dean Constable as leader at its annual convention in Summerside on 22 April. Barbara Anne Hagerman was installed – the fortieth lieutenant governor since the creation of PEI as a colony in 1769 – on 31 July 2006. Municipal elections – including acclamations – were held 6 November for PEI's 75 incorporated and unincorporated municipalities. Mayoralty results for the four major municipalities were Charlottetown – Clifford Lee; Summerside – Basil Stewart; Stratford – Kevin Jenkins; and Cornwall – Patrick MacFadyen.

The year 2006 saw much political debate over the changing of provincial electoral boundaries; on 4 May the Special Committee of the Legislative Assembly on Electoral Boundaries recommended to the Legislative Assembly that the *Report of the PEI Electoral Boundaries Commission* (2004) should be rejected and instructed Elections PEI to design a new electoral map with boundaries redistributed to balance community concerns with voter parity. This new map was presented as a bill, debated, rejected, and amended in the assembly on 28 June and got assent the same day to form the new electoral boundaries for PEI. In the spring, Liberal Opposition leader Robert Ghiz proposed legislation for fixed-date provincial elections; the government agreed to a plebiscite to be held in conjunction with the next provincial election on whether PEI should adopt fixed-date elections.

On 21 September Premier Binns announced that 30 per cent of PEI's total energy needs would be derived from local renewable resources by 2016. A new forestry policy for PEI – Moving to Restore a Balance in Island Forests – was released 25 October by the provincial government. The Department of Health released a report they commissioned, *Gambling and Problem Gambling in Prince Edward Island*, on 10 November; it reported no significant change in the number of problem gamblers since a 1999 study.

Provincial health initiatives were many in 2006. In February the provincial government changed the Registered Nurses Act to allow for the development of nurse-practitioner proposals. The minister of health announced the PEI Pandemic Influenza Contingency Plan 18 December; the plan included public education, limiting indoor public gatherings, infection prevention and control, vaccination of the population, the use of antiviral medications, essential service plans, and business continuity plans. The PEI government signed a ten-year contract in October with Island EMS to establish a centralized, province-wide ambulance service starting 1 April 2007. In May the government approved $47 million for the first redevelopment phase of Charlottetown's Queen Elizabeth Hospital to enhance the emergency department, ambulatory care, and day surgery services. In October the government announced that it endorsed the report from the West Prince Consultation Project Committee recommending a new single acute-care hospital in the Bloomfield area of West Prince to replace the existing hospitals in O'Leary and Alberton. Federal, provincial, and territorial ministers responsible for seniors met in Roseneath, Prince Edward Island, on 11–12 September to discuss advancing the well-being of seniors in Canada.

The PEI government released the report of the Task Force on Student Achievement to the public 25 January and outlined its response to the report's recommendations.

On 16 February PEI's Supreme Court attacked PEI's long tradition of political patronage by ruling that the Binns government acted unconstitutionally by limiting payouts to seasonal workers fired after the 1996 provincial election.

Other events

PEI hosted several major conferences in 2006. Over 300 delegates from across North America attended the Canadian Council of Motor Transport Administrators' annual conference in Charlottetown 13–18 May. On 18–20 June more than 250 participants attended the Canadian Language and Literacy Research Network's fifth annual conference in Charlottetown. More than 500 delegates met in Charlottetown for the annual conference of the Institute of Public Administration of Canada 27–30 August. From 10 to 12 September, PEI hosted the twenty-seventh annual conference of the Canadian Council of Public Accounts / Canadian Council of Legislative Auditors. The fifth annual Atlantic 911 Conference was held 11–13 October in Summerside for the region's 911 professionals.

The term for PEI's poet laureate was extended from two years to three; incumbent Frank Ledwell agreed to serve for a third year. Catherine Edward of Belfast was given the Department of Community and Cultural Affairs first biennial PEI Book Award for her work *The Brow of Dawn* in June. The 2006 recipients of the Order of PEI were announced 7 June: Dr Sheldon R. Cameron of Summerside, Frank J. Ledwell of Loyalist Road, and Dorothy Lewis of York.

The premier proclaimed 13 January 'Mark MacDonald Day' in PEI in honour of the record-setting island harness driver. On 23–27 February, PEI hosted the East Coast Music Awards in Charlottetown. On 21 March, 375 professors and librarians at University of Prince Edward Island went on strike; the 15-day strike ended 6 April. In June, a case of H5 avian flu virus was detected in the western end of PEI. The island's promotional and charity event 'Making the Connection' Legends of Golf teed off at the Rodd Brudenell River Resort on 19–20 June, featuring Jack Nicklaus and Tom Watson. In Charlottetown on 6 August the group Barenaked Ladies played to 4,000 people; on 5 September the group Black Eyed Peas played to an audience of 18,000. Island storyteller, comic, and musician Urban Carmichael died 13 February at age 54. Lorne Bonnell, physician and former MLA, provincial Cabinet minister, and member of the Senate of Canada, died 9 October.

ROBERT FINBOW

Nova Scotia

It was a year that portended change in public life but eventually produced much continuity. In an important symbolic move, Mayann Francis was appointed the first African Canadian lieutenant governor of Nova Scotia. But, despite the selection of a new premier, the political situation remained unchanged, with a minority Conservative government and Liberal disarray and weakness. Yet the potential for future change was evident – the NDP opposition gained strength and made historic breakthroughs in previously hostile rural regions of the province. The province held its own economically, despite high energy costs, with slow progress offshore and in economic modernization. The new federal government posed challenges for Nova Scotia, in a region that Conservative prime minister Stephen Harper had labelled 'defeatist.' The minority status of the federal government, however, gave it a pragmatic cast; despite policy differences, there was no sharp ideological break between the province and Ottawa.

Politics

The Conservatives elected a leader to replace retiring premier John Hamm. In a surprise result rookie Cape Breton MLA Rodney MacDonald beat out two high-profile opponents – former finance minister Neil LeBlanc and prominent businessman Bill Black. Leblanc had been the front runner but was criticized for suggesting he would leave politics if he did not win the leadership. Black, a former CEO of Maritime Life, was praised for business skills and survived to the final ballot despite a lack of political experience. MacDonald was a fresh face – youthful, with a sense of humour and unique talent as a Cape Breton fiddler. But he soon began to falter and cost himself support.

The Opposition questioned the secrecy surrounding contributors to MacDonald's campaign. One of his supporters, Ernie Fage, resigned as minister of economic development over a loan to S. and J. Potato

Farms, which leased land from Fage. (Fage was reappointed to Cabinet as minister of human resources four months later.) The Opposition queried whether companies that received government loans funded MacDonald's leadership bid. MacDonald made a series of pre-election spending announcements that caused some to question his sense of fiscal responsibility. He reversed course by implementing gas regulation as prices rose. He was criticized for stealing Opposition policies to court voters while abandoning principles – he was portrayed as opportunistic and indecisive, qualities that harmed his approval ratings.

The Tories, however, boasted 40 per cent public support and were confident they could win a majority. NDP leader Darrel Dexter promised his party would support the government if its proposal for elimination of the HST on heating and fuel costs was adopted. The premier nonetheless called a June election before passing his first budget, to take advantage of his new position. Despite the Conservatives' cooperation with the NDP over the last three years – and their adoption of its policies on health care for seniors in nursing homes, higher minimum wages and overtime pay, a ban on school closures, and removal of the HST on heating fuel – MacDonald portrayed the NDP as a threat to the economy. Late in the campaign the tone worsened as the premier feared NDP strength; he called Dexter soft on crime and also claimed public auto insurance would cost jobs and increase deficits. The tactic did not undermine support for Dexter's perceived moderate approach.

In a campaign with no major theme, MacDonald eked out a win, whereas the NDP increased in strength. The government lost 2 seats, down to 23, the NDP gained 5 to reach 20 seats, while the Liberals weakened to 9 seats as their vote share eroded. The government fared poorly in Halifax as star candidate Bill Black was defeated in the affluent south end. The NDP increased its support in rural areas, giving it representation across the province. Two more women were elected, bringing the total to 9 out of 52 MLAs, a lower percentage than most other provinces. A Nova Scotia Green Party was launched, which hoped to succeed where minor parties often foundered, but it garnered limited support in its initial electoral foray.

The government still relied on support from the Opposition parties to secure its agenda. Having enjoyed a collaborative minority situation since 2003, the government faced an emboldened NDP ready to provide a more assertive challenge as a government in waiting. The NDP's success was credited to the leadership of Dexter, who reassured skeptical voters while retaining core support from loyalists. The Liberals were weakened and leader Francis Mackenzie (who was widely blamed for the poor performance) announced his intention to step aside; veteran MLA Michel Samson was selected as interim leader. Dartmouth MP Mike Savage declined to run, but potential candidates included MLAs Diana Whalen and Stephen MacNeil and Colchester mayor Mike Smith. By year end, leadership contenders had not yet declared. The party was further embarrassed by the trial of former MLA Brian Boudreau on forgery charges.

Problems continued for the premier after the election. The government tried to address the Sunday shopping controversy. In the summer, it passed a Cabinet order to enforce closures against challenges from major retailers, but the courts found this measure exceeded authority delegated to Cabinet by the legislature. Then MacDonald tried another Cabinet order making Sunday openings legal, which brought Opposition charges of undemocratic behaviour because the population had rejected the idea in an earlier plebiscite. In addition, it eroded rural support for the party when the Opposition was cutting into these formerly solid Conservative districts. Also, the premier was criticized for appointing his former chief of staff, Heather Foley Melvin, as CEO of Conserve Nova Scotia, the new energy conservation agency. The NDP wanted her ruled in contempt of the House for her failure to answer questions from a legislature committee about her appointment, which paid $131,613.82. The Opposition challenged composition of the commission to investigate social and economic effects of gambling, dominated as it was by bureaucrats, because it lacked representation from gamblers and their families. The premier's popularity declined substantially by year's end.

Nova Scotia's education minister fired the entire Halifax Regional School Board after infighting had paralyzed and discredited the board; Howard Windsor was appointed a one-person board in an interim capacity until reforms could be enacted. Some officials mused about the benefits of eliminating elected local boards altogether, whereas others contemplated giving the boards power to raise supplementary funds for special programs such as art and music to end their dependency on overstretched provincial budgets.

The legislature

The legislature had an inactive year, with few sitting days, as the government avoided opportunities for a surprise defeat. When possible, the Opposition did press issues to knock the sheen off the new leader. A major target was an increase in the Industrial Expansion Fund, which the Opposition claimed suggested conflicts of interest; government supplied only redacted documents in response to legislative queries about the $50 million hike, some of which went to Michelin Tire, Magic Valley Family Fun Park (owned by friends of former premier Hamm), and S. and J. Potato Farms, which leased land from Fage, who was minister in charge of the fund. The Liberals introduced a motion to tighten conflict of interest rules for ministers. The NDP targeted high costs of heating oil and proposed ending the HST on this commodity, but the spring session met only a few days for the budget speech and was dissolved before a vote could be taken.

The 2005 agreement with Ottawa on offshore revenues and increased royalties from the offshore industry temporarily bolstered the province's financial situation, and it put $830 million towards the province's cash debt, reducing debt-servicing costs and permitting a surplus. Minister of finance Michael Baker indicated that the surplus would permit real tax savings for average Nova Scotians, but the government also faced pressures for corporate tax cuts to improve the province's competitive position as a location for manufacturing and other investments. In pre-election fashion, the budget sought to please many constituencies. It assisted families by eliminating the 8 per cent HST on electricity and heating fuel. This step was taken despite the Tories having criticized the NDP plan as too costly. The budget proposed future income tax cuts, starting by 2011 when tax brackets would be linked to inflation; corporate investments would not be taxed after 2012. The budget included $339 million in spending on doctors and teachers, tax credits for post-secondary graduates who worked locally, increased spending on highways and long-term care, and Pharmacare for children of low-income parents (*Daily News*, May 10). The budget included a 10-year 'Route to Prosperity' plan for investment in infrastructure. The government announced a tuition rebate using federal funds; students still faced the most expensive tuition in the country.

The government anticipated a surplus of $72 million. The ratio of overall debt to GDP decreased, although most hard choices over spending were not addressed. Credit rating agencies noted the commitment to balanced budgets, elimination of unprofitable agencies, and improved and diverse economy made the provincial situation stable. Moody's Investors Service raised the province's credit rating from A2 to A1. Business supported the tax cuts, though unions feared it could produce a Conservative majority that would have to cut public services to pay for these promises. The Liberals criticized the budget for overlooking rural needs and tourism and encouraging energy use via the HST rebate.

The NDP insisted that the budget be brought to a vote before an election, to ensure these pledges were kept. Because it included an HST cut on energy and tuition relief, the NDP planned to vote in support, but MacDonald opted for an election instead.

The legislature reconvened in June. Students remained unhappy about rising costs, and the NDP seized upon this issue – and the government's apparent reversal after the election of a planned use of federal funds to support tuition cuts. The NDP threatened to derail the budget unless tuition cuts were enacted. The provincial minister pointed at changes in the federal budget that forced the province's hand on this issue by requiring spending on infrastructure. The province proceeded with Pharmacare expansion, with 35,000 children in families earning less than $20,921 receiving coverage for prescriptions with limited copayment. The Opposition approved the plan but claimed the province was diverting federal child-care funding for this purpose and noted not all families below the poverty line of $26,000 were covered; the government responded that by 2008 it would introduce Pharmacare for all uninsured families. The assembly adjourned in July after adopting the budget with Liberal support.

By late fall, the budget situation worsened. The province was on track to spend a record $6 billion, up 8 per cent from the previous year, and faced a return to deficits. The budget had omitted spending by health authorities; the Capital District Authority overspent by $21 million, erasing much of the surplus. A computer system for the province and its school boards also went over budget by $20 million, much of it for fees and hotel bills for external consultants on the multi-year project. The government asked departments to cut $20 million and warned of further austerity measures. Changes in federal tax policies (such as income splitting for pensioners), rising pension costs, a settlement with health care workers, and uncertain tax revenues created fears of widening deficits. In this context, the announcement by an arm's-length commission that legislators would receive a 21 per cent pay raise was greeted with disdain, given that the province limited wage increases for others in public service. The commission recommendations – designed to prevent political interference – were binding on the legislature.

Although the budget dominated the agenda, a few other measures were adopted, with new cooperation between the Conservatives and Liberals as the NDP moved to a more oppositional stance. The short fall session passed 44 bills, covering consumer protection, property assessments, and midwifery. A contentious bill on campaign financing stalled as the Tories and Liberals sought a $5,000 cap on corporate and union donations, while the NDP preferred a total ban on large contributions which favoured the Tories and sought to prevent the Liberals from using their $3.4 million trust fund, raised through kickbacks to a past government. An all-party compromise was short-lived, and the government proposed a rare January sitting in 2007 to pass the legislation over NDP objections. The premier also introduced a bill to regulate private health clinics, while the NDP pledged to defend the public system from growing encroachments by for-profit operations.

An Opposition motion sought to restore the arm's-length arts council, which Premier MacDonald (as minister of tourism in 2002) had replaced with a government-controlled body; he claimed the old council was inefficient and would not be revived, whereas the Opposition sought an independent entity to approve grants to artists. The Tories put forth a bill on long-term care to ensure seniors did not have to sell their homes to fund this, although specifics were to be worked out in regulations. The Opposition accused the government of frequently leaving the details out of bills so it could make policy via regulations after laws were enacted. Despite the controversial bills on the agenda, the legislature adjourned quickly. Criticized for keeping the House idle, Premier MacDonald suggested, 'I don't think Nova Scotians want us to be wasting time in the legislature,' and noted that the 'co-operative nature' of the minority government meant fewer debates were required (ibid., Oct. 30).

The economy

The provincial economy was relatively strong, with growth around 2.6 per cent; consumer demand, a strong housing market, and the improved fiscal position were key factors. Total employment was down 0.4 per cent, although unemployment rates remained level because of a contracting workforce. Layoffs in manufacturing hurt, such as Trenton Works, whose flat railcars for lumber transport were in less demand in the US economic slump. Unemployment in Halifax declined to 5.2 per cent, well below national averages. Canjet ended regular service in Halifax, to concentrate on charters, with the loss of 375 jobs. Irving Shipyards announced construction of two cruise ships, creating up to 200 jobs. Production estimates for the Deep Panuke offshore gas site were reduced some 25 per cent, but Encana announced it would proceed. Production at Sable was 7 per cent lower than in 2005 but was expected to increase after new facilities at the Thebaud site came online late in the year. New exploration activity was down with attention focused on western tar sands ('Outlook 2007: Opportunities for Growth Amidst Diverging Economic Trends' 41, no. 3 (fall 2006): 14).

Energy prices were high, but the government declined to intervene to overturn a Utility and Review Board (URB) decision in favour of a fee hike for Nova Scotia Power. There was controversy when two big industrial users, Stora Enso and Bowater, sought to reduce costs for power at their two mills; Nova Scotia Power declared it would have to transfer costs to residential power bills. The companies responded that reduced peak use should save the utility money and forestall the need for new generating facilities. The Finnish owners of Stora threatened to close the mill if it could not get a reduction in power costs of 15 per cent. The URB enacted a compromise around a real-time formula allowing the companies to determine when to draw power and permit savings from more off-peak usage. The Stora mill restarted after the lockout, and the municipality granted tax breaks, although only 300 of 600 workers were immediately recalled to work. The lockout harmed nearby linkage industries, including woodlots and railways. Nova Scotia Power applied for rate increases of 7–11 per cent for its other customers after the URB decision.

Construction projects in Metro Halifax – such as the Halifax Harbour Solutions cleanup project, the Dartmouth Crossing retail development, Halifax airport, the Port of Halifax expansion, and a $100 million upgrade to Imperial Oil's refinery – boosted employment. The cleanup of the Sydney tar ponds and construction of a compression deck at the Sable Offshore Energy Project created more jobs. Future employment was expected from the Bear Head liquid natural gas terminal and proposed petrochemical, liquid natural gas terminal and electricity plants in Guysborough County, but these remained uncertain. The government removed the financial firm in charge of its immigration nominee program, amidst allegations that newcomers were charged too much with minimal benefits in return; economic immigrants paid as much as $130,500 in fees to enter Canada via the controversial program; the company launched legal action against the province for damage to its reputation and lost revenues.

The spread of post-weaning multi-systemic wasting syndrome felled 20–40 per cent of livestock on some hog farms. This, plus continued low hog prices, made some farmers threaten to liquidate pig stocks rather than absorb more losses. The province budgeted $2.8 million to help farmers withstand low prices. Consolidation of Maple Leaf processing plants also threatened producers. Michelin received $10 million from the province to revamp facilities at Waterville. Marking 35 years in Nova Scotia, the French tire maker produced its 200-millionth tire in local plants. In high technology, a Research in Motion technical support centre (and construction of its regional facilities) provided a boost. Although skilled jobs were welcome, most IT work was still in low-wage call centres. Payroll rebates kept a call centre in Yarmouth and a corporate services firm in Halifax.

The overheated economy in the west robbed Nova Scotia of skilled workers as many migrated to accept lucrative jobs in the energy sector and public services; even prosperous communities in the lobster fishery lost essential workers to outmigration. Many communities experienced a loss of people even where employment openings existed, leading to shortages of workers with needed skills. Nova Scotia engaged in a competitive advertising war with Alberta and other western provinces by responding to ads luring the skilled with ones of its own extolling the opportunities and lifestyles which the oil-patch could not offer expatriates, such as a low cost of living, community spirit, and scenic beauty.

Intergovernmental relations

The federal government of the 'new' Conservatives (based on the Conservative, Reform, and Alliance Parties) presented opportunities and challenges. Nova Scotia and other Atlantic provinces had exerted strong influence in the minority government of Paul Martin, but Stephen Harper's government had its roots in western protest politics, although most local Tories supported the prime minister. Some feared Harper would follow through on past pledges to decentralize the federation and limit transfers to individuals and less prosperous provinces. The termination of the proposed national child-care agreements and their replacement by modest payments to individuals for child care was taken by some as a portent that 'have-not' provinces would be on their own and forced to adopt less generous programs than 'have' regions which did not require federal funds. Under Harper's plan, Nova Scotia would lose all but $20 million of the $137 million pledged over five years for child care, and families would receive only $1,200 annually to pay for child-care spaces, which often ran to $700 or more per month.

Despite skepticism about the prime minister's views on the Maritimes, the provincial and federal governments found some common ground. Premier MacDonald supported Harper's bill to limit Senate terms and provide for elected senators, a core Reform Party plank. The province and Halifax regional municipality welcomed federal support for their bid to host the Commonwealth Games in 2014. The province expected spin-offs from increased federal attention to military upgrades; the premier appointed justice minister Murray Scott as minister of military relations to coordinate with the Department of National Defence, maximize economic benefits, and address social impacts from military contracts and facilities. Contracts for new or upgraded equipment were pending or issued for marine helicopters, support ships, patrol frigates, armed Arctic patrol vessels, and an amphibious assault ship. The province hoped this could reverse the decline in military-related jobs, but some contracts were expected to go to outside rivals and Ottawa declined to use Shearwater to house its proposed new rapid reaction force. On another federal priority, Nova Scotia chaired a ministerial meeting which worked to improve worker mobility and recognition of professional and occupational qualifications, credentials, and licences across provincial borders.

Harper was not pleased with the offshore accord reached with Paul Martin, to eliminate clawbacks for the province's offshore royalties, although he pledged during the election to honour it. The new government re-examined the entire equalization system, with a plan to enrich the pot overall, but a December federal-provincial meeting was inconclusive, despite consensus on a 10-province standard for calculating revenues. The provinces remained split on how non-renewable resource revenues should be treated in the equalization formula. Alberta, Saskatchewan, and Newfoundland – primary resource-producing provinces – opposed inclusion of non-renewable revenues. Nova Scotia joined Ontario and New Brunswick in seeking their inclusion despite its success in getting such revenues excluded from equalization clawbacks. Some rich provinces preferred a per capita increase in social transfers from Ottawa to enrichment of equalization. There was pressure to make the provinces collectively responsible for social transfers and reduce the federal role in determining such funding for health, welfare, and higher education. MacDonald, however, remained hopeful the provinces could work out a compromise position; he hoped the 10-province approach would provide an additional $100 million annually, although depending on the specifics of a new formula, the province could be a net loser.

In a bid to increase the province's influence in Ottawa, then-premier Hamm appointed Ian Thompson as provincial representative. Thompson spent the year trying to work on core issues such as health care, environmental and social sustainability, human resources, and fiscal issues; he focused attention on the Atlantic Gateway proposal to invest in infrastructure to allow Nova Scotia's ports to compete for the so-called

Post-Panamax generation of giant container vessels. This was considered a major opportunity for the province to improve its economic performance. The province sought around $400 million for highway and port upgrades, to match what Harper had already promised British Columbia for a similar Western Gateway. In promoting the provincial case, Thompson had to battle a negative image of the have-not province, which was not a priority in national decision-making because of its smaller population and weaker economy (Canadian Press NewsWire, 28 Dec.). This challenge was increased by the perception that the offshore accords allowed Nova Scotia to have it both ways – retaining both resource royalties and equalization entitlements unfairly compared to some other provinces.

The province asked Ottawa to compensate it for its large intake of out-of-province college and university students. Unlike medical costs, there was no system to compensate Nova Scotia for providing this service to students from other regions of Canada, who paid the same fees as local residents. Premier MacDonald suggested a figure of $20 million for these costs, although this estimate might be low. Student groups felt that the textbook tax credit and tax relief on bursaries and scholarships announced in the federal budget were too small to improve access to higher education for many now excluded by escalating costs. The federal government, however, responded that the $28.8 million in infrastructure monies could help fund higher education in the province. Nova Scotia's extra funds from the offshore accords could be used as compensation, with future changes to equalization addressing the issue in the long term.

The federal Conservative government provided additional funds to upgrade key harbours important to the south shore fisheries; the overall amount spent on such 'Small Craft Harbours' was $17.4 million for 2006. The province lost funds when the new government terminated funding for climate change initiatives as part of its rejection of the Kyoto Protocol, although the government promised a 'made in Canada' plan for clean air in the near future. The premier pressed Ottawa to double its contribution to provincial highway upgrades to $160 million, claiming it returned only a small fraction of gas taxes collected in the province. This infusion of cash was essential to prevent the province from falling farther behind in highway quality. The province joined others in criticism of a 'fiscal imbalance' as federal health and social transfers were expected to decline, and the equalization system remained in flux. The provincial Opposition criticized the premier – an early supporter of Stephen Harper who had chaired the Tories' federal campaign in the province – for his alleged inability to get the federal Conservatives to respond sympathetically to provincial needs.

The province continued work on a framework agreement to move forward negotiations with the federal government and its Mi'kmaq communities. The aim was to develop a Mi'kmaq Rights Initiative to clarify issues governing natural resources such as timber, hunting and fishing, and access to Crown lands in the province. It would also permit negotiations for improvements in housing, economic opportunity, health, education, and policing. Despite financial weakness in some bands, progress continued in economic and cultural spheres, exemplified by the opening of the Glooscap Heritage Centre, which displayed priceless cultural artefacts. Conflicts remained over fishing rights, with vandals cutting loose native lobster traps, and tension spilled over into some communities and schools.

Cape Breton Regional Municipality continued to demand changes to funding arrangements that it claimed cost the region some $20 million per year. The municipality noted it received an unfair share of grants to compensate for lost revenue from Nova Scotia Power facilities. The region invoked the provincial rhetoric of Premier Hamm's 'Campaign for Fairness' on equalization, noting that the same principles respecting access to quality services at comparable tax rates should apply within the province. Halifax regional councillors complained that increases in property assessments, done provincially, far exceeded the cost of living increase and wanted a more reasonable figure to avoid burdens to residents. Municipalities viewed it as unfair that the province charged them for key services, imposing burdens on their budgets, while it let the finance minister falsely claim a surplus. The Union of Nova Scotia Municipalities called for full funding of municipal equalization and for the province to cover all costs of incarceration, education, and low-income housing. The minister indicted that municipal restructuring and amalgamation were not on the government's agenda at present.

MELVIN BAKER AND PETER NEARY

Newfoundland and Labrador

At the beginning of 2006 the attention of Newfoundlanders and Labradorians was focused on the federal election scheduled for 23 January. On 28 November 2005, Premier Danny Williams (Humber West) wrote the Liberal, Conservative, and NDP leaders inquiring about their positions on various issues affecting the province. His purpose was to help provincial residents decide how to vote. Stephen Harper replied on 4 January, Jack Layton on 15 January, and Prime Minister Paul Martin on 16 January. Crucially, Harper promised that a Conservative government would 'ensure that no province' would be 'adversely affected from changes to the equalization formula' (Executive Council, *News Release*, 16 Jan.). With all the replies in hand, Williams declared the Conservative and NDP answers 'very encouraging on several fronts' (ibid., 17 Jan.). By contrast, Martin's reply was 'disappointing' (ibid.). Whether any of this mattered can only be speculated upon, but Williams urged voters to take account of the information he had solicited.

In 2004 the Liberals won 5 seats in the province and the Conservatives 2. This time 28 candidates stood for election, with the Liberal, Conservative, New Democratic, and Green Parties being represented in all 7 ridings. Nine women were nominated: 4 by the NDP, 3 by the Green Party and 1 each by the Liberals and Conservatives. In the event, 4 Liberals and 3 Conservatives, all male, were elected. The Conservative gain was in Avalon, where Fabian Manning, who (in May 2005) had been expelled from the Conservative caucus in the House of Assembly, was victorious. In the other 6 constituencies the incumbents were returned. Geographically, the Conservatives carried the 3 seats on the Avalon Peninsula and the Liberals won everywhere else. Voter turnout in the province was 56.7 per cent, compared with 64.7 per cent nationally.

On 6 February, when the Conservative government of Stephen Harper took office, Loyola Hearn (St. John's South – Mount Pearl) was sworn in as minister of fisheries and oceans and became the province's sole representative in the federal Cabinet. On 12 April, on his first visit to the province as prime minister, Harper announced that the weather forecasting centre at Gander, closed by the federal Liberals, would be reopened. Williams described Harper on this occasion as a leader who didn't 'have to be dragged kicking and screaming into a room to fulfill a promise' (*Globe and Mail*, 13 April).

While the dust was still settling from the federal election, the province was electrified when, on 24 February, the curling team of Brad Gushue, Mark Nichols, Russ Howard, Jamie Korab, and Mike Adam won gold for Canada at the winter Olympic Games in Torino, Italy, defeating Finland 10–4. All but Howard were born in Newfoundland and Labrador, and on the day of the final game schools were closed in the province at 12:30 p.m. so that pupils could watch on television the heroics of Team Gushue. On 4 March Williams welcomed the Olympic gold medallists home at a photo and autograph session, and on 8 December the golden five, along with coach Tobias F. McDonald, were invested into the Order of Newfoundland and Labrador. On 29 December Team Gushue was named Canadian team of the year by *Canadian Press and Broadcast News*.

For some years, the advent of spring in Newfoundland and Labrador had been accompanied by battling between advocates and opponents of the annual seal hunt. In 2006 this continuing tussle attracted more attention than usual, thanks to the efforts of ex-Beatle Sir Paul McCartney and his wife, Heather Mills-McCartney, who took to the ice floes off the Îles de la Madeleine on behalf of the anti – seal hunt cause. En route to their offshore photo-op, which drew international attention, the McCartneys passed through St. John's on 1 March. Williams seized this opportunity to invite Sir Paul to discuss the Newfoundland and Labrador point of view on the annual harvest. Two days later he got his chance when, to great hometown acclaim, he debated the McCartneys on the popular US television program *Larry King Live*. 'Mr. and Mrs. McCartney are vegans,' he said afterwards, '[a]nd what they stand for is the complete elimination of the killing of anything that is breathing' (ibid., 4 March).

Memorial University was also prominent in the news in the first part of the year. On 13 January President and Vice-Chancellor Axel Meisen announced the appointment of Dr Shirley Katz of York University to look into 'the employment-related experience of Dr. Deepa Khosla,' who had joined the Memorial faculty on 1 August 2005 and died on 21 November (http://www.today.mun.ca/news.php?news_id=1730). It was alleged that she had 'felt a lack of support for her safety and an unwelcoming environment for women at Memorial University' (ibid.). Dr Katz submitted her report, which included many recommendations for change, in August. On 27 January the Supreme Court of Canada ordered Memorial to pay former social work student Wanda Young $839,400 plus interest and court costs for wrongful action taken against her, without her knowledge, based on a paper she had submitted in a course. Hard on the heels of this judgment, Auditor General John Noseworthy in his annual report, presented to the Speaker of the House of Assembly on 31 January, found much to criticize in various practices and procedures at Memorial. The previous day, moreover, *The National*, the flagship news program of CBC television, had started a three-part series featuring reporter Chris O'Neill-Yates on alleged irregularities in the research record of nutrition and immunology expert Dr Ranjit Kumar Chandra, one of Memorial's most prominent faculty members before his retirement in 2002.

On 6 February the *dramatis personae* of provincial politics changed when Jim Bennett, a 52-year-old lawyer from Daniel's Harbour, became leader of the provincial Liberal Party. Following the resignation of Roger Grimes, the Liberals had scheduled a leadership convention for 9–10 June 2006, but when nominations for the position of leader closed on 6 February, Bennett was the only candidate and was therefore elected by acclamation. He was not a member of the House of Assembly and, on becoming leader, said that he would devote his time to rebuilding the party and paying down its debt and then run in the general election. His first taste of electoral politics came the same month in the campaign leading up to a by-election on 21 February in Placentia – St. Mary's, the seat vacated by Fabian Manning. When the votes were counted, Felix Collins easily held the seat for the Conservatives, winning 2,246 (46.2 per cent) of the 4,857 votes cast. Kevin Power, the Liberal candidate, came in third (behind independent and former Tory Nick Careen) and won 931 votes (19.2 per cent). Williams interpreted the result as a 'wake-up call … for the Liberals' (*Telegram*, St. John's, 22 Feb.).

The third session of the 45th General Assembly began on 22 March, with Liberal Gerry Reid (Twillingate and Fogo) still in the role of leader of the Opposition. In the Speech from the Throne the government promised to give priority to fostering a well-educated workforce. Legislation passed and given assent in 2006 included acts relating to fishing industry collective bargaining, forestry, student financial assistance, highway traffic, public utilities, the Human Rights Code, physiotherapy, support orders enforcement, and workplace health, safety, and compensation.

The 2006 budget speech, 'The Right Choices: Momentum for Growth and Prosperity,' was delivered by finance minister and president of Treasury Board Loyola Sullivan (Ferryland) on 30 March. He reported a surplus of $76.5 million in fiscal 2005–6 versus a forecast deficit of $492.5 million. For 2006–7 he predicted a surplus of $6.2 million on revenue of $5,188.8 million, net income from government business enterprises of $177 million, and total net expenses of $5,359.6 million. The government, the minister said, had 'inherited fiscal challenges that were clearly troubling and unsustainable,' but the province was now 'on the right track,' and the 'goal of a strong and self-reliant Newfoundland and Labrador' was within sight (http://www.budget.gov.nl.ca/budget2006/intro.htm). The 'right choices' specified in the budget were detailed under nine headings, and the St. John's *Telegram* described the government's plan as 'what many political pundits would call an election-style budget, one that's wrapped in plenty of spending and goodies for many sectors of society' (31 March). On 9 March Sullivan and education minister Joan Burke (St. George's – Stephenville East) announced that a four-year memorandum of agreement had been reached with the Newfoundland and Labrador Teachers' Association. Included in this was an allocation, announced earlier, of $1.953 billion to bolster the teachers' pension plan. On 6 June Sullivan announced that the Dominion Bond Rating Service had raised the province's credit rating from BBB (high) to A (low) and that Moody's Investor Service had moved the province from A3 to A2. In July he announced that Standard & Poor's Rating Services had moved the province from A– to A. The province, he said, still had 'quite a ways to go' in overcoming its accumulated debt but each rating change was 'a step in the right direction' (Finance, *News Release*, 20 July).

On 3 April, in the wake of the sunny budget news, a long-simmering dispute between the government and Chevron over the development of the Hebron – Ben Nevis offshore oilfield came to a rolling boil when the company, which had as partners on the project Exxon Mobil, Petro-Canada, and Norsk Hydro ASA, decided to abandon the venture because of the province's demand for an equity position. Williams was now pilloried in the national press for his negotiating stance with the oil companies, and the *Globe and Mail* called him 'Canada's Hugo Chavez' (13 April). But the premier stood his ground, having explained himself in the same paper in no uncertain terms on 5 April: 'We welcome and encourage development in Newfoundland and Labrador. But not at any cost … The oil is not going anywhere. And neither are we.' The stand-off over Hebron – Ben Nevis continued for the remainder of the year, but so too did the departure of workers from the province for jobs in booming Alberta. According to one report, in the year ending 30 June 2006, 4,991 people left Newfoundland and Labrador for that province, and when a group of Alberta companies held a job fair at the Capital Hotel, St. John's, in the fall, more than 9,000 turned out to be considered for work. On 6–8 November, with some provincial employers finding it difficult to attract and keep skilled workers, the Newfoundland and Labrador Employers' Council held a conference in Gander on outmigration. Against this high-stakes employment backdrop, it was reported on 16 December that a cutback in production at the Hibernia offshore oilfield was likely because the project partners had not been able to secure a permit to cover operations on the field's southern extension. The delay in granting the permit, it was ventured, was related to the province's strategy to advance its position in relation to the proposed Hebron – Ben Nevis project. Just how much was at stake in all this was underlined in June when it was reported that the Hibernia oilfield was 44 per cent larger than previously estimated. In December it was reported that Norsk Hydro ASA and Husky Energy had made a sizable oil and gas discovery in the West Bonne Bay formation of the Jeanne d'Arc basin and near the existing Terra Nova oilfield.

On 8 May Jim Bennett resigned as leader of the provincial Liberal Party, after just over three months on the job. 'I think we're moving in the right direction,' he explained, 'although I think we could make better progress … I think had I been in caucus I would've had the opportunity to gel with the existing members … We'll be able to move forward with another leader, possibly someone from within caucus' (*Telegram*, St. John's, 9 May). Following Bennett's sudden exit (he still intended to run in the next provincial election) Gerry Reid became first interim leader of the party and then – this was announced by the party executive on 29 May – leader. His selection was subject to ratification by delegates at a two-day convention to be held at Gander beginning 9 June, and this action duly followed. On 29 May the provincial NDP also got a new leader when Lorraine Michael, a former Roman Catholic nun and well-known social activist, was chosen to succeed Jack Harris (Signal Hill – Quidi Vidi). She was elected at a party convention held in St. John's and defeated writer Nina Patey 107–5.

While his opponents were busy sorting out their internal affairs, Williams was again on the offensive in relation to resource development. On 8 May he announced that the province, which had dickered for years with Hydro-Québec for a joint power development project on the Lower Churchill River, had decided to lead the venture on its own. 'We know,' he asserted, 'that we are capable of executing this project in a way that will ensure we maximize the returns while mitigating the risks … This is about doing it by ourselves, for ourselves. We are on a path to be masters of our own destiny' (Executive Council, *News Release*, 8 May). The planning schedule being followed by the province called for 'a project sanctioning decision by 2009 and potentially first power by 2015' (ibid.). On 1 December Newfoundland and Labrador Hydro filed requests for federal and provincial environmental assessments of its Lower Churchill plans. Williams now said that the province was confident that TransÉnergie of Québec would accommodate the export across that province of the electricity to be generated. As a company transmitting power to the United States, he noted, TransÉnergie was constrained by the requirement of the US Federal Energy Regulatory Commission that it facilitate the needs of other suppliers. But the possibility of exporting power down through Newfoundland and across the Cabot Strait was also being explored.

Other initiatives by the Williams government in 2006 included the 27 March release of *Innovation Newfoundland and Labrador: A Blueprint for Prosperity*; the 4 April launch of a six-year violence prevention plan; the implementation of various training, agricultural, and tourism recommendations of the Bay St. GeorgeTask Force on behalf of a part of the province hit hard by the national downturn in the forest industry; the investment of $50 million in the transportation infrastructure of Labrador; the re-registration of everyone covered by the province's Medical Care Plan; the enhancement of French-language services in the province; a review, as part of a continuing Red Tape Reduction Initiative, of the fees imposed by government departments; and the start of construction of the Humberwood Provincial Treatment Addictions Centre in Corner Brook. On 3 October Williams and business minister Kevin O'Brien (Gander) unveiled a new 'brand signature' for the province (Executive Council, *News Release*, 3 Oct.). This featured a stylized pitcher plant, the provincial flower, and was said by the premier to be 'truly representative of the essence of our province: creativity, resiliency, and a modern society shaped by our rich history' (ibid.).

Public appointees in 2006 included former provincial Liberal Cabinet minister Charles J. Furey (chief electoral officer); Leslie MacLeod (president, Provincial Advisory Council on the Status of Women); Joe Browne (chief of the Royal Newfoundland Constabulary); John FitzGerald (provincial representative in the Newfoundland and Labrador Office of Federal-Provincial Relations, Ottawa); and Max Ruelokke (chairman and CEO of the Canada-Newfoundland and Labrador Offshore

Petroleum Board). Ruelokke's appointment had been recommended by a panel named by the federal and provincial governments under the terms of the Atlantic Accord after they had been unable to agree on an appointee. Williams, who favoured St. John's mayor Andy Wells for the job, resisted this recommendation but was eventually bested in a court action started by Ruelokke. In March an electoral boundaries commission, chaired by retired justice John J. O'Neill, was appointed under statute. It reported on 30 November. On 31 August clerk of the House of Assembly John Noel retired from the public service and, effective 30 October, was replaced by William MacKenzie. On 30 May justice minister Tom Marshall (Humber East) received the report of retired Supreme Court of Canada justice Antonio Lamer about the wrongful convictions of Gregory Parsons, Randy Druken, and Ronald Dalton. On 28 June, in applauding the apology of the government of Canada for the Chinese head tax and Chinese Exclusion Act, Williams made a separate apology for the head tax Newfoundland had imposed on Chinese immigrants before it had become part of Canada in 1949. In October, a report was released by child and youth advocate Darlene Neville into the 2003 suicide of Dr Shirley Turner, who had drowned herself along with her 13-month-old son, Zachary. At the time, Turner had custody of Zachary while fighting extradition to the United States to stand trial for the murder of his father, Dr Andrew Bagby. Prepared by Dr Peter H. Markesteyn, the report exposed serious failings in the province's child protection system.

On 24 May, the day before the House of Assembly adjourned, Williams held a meeting in St. John's with stakeholders in the fishing industry. The backdrop to this gathering, which was also attended by Loyola Hearn, was the closure of three plants by Sea Treat Ltd, falling prices, and the prospect of further restructuring in the industry. The meeting heard about fifty presentations and was billed as a 'fisheries summit' by the *Telegram* (25 May). On 28 June, fisheries and aquaculture minister Tom Rideout (Lewisporte) announced 'a framework to assist plant workers and regions impacted by fish plant closures' (Executive Council, *News Release*, 28 June). Next, on 14 August, Williams met with Hearn to review accomplishments by the two levels of government since the May meeting in St. John's to provide the fishing industry with 'greater stability' through an 'ocean to plate' integrated approach (ibid., 14 Aug.). Then, on 20 October, Williams, Hearn, and Rideout announced the start of 'a comprehensive consultation process on the future of the fishery in Newfoundland and Labrador' (ibid., 20 Oct.). This would be guided by a discussion paper – *Canada – Newfoundland*

and Labrador Fishing Industry Renewal – released simultaneously. Good news for the industry followed on 27 October when Glen Cooke of New Brunswick – based Cooke Aquaculture announced in St. John's that his company would invest $135 million to triple farmed salmon production in the province. By contrast, a November article in *Science* by an international team of researchers led by fisheries biologist Boris Worm of Dalhousie University, which cited the catastrophe that had overtaken Atlantic cod stocks, forecast the collapse of world commercial fish stocks by mid-century unless radical new management practices were introduced. In response Hearn defended current Canadian fisheries policy, which was taking an ecosystem approach and trying 'to counteract some of the mistakes of the past' (*London Free Press*, 4 Nov.).

Summer 2006 began in the province with a political eruption. At 6:15 p.m. on 21 June, Williams went on radio and television and announced that natural resources minister Ed Byrne (Kilbride), his predecessor as leader of the provincial Progressive Conservative Party, had resigned from the Cabinet at his request. The reason, the premier explained, was 'a serious investigation going on within the Internal Economy Commission ... and within the House of Assembly by the auditor general' (*Telegram*, St. John's, 22 June). The following day Auditor General Noseworthy released the first of a series of reports that rocked the province. This found that between 2002 and 2004 the outgoing minister had considerably overspent his tax-free constituency allowance. On 27 June Noseworthy reported that over a seven-year period ending 31 December 2005, $2,651,644 had been spent on 'low-value novelty items' (http://www.cbc.ca/news/canada/newfoundland-labrador/story/2006/06/27/audit-companies.html) for members of the House of Assembly and that 'improper retention or misappropriation of public money' may have been involved (*Telegram*. St. John's, 28 June). Included among the purchases, made without tender, were 79 'customized MHA gold rings,' which had rung in at $750 each plus HST for a total of $69,000 (ibid.). In three more reports, submitted on 4 July, Noseworthy found that two other sitting MHAs – one NDP and one Liberal – and a former Liberal member had overspent their office allowances by $766,831. Subsequently, Noseworthy began a review of constituency allowance spending back to 1989 and an audit of the accounts of the House of Assembly for the fiscal years 1999–2000 to 2003–4.

With politicians on all sides scrambling for cover, Williams played a cool hand. On 26 June – this was strategic – he reaffirmed the government's commitment to accountability and transparency and announced that Chief Justice Derek Green of the Supreme Court of Newfoundland

and Labrador would review existing practice and render 'an opinion as to the appropriate manner in which to preserve the democratic requirement to have an autonomous legislature, while also guaranteeing public accountability' (Executive Council, *News Release*, 26 June). This review would be done 'on a go-forward basis' and would 'not include a review of the Auditor General's findings' (ibid.).

Having responded positively to this uproar, Williams left for France, where, on 1 July, he participated in a ceremony to mark the 90th anniversary of the action at Beaumont Hamel on the first day of the Battle of the Somme. Of 801 members of the Newfoundland Regiment (later the Royal Newfoundland Regiment) who took part in this action on 1 July 1916, only 68 survived. On his return to St. John's, Williams shuffled his Cabinet, moving Kathy Dunderdale (Virginia Waters) from trade to natural resources.

What was probably the high point of Williams's year came later in the month when, from 26 to 28 July, as chair of the Council of the Federation, he hosted the annual summer meeting of provincial and territorial premiers. This event, which attracted 12 corporate partners, kicked off in Corner Brook with a pre-conference meeting with national Aboriginal leaders. The gathering then moved on to St. John's, where meetings were interspersed with some lively entertainment. On 26 July dinner was served in a tent at Cape Spear, and the guests 'were treated to a gorgeous sunset and frolicking whales' at Canada's easternmost point (*Globe and Mail*, 29 July). The visiting first ministers were also given 'goodie bags containing hand-knit traditional sweaters and Newfoundland pottery' (ibid.). A good time seems to have been enjoyed by all who attended, but agreement on a new equalization formula was a non-starter, and the conference ended with each province left to fend for itself vis-à-vis Ottawa.

In late August, shortly before leaving for a trip to Iceland and Norway, Williams called on former NDP leader Jack Harris to get on with his retirement and resign as the member for Signal Hill – Quidi Vidi. Harris, the premier said, was going door to door in the riding with NDP leader Lorraine Michael, and the Tories should have an equal chance to campaign there. The NDP did not take this bait, but on 29 September the premier got his wish when Harris resigned from the House. On 10 October Williams announced that a by-election would be held in the district on 1 November. During the short but intense campaign that followed, a decidedly chill wind was felt in the province's relations with Ottawa when Prime Minister Harper flew in to attend the provincial Progressive Conservative convention in Gander. At a meeting with Williams on 14 October, Harper confirmed that, although the Atlantic Accord would not be affected by any change in the equalization formula, a scheme put forward by an expert panel headed by former Alberta deputy treasurer Al O'Brien remained under consideration. Under this plan, which would take account of resource revenue, Newfoundland and Labrador would lose equalization dollars. In his speech to the convention Harper sounded another discordant note when he publicly rejected provincial pressure for 'fallow-field' legislation to force oil companies to develop a resource under rights or lose it (*Globe and Mail*, 16 Oct.).

All of this ignited Williams, who – after the prime minister had left – told the convention that if the commitment about equalization Harper had put in writing during the federal election campaign was broken, there would be a 'very strong response from the electorate of Newfoundland and Labrador' (*National Post*, 17 Oct.). Harking back to his battle over the Atlantic Accord with Prime Minister Martin following the federal election of 2004, Williams advised convention delegates, 'Stay tuned, you might be into round two before this one is all over' (*Globe and Mail*, 16 Oct.). 'This Prime Minister,' he lashed out, 'is telling me when he comes into my province, into our town, to our convention, that he hasn't made up his mind yet … He better make his mind up, I can tell you right now … Because if not, when those federal election results come in across the country and they come to Newfoundland and Labrador … there better be a big goose egg for the Conservatives if they haven't delivered on their promise' (ibid.).

This blunt talk undoubtedly found a receptive audience on the home front but nationally it played to mixed reviews. According to the *Globe and Mail*, the premier's 'grandstanding' was 'costing the province' and it was time for him 'to stop acting as if everyone were out to cheat his province and to look for genuine solutions to the offshore dispute, to equalization reform and to other issues too important to be used as demagogic fodder' (18 Oct.). Another, and perhaps more consequential, knock for Williams followed on 1 November when the electors of Signal Hill – Quidi Vidi returned Lorraine Michael, who defeated Conservative Jerome Kennedy, a St. John's lawyer, 1,968–1,595. The Liberals, who had stayed out of the by-election, were now said by the premier to no longer be 'a factor in provincial politics' (http://www.cbc.ca/canada/newfoundland-labrador/story/2006/11/03/williams-liberals.html). On 18 December, after a meeting on the hot topic of equalization between the provincial ministers of finance and federal finance minister Jim Flaherty, Williams said that he and Premier Lorne Calvert of Saskatchewan would campaign together across the country for a fair settlement.

On 16 November, four days before the House of Assembly resumed sitting, Finance Minister Sullivan released a mid-year financial update. This forecast a $39.8 million deficit in 2006–7 as compared with the $6.2 million surplus forecast in the budget. The explanation offered by the minister for this change was a revenue shortfall brought on by an unexpectedly long shutdown, at a time of high oil prices, at the Terra Nova production facility. When the House reopened, attention quickly turned to a controversy that had blown up over the government's announcement, on 2 November, that it would invest $15 million in a fibre-optic link connecting Newfoundland with Nova Scotia, to be built jointly by Rogers Communications, Persona Communications, and MTS Allstream. This deal was criticized by Liberal Opposition leader Gerry Reid on the grounds of previous close ties between Williams and two of the executives involved: Persona CEO Dean MacDonald (described by Reid as the premier's 'first lieutenant') and Rogers Communications vice president Ken Marshall, who had worked for Williams when the latter owned Cable Atlantic (http://www.cbc.ca/canada/newfoundland-labrador/story/2006/11/07/fibre-optic.html). The premier vigorously denied any conflict of interest and challenged Opposition members to repeat their claims outside the protected forum of the House of Assembly.

On 28 November Ed Byrne announced his resignation from the legislature, effective 1 January 2007. This news was followed, on 5 December, by the release of five more reports submitted by the auditor general to the Speaker of the House. These gave further details of the excess constituency allowance spending of five sitting and former members of the Assembly, whose affairs had called for scrutiny. The House adjourned again on 12 December, a few days after Williams had hosted the 13th session of the Council of Atlantic Premiers.

The year 2006 brought positive developments in the province's relations with its First Peoples. From 13 to15 March an Aboriginal women's conference was held at Happy Valley – Goose Bay, and from 24 to 26 November a conference was held at Stephenville for Innu, Inuit, Métis, and Mi'kmaq women. On 8 September Tom Rideout, as minister responsible for Aboriginal affairs, announced that the province had agreed to transfer Crown lands to the government of Canada for the creation of a reserve for the Innu First Nation at Sheshatshiu, Labrador. In October the first general election was held for the Assembly of Nunatsiavut (the Inuit-governed territory in Labrador). The Assembly was composed of eight ordinary members and Speaker Todd Broomfield.

Culturally, the province had another banner year. On 28 March the premier and culture, tourism, and recreation minister Tom Hedderson

(Harbour Main – Whitbourne) launched a strategic cultural plan, *Creative Newfoundland and Labrador: The Blueprint for Development and Investment in Culture*, and announced a $17.6 million three-year investment to implement it. The first anniversary of the Rooms, the big new gallery / museum / archives complex in St. John's, was celebrated on 29 June with the start of four days of events. Three Newfoundland and Labrador writers were included in the finalists for the 2006 Giller Prize: Kenneth J. Harvey, Wayne Johnston, and Russell Wangersky.

The 2006 necrology of persons resident in or connected with the province included Bill Adams (mayor of St. John's, provincial Cabinet minister, and district court judge); Tom Cahill (writer of the celebrated song 'Thank God We're Surrounded by Water'); Patricia Cowan (MHA and first female president of the Newfoundland and Labrador Teachers' Association); Craig Dobbin (the most flamboyant provincial businessman of his generation); C. William Doody (provincial Cabinet minister and senator); Kenneth Lochhead (painter of the mural in the international lounge at Gander International Airport); John Mahoney (provincial Cabinet minister and Supreme Court justice); Rae Perlin (artist); David Rooney (MP); Doris Saunders (editor of the Labrador publication *Them Days*); Ramon (Ray) Winsor (MHA); Rick Woodford (MHA); and Leslie Yeo (stalwart of the St. John's – based 1950s London Theatre Company). Numbered among Canada's 2006 fallen in Afghanistan were three brave Newfoundland and Labrador sons: Sergeant Craig Paul Gillam, Sergeant Vaughan Ingram, and Warrant Officer Richard Francis Nolan. Master Corporal Kirk Noel and Sergeant Duane Brazil, two of the three Canadian Forces members killed in a helicopter crash off Nova Scotia in July, were also from the province.

In 2006 Newfoundland and Labrador continued along its particular path of economic development and province-building. Although enjoying the revenue gains of 'peak oil,' it also attempted to assist the casualties of the steep decline in the Canadian forest industry, continue the rebuilding of its fishing economy, and counter the exodus of its population, especially to skill-hungry Alberta. St. John's in particular prospered during 2006, though it lost its direct air service to London, England. The year ended with a big political surprise when, on 29 December, Loyola Sullivan announced his retirement from politics. He was immediately replaced as finance minister by Tom Marshall. As residents digested this news, they could look forward to a provincial election, scheduled, by a 2004 statute, for 9 October 2007.

Obituaries

ANDRE, MARION (9 May, age 86). Theatre director, professor, and founding artistic director of the Saidye Bronfman Theatre Centre in Montreal.

BAIN, GEORGE (14 May, age 86). Newspaper reporter and editor, Member of the Order of Canada.

BALDING, ALLAN (30 July, age 82). Professional golfer and member of the Canadian Sports Hall of Fame.

BANKS, SYDNEY (14 November, age 89). Co-founder of the Global Television network.

BARRON, SID (29 April, age 88). Cartoonist.

BERRY, GLYN (15 January, age 59). Diplomat, Department of Foreign Affairs.

BLACKBURN, GEORGE (15 November, age 90). Non-fiction author, Member of the Order of Canada.

BOUCHARD, JACQUES (29 May, age 75). Pioneering French-language advertising executive, Member of the Order of Canada.

BROOKS, NORMAN (14 September, age 78). Musician, actor, and Al Jolson imitator.

BROWN, JAMES (25 December, age 73). Wildly popular and flamboyant American soul singer.

CALDER, FRANK ARTHUR (4 November, age 91). Namesake of the Supreme Court of Canada case that established Aboriginal title exists in modern Canadian law, Officer of the Order of Canada.

CAMERON, JOHN ALLAN (22 November, age 67). Influential folk and Celtic singer, Member of the Order of Canada.

CARLSON, LEN (26 January, age 68). Voice actor.

COULL, GARY (26 October, age 52). Co-founder of CLSA Asia-Pacific Markets, one of the largest brokerage firms in the Asia-Pacific region.

CROWE, HEATHER (22 May, age 61). Public face of Canada's anti-smoking campaign.

CURRY, FLOYD (16 September, age 81). Four-time winner of the Stanley Cup with the Montreal Canadiens.

DESBIENS, JEAN-PAUL (23 July, age 79). Author of *Les Insolences du Frere Untel*, which is credited with inspiring the Quiet Revolution, Officer of the Order of Canada.

DUKE, DARLY (21 October, age 77). Director of Emmy Award – winning miniseries *The Thorn Birds*.

FALLON, JACK (22 May, age 90). Jazz musician who performed with Ella Fitzgerald and Duke Ellington and played the violin on the Beatles' White Album.

FARAGALLI, JOE (10 April, Age 76). Professional football coach in the CFL.

FERGUSON, WALTER 'MAYNARD' (23 August, age 78). Musician who performed with such jazz legends as Duke Ellington.

FORD, GERALD (26 December, age 93). Former president of the United States of America (1974–7).

FORRESTALL, MICHAEL (9 June, age 73). Former member of the House of Commons and the Senate.

GAINEY, LAURA (9 December, age 25). Daughter of Montreal Canadiens general manager and former player Bob Gainey.

GEERTZ, CLIFFORD (30 October, age 80). Influential American cultural anthropologist.

GEOFFRION, BERNIE 'BOOM BOOM' (11 March, age 75). Six time Stanley Cup Champion with the Montreal Canadiens, member of the Hockey Hall of Fame.

GIBSON, MARGARET (25 February, age 57). Non-fiction writer and novelist.

GREGOIRE, GILLES (22 November, age 80). Former member of the House of Commons and the National Assembly of Quebec, co-founder of the Parti Québ́écois.

HAYDEN, MELISSA (9 August, age 83). Ballerina and former principal dancer for the New York City Ballet.

HENDERSON, LARRY (27 November, age 89). First regular news reader for the national news on CBC television.

HEPPNER, BEN (24 September, age 63). Member of the Legislative Assembly of Saskatchewan.

HILL, ARTHUR (22 October, age 84). Tony Award – winning actor.

HILEBRAND, IKE (27 August, age 79). Member of the Canadian Sports Hall of Fame.

HORWOOD, HAROLD (16 April, age 82). Literary and political author, Member of the Order of Canada.

HUSSEIN, SADDAM (30 December, age 69). Former Iraqi president (1979–2003). Executed for crimes against humanity.

JACOBS, JANE (25 April, age 89). Influential urban activist who authored *The Death and Life of Great American Cities*.

KENNEY, MATT (8 February, age 95). Jazz and big-band musician, Member of the Order of Canada.

LAYTON, IRVING (4 January, age 93). Poet, recipient of the Governor General's Award, Officer of the Order of Canada.

LEHOTSKY, HARRY (11 November, age 49). Pastor, anti-poverty advocate, Member of the Order of Canada.

LENNON, FRANK (22 August, age 79). Photographer who captured Paul Henderson's winning goal in the 1972 Summit Series.

LOCHHEAD, KENNETH (15 July, age 80). Professor, painter, Officer of the Order of Canada.

MARSDEN, PAT (27 April, age 69). Sportscaster.

MARTIN, JOHN (24 February, age 60). Pioneer of music television in Canada.

MASON, DUTCH (23 December, age 68). Blues musician.

MONDOR, EMILIE (9 September, age 25). Olympic distance runner.

MORSELLI, GIUSEPPE (30 March, age 67). Key fundraiser for the Liberal Party of Canada in Quebec.

MOOR, MAVOR (18 December, age 87). Writer, actor, and radio and television producer.

NAULT, FERNAND (26 December, age 85). Ballet dancer, choreographer, and assistant director of Les Grands Ballets Canadiens; Officer of the Order of Canada; Knight of the National Order of Quebec.

OSTRY, BERNARD (24 May, age 78). Author, civil servant, and former CEO of TVOntario, Companion of the Order of Canada.

PARKER, JACKIE (7 November, age 74). Three-time Grey Cup champion, member of the Canadian Football Hall of Fame, member of the Canadian Sports Hall of Fame.

PEPIN, CLERMONT (2 September, age 80). Pianist, composer, and teacher, Officer of the Order of Canada, Officer of the Order of Quebec.

PICKETT, HUGH (13 February, age 92). Vancouver-based music promoter, dubbed 'Mr. Showbiz,' booked such acts as the Rolling Stones, Frank Sinatra, and Elvis.

PLASSE, MICHEL (30 December, age 58). Canadian hockey player.

POWNALL, LEON (2 June, age 63). Film and television actor and director.

RAE, JOHN 'JACKIE' (5 October, age 84). Singer and television performer, Member of the Order of Canada.

ROSENTHAL, ABRAHAM MICHAEL (10 May, age 84). Former executive editor of the *New York Times* and Pulitzer Prize winner.

RUSSELL, ANNA (18 October, age 94). Comedian and satirist of classical music.

SAUVAGEAU, BENOIT (28 August, age 42). Bloc Québécois Member of House of Commons.

SAXBERG, LORNE (6 May, age 48). Journalist and broadcaster, recipient of the Edward R. Murrow Award.

SCOTT, IAN (10 October, age 72). Former attorney general of Ontario (1985–90).

SHOYAMA, THOMAS (22 December, age 90). Reporter-editor of Japanese Canadian newspaper the *New Canadian*, civil servant who worked with Tommy Douglas on Medicare, head of Atomic Energy of Canada, professor.

SIMONEAU, LEOPOLD (24 August, age 90). Opera performer, Companion of the Order of Canada.

SINCLAIR, IAN (7 April, age 92). Former chair and CEO of Canadian Pacific Ltd, Member of the Order of Canada.

SINCLAIR, LISTER (16 October, age 85). Influential and controversial playwright and broadcaster, Officer of the Order of Canada.

STAEBLER, EDNA (12 September, age 100). Author of cookbooks, Member of the Order of Canada.

STAVRO, STEVE (24 April, age 78). Founder of the now defunct Knob Hills Farm grocery store chain and former owner of the Toronto Maple Leafs.

STOERY, ROY 'RED' (15 March, age 88). Former NHL referee who officiated in six Stanley Cups in the 1950s.

STUKUS, ANNIS (20 May, age 91). Football player, coach, and general manager, member of the Canadian Sports Hall of Fame.

THOMSON, KENNETH (12 June, age 88). Patriarch of the Thompson Corporation and Canada's wealthiest person.

TURVEY, JOHN (11 October, age 61). Social worker and youth activist, Member of the Order of Canada.

VACHON, LOUIS-ALBERT (29 September, age 94). Archbishop Emeritus of Quebec, Companion of the Order of Canada.

VIGER, ANDRE (1 October, age 54). Wheelchair marathoner, member of the Paralympic Hall of Fame, Knight of the Order of Quebec, Officer of the Order of Canada.

WEINZWEIG, JOHN (24 August, age 93). Classical music composer, Officer of the Order of Canada.

Election tables

Nova Scotia Thirty-seventh Provincial General Election 13 June 2006

Political party	Votes received (Valid)	Percentage of popular vote	Candidates elected
Progressive Conservative Party	160,119	39.57	23
New Democratic Party	140,128	34.63	20
Liberal Party	94,872	23.44	9
Green Party of Nova Scotia	9,411	2.33	0
Independent	153	0.4	0
Rejected Ballots	1,363		
Total	406,046		82

Source: Elections Nova Scotia

Canada Thirty-ninth General Election 23 January 2006

Political party	Votes received (Valid)	Percentage of popular vote	Candidates elected
Animal Alliance Environment Voters Party of Canada	72	0.0	0
Bloc Québécois	1,553,201	10.5	51
Canadian Action Party	6,102	0.0	0
Christian Heritage Party of Canada	28,152	0.2	0
Communist Party of Canada	3,022	0.0	0
Conservative Party of Canada	5,374,071	36.6	124
First Peoples National Party of Canada	1,201	0.0	0
Green Party of Canada	664,068	4.5	0
Liberal Party of Canada	4,479,415	30.2	103
Libertarian Party of Canada	3,002	0.0	0
Marijuana Party	9,171	0.1	0
Marxist-Leninist Party of Canada	8,980	0.1	0

Continued

(Continued)

Political party	Votes received (Valid)	Percentage of popular vote	Candidates elected
New Democratic Party of Canada	2,589,597	17.5	29
Progressive Canadian Party	14,151	0.1	0
Western Block Party	1,094	0.0	0
Independent	76,696	0.5	1
No Affiliation	5,164	0.0	0
Total	14,817,159	100	308

Source: Elections Canada

Index of names

Ablonczy, Diane, 149
Adam, Mike, 256
Adams, Bill, 266
Aglukark, David, Sr., 175
Aitken, Maxwell III, 234
Aitken, William Maxwell "Max." *See* Beaverbrook (Lord)
El-Akhras family, 68
Alcock, Reg, 170
Almalki, Abdullah, 6, 50
Ambrose, Rona, 25, 149
Anderson, Doris, 19
Andre, Marion, 267
Annan, Kofi, 68
Arar, Maher, xxxi, 5–6, 49–50, 63–6
Arar, Mehar, 49
Arthur, Andre, 18
Arvaluk, James, 179
Ashfield, Keith, 231
Ashton, Steve, 169
Austin, Jack, 30

Bachand, Raymond, 205
Bagby, Andrew, 261
Bagnall, Jim, 241
Bagnell, Larry, 175, 176
Bagri, Ajaib Singh, 59
Bain, George, 267
Baird, John, 25, 36, 95
Baker, Michael, 247
Bakken-Lackey, Brenda, 153
Balding, Allan, 267
Balfour, Marcel, 109
Ban Ki-moon, xxxvi
Banks, Sydney, 267
Barron, Sid, 267
Basrur, Sheela, 190
Bastarache, Michel, 115
Beardy, Stan, 103
Beaverbrook (Lord), 234–5
Béchard, Claude, 205
Bennett, Carolyn, 20
Bennett, Jim, 257, 259
Bentley, Chris, 192
Berger, Thomas, 116, 117, 117n4, 182
Bernard, Joshua, 115
Bernardo, Paul, xv
Bernier, Maxime, 25
Berry, Glyn, xv, 77, 267
Bevilacqua, Maurizio, 20
Bevington, Dennis, 175
Binns, Pat, 241, 242
Black, Bill, 244, 245
Black, Dawn, 76
Blackburn, George, 267
Blackburn, Jean-Pierre, 25
Blais, Pierre, 109
Blondin-Andrew, Ethel, 18, 175
Boisclair, André, 206
Boniface, Gwen, 199

Bonnell, Lorne, 243
Bouchard, Jacques, 267
Bouchard, Lucien, 203, 205
Boudreau, Brian, 246
Boudreau, Victor, 235, 237
Bourassa, Robert, 204
Boyde, Pam, 175
Bracken, John, 169
Branch, Frank, 222, 223
Brault, Jean, xxxi, 48, 49
Brazeau, Patrick, 100, 114
Brazil, Duane, 266
Brewer, Allison, 226, 237
Brison, Scott, 20, 22, 84
Bronfman, Saidye, 267
Brooks, Norman, 267
Broomfield, Todd, 265
Brown, James, 267
Browne, Joe, 260
Bruinooge, Rod, 100, 170
Bryant, Michael, 199
Burke, Joan, 258
Burke, T.J., 236, 237
Bush, George W., 57, 62, 66, 78, 83
Byrne, Ed, 262, 265
Byrne, Greg, 236

Cadman, Chuck, 18
Cahill, Tom, 266
Calder, Frank Arthur, 267
Calvert, Lorne, 154, 157, 160, 264
Cameron, John Allan, 267
Cameron, Sheldon R., 243
Campagnolo, Iona, 121
Campbell, Gordon, 106, 118, 120, 122, 124, 126, 127–8, 129, 132, 134, 142
Campbell, Kim, 119
Cannon, Lawrence, 25, 98
Cansfield, Donna, 185, 194
Caplan, Eleanor, 188
Carle, Guillaume, 114
Carlson, Len, 267
Carmichael, Urban, 243
Carr, Jody, 230
Casselman, Leah, 185
Castro, Fidel, xxviii
Castro, Raúl, xxviii
Celil, Huseyin, 74
Chandra, Ranjit Kumar, 257
Chaoulli, Jacques, 207–208, 208n2, 209
Charest, Jean, 41, 204, 205, 209, 210, 213, 218, 219, 220
Charlie, Sherry, 129
Chartier, Clement, 102
Chavez, Hugo, 258
Chiarelli, Bob, 95
Chong, Michael, 24, 25, 41, 215
Chrétien, Jean, 21, 40, 42, 60, 75, 79
Christensen, Tom, 129
Clement, Tony, 25, 75, 150
Clinton, Bill, 74
Coffin, Paul, xxi, 48, 49
Coleman, Rich, 133
Collins, Felix, 257
Comuzzi, Joe, 46
Constable, Dean, 241
Cooke, Glen, 262
Coon, David, 232
Copeman, Don, 189
Copps, Sheila, 4, 19
Cordiano, Joe, 185, 192
Cory, Peter, 187, 234
Coull, Gary, 267
Couturier, Norman, 81
Cowan, Patricia, 266
Crabbe, Ray, 85
Craig, John, 229
Crane, Olive, 241
Crofford, Joanne, 157
Crowe, Heather, 267
Currier, Shawn, 131
Curry, Bill, 29
Curry, Floyd, 268

Dalai Lama, 73
Dalton, Ronald, 261
Davies, Tim, 135
Day, Brian, 136
Day, Stockwell, 25, 51, 54n2, 65, 121
DeCicco Best, Anne-Marie, 96
DeLong, Alana, 145
Desbiens, Jean-Paul, 268
Deschamps, Marie, 207–208
Dexter, Darrel, 245
Diefenbaker, John, 172
Dinning, Jim, xxxiv, 145, 146–7
Di Novo, Cheri, 201
Dinsdale, Peter, 101
Dion, Stéphane, xxxiv, 4, 10, 12, 20, 21, 22, 30, 41, 53, 174, 177, 216
Dobbin, Craig, 266
Doer, Gary, 164, 168–9, 170
Doerksen, Victor, 145, 147
Doody, C. William, 266
Dorey, Dwight, 100
Dorval, Michel, 43
Dosanjh, Ujjal, 56, 76, 78, 85
Douglas, Tommy, 270
Druken, Randy, 261
Dryden, Ken, 20, 22, 41
Duceppe, Gilles, 9, 13, 16, 18, 22, 27, 41, 211
Duke, Darly, 268
Dumont, Luc, 105
Duncan, Dustin, 153
Duncan, Dwight, 185, 195
Dunderdale, Kathy, 263
Durelle, Yvon, 233

Edjericon, Richard, 175
Edward, Catherine, 243
Edzerza, John, 177
Egeland, Jan, 67
Ehman, Diana, 178
Ellington, Duke, 268
Emerson, David, xvi, 23, 24, 25, 27, 43–4, 55, 72, 118, 119–20, 121, 131, 132, 133, 134, 149
Emery, Marc, 133
Erickson, Douglas Lloyd, 131
Evans, Iris, 147
Evans, Ron, 109
Eves, Ernie, 185

Fabrikant, Valery, 213
Fage, Ernie, 244–5, 247
Fallon, Jack, 268
Fantino, Julian, xxxii, 199
Faragalli, Joe, 268
Fellegi, Ivan, 137
Fentie, Dennis, 176, 177, 178
Ferguson, Michael, 227, 237
Ferguson, Walter "Maynard," 268
Fiacco, Pat, 97
Filmon, Gary, 170
Finlayson, Hugh, 125
Finley, Diane, 25
Finley, Doug, 21
Fitzgerald, Ella, 268
FitzGerald, John, 260
Flaherty, Jim, xxxii, 25, 34–7, 38, 39, 264
Fletcher, Steven, 170
Fogarassy, Tony, 119
Fontaine, Phil, 99–100, 105, 106, 115, 217
Fontana, Joe, 27, 96
Foran, John, 236
Ford, Gerald, 268
Forgeron, Don, 226
Forrestall, Michael, 268
Fortier, Michael, xvi, 24, 25, 149
Fowlie, Brenda, 227
Fox, Tom, 60, 61
Francis, Mayann, 244
Fraser, David, xviii, 76
Fraser, Sheila, 32, 53, 108, 179

Frastacky, Mike, xxviii
Freiman, Mark, 43
Frulla, Liza, 18
Fry, Hedy, 20, 119
Furey, Charles J., 260
Furlong, Dennis, 235

Gainey, Bob, 268
Gainey, Laura, 268
Galloway, Gloria, 13
Gates, Bill, 74
Gates, Melinda, 74
Geertz, Clifford, 268
Gélinas, Johanne, 45
Geoffrion, Bernie "Boom Boom," 268
George, Dudley, 196–7
Gerrard, John, 170
Gerretsen, John, 201
Getty, Don, 148
Gharbi, Gamil, 213. *See also* Lepine, Marc
Ghiz, Robert, 241
Gibson, Margaret, 268
Gill, Kimveer, 212, 213
Gillam, Craig Paul, 266
Girtel, Kim, 69
Goddard, Nichola, 77
Goddard, Tim, 78
Godfrey, John, 20
Godin, Ronald, 237
Gomery, John, xvi, 3, 5, 47, 48, 203, 204, 220
Gonzales, Alberto, 63
Goodale, Ralph, 16, 153
Gore, Al, 143, 173
Graham, Bill, xv, xix, 19, 26, 37, 46, 56, 65, 68
Graham, Shawn, xxx, 10, 222, 224, 225, 226, 227, 228, 229–30, 231, 235, 236–7
Gravel, Raymond, 27
Gray, Darrell, 114
Green, Brad, 227, 229
Green, Derek, 262
Green, Jim, 91
Greetham, Sue, 175
Gregoire, Gilles, 268
Grimes, Roger, 257
Guité, Chuck, xxv, 49
Gushue, Brad, 256

Hagerman, Barbara Anne, 241
Hahn, David, 126
Hall Findlay, Martha, 20, 22
Hamm, John, 244, 247, 254
Hancock, Dave, 145, 146–7, 152
Handley, Joe, 176
Hansen, Colin, 127
Hansen, Rick, 122
Hardy, Todd, 177, 178
Harper, Stephen, xvi, xvii, xix, xxvi, xxix, 3, 5–6, 6–7, 8, 9–10, 11, 12, 13, 14, 15–16, 17, 23, 24, 25, 26, 28, 29, 30, 31, 33, 41, 42, 45, 46, 48, 50, 43, 52, 53, 54–5, 56, 58, 59, 60, 61, 65, 66, 67, 68, 69, 72, 73, 74, 76, 78, 79, 80, 82, 83, 87, 93, 98, 99, 100, 102, 107, 113, 118, 127, 134, 141, 148, 149, 150, 153, 157, 160, 162, 173, 173n1, 176, 204, 211, 215, 218, 220, 223, 236, 244, 251, 252, 253, 254, 255, 256, 263, 264
Harris, Jack, 259, 263
Harris, Jim, 15, 23
Harris, Mike, 188, 191, 192, 196–7
Harrison, Jeremy, 153
Harvey, Kenneth J., 266
Hatchen, Dan, 102
Haverstock, Lynda, 157
Hawes, Randy, 123

Hawn, Laurie, 148
Hayden, Melissa, 268
Hearn, Loyola, 25, 255, 261, 262
Hedderson, Tom, 265
Heinbecker, Paul, 56
Henderson, Larry, 268
Henderson, Paul, 269
Heppner, Ben, 155, 268
Hermanson, Elwin, 155
Hess-von Kruedener, Paeta, 68
Hilebrand, Ike, 268
Hill, Arthur, 268
Hill, Jay, 121
Hillier, Rick, 47, 79, 84–5, 85n13, 86n14
Hinman, Paul, 146
Hodgson, Chris, 196
Hogg, Peter, 31
Homolka, Karla, xv
Hope, Ian, 79
Horwood, Harold, 268
Howard, Russ, 256
Hudak, Tim, 201–2
Hughes, Ted, 118, 129–31
Hu Jintao, 74
Hunt, Constance, 31
Huntjens, Tony, 222
Hussein, Saddam, 269

Iacobucci, Frank, 6, 50, 193
Ignatieff, Michael, xxxiv, 4, 9, 20, 21, 22, 41, 74, 176, 216
Ingram, Vaughan, 266
Ip, James, 192

Jackson, Cam, 185
Jacobs, Jane, 269
Jamieson, Stuart, 236
Jean, Michaëlle, 24, 75
Jenkins, Kevin, 241
John, Edward, 107
Johnson, Pierre Marc, 207
Johnston, Wayne, 266
Jolson, Al, 267
Joseph, Lawrence, 162

Karagianis, Maurine, 123
Karetak-Lindell, Nancy, 175–6
Karwacki, David, 153
Karzai, Hamid, xxxi, 7, 76, 77
Katz, Sam, 95, 97, 170, 171
Katz, Shirley, 256–7
Keir, Jack, 228
Kember, Norman, 60
Kennedy, Gerard, xxxiv, 4, 20, 21, 22, 41, 184, 185, 191, 192, 215, 216
Kennedy, Jerome, 264
Kennedy, John F., 64
Kennedy, Larry, 230
Kenney, Jason, 73, 149
Kenney, Matt, 269
Kenny, Colin, 84
Khadr, Abdullah, 63
Khadr, Ahmed Said, 61, 63
Khadr, Omar, 6, 61–2
Khosla, Deepa, 256
Kilabuk, Peter, 179
Kilgour, David, 148
King, Larry, 256
King, Peter, 59
Kirby, Michael, 186
Kirkpatrick, Pamela, 107
Kitchen, William, 106
Klassen, Cindy, xviii
Klein, Ralph, xix, xx, xxxi, xxxv, 10, 126, 140, 142, 144, 145, 146, 148, 150–1
Klinkenberg, Marty, 234
Klippenstein, Murray, 103
Korab, Jamie, 256

Kusugak, Jose, 179
Kwinter, Monte, 200

LaForme, Bryan, 106
Lamrock, Kelly, 235–6
Lamy, Pascal, 70
La Rose, Lauren, 190
Lay, Kenneth, xxiv
Layton, Irving, 269
Layton, Jack, 11, 16, 18, 22, 174, 255
LeBlanc, Neil, 244
LeBreton, Marjory, 25
Ledwell, Frank, 243
Lee, Clifford, 241
Lefebvre, Henri, 91
Lehotsky, Harry, 269
Lennon, Frank, 269
Lepage, Guy A., 213
Lepine, Marc, 212, 213
Leslie, Keith, 192
Lewis, Dorothy, 243
Lewis, Stephen, 74
Linden, Sidney, 196, 197
Lochhead, Kenneth, 266, 269
Lonechild, Guy, 162
Loney, James, xix–xx, 60, 61
Lord, Bernard, 10, 222, 223, 224, 225, 226, 227, 228, 229, 230, 231, 237
Lougheed, Peter, 10, 143–4
Love, Rod, 146
Lunn, Gary, 25

Al Maati, Ahmed, 6
El Maati, Ahmad, 50
MacAdam, Kevin, 241
MacDonald, Dean, 265
MacDonald, Mark, 243
MacDonald, Rodney, xvii, xviii, 244, 245, 246, 248, 249, 251, 252, 253
MacFadyen, Patrick, 241
MacKay, Peter, xxiii, 25, 47, 54–5, 57, 66, 67, 69, 70, 73, 76, 241
MacKay, Wayne, 230, 231
Mackenzie, Francis, 245
MacKenzie, William, 261
MacKinnon, Peter, 31, 159
MacLeod, Leslie, 260
MacNeil, Stephen, 246
Mahoney, John, 266
Major, John, 6, 31, 43, 60
Major, John C., 135
Malavoy, Marie, 206
Malik, Ripudaman Singh, 43, 59
Malley, Michael “Tanker,” 222, 223, 224, 227
Manley, John, 4, 20
Mann, Tom, 231
Manning, Fabian, 255, 257
Mar, Gary, 127, 152
Markesteyn, Peter H., 261
Marsden, Pat, 269
Marshall, David, 110, 199
Marshall, Ken, 265
Marshall, Stephen, 115
Marshall, Tom, 261, 266
Martel, Leo, 65
Martel, Shelley, 188, 191–2
Martin, John, 269
Martin, Paul, xv, xix, xxxvii–xxxviii, 7, 11, 12, 13, 15–16, 19–20, 21, 23, 27, 40, 46, 55, 56n4, 60, 63, 87, 99, 118, 119, 153, 157, 174, 175, 204, 251, 252, 255, 264
Masciulli, Joseph, 224
Mason, Dutch, 269
May, Elizabeth, xxx, 23, 27, 28
Mayes, Colin, 102
Mazigh, Monia, 65
McCall, Warren, 157
McCallion, Hazel, 95
McCartney, Paul, 256

McDonald, Tobias F., 256
McDougall, Barbara, 198
McFadyen, Hugh, 164, 170
McFarlane, Norm, 236
McGuinty, Dalton, 142, 184, 197, 200
McKenna, Frank, 4, 20, 56n4, 83, 227, 236
McKeown, David, 190
McLellan, Anne, 18, 148
McPherson, Gary, 145, 147
McQuaig, Linda, 18
Measner, Adrian, 52, 53
Meisen, Axel, 256
Melvin, Heather Foley, 246
Merasty, Gary, 153
Mesheau, Peter, 224
Michael, Lorraine, 259, 255, 264
Mickleborough, Graham, 153
Miller, David, 87, 95, 96, 97, 98
Mills-McCartney, Heather, 256
Mitchell, Arthur, 177
Mohammed, 57, 57n5
Moisan, Jean, 49
Molloy, John, 68
Mondor, Emilie, 269
Montaner, Julio, 75
Moor, Mavor, 269
Moore, James, 121
Morgan, Gwyn, 30
Morris, Layne, 63
Morselli, Giuseppe, 269
Morton, Alexandra, 134
Morton, Ted, 145, 146–7, 151–2
Mulcair, Thomas, 205
Mulroney, Brian, 75, 149
Multani, Gurbaj Singh, 214, 206n8, 215
Munson, Ken, 102
Munter, Alex, 96
Murphy, Mike, 230, 235
Murray, Lowell, 30
Murray, Stuart, 169
Murrow, Edward R., 270
Muskego, Fred, 109

Namagoose, Bill, 114
Nasrallah, Hassan, 67
Nault, Fernand, 269
Netster, Patterk, 179
Neve, Alex, 105
Neville, Darlene, 261
Newcombe, Bob, 131
Nichols, Mark, 256
Nicholson, Robert, 25
Nicklaus, Jack, 243
Noel, John, 261
Noel, Kirk, 266
Nolan, Richard Francis, 266
Nordheimer, Ian, 185
Norris, Mark, 145, 146–7
Norris, Rob, 154
Noseworthy, John, 257, 262
Nurredin, Muued, 6
Nurredin, Muyyed, 50
Nutarak, Jobie, 179

Oberg, Lyle, 145, 147
O'Brien, Al, 264
O'Brien, Kevin, 260
O'Brien, Larry, 95, 96
O'Connor, Dennis, 5–6, 49, 50, 64–5
O'Connor, Gordon, xix, 25, 47, 55, 56, 57, 58, 78, 79, 80, 82, 83, 85–6, 85n12, 85n13, 86n14
Oda, Bev, 25
Okalik, Paul, 176, 179
Okulitch, Andrew, 27
Olhmert, Ehud, 67, 68
O'Neill, John J., 261
O'Neill-Yates, Chris, 257
Ostry, Bernard, 269

Pacienza, Angela, 192
Pallister, Brian, 171
Palmeter, Frank, 100
Paradis, Pierre, 210
Parker, Jackie, 269
Parkin, Tony, 196
Parsons, Gregory, 261
Patey, Nina, 259
Pellegrini, Alain, 68
Pelletier, Benoît, 219
Penn, Sean, 190
Pepin, Clermont, 269
Perlin, Rae, 266
Person, Glen, 27
Peterson, David, 198
Pettigrew, Pierre, 17–18
Picard, Ghislain, 217
Picard, Raphael, 113
Pickett, Hugh, 269
Pickton, Robert, 135
Pillarella, Franco, 65
Piper, Martha, 136
Plasse, Michel, 269
Point, Steven, 107
Polchies, Clark, 115
Pope, Alan, 111, 200
Power, Kevin, 257
Pownall, Leon, 269
Pralle, Sarah, 92n5
Prebble, Peter, 157
Prentice, Jim, 25, 100, 104, 107, 111, 128, 141, 176, 199
Presley, Elvis, 269
Prudori, Tony, 111
Pupatello, Sandra, 192

Rae, Bob, 4, 20–1, 22, 41, 43, 60, 184, 216
Rae, John "Jackie," 270
Ramsay, David, 40, 199, 200
Reid, Gerry, 257, 259, 265
Reyat, Inderjit Singh, 43, 135
Rice, Condoleezza, 59, 66
Riddell, Bill, 175
Rideout, Tom, 261, 265
Riley, Susan, 42
Robichaud, Elvy, 229
Robinson, Svend, 119
Rock, Alan, 4, 20
Rodin, 234
Rodriguez, Pablo, 45
Rooney, David, 266
Rosenthal, Abraham Michael, 270
Ross, Ronald, 233
Rothstein, Marshall, xvii, xviii, 31, 32
Rudd, David, 54
Ruelokke, Max, 260–1
Rumsfeld, Donald, xxxiii
Runciman, Robert, 196
Russell, Anna, 270

Saada, Jacques, 10
Sale, Tim, 168–9
Samson, Michel, 246
Sappier, Dale, 115
Sarsfield, Peter, 111
Saunders, Doris, 266
Sauvageau, Benoit, 27, 270
Savage, Larry, 97n7
Savage, Mike, 246
Saxberg, Lorne, 270
Schmidt, Grant, 155
Schreyer, Ed, 171
Schuler, Ron, 170
Schwab, Susan, 72, 132
Scott, Ian, 270
Scott, Murray, 252
Selinger, Greg, 166
Shakespeare, William, 165
Shapiro, Bernard, 33, 52
Shoyama, Thomas, 270
Sihota, Moe, 123

Simon, Mary, 173, 179
Simoneau, Leopold, 270
Simpson, Jeffrey, 24, 219, 211n13
Sims, Jenny, 125
Sinatra, Frank, 269
Sinclair, Ian, 270
Sinclair, Lister, 270
Sinclair, Phoenix, 171
Skelton, Carol, 25
Slack, Enid, 90
Smith, Mike, 246
Smitherman, George, 186, 189
Snelgrove, Lloyd, 147
Snyder, Stephen, 194
Solberg, Monte, 25, 99, 128, 141
Sooden, Harmeet Singh, xix–xx, 60, 61
Sorbara, Greg, 185
Spearin, Donald, 54n1
Speer, Christopher, 63
Speer, Tabitha, 63
Staebler, Edna, 270
Stavro, Steve, 270
Stelmach, Ed, xxxiv, 10, 144, 145, 146–7, 148, 151
Stevenson, Mark, 107
Stewart, Basil, 241
Stewart, Jane, 198
Stewart, Ron, 32, 53
Stoery, Roy "Red," 270
Strahl, Chuck, 25, 52
Strom, Harry, 148
Stukus, Annis, 270
Stymiest, Drew, 233
Sullivan, Loyola, 258, 265, 266
Sullivan, Sam, 93, 134
Sullivan, Terry, 190
Svekla, Thomas, 152
Sylvain, Matthew, 189

Takhar, Harinder, 185
Tarchuk, Janis, 147
Taylor, Carole, 118, 123–4, 131, 137
Thira, Sharon, 104
Thompson, Gregory, 25, 229, 235
Thompson, Ian, 252, 253
Thompson, Richard, 82
Thomson, Kenneth, 270
Thornton, Grant, 237
Tkachuk, David, 31
Tobin, Brian, 4, 20
Toews, Vic, 25, 170
Tomah, Jeff, 115
Toope, Stephen, 49, 136
Tory, John, 197
Tout, Anne Marie, 178
Trudeau, Pierre, 5, 20, 136
Turner, Garth, 27, 41, 120
Turner, Shirley, 261
Turner, Zachary, 261
Turvey, John, 270

Vachon, Louis-Albert, 270
Valeri, Tony, 18
Vanier, Dana J., 90
Van Iersel, Arn, 134
Van Loan, Peter, 24
Van Tighem, Gordon, 178
Vellacott, Maurice, 102
Verner, Josée, 25
Viger, Andre, 270
Volpe, Jeannot, 223
Volpe, Joe, 41
Volpe, Tom, 20, 21, 22

Waddell, Ken, 170
Wainberg, Mark, 75
Waldman, Lorne, 50
Wangersky, Russell, 266
Wark, Wesley, 59
Watson, Tom, 243
Watt, Sheila, 173
Weinzweig, John, 270

Weir, Elizabeth, 225, 226
Weitzel, Kim, 131
Wells, Andy, 261
Whalen, Diana, 246
Wilkins, David, 80, 83
Williams, Claude, 230
Williams, Danny, 160, 255, 256, 257, 258, 259, 260, 261, 262, 255, 264, 265
Wilson, Bill, 105
Wilson, Michael, 39, 56, 71
Windsor, Howard, 246
Winsor, Ramon "Ray," 266
Wong, Jan, 213, 205n4, 215
Wong, Tony, 185
Woodford, Rick, 266
Worm, Boris, 262
Wynne, Kathleen, 192

Yates, Kevin, 154, 157
Yeo, Leslie, 266
Young, Alan, 43
Young, Wanda, 257

Zaccardelli, Giuliano, 5, 49–50, 65–6
Zucker, Jerry, xvi, xvii

Index of subjects

Aborigines: aboriginal affairs and, 40–1; with Aboriginal Affairs Committee, 102; with aboriginal pilot sales program, 106–7; with CAP, 100, 114; employment rates for, 88; with familial abuse, xxv; housing, 27; Hughes Report and, 129–31; Kelowna Accord and, 7–8, 27, 40–1, 99, 127–9, 174–5; with Maritimes and treaty rights, 114–15; NCLA, 116–17, 116n3; QNA, 114; in Saskatchewan, 162–3
abortions, xix, 14
abuse: of children, 171; familial, xxv, xxvii, xxxi
Access to Health Care Services in Canada, xvi
activists, environmental, 92, 134, 143
activities, leisure, xxviii
adult education, xx, 36
Afghanistan: Canadian casualties in, xv, xx, xxiii, xxvii, xxviii, xxix, xxx, xxxi, xxxii, xxxiv, 46, 77–8; Canadian troops in, xviii; civilians killed by Canadian troops, xix; Harper's visit to Kandahar, 79; mission and debate, xxxi, 75–7; mission extended, xxiii, 6–7, 46–7; mission support, xxiii
AFN. *See* Assembly of First Nations
age: life expectancy, xxxvi; median, xxxii; seniors and, 32; of sexual consent, 43
Agent Orange, 235
agriculture, 165
AIDS / HIV, xxix, 74–5
Air India, 50–1, 59–60, 135
airplanes, flown over Arctic, 81n10
Alberta: boom in, 139–40; Calgary, 90–1; with federal election in 2006, 148–9; growth in, xxii, 140–4; health care reform founders and, 149–51; legislature, 151–2; new premier in, 144–8; oil in, 139, 142–3; other news in, 152; trade between BC and, 126–7; unemployment in, 141
alcohol sales, xxx
Anti-Terrorism Act, xxiv
appointees: merit and government, 29; Newfoundl and and Labrador with public, 260–1
Arar, Mehar, xxxi, 5, 49–50, 63–6
Arctic: commercial flights flown daily over, 81n10; defence policies in, 80–1; ice cap, 173–6; Operation Nunalivut, 81; resources, 172–3; sovereignty, 172–6, 183
Arctic Climate Impact Assessment, 173
arrests, terrorism, 201
art galleries, xxviii
Asia-Pacific trade, 138
Assembly of First Nations (AFN): elections, 105–6; leadership, 99–100

auditor: general, 29, 32;
of procurements, 29
autism, 192

Ballistic Missile Defence (BMD), 82–4
Bandidos motorcycle gang, xxi, xxv
Bank of Canada, 38
bankruptcy, xxxii
bargaining, BC labour issues and, 123–6
BC. *See* British Columbia
bears. *See* Spirit Bears
Beaverbrook, (Lord), 234–5
beetles. *See* western mountain pine beetles
bills, crime, 43–4
birth rate, crude, xxviii
BMD. *See* Ballistic Missile Defence
boil water advisory, 136–7
bombings. *See* Air India
boom: in Alberta, 139–40; oil and gas, xviii
borders, North American trade, 72–3
British Columbia (BC): Aboriginal pilot sales program and, 106–7; Air India bombing and, 135; with boil water advisory, 136–7; budget, 123; CMAs, 136; economy, 137–8; Emerson fall-out after election in, 119–20; Emery and, 133; federal election and seats in, 120; federal election in, 119; ferry sinking in, xix, 126; First Nations in, 32, 106–8; forest fires in, 133; with four BC ministers on federal cabinet, 121; with government spending, 106; growth in, xxii, 137–8; with health systems issues, 131; with highway of tears, 126; interprovincial cooperation in, 126–7; Kelowna Accord and, 7–9, 27, 40–1, 99, 127–9, 174–5; labour issues with marathon public-sector bargaining, 123–4; labour issues with teachers bargaining, 124–6; mining accident in, 131; Olympics and, 133–4; Pickton trial and, 135; salmon farming in, 106–7, 134–5; with social services and Hughes Report, 129–31; softwood lumber and, xxii, 131–3; Speech from Throne in, 121–3; Spirit Bear and environmental protection in, 134; summary, 118; treaty firsts in, 107–8; with UBC's new president, 136; unions, 124
budgets: BC, 123; concerns, 32; conservatives' first, 34–5; cuts, 27–9; First Nations and, 101–4; Manitoba, 166–7; military, 27, 80–2; Newfoundland and Labrador, 258; Nova Scotia, 247–8; with parliamentary budget authority, 29; Saskatchewan, 157–8
building permits, xv, xvi, xviii, xxi, xxii, xxv, xxvi, xxix, xxx, xxxi, xxxiii, xxxiv
bureaucracy, in Quebec, 206–209

cabinets: BC ministers on federal, 121; Manitoba, 168–9; members, 54–7; national institutions, 23–4; Saskatchewan, 157
calendar, Canadian, xv–xxxvi
Calgary, Alberta, 90–1
caloric intake, xxiv
Camp Gagetown, 235
Canada: calendar for, xv–xxxvi; with Canadians kidnapped in Iraq, 60–1; with casualties in Afghanistan, xv, xix, xx, xxiii, xxvii, xxviii, xxix, xxx, xxxi, xxxii, xxxiv, 46, 77–8; China and trade with, 73–4; growth in, 33; Jan. 2006 general election table for, 271–2; new government and conservatives' style, 26–27; sovereignty, 80–1, 172–6; terrorism and, 57–70

Canadian Council of Motor Transport Administrators, 242
Canadian Labour Congress (CLC), 97
Canadian Wheat Board (CWB), 52–3
cancer, 27, 186
CAP. *See* Congress of Aboriginal Peoples
cartoons, Mohammed, 57–8
casualties: in Afghanistan, xv, xix, xx, xxiii, xxvii, xxviii, xxix, xxx, xxxi, xxxii, xxxiv, 46, 77–8; in Lebanon, 68
caucus changes, 27–8
census metropolitan areas (CMAs), 87–8, 136
Charter of Rights and Freedoms, 16
children: abuse of, 171; autism in, 192; child care and, xxi, 27; child protection system, 118; household income and influence on, xxiii; social services and, 129–31, 171; youth, xx–xxi, 18, 36
China: Canada and trade with, 73–4; foreign takeovers and, 40
Chinese Head Tax, xxvi
cities: in confederation, 98; in marketplace and municipal affairs, 87–91; municipal affairs and culture of, 91–3. *See also specific cities*
CLC. *See* Canadian Labour Congress
Clean Air Act, 8, 44–5
climate change: Calgary's plan for, 90–1; Clean Air Act and, 8, 44–5; films about, 143, 173; Kyoto Protocol, 8–9, 27, 44–5; UN Convention on, 8
CMAs. *See* census metropolitan areas
commissioners: ethics, 29, 25, 43–4; patronage, 29–2
commissions. *See* special commissions
commuters, xxvii
composting facilities, 92
computers, 34
confederation, cities in, 98
Congress of Aboriginal Peoples (CAP), 100, 114
Conservative Party of Canada, xv
conservatives: with first budget, 34–5; style of, 26–27; thirty-ninth general election and swing to, 16–17; with voter preferences by political party, Dec. 2005 to Jan 2006, 17
Consumer Price Index (CPI), xv, xvii, xix, xxvi, xxviii, xxix, xxxi, xxxvi
contestants, in thirty-ninth general election, 13–14
controversies: Crocus Fund, 167; Emerson, David, and ethics commissioner, 51–2; fraud, xvi, xxiv, xxv, xxxi, 5, 32, 47–9, 233; office of correctional investigator, 53; sponsorship scandals, xvi, xxv, xxxi, 5, 47–9; wheat board, 52–3
corporations, xxiv, xxix, xxxiv; with ban on donations, 29; with mergers and takeovers, 33–4
corrections: office of correctional investigator, 53; penitentiaries and jails, xxxii, 53; re-offence rate, xxxv
CPI. *See* Consumer Price Index
crimes, 14; bills, 43–4; corrections and, xxxii, xxxv, 53; determinants, xxv; guns, xxii, xxx, xxxiii, 200; hate, 198; Karla and, xv; national crime rate, xxviii; punishment and, 42–4; re-offence rate, xxxv, 43; shootings, xxii, xxx, 212–3; the Territories and, xxxii; violence and, 22
Criminal Code, 29
Crocus Fund, 167
culture: of cities and municipal affairs, 91–3; in Newfoundland and Labrador, 265–6
CWB. *See* Canadian Wheat Board

debt: financing, xvii; load, xxxv, 27
defence policies: Afghanistan, 75–9; Arctic, 80–1; BMD and, 82–4; with defence procurement, 81–2; foreign affairs and, 75–86; Hillier and, 84–6; NORAD and, 84, 84n11
defence procurement, 81–2
democracy, municipal affairs and local, 95–7
Department of Public Safety, 32
diamonds, 81, 179, 180, 181
doctors, 124
dollar, value of Canadian, xxii, 37
donations, ban on political, 29
Douglas Creek Estates, xviii, xix, xxi, xxiii, xxv, 197–9
driving: under influence, 44; street racing, 43

ecology, industrial, 90
economy: BC, 137–8; with economic hardship and senior women, xxvii; indicators, 33–4; Manitoba, 164–6; national, xxxii, 14, 33–40; Newfoundland and Labrador, 262–3, 266; Nova Scotia, 249–51; OECD, 95; PEI, 238–9; Saskatchewan, 158–9; Territories, 180–1
education: adult, xx, 36; autism and, 192; with Indian residential school settlement, 103–5; literacy rates, 117; Manitoba, 167; of minority youth, xx–xxi; NB, 230–1; Nova Scotia, 253; Ontario, 191–3; Post-Secondary Learning Amendment Act, 151; public school system reform, 122; students and funding for college, xxii, xxx; with tax-exempt scholarships, 34; teachers, 124–6, 191; Territories, 181, 182–5; with university enrolment, xxxiii
educators, xxxiv
elections: AFN, 105–6; democracy and municipal, 95–7; fixed election dates, 28; NB, xxx, 10, 224–7; Nova Scotia, xxiii; Ontario, 96; politics and, xxxvii–xxxix; Saskatchewan, 153–4; tables for Canada's Jan. 2006 general, 271–2; tables for Nova Scotia's June 2006 general, 271; tampering, 162; U.S., xxxiii
elections, federal: Alberta, 2006, 148–9; BC, 119–20; Emerson and fallout after, 119–12; First Nations and, 99–100; Manitoba, 2006, 170–1; Newfoundland and Labrador, 255–6, 263–4
elections, in parliament: contestants, 13–14; with fixed election dates, 28; Green Party leadership, 23; with house by-elections, 27–8; liberal leadership transfer, 19–22; major party platforms and issues, 14–16; NDP and bloc hold steady, 22; results, 17–9; results from 2006 with changes from prior election, 19; with swing to conservatives, 16–17; thirty-ninth general, 11–23; voter preferences by political party, Dec. 2005 to Jan. 2006, 17
11 September 2001, 70
Emerson, David: with election fallout, 119–20; ethics commissioner and, 51–2
Emery, Marc, 133
employment: Aborigines and, 88; credit, 34; rate, xv, xvi, xvii, xix, xxi, xxii, xxiii, xxiv, xxviii; students and summer, xxii; with unemployment, 34, 89, 141; with unemployment rate, xxv, xxvii, xxxi, xxxiii, xxxiv, 34; youth, 36

energy: in NB, 223, 225, 228; in Nova Scotia, 250; in Ontario, 194–6; plan, 89–90
engineers, xxiii, 206–7
environmental activists, 92, 134, 143
ethics commissioner, 29, 33, 43–4
Ethnic Diversity Survey, xxii
ethnicity, in Quebec, 212–17
evacuees, from Lebanon, 68–70
events: Alberta, 152; Manitoba, 171; NB, 233–5; PEI, 242–3
expectancy, life, xxxvi
exports: diamonds, 179; to U.S., 34. *See also* trade

families: abuse in, xxv, xxvii, xxxi; with wealth, xxxv
Family Violence in Canada: A Statistical Profile, xxvii
farming, salmon, 106–7, 134–5
Federal Accountability Act, 29
federalism, in Quebec, 217–20
ferry sinking, in BC, xix, 126
films: *An Inconvenient Truth*, 143, 173; *Karla*, xv
fires, forest, 133
First Nations: Aboriginal Affairs Committee and, 102; with AFN, 99–100, 105–6; in BC, 32, 106–8; budgets and, 101–2; CAP and, 100, 114; federal developments and, 99–106; with federal election, 99–100; Governance Act, 8, 102–3; Human Rights Act and, 103; Indian residential school settlement and, 103–5; KI, 112–13; Lheidli T'enneh, 107; with Maritimes and treaty rights, 114–15; Mississaugas, 106; NAN, 103; in Newfoundland and Labrador, 265; Nisga'a, 107; in North, 115–17; Norway House Cree Nation, 109; in Ontario, 109–13, 196–200; Pabineau, 115; Pessamit, 113; with provincial and territorial developments, 106–17; in Quebec, 113–14; with realignment of federal spending, 101; salmon farming and, 106–7; Six Nations, 109–11; with UN declaration on rights of indigenous peoples, 105; in West, 108–9. *See also* Aborigines
fiscal crisis, 89
fiscal events, in PEI, 239–40
fishing industry: in Newfoundland and Labrador, 261–2; salmon farming, 106–7, 134–5
football, xxxiv
foreign affairs: defence policy and, 75–86; international AIDS conference and, 74–5; with major trade issues, 62–6; summary, 54–7; with terrorism and Canada, 57–70
foreign direct investment, xxiii
forest fires, 133
francophonie, Canadian, 219–20
fraud: at Department of Public Safety, 32; Miramichi Hospital case, 233; securities, xxiv; sponsorship, xvi, xxv, xxxi, 47–9. *See also* controversies
Freedom of Information and Protection of Privacy Act, 151
friendly fire, xxx, 46
fuel costs, xxiii, 33
funding: marijuana science, 36; students and college, xxii, xxx. *See also* spending

Gagetown, Camp, 235
gas: boom, xviii; prices, 33, 139
gateway pipeline, 108
GDP. *See* gross domestic product
global warming. *See* climate change
Gomery inquiry, xvi, xxv, xxxi, 5, 47–9

goods and services, xv
Goods and Services Tax (GST), xxvi, 14, 38
governance: accountability, 29; First Nations Governance Act, 8, 102–3; with merit of appointees, 29; municipal affairs and regional, 93–4; in NB with Graham, 235–7; Saskatchewan and intergovernmental relations, 160–2; in West with First Nations, 109
Graham, Shawn, 235–7
Grand Manan Five case, 233–4
Greater Toronto Transportation Authority (GTTA), 94–5
greenhouse gas emissions: transportation and, xxxiii. *See also* Kyoto Protocol
Green Party, 23, 28
gross domestic product (GDP), xviii, xxiv, xxx, xxxiii, xxxiv
growth: in Alberta, xxii, 140–4; in BC, xxii, 137–8
GST. *See* Goods and Services Tax
GTTA. *See* Greater Toronto Transportation Authority
guns, xxii, xxx, xxxiii, 200, 212–13

Hamas, 68n8
Harper, Stephen, 79
hate crimes, 198
Haudensaunee, 109–11
health, xvi; *Access to Health Care Services in Canada*, xvi; in Alberta, 149–51; in BC, 131; caloric intake, xxiv; cancer and, 27, 186; doctors, 124; HIV / AIDS, xxix, 74–5; home care providers, 188; hospitals, 27, 166, 188–1, 207, 233; in NB, 226, 229–30; nurses, xxxv, 111, 188; obesity, xxix; in Ontario, 185–91; pandemics, 27; with pharmaceutical companies, 186–7; in Quebec, 208–209; reforms, 150–1; smoking ban, 190
Health Canada, budget, 32
Hebron – Ben Nevis offshore oilfield, 258–9
Hezbollah, xxvii, 7, 67
High-Frequency Surface Wave Radar Project, 36
highway of tears, in BC, 126
Hillier, Rick (General), 84–6, 85n13
HIV / AIDS, xxix, 74–5
hockey, xv, xxvi, 152
home care providers, 188
hospitals, 27, 166, 188–9, 207, 233
households: income, xxiii; spending, xxxv
housing, 27, 36
Hudson's Bay Company, xvi, xvii
Hughes Report, 129–31
Human Rights Act, 103

ice cap, Arctic, 173–4
identity, in Quebec, 212–17
immigration, xxxi; males and, xviii; Manitoba, 165–6
income: children influenced by household, xxiii; with taxes on income trusts, xxxii, 14, 39
An Inconvenient Truth (film), 143, 173
India. *See* Air India
Indian residential school settlement, 103–5
indicators, economic, 33–4
indigenous peoples: UN declaration on rights of, 105. *See also* Aborigines; First Nations
industrial ecology, 90
inflation, 38
inquiries: Air India bombing, 50–1, 59–60, 135; Arar, xxxi, 5, 49–50, 63–6; Gomery, xvi, xxv, xxxi, 5, 47–9

institutions. *See* national institutions
intergovernmental relations: Nova Scotia, 251–6; Saskatchewan, 160–2
Internal Economy Commission investigation, 262–3
Internet, 5
interprovincial cooperation, in BC, 126–7
Iraq, 60–1
Israel, in Lebanon, xxvii, xxix, 7, 67–62

jails, xxxii
job satisfaction, xxxii
Joint Task Force 2, 61
judiciary, in Saskatchewan, 159

Kandahar, Afghanistan, 46, 79. *See also* Afghanistan
Karla (film), xv
Kelowna Accord, in BC, 7–8, 27, 40–1, 99, 127–9, 174–5
Khadrs, terrorism and, 61–5
KI. *See* Kitchenuhmaykoosib Inninuwug
kidnappings, 60–1, 64
Kitchenuhmaykoosib Inninuwug (KI), 112–13
Ku Klux Klan, 198
Kyoto Protocol, 8–9, 27, 44–5

labour issues: BC and marathon public-sector bargaining, 123–4; BC and teachers bargaining, 124–6; Ontario, 200–2; Quebec, 211–12
Labrador. *See* Newfoundland, Labrador and
land use, 90, 205, 210
leadership: AFN, 99–100; Green Party, 23; liberals and transfer of, 19–22
Lebanon: casualties in, 68; evacuees from, 68–70; Israel with siege of, xxvii, xxix, 7, 67–70; terrorism and crisis in, 67–70
legal issues: First Nations and Quebec, 113; Ontario, 200–2
legislation. *See specific legislation*
legislature: Alberta, 151–2; Manitoba, 167–9; Nova Scotia, 246–9; PEI, 240–2; Saskatchewan, 155–8
leisure activities, xxviii
Lheidli T'enneh, 107
liberals: leadership transfer, 19–22; in Newfoundland and Labrador, 257, 259
life expectancy, xxxvi
literacy rates, 117
lobbyists, 29
Lord, Bernard, 222–4
lumber: softwood, xxii, xxvi, 36, 71–2, 131–3, 160; with western mountain pine beetle infestation, 36, 132

Mackenzie Valley Pipeline Project, 115–16, 174, 180
Manitoba: agriculture in, 165; budget in, 166–7; cabinet, 168–9; economic developments in, 164–6; education in, 167; with federal election of 2006, 170–1; immigrants in, 165–6; legislative session in, 167–9; mining in, 165; other events in, 171; politics and political parties in, 169–70
marathon public-sector bargaining, 123–4
marijuana: growers, 42; legalization, 133; science funding, 36
Maritimes, with First Nations and treaty rights, 114–15
marketplace, municipal affairs and, 87–91
marriage: same-sex, 9–10, 14, 16, 45–6, 151–2; statistics, xxvi

mayors, 98
Memorial University, 256–9
men: adult education and, xx; immigrants, xviii; with leisure activities, xxviii; wages earned by, xix, xxix
mergers, 33–4
military, 85n13; BMD and, 82–4; budgets and spending on, 27, 80–2; Joint Task Force 2, 61; Operation Nunalivut, 81; presence in Arctic, 80. *See also* Afghanistan
minimum wage, 201
mining: BC accidents, 131; diamonds, 81, 181; Manitoba, 165; Saskatchewan, 159; Territories, 181
Miramichi Hospital fraud case, 233
Mississaugas, 106
Mohammed, cartoons, 57–8
Mumbai, terrorism in, xxvii
municipal affairs: cities, culture and, 91–3; cities in confederation and, 98; cities in marketplace and, 87–91; with local democracy, 95–7; with regional governance, 93–4
Municipal Revenue Sharing Amendment Act, 156
museums, xxviii, 36

NAN. *See* Nishnawbe Aski Nation
national economy: autumn economic update and, 37–8; budget cuts, 35–7; conservatives' first budget and, 34–5; with economic indicators, 33–4; income trusts and, xxxii, 14, 39; trade and, 39–40
national institutions: auditor general, 29, 32; branding new government and conservatives' style, 26–27; cabinet, 23–24; ethics commissioner, 33; first conservative ministry, Feb. 2006, 25; fixed election dates, 28; with government accountability, 29; house by-elections and caucus change, 27–28; party standings, 31 Dec. 2006, 28; patronage commissioner, 29–3; with Senate reform, 30–1; Speech from Throne in, 24–5; Supreme Court, 31–4
national net worth, xxvi, xxx, xxxv
national spending, 27
NATO, xxxiii
NB. *See* New Brunswick
NCLA. *See* Nunavut Land Claims Agreement
NDP. *See* New Democratic Party
net worth, national, xxvi, xxx, xxxv
New Brunswick (NB): with Agent Orange fallout at Camp Gagetown, 235; with decline in natural resources, 231–3; education in, 230–1; energy in, 223, 225, 228; events in, 233–5; with fight over Lord Beaverbrook's art gifts, 234–5; general election in, xxx, 10, 224–7; Graham's cautious approach to governing in, 235–7; Grand Manan Five case, 233–4; health in, 226, 229–30; Lord's last session in, 222–4; Miramichi Hospital fraud case, 233; power in, 219–21; public sector challenges in, 227–31
New Democratic Party (NDP), 22
Newfoundland, Labrador and: budget in, 258; culture in, 265–6; economic development in, 266; federal election of 2006 and, 255–6, 263–4; First Nations in, 265; fishing industry in, 261–2; Hebron – Ben Nevis offshore oilfield and, 258–9; Internal Economy Commission investigation and, 262–3; Liberal Party in, 257, 259; Memorial University and, 256–7; other initiatives, 260; public appointees

and, 260–1; resource development and, 259–60; seal hunting in, 256; Speech from Throne in, 257; spending in, 265; Williams, Danny, and, 263; Winter Olympics and, 256
9/11. *See* 11 September 2001
Nisga'a, 107
Nishnawbe Aski Nation (NAN), 103
NORAD. *See* North American Aerospace Defence Command
North: First Nations in, 115–17; Kelowna Accord and, 174–5; Mackenzie Valley Pipeline Project in, 115–16, 174, 180; military presence in, 80; Nunavut Project, 116–17; Territories and national politics in, 172–7. *See also* Arctic; Territories
North America, trade and borders, 72–3
North American Aerospace Defence Command (NORAD), 84, 84n11
Norway House Cree Nation, 109
Nova Scotia: budget in, 247–8; economy in, 249–51; education in, 253; elections in, xxiii; energy in, 250; intergovernmental relations in, 251–4; June 2006 general election table for, 271; legislature in, 246–9; political parties in, xxv; politics in, 244–6; taxes, 247
nuclear power plants, 195
nuclear weapons, xxxii
Nunavut Land Claims Agreement (NCLA), 116–17, 116n3
Nunavut Project, 116–17
nurses, xxxv, 111, 188

obesity, xxix
obituaries, 267–70
OECD. *See* Organization for Economic Cooperation
office of correctional investigator, 53
oil: in Alberta, 139, 142–3; boom, xviii; Hebron – Ben Nevis offshore oilfield, 258–9; pipelines, 108, 115–16, 174, 180; prices, 33
Olympics, 88, 93; BC and, 133–4; Newfoundland, Labrador and, 256
Ontario: with Caledonia and Haudensaunee, 109–11; education in, 191–3; elections in, 96; energy in, 194–6; First Nations in, 109–13, 196–200; health in, 185–91; home care providers in, 188; KI in, 112–13; minimum wage in, 201; with ongoing water crisis, 111–12; pharmaceutical companies in, 186–7; protestors in, 184; social, labour, and legal issues in, 200–2; summary, 184–5; Toronto, xxiv, xxxv, 6, 58–9, 94–5; transit workers strike in, xxiv; TSX, xxxv
Operation Nunalivut, 81
Organization for Economic Cooperation (OECD), 95
overpass collapse, 206–7

Pabineau, 115
Pacific Gateway, 122
Palestinian Authority, xx, 68n8
pandemics, 35
parliament: major policy areas, 40–7; national economy, 33–40; national institutions, 23–33; with parliamentary budget authority, 29; personalities and controversies, 51–3; special commission and inquiries, 47–51; summary, 3–4; thirty-ninth general election, 3–15
patents, xxxi
patronage commissioner, 29–2
PEI. *See* Prince Edward Island
penitentiaries, xxxii, 53
pension fund, of RCMP, 32

Pessamit, 113
pesticides, 91–2
pharmaceutical companies, 186–7
Pickton, Robert, trial of, 135
pipelines: First Nations in West and gateway, 108; Mackenzie Valley Pipeline Project, 115–16, 174, 180
poet laureate, of PEI, 243
police officers, xxxiii. *See also* Royal Canadian Mounted Police
policies: Aboriginal affairs, 40–1; Afghanistan, xxiii, 46–7; crime and punishment, 42–4; defence, 75–86; Kyoto Protocol, 8–9, 35, 44–5; Québécois, xxxiv, 9, 41–2; in Quebec with public disapproval, 209–11; same-sex marriage, 9–10, 14, 16, 45–6, 151–2
political parties: CLC, 97; Conservative Party of Canada, xv; donations for, 29; Green Party, 23, 28; major party platforms and issues, 14–16; Manitoba, 169–70; minor, 13–14; NDP, 22; Nova Scotia, xxv; party standings, 39 Dec. 2006, 28; Saskatchewan, 154–5; voter preferences, Dec. 2005 to Jan 2006, by, 17. *See also* elections; elections, federal; elections, in parliament
politics: elections and, xxxvii–xxxix; Manitoba, 169–70; North in national, 172–7; Nova Scotia, 244–6; PEI, 240–2; Territories, 177–80
pollution: Clean Air Act, 44–5; water, 111
Post-Secondary Learning Amendment Act, 151
power, in NB, 219–21
premiers, Alberta, 144–8
Prince Edward Island (PEI): economy in, 238–9; electoral map, 241; fiscal events in, 239–40; other events in, 242–3; poet laureate, 243; politics and legislature in, 240–2
procurements: auditor of, 29; defence, 81–2
Project KARE, 152
protestors: activists and, 92, 134, 143; Douglas Creek Estates and, xviii, xix, xxi, xxiii, xxv, 197–9; in Ontario, 184
public appointees, in Newfoundland and Labrador, 260–1
public school system, reform and, 122
public sector, in NB, 227–31
publishing, xxvi
punishment, crime and, 42–4

al-Qaeda, 58–9, 61, 75
QNA. *See* Quebec native alliance
Quebec: bracing up, 220–1; with ethnicity, difference, and national identity, 212–17; federalism in, 217–20; First Nations in, 113–14; francophonie, 219–20; health in, 200–1; labour, jobs lost and added, and old conflicts resolved in, 211–12; lawsuit, 113; with policy and public disapproval, 209–11; QNA and, 114; rejection consensus in, 204–6; RRDP and, 113–14; shootings in, xxx, 212–13; state bureaucracy questioned in, 206–17; summary, 203–4
Quebec native alliance (QNA), 114
Québécois, sovereignty and, xxxiv, 9, 15, 41–2, 204, 206, 215–6

radar project, 36
RCMP. *See* Royal Canadian Mounted Police
reform: health, 149–51; public school system, 122; Senate, 30–1
rejection, in Quebec, 204–8
religion, rights, 214

Remembrance Day, 78
re-offence rate, xxxv, 43
resources: Arctic, 172–3; NB, 231–3; Newfoundland and Labrador, 259–60
rights: *Charter of Rights and Freedoms*, 16; First Nations in Maritimes and treaty, 114–15; Human Rights Act, 103; religious, 214; UN declaration on rights of indigenous peoples, 105
Royal Canadian Mounted Police (RCMP), 53; Air India and, 60; with Arar inquiry, 64, 66; budgets and spending on, 35; with Canadians kidnapped in Iraq, 61; drug-impaired-driving program's training, 36; pension fund of, 24
Rupert River Diversion Project (RRDP), 113–14

sales, alcohol, xxx
salmon farming: in BC, 134–5; First Nations and, 106–7
same-sex marriage, 9–10, 14, 8, 45–6, 151–2
Saskatchewan: Aboriginal affairs, 162–3; budget, 157–50; economy, 158–9; elections, 153–4; executive, 157; intergovernmental relations, 160–2; judiciary, 159; legislature, 155–8; mining in, 159; political parties in, 154–5; property tax relief, 161; softwood lumber in, 160; Speech from Throne in, 156
satisfaction, job, xxxii
scandals: Crocus Fund, 167; sponsorship, xvi, xxv, xxxi, 5, 47–9. *See also* controversies
scholarships, tax-exempt, 34
scientists, xxiii
seal hunting, in Newfoundland and Labrador, 256
securities fraud, xxiv
Senate, reform in, 30–1
seniors, 32
sex offenders, 44
sex-trade workers, 152
sexual consent, age of, 43
shootings, xxii, xxx, 212–13
Six Nations, 109–11
smoking ban, 190
social issues: Ontario, 200–2; Territories, 181–3
social services: children and, 129–31, 171; Hughes Report and, 129–31
softwood lumber: in BC, xxii, 131–3; in Saskatchewan, 160; trade, xxvi, 71–2; trade litigation, 36
sovereignty: Arctic, 172–6, 183; Canada, 80–1, 172–6; Québécois, xxxiv, 9, 15, 41–2, 204, 206, 215–16. *See also* Aborigines; First Nations
special commissions: with Air India bombing inquiry, 50–1, 59–60, 135; with Arar inquiry, 49–50; Gomery commission and sponsorship scandal, xvi, xxv, xxxi, 5, 47–9
Speech from the Throne: BC, 121–3; national institutions, 24–5; Newfoundland and Labrador, 257; Saskatchewan, 156
spending: BC, First Nations and government, 106; household, xxxv; on military, 35, 80–2; national, 35; in Newfoundland and Labrador, 265; realignment of federal, 101
Spirit Bears, 134
sponsorship scandal, xvi, xxv, xxxi, 5, 47–9
sports: facilities, 92; football, xxxiv; hockey, xv, xxvi, 152
Spraytech, 91–2

Statistics Canada: abortions, xix; abuse in families, xxv, xxvii, xxxi; alcohol sales, xxx; bankruptcy, xxxii; building permits, xv, xvi, xviii, xxi, xxii, xxv, xxvi, xxix, xxx, xxxi, xxxiii, xxxiv; caloric intake, xxvi–xxvii; charitable organizations, xxiv; children, xxi, xxiii; commuters, xxvii; corporations, xxiv, xxix, xxxiv; CPI, xv, xvii, xix, xxvi, xxviii, xxix, xxxi, xxxvi; crime, xxv, xxviii, xxxii, xxxiii; crude birth rate, xxviii; debt financing, xvii; debt load, xxxv; earnings and single mothers, xxv; economy, xx; educators, xxxiv; employment, xv, xvi, xvii, xix, xxi, xxii, xxiii, xxiv, xxviii; foreign direct investment, xxiii; fuel costs, xxiii; GDP, xviii, xxiv, xxx, xxxiii, xxxiv; goods and services, xv; health, xvi; household spending, xxxv; immigration, xxxi; Internet access, xxix; job satisfaction, xxxii; leisure activities, xxviii; life expectancy, xxxvi; male immigrants, xviii; on marriage, xxvi; median age of Canadians, xxxii; men, xx; national net worth, xxvi, xxx, xxxv; nurses, xxxv; obesity, xxix; penitentiaries and jails, xxxii; police officers, xxxiii; publishing revenues, xxvi; re-offence rate, xxxv; on scientists and engineers, xxiii; senior women, xxvii; sugar consumption, xxiv; trade, xvii; transportation and greenhouse gas emissions, xxxiii; unemployment rate, xxv, xxvii, xxxi, xxxiii, xxxiv; university degrees awarded, xxxiii; university enrolment, xxxiii; wealthiest families, xxxv; women, xvii, xviii, xx, xxix; workday total, xxiii, xxviii

street racing, 43

strikes: teachers, 125; transit workers, xxiv

students: with college education funding, xxii, xxx; summer employment for, xxii

sugar, consumption of, xxiv

Supreme Court of Canada: as national institution, 31–2; *Spraytech* and, 91–2

sustainability, with unsustainable sprawl, 90

Syria, 64

takeovers, 33–4, 40

taxes: Chinese Head Tax, xxvi; education scholarships exempt from, 34; GST, xxvi, 14, 38; on income trusts, xxxii, 14, 39; in Nova Scotia, 247; property tax relief, 161

teachers: bargaining with BC labour issues, 124–6; strikes, 125; substitute, 191

technology: computers, 34; initiatives and setbacks, 32, 36; Wi-Fi, 91

Territories: crime in, xxxii; devolution, 36; economy, 180–1; education in, 181, 182–3; mining, 181; with North in national politics, 172–7; social issues in, 181–5; with territorial politics, 177–80

terrorism: Air India bombing and, 50–1, 59–60, 135; Anti-Terrorism Act, xxiv; Arar inquiry and, xxxi, 5, 49–50, 63–6; arrests, 201; Canada and, 57–62; with Canadians kidnapped in Iraq, 60–1; crime bills and, 43; with crisis in Lebanon, 67–70; 11 September 2001, 70; Khadrs and, 61–3; on Mumbai commuter train, xxvii; prophet Mohammed cartoons and, 57–8; al-Qaeda and, 58–9, 61, 75; Toronto 17 and, xxiv, 58–9; Toronto 18 and, 6, 58

Toronto, Ontario: 17, xxiv, 58–9; 18, 6, 58; GTTA, 94–5

Toronto Stock Exchange (TSX), xxxv
torture, 64
trade, xvii; Asia-Pacific, 138; between BC and Alberta, 126–7; with Canada-China relations, 73–4; exports and, 34, 179; national economy and, 39–40; North American borders and, 72–3; softwood lumber and, xxvi, 71–2; WTO, 39, 70–1
transportation: commuters, xxvii; greenhouse gas emissions and, xxiii; GTTA, 94–5
treaties: in BC with First Nations, 107–8; with First Nations in Maritimes and treaty rights, 114–15
trusts, income, xxxii, 14, 39
TSX. *See* Toronto Stock Exchange

UBC. *See* University of British Columbia
UN. *See* United Nations
unemployment: in Alberta, 141; fiscal crisis influencing, 89; rate, xxv, xxvii, xxxi, xxxiii, xxxiv, 34. *See also* employment
UNESCO, 41, 218
UN-Habitat, 87
uniforms, 34
unions: with ban on donations, 29; in BC, 124
United Nations (UN), xxxvi; Convention on Climate Change, 8; declaration on rights of indigenous peoples, 105; on Israel's attack on Lebanon, 68; in West, 108–9
United States (U.S.): elections in, xxxiii; exports to, 34; torture and, 64
universities: enrolment and degrees awarded, xxxiii; Memorial, 256–7. *See also specific universities*
University of British Columbia (UBC), 136
U.S. *See* United States

violence, crime and, 30
volunteerism, 36
voters: preferences by political party, Dec. 2005 to Jan 2006, 17; youth, 18. *See also* elections; elections, federal; elections, in parliament

wages: men and earned, xix, xxix; minimum, 201; women and earned, xviii, xxv, xxix
water: Arctic ice cap, 173–4; with boil water advisory, 136–7; crisis in Ontario and First Nations, 111–12; RRDP, 113–14
wealth, families with, xxxv
West: First Nations in, 108–9; gateway pipeline in, 108; governance in, 109; UN in, 108–9
western mountain pine beetles, 36, 132
wheat board controversy, 52–3
Wi-Fi, 91
Williams, Danny, 263
women, 36; abortion and, xix, 14; adult education and, xx; economic hardship and senior, xxvii; studies on, xvii; wages earned, xviii, xxv, xxix
workers: sex-trade, 152; with transit strike, xxiv; with workday total, xxiii, xxviii
World Trade Organization (WTO), 39, 70–1
World Urban Forum, 87
WTO. *See* World Trade Organization

youth: education and minority, xx–xxi; employment, 36; voters, 18. *See also* children
Youth Criminal Justice Act, xx

zoos, xxviii

FSC
www.fsc.org
MIX
Papier | Fördert gute Waldnutzung
FSC® C083411

Kolibri 360 GmbH
Ferdinand-Jühlke-Straße 7
99095 Erfurt, Deutschland
produktsicherheit@kolibri360.de